PELICAN BOOKS
African Affairs

EDITOR: RONALD SEGA

Africa Undermine

Greg Lanning is a freelance writer and documentary film director,
who made eight documentaries for UNICEF (United Nations
Children's Fund) in Africa and is currently working as a
producer and director for a British television company.
A law graduate from Sheffield University, he has travelled
widely, visiting India and Pakistan, as well as many countries
in Africa, where he worked for four years and where the bulk
of the research and writing for this book was done.

Marti Mueller is an American writer, journalist and
photographer residing in France. She has written articles
on Africa which have appeared in the London *Guardian*,
the Paris *Le Monde*, the *New York Times*, the *Washington
Post*, and the *Boston Globe* and has contributed to American
and European magazines. A former staff writer for *Science*,
she has done postgraduate grant research at Harvard University.
She has an MA in journalism from Northwestern University
in Chicago, and is a Phi Beta Kappa. She has travelled
extensively in Europe, the Middle East and central Asia
and spent two years freelancing in a wide variety of countries
in Africa.

GREG LANNING
WITH MARTI MUELLER

Africa Undermined

**Mining Companies and the
Underdevelopment of Africa**

Penguin Books

Penguin Books Ltd, Harmondsworth,
Middlesex, England
Penguin Books, 625 Madison Avenue,
New York, New York 10022, U.S.A.
Penguin Books Australia Ltd, Ringwood,
Victoria, Australia
Penguin Books Canada Ltd, 2801 John Street,
Markham, Ontario, Canada L3R 1B4
Penguin Books (N.Z.) Ltd, 182–190 Wairau Road,
Auckland 10, New Zealand

First published 1979

Copyright © Greg Lanning and Marti Mueller, 1979
All rights reserved

Made and printed in Great Britain by
Hazell Watson & Viney Ltd, Aylesbury, Bucks
Set in Monotype Plantin

'Big business doesn't really have the power most people think it has, does it?'

Harry Oppenheimer, quoted in the Johannesburg *Sunday Times*, 26 May 1963

Contents

List of Figures

List of Tables

Preface

This book grew out of a detailed study of the political and economic role of the Anglo American Corporation in South Africa. At Ronald Segal's suggestion this report was expanded to cover mining companies in all of Africa. We soon realized the enormity of the task, as there has been no major survey of the African mining industry since Professor S. H. Frankel's *Capital Investment in Africa* published in 1938. It has taken us several years to complete this book, which is based largely on secondary sources supplemented by visits to many parts of Africa and to Europe and America. The book is the product of a long period of mutual effort, although in the final drafts Chapters 1–18 and Chapter 21 were written by Greg Lanning and Chapters 19 and 20 were written jointly. We hope that by collecting information together in one volume we have contributed to a clearer understanding of the role of mining companies in the underdevelopment of Africa.

G.L.
M.M.

Acknowledgements

In the course of researching and writing this book we have travelled widely. We have many people to thank for their hospitality, kindness, perceptive criticism and encouragement, and in particular: Don Brind, Michael Barratt-Brown, Oliver Carruthers, Bruce Detwiler, Bob Fitch, Sean Gervasi, Richard Hall, John Kane-Berman, Martyn Marriott, Neil Middleton, Robert Molteno, Ann Seidman and Rick Wolff; our thanks too to Roger Murray for compiling Appendix 2, to the many individuals in research groups who provided us with library materials, and to Ronald Segal and Michael Dover at Penguin for coaxing us through the book's many stages; and most of all to Ian Margo for his invaluable support throughout the book's evolution, and to Barbara Dinham for putting up with an ever-growing library of books, magazines and newspaper cuttings and for typing the manuscript through innumerable drafts. Notwithstanding all this generous assistance we alone are responsible for any errors that remain.

Acknowledgements are also due to the publishers of the following for permission to quote copyright material: S. H. Frankel, *Capital Investment in Africa*, Oxford University Press, 1938; Francis Wilson, *Labour in the South African Gold Mines 1911–1969*, Cambridge University Press, 1972; *Africa 74/75*, Africa Journal 1974; J. G. Lockhart, C. M. Woodhouse, *Rhodes*, Hodder & Stoughton, 1963; A. Sutulov, *Minerals in World Affairs*, University of Utah, 1973; *African Development* magazine; *Mining Annual Review* (various), *Annual Survey of Mining Activity* (1978), Mining Journal; *Financial Mail*; and *Harvard Business Review*.

Greg Lanning
London

Marti Mueller
Pezeral, France

A Note on Financial and Other Statistical Information

Inevitably in a work of this nature the statistics are gathered and analysed well in advance of publication. Unless otherwise stated all financial and statistical information given is that available at 31 December 1977. This means that for most of the mining companies the latest available data covered either the financial year 1976–7 or the calendar year 1977 according to the company's reporting practice. But national and continental statistics derived from African sources are generally two or three years further adrift – the underdevelopment of the continent's statistical services is but another facet of Africa's general underdevelopment.

CURRENCIES

This book was written in a period of rapid currency fluctuations. We have not attempted to convert figures to current values. All conversions and financial statements are given at their historical value. These are some of the more important currency realignments and conversion values in the post-war era:

United Kingdom

Sterling was exchanged at the rate of £1.00 = US $2.80 from 1947. It was devalued in 1967, when £1.00 = US $2.40. The pound was allowed to float in 1971 and in December 1977 £1.00 = $1.917.

South Africa

In 1960 the South African pound was replaced by a new decimal currency (one Rand = 100 cents), and R2 = £1 sterling. After the 1967 sterling devaluation R1.71 = £1.00. The Rand was devalued by 12·28 per cent in 1971 and a further 17·9 per cent in 1975. In December 1977 R1.669 = £1.00 and R1.00 = US $1.15.

Zambia

The Zambian pound was replaced in January 1968 by a new decimal currency (one Kwacha – 'freedom' = 100 ngwee – 'dawns'). After the 1967 sterling devaluation K1 = £0.58. In 1971 the Kwacha was pegged to the US dollar and K1 = £0.54. In December 1977 K1.42 = £1.00, and K0.76 = US$1.00.

Zaïre

Before 1960 50 Belgian francs equalled one US dollar. In June 1967 a new decimal currency (one Zaïre = 100 makutas) was introduced. One Zaïre = US$2.00. In December 1977 Z1.59 = £1.00, and Z0.83 = US$1.00.

WEIGHTS

One short ton = 20 cwt (@ 100 lb a cwt) = 2,000 lb.
One metric ton = 1,000 kilograms = 2,204·62 lb.
One long tonne = 20 cwt (@ 112 lb a cwt) = 2,240 lb.

Introduction

Mining companies and minerals have played an important role in the development of Africa during the last hundred years. From Cecil Rhodes to Harry Oppenheimer, the mining magnates and their companies have dominated the political economy of Africa. Nevertheless, there have been relatively few attempts to identify and analyse the effect that the mining companies have had on the political, economic and social structures of Africa.[1] The task is made more difficult by the absence of a widely available history of mining in Africa. It is made more urgent by worldwide concern over the extent of the planet's natural resources, and by the insistence of the poor countries of Africa, Asia and South America that they receive a fair price for the minerals they sell on world markets. But in Africa and the rest of the Third World, control of mineral resources lies not with governments, or even with local capitalists, but with giant international companies. The problem for Africa, whose social and economic structure was heavily distorted by colonialism, is whether the activities of the international mining companies are compatible with the continent's economic development, or whether the companies are in fact the greatest obstacle to that development.

ECONOMIC DEVELOPMENT

To consider the economic state of Africa today is to confront a baffling paradox. Africa is already a major producer of minerals, accounting for 80 per cent of the world's annual gold production, 75 per cent of the diamonds, and over 30 per cent of the vanadium, the antimony, the chrome, and the manganese as well as significant quantities of copper, uranium and petroleum. The continent also has large, as yet unexploited deposits of iron ore, bauxite, phosphate, uranium, platinum, copper, nickel, vanadium, tin and fluorspar. And yet Africa is falling further and further behind the industrialized nations of Europe, North America and Asia. Whereas in 1850 the gap in economic output *per capita* between the developed nations and Africa was somewhere between $100 and $200, by 1970 this gap had grown to $2,000.* It is estimated that this gap will have widened to $7,000 by the end of this century.[2]

In the 1960s the economies of the developing countries grew at an average rate of 5 per cent a year. At a comparable stage in their development, from 1850 to 1920, the industrialized nations of Europe and America grew at an average rate of only 2 per cent a year. For the 1970s the Pearson Report[3] suggested that the developing countries aim at a growth rate of at least 6 per cent a year. The Pearson Report recommended that the developing countries concentrate on producing and exporting those items (largely primary goods) which they could produce more cheaply or more conveniently than the developed nations. By participating in international trade and selling their agricultural produce and minerals in an expanding world market, the developing nations, it was argued, could generate sufficient capital to build up their own economic structures and invest in a growing range of industries producing manufactured goods for the home and international market. Yet the best that the distinguished and knowledgeable men who compiled the Pearson Report could hope for at the end of the century was that after a prodigious effort the developing countries would double their output *per capita* but would be even further from the economic level of the industrialized countries than they are today.

Critics of orthodox development economists and of the Pearson Report have argued against the belief that an expansion of trade in itself can promote economic development. Pearson assumed that there is a developmental continuum along which the developed nations and the developing nations can be placed, and that this continuum is stable and unaffected by the previous development of the first countries to industrialize. To put it

*US $ at 1969 value.

another way: there is a 'road to development' along which Britain, Western Europe and the United States have travelled. In order to get from A to D (in this case from poverty and economic stagnation to wealth and development), all that a nation has to do is steer the same course through B and C as its predecessors. In fact, however, the very process of development and industrialization in Western Europe and the United States has totally altered the global economy. As a direct consequence of that original accumulation of wealth an artificial international division of labour was created. The first-comers are now rich, industrialized and powerful. The late-comers are poor, weak and lacking in industry. The poor countries produce the raw materials which the rich nations turn into manufactured goods. By virtue of their immense wealth and their industrial, managerial, educational and marketing ability, those countries who were first to develop are able to go on appropriating more and more of the planet's wealth. Because of these disparities in economic and political power, the poor nations at each stage of their development find their way barred by the powerful industrialized ones. No matter what they produce, they are always liable to be forced out of the world market by the developed countries, with their greater resources of both skilled labour and capital. The very development of the industrialized nations has created an obstacle to the future development of the late-comers. Therefore, in order to develop, a country will have to steer a different path from that followed by Western Europe and America, if only to avoid direct confrontation with these more powerful nations. It is a different world today from that in which earlier industrialization took place.

UNDERDEVELOPMENT

What is needed is a theory of development which is rooted in and corresponds to the historical experience of Africa, Asia and Latin America. In the 1960s the task of developing such a theory was tackled most resolutely in South America. Where the Pearson Report speaks of developing nations, Latin American economists, such as André Gunder Frank, spoke of underdeveloped nations.[4]

They argued that the present condition of the developing nations was the historical product of the relations between the developed nations and the poorer countries. These relations were a key element in the evolution of the world capitalist system because the developed nations

destroyed or totally transformed the earlier viable social and economic systems of these societies, incorporated them into the metropolitan dominated world-wide capitalist system, and converted them into sources for its own metropolitan capital accumulation and development. The resulting fate for these conquered, transformed, or newly-acquired established societies was, and remains, their decapitalisation, structurally generated unproductiveness, ever increasing misery for the masses – in a word their UNDERDEVELOPMENT.[5]

Once their resources have been incorporated into the world capitalist economy, the underdeveloped areas suffer from their relationship with the advanced industrial states in two major ways. They pay a heavy economic tribute, which aids the further industrial development of the metropolitan centres, and their own social, economic and political structures are heavily distorted. Colonial rule, the companies, and free trade confine their economies to the production of primary goods. Their mineral and agricultural exports feed the factories of the industrialized states which then export back manufactured goods, to make a handsome profit from the transaction. The process strengthens the position of the manufacturers in the developed states and destroys the possibilities of independent industrial growth in the underdeveloped ones. What industrial activity there is in the Third World is largely owned and controlled by the giant multinational companies with their base in the industrialized nations.[6] For as long as the poor countries remain economic satellites of the advanced capitalist metropoles, they will be prevented by the operation of economic, political and military forces from achieving significant economic development.

MINING COMPANIES IN AFRICA

The theory of underdevelopment was an important advance, but it has been criticized, and subsequent work has developed a deeper understanding of the mechanisms of inequality in the world economy.[7] To examine some of the economic, political and social implications of the existing relationship between the developed nations and the continent of Africa, we have picked one aspect of this relationship: the movement of African minerals in world trade, through the agency of the international mining companies. A close examination of this trade will explain some of the reasons why the gap between the poor nations of the world and the industrialized nations of America and Western Europe is constantly widening. It will, in particular, indicate whether the orthodox strategy of development can lead to autonomous, self-generating, and balanced economic development; or whether the prospects for Africa's future economic development are being undermined by the operations of the metropolitan owned and controlled mining companies and Africa's integration into the world economy. By concentrating our attention on the companies, we hope to illuminate the debate about development, underdevelopment and the post-colonial state in Africa; and to contribute to the analysis and understanding of the international companies in Africa.

Mining companies have been the subject of much criticism both within Africa and without. But they are not the only international companies in Africa. Much of the production and export of Africa's agricultural goods is controlled by international companies, like Unilever, Brooke Bond, Rowntrees and Firestone Rubber. But whereas Africa's tea, coffee and cocoa production is annually renewed, Africa's mineral resources are essentially non-renewable and are of much greater strategic importance both for Africa and for the industrialized nations. Outside South Africa, the multinational manufacturing companies, although they are expanding their interests, have not yet assumed such importance as the mining companies in Africa.

Mining companies are particularly important because, compared with multinational manufacturing companies, they generally operate on a much larger scale and yet require less labour and fewer local supplies. In Africa the mining companies produce almost exclusively for export, using highly capital-intensive methods of mining. This often leads to isolated mining enclaves with few employees and few linkages with the local economy. The question is whether such a form of production can contribute to African economic development. When the companies have exhausted Africa's major mineral deposits, will the continent have anything more to show than huge holes in the ground?

Another important question raised by a study of the mining companies in Africa is why South Africa has achieved a measure of economic development based on a large and expanding mining industry producing for export. If South Africa's experience is repeatable, then other African states can hope to follow the capitalist path to development. If it is not, then they may be condemned to permanent poverty. But to adopt an alternative strategy presupposes economic independence. And after more than ten years of political independence, is Africa any nearer to economic independence; or are the mining companies blocking the way?

In the pages that follow we analyse the role of the international mining companies in Africa. We examine the incorporation of African mineral resources into the world capitalist economy (Part 1); the role of the companies in the political economy of several African countries (Part 2); and the aims, structure, and operations of international mining companies today (Part 3). Our examination is limited in two significant respects: the geographical area under consideration is not the whole of Africa, but only sub-Saharan Africa; and our survey of mineral exploitation excludes oil. We feel that, although much of our general argument applies, the political economy of North Africa and the relationship between the international oil companies and African oil-producing countries are best considered separately. This book is then a study of the role of the international mining companies in the political economy of sub-Saharan Africa.

Part One

African Minerals in the World Economy

1 The Incorporation of African Minerals into the World Economy

For many centuries before the arrival of the Europeans, minerals were produced in Africa by Africans for African societies. The scale and techniques of mining and metal working in Africa were clearly comparable with those both in Europe and in the great Eastern civilizations of India and China – at least until towards the end of the seventeenth century. Even in the nineteenth century David Livingstone reported that the African iron workers of Mozambique considered English iron 'rotten'. He took some hoes back to England; and they were 'found of such good quality that a friend of mine in Birmingham has made an Enfield rifle of them', he wrote.[1] The first minerals were intended only for local consumption, but gradually they began to enter into intra-continental trade along the well-established routes which criss-crossed the continent (see Figure 1). There was some mineral trade with Europe, but this was relatively unimportant. Most of the production was for use or sale in markets close to the mine. But by the late nineteenth century the balance of power between Europe and Africa had changed beyond recognition, and with it the pattern of trade.

The slave trade, begun in the seventeenth century, irrevocably altered the relationship between Europe and Africa. Until that era, Africa and Europe had dealt with each other on the basis of equality and mutual respect. Europe did not impose the slave trade on Africa. At the start both were jointly involved. But it was Europe which dominated the connection as a result of both superior firepower and the wealth which accrued from the trade. Europe continually shaped and promoted the trade, turning it to Europe's profit and Africa's cost.[2] The debilitation of Africa, together with the superior firepower of Europe, enabled the European powers to occupy the entire African continent. Although well into the twentieth century much of this control was nominal, Europe was now in a position to proceed with the exploitation of Africa's natural resources. In 1861, King Leopold of the Belgians spoke for a confident, aggressive and expansionist Europe:

'The sea bathes our coast, the world lies before us. Steam and electricity have annihilated distance. All the non-appropriated lands on the surface of the globe [mostly in Africa] can become the field of our operations and our success.'[3]

PRE-CAPITALIST MINING IN AFRICA

The earliest mine archaeologists have yet discovered is in the small southern African state of Swaziland. Archaeologists estimate that mining began there around 43,000 B.C.[4] The mine is fifteen kilometres to the west of Swaziland's largest town, Mbabane, and today is the site of a modern open-cast iron mine owned by the Anglo American Corporation of South Africa. The mine lies in a range of hills known to the local people for centuries as Emabovini, which means 'where the red ochres are'. The dust from the red haematite ore* and the glistening black oxide of iron, called specularite, provided the earliest cosmetics. To these people, the red substance in blood seemed to be the essence of life, and so the red dust was widely regarded as a surrogate for blood in all its life-giving and sustaining aspects. During rituals, the red ochre and the shiny specularite were used as body decoration; and at death the corpses were smeared with red to ensure blood (and therefore life) after death. The attraction of red colouring matter led to the exploitation of surface deposits and later to the first underground mines. As early societies strove to adapt the coloured minerals to their taste in cosmetics and ornaments, by crushing, hammering and heating, they produced the first metals. Those metals which were easily worked – gold, copper and iron – were the first to be produced in Africa.

Gold is commonly found in alluvial deposits where individual miners can pan the river-beds for small grains and even an occasional nugget. Apart from its attractive colour, gold is highly

---

*Today widely exploited as a source of iron ore.

malleable and has a low melting-point. These qualities mean that, with only simple equipment, it is possible to create ornate masks and elaborate decorations. Gold played a central part in the government and life of the great West African kingdoms of Ghana, Mali and Songhai. According to an Arab chronicler, when one king gave audience and listened to the complaints of his people, he sat 'in a pavilion around which stand ten pages with gold-mounted swords: and on his right hand are the sons of the princes of his Empire splendidly clad and with gold plaited in their hair'.[5] Even the dogs wore ornamental collars of gold and silver. Taxes and tributes were levied in gold, and it was also used as a currency. West African gold is known to have moved in international commerce since the eighth century, if not earlier. Between the Portuguese entry into the region and 1900, one historian has estimated that the gold traded was worth £600 million.[6] This may be an overestimate, but certainly by the beginning of the eighteenth century the value of gold exports was running at £200,000 a year.[7] In the early days of the slave trade, the West African traders would accept only gold from the European slave captains for their human merchandise. In 1771 a slave trader wrote: 'There is no buying a slave without one ounce of gold at least.' Proof that inflation is not a modern phenomenon came a year later, when he complained: 'There is no buying slaves now without you give two ounces of gold on each.'[8]

Copper was found in surface deposits near the watersheds of the Congo and the Zambezi rivers in Central Africa. It was used both for ornamental masks and, in the form of crosses, as currency. Mining engineers estimate that more than 100,000 tons of copper were produced from the Katanga mines before the Europeans came. The main shafts might go down to 100 feet and were often shored with timber supports. Furnaces produced up to 30 pounds of metal at a time, and a copper cross one foot long weighed about 20 pounds. Such a cross would buy a beautiful woman. A man, however, was worth somewhat less.[9]

The melting, casting and working of iron ore is a more skilled technique. Between two and three hundred years B.C., the great iron age civilization of Meroe flourished on the banks of the upper reaches of the Nile. Products of this Birmingham of ancient Africa were traded south and west over the continent. The techniques of iron working spread more slowly, because mastery of the technique conferred power and was therefore a closely guarded secret. Even in the nineteenth century, a Portuguese traveller in the Tete district of Mozambique reported that he was not allowed to see the mining or the working of the iron because 'there is a superstition that the work may be seen only by those who actually perform it, for otherwise the metal will be lost'.[10] As iron working techniques spread southwards across the continent, they promoted an agricultural revolution. Simple iron agricultural implements enabled more intensive methods of cultivation to be developed. This increased productivity, which in turn led to greater concentrations of population and more complex forms of social organization.

As the iron age culture of the interior grew and flourished, trade from the east coast of Africa across the Indian Ocean increased dramatically. Coastal traders demanded ivory, iron and gold from the interior. The capacity of the interior to buy imports from the coast grew, along with the volume of trade. The mature iron age of central and southern Africa begins about the twelfth century A.D. and it is from this period that the magnificent stone ruins of Zimbabwe date.

A Moroccan scholar wrote in the twelfth century:

There are in fact a great number of iron mines in the mountains of Sofala [Mozambique]. The people of the Zanedj Islands and other neighbouring islands come here for iron, which they carry to the continent and islands of India where they sell it at a good price – for it is a material of great trade and consumption in India.[11]

Although trade with the East was important, the main trade routes were still within the continent, and it was along these trade routes that the continental economy flowed. The export and import trade was mainly confined to high-value, low-volume, luxury goods such as gold, ivory and spices.

As early as the seventeenth century both Africa and Europe were well aware of the potential rewards and perils of an increased trade in minerals. One traveller, after a visit to northern Mozambique, wrote to the Portuguese authorities:

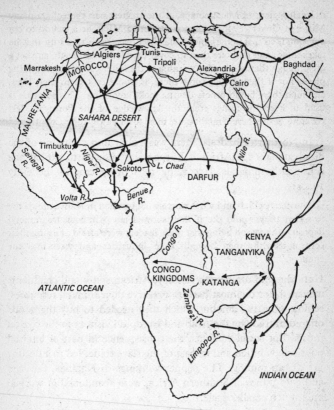

Fig. 1. Principal lines of trade in Africa from the ninth to the six-teenth century

SOURCE: Basil Davidson, *Africa: History of a Continent*, Hamlyn, 1972, p. 84.

It would be proper to conquer the whole of the kingdom, and divide the lands among the Portuguese, by which there would be great favours and rich appointments for the deserving. Then the natives would dig as much gold as their masters, the Portuguese, required...[12]

But another traveller in Mozambique reported that Africa was wary of the rapacious Europe.

In all regions of Manamotapa, or the greatest part thereof are many Mines of Gold; . . . if by chance any find a Mine, he is bound to cry out aloud, so that some other Cafar [*sic*] may come to testify that he takes none; and both are then to cover the place with Earth, and set a great bough thereon, to give warning to the other Cafares to avoyd the place. For if they should come there, it would cost them their lives, although there be no proofs that he tooke any thing. This severitie is used to keep the mines from the knowledge of the Portugals, lest covetous desire thereof might cause them to take away their Countrey.[13]

In Northern Rhodesia, there was a clear understanding of the disadvantages for Africa if Europe was allowed to exploit the continent's minerals. According to a prospector in the early 1920s:

The native chiefs and witch doctors . . . instilled in Native minds the fear that they would die if they showed any white man a mineral deposit – the reason being that these leaders were afraid of losing their control if white men brought their industries and vices into the country.[14]

Until the mid nineteenth century, African states and chiefdoms managed, for the most part, to preserve their mineral resources, selling only that amount which they needed to buy the goods offered in trade by the Arab and European visitors to the coastal towns. But social conflicts, the consequence in part of internal political evolution and in part of the slave trade, led to a decline in African mining. The copper workings in Katanga, the iron and gold mines of Southern Africa, were abandoned or worked on a much smaller scale.

The European presence on the continent increased during the nineteenth century and began to make itself felt farther inland. In Southern Africa, a large number of Dutch-speaking settlers had moved from the Western Cape into the interior and established a precarious existence there. In 1867 some of their children playing on the banks of the Vaal river discovered a rough glittering stone. A passing traveller tried and failed to sell it for a penny in the nearby towns of Colesberg and Hopetown. Some time later he was in Grahamstown, and a local doctor recognized that the stone was a twenty-carat diamond. The stone was sold to Sir Philip Wodehouse, the British governor of Cape Colony, for

£500. In 1871 Britain annexed the area, over the protests of the local Griqua tribesmen and the neighbouring Boer Republics, and established the new colony of Griqualand West.*

THE KIMBERLEY DIAMOND RUSH

The discovery of diamonds precipitated a rush of fortune-hunters to the interior. Farmers, diggers, speculators and tradesmen poured into the area, where they lived in rough and insanitary conditions. There was no housing, no medical service, no power, and very little transport. The nearest spring was seven miles away, and water cost two shillings and sixpence a bucket. All this did not discourage the diggers. Many men, like Barney Barnato (the younger half of a vaudeville team from London's East End), walked the six hundred miles from Cape Town to the diggings. By 1871 the population of Kimberley had risen to 37,000. Among those flooding into the area in the next few years were the rough-cut tycoons who decisively shaped the gold and diamond mining industries of South Africa. Cape-Town born Joseph Robinson came in 1870, Barney Barnato in 1873, Charles Rudd in 1874, Lionel Philips and Alfred Beit in 1875, and Julius Wernher in 1876. Over half the new arrivals in these early years at Kimberley were Africans. They came largely to earn the £6 needed to buy a gun to protect their land and cattle from the encroaching white man. So strong was the demand for labour at Kimberley that the lieutenant-governor of the British colony of Griqualand West, Richard Southey, deliberately encouraged the traffic in guns and ammunition so as to attract Africans to the

---

*In 1846 Britain had acknowledged that the area belonged to the Griqua tribe, who numbered about 3,000. Wodehouse wrote to Kimberley, the British secretary of state: 'As a matter of right the native . . . tribes are fairly entitled to that tract of country in which for the present the diamonds appear to be chiefly found.' Unfortunately it was a matter of might not right, and in October 1871 Britain annexed the land under the title of Griqualand West in the face of protests from the Griquas; from the diamond diggers who had declared a diggers' republic with an ex-able bodied seaman as president; and from the adjoining Afrikaner republics of Orange Free State and Transvaal. The Orange Free State was later compensated with £90,000 by Britain. The Griquas received no compensation at all.

diggings. Guns stimulated the trade with interior tribes and drew them into the cash economy. During the last nine months of 1873, over 18,000 guns were introduced into Griqualand West.[15] By that year four diamond mines had been established: Kimberley, De Beers, Bultfontein and Dutoitspan.

Among the early arrivals was an eighteen-year-old schoolboy from England, who had followed his elder brother to the diamond fields. He described the scene in a letter to his mother:

Imagine a small round hill, at its very highest point only 30 feet above the level of the surrounding country, about 180 yards broad and 220 feet long; all round it a mass of white tents . . . It is like an immense number of antheaps covered with black ants, as thick as can be . . . Peg the whole off into squares or claims 31 feet by 31 feet and the question is how to take all the earth out and sort and sieve it. All through the kopje* roads have been left to carry the stuff off in carts [each of these roads was seven and a half feet wide]. The carting on the kopje is done chiefly by mules, as they are so very handy and have so few diseases. There are constantly mule carts and all going head over heels into the mines below.

The diamonds are found in all ways, the big ones generally in the hole by the caffre [*sic*], or else in the sieving; and the small ones on the table. They are only found on these kopjes and along the river where they very likely have been carried by water. There are reefs all round these diamond mines, inside which the diamonds are found. The reef is the usual soil of the country around, red sand just at the top and then a black and white stony shale below. Inside the reef is the diamondiferous soil. It . . . is as like the composition of Stilton cheese as anything I can compare it to . . . They have been able to find no bottom yet, and keep on finding steadily at 70 feet. You will understand how enormously rich it is, when I say that a good claim would certainly average a diamond to every load of stuff that was being sorted – a load being about fifty buckets.[16]

What the young Cecil Rhodes fails to make clear is that the work was done almost entirely by the Africans, who broke the ground, hauled and then sifted the earth. It was, as another white man wrote, 'a veritable tom tiddlers ground', where the diggers could not only make a fortune 'but have it done for them by niggers'.[17]

*Afrikaans for 'hill'.

The white man sat under an awning and did the sorting, 'leaving the kaffirs to perform all the other stages of work'.[18]

Cheap African labour was from the very start the basis of the diamond industry. When the production of diamonds passed a value of £1½ million in 1872, the weekly wage for the black man was around 7s.6d., with rations worth maybe 6s.6d.[19] So obvious was the disparity between the value of the stones and the level of the wages that illicit diamond mining grew into a major industry, with African and Coloured labourers providing the stones. Many wealthy dealers laid the basis of their fortunes by buying these stolen gems, and then with the proceeds buying claims from the small diggers, to become big mineowners themselves. As the illicit business grew, so also did the myths. Some claimed that at least half the output was stolen by the Africans. 'Above all things,' advised one digger, 'mistrust a kaffir who speaks English and wears trousers.'[20]

RISE OF THE MINING COMPANIES

Originally there were 3,600 claims in the four mines, and each claim was worked independently of the next. The diggings grew deeper, and an amazing collection of wires and pulleys was used to haul up the soil. Diggings were worked to varying depths, and the narrow seven-foot paths that divided the individual claims were rapidly and sometimes catastrophically undermined, to bury men, equipment and claims under tons of soil. The costs of mining increased sharply. Pumps to deal with the frequent flooding, and other mining equipment, had to be imported from Europe and hauled up from the Cape by road. The railway did not reach Kimberley until 1886.

To spread the costs, diggers formed companies by exchanging shares in their respective claims. Some men wanted to raise cash, and so a local market in shares developed. Diggers began buying up the claims which bordered on their own. Government regulations which had prevented diggers from owning more than one claim each were amended. Diggers were first allowed three claims, and then in 1874 a person or company was given the right to hold as many as ten. Cecil Rhodes merged his three claims with those of his brother and of Charles Rudd. As the diamond fields boomed, the rich banks and diamond merchants of the Cape granted credit liberally. Reckless trading and speculation ensued, although the lowest rate of interest on good security was 12 per cent.[21] The government of Griqualand West was heavily in debt to the banks and in no position to restrict their activities. The boom could not last.

In the early 1870s world trade in diamonds had boomed, due to increased demand from America after the California Gold Rush;[22] but by 1874 the sheer quantity of diamonds from Kimberley was beginning to depress prices.* Sales fell sharply in the worldwide financial crisis that had begun with the collapse of the Vienna Bourse in 1873. At the close of 1874, the diamond fields were on the verge of collapse. The banks and merchants called in their loans. Despite increases in taxation, the government of the colony was in severe financial difficulties and the independent diggers were struggling to survive.

But 'the embarrassment of the small man was the opportunity of the strong'.[23] The banks and merchants brought every conceivable pressure to bear on independent diggers. The European population on the diggings fell to 6,000. Capitalists and company promoters with money from London approached members of the government with bribes and schemed to buy out the claimholders and work the mines themselves.

The responsibilities of Southey's inexperienced and incompetent government in Griqualand West were growing in magnitude just as revenues declined. Conditions on the diamond fields were appalling, and a fragmented and disorganized industry was incapable of bearing the increased load of taxation needed to support the administration. In addition, Southey was harassed by emphatic orders from the British Treasury to minimize expenditure. While he wrestled with these administrative problems, Southey saw that the issue being decided at Kimberley was

---

*Before Kimberley, Brazil was the leading producer with an annual production of 180,000 carats. By 1874 Kimberley was producing 1·3 million carats annually. By 1872 Kimberley's diamond exports were worth £1·6 million per annum.

how mining enterprise, with which the whole economic and social future of South Africa was destined to be bound up, was to be organised and controlled. Could South Africa at the outset of its industrial history discipline the resourceful and powerful interests that came to draw profit from her unusual wealth ? . . . To the company promoters he [Southey] let it be known 'that the immense wealth yet to be obtained from our diamond mines should be carefully guarded, in order that the people of South Africa may derive the profits accruing from them rather than that such profits should go out of the country to foreign companies'.[24]

Southey secured the passage of regulations to protect the small diggers from capitalist proprietors. His government took powers to claim the mineral rights, and regulate the ground rents. But to a British government determined to reduce the expenses and responsibilities of the turbulent colony, the diggers were disturbers of the peace and enemies of property rights. The Colonial Secretary in London disallowed the legislation. The proprietors immediately put up ground rents and ejected diggers who could not pay.

The diggers were bitter and were further enraged by Southey's limited attempts to protect the migrant African labourer:

In Southey's attempt to regulate mining they could see only a bungling officiousness. To his defence of their interests they were blinded by their horror of his native policy.[25]

The diggers established the Kimberley Defence League and organized armed vigilantes. The proprietors and company promoters hired agitators to inflame the tense situation. Southey was forced to appeal to the Cape for military aid. It was the end of the separate colony of Griqualand West. Southey and his government were lost, but so also were the diggers whose actions had played into the hands of the proprietors and company promoters. Southey was recalled, and an inquiry into the financial position of the diamond fields at the end of 1875 recommended the revocation of the restrictive ten-claim clause. The way was now open for the transformation of the diamond industry.

Financiers like Alfred Beit, Cecil Rhodes and Barney Barnato were quick to recognize the opportunities now open to them.

Joint stock companies which could raise large amounts of capital, and exploit the Kimberley field more efficiently and profitably, were now possible. Although the overseas market in diamond shares was not yet organized, connections were being established with European investors attracted by the fabulous wealth of Kimberley. The colonial authorities expected the larger units to provide a solid base for colonial taxation. However, one further change was necessary. The possibility that Africans might thrust above the status of unskilled low-paid labourers had to be eliminated. Africans were barred from holding claims or from washing the debris. The victory of the wealthy white bankers, company promoters and financiers was complete.

Companies and diamond buyers bought out the claims of individual diggers and amalgamated them. The leading Paris merchant, Jules Porges, having bought interests in all four mines, now concentrated on the Kimberley mine. He formed the Compagnie Française de Diamant du Cap de Bonne Espérance to look after these interests. It was known as the French Company. In 1876, at the age of only twenty-three, Barney Barnato, the most successful *kopje walloper* (diamond buyer) in Kimberley, bought four claims for £3,000. These claims produced diamonds worth £200,000. He bought another four claims for £180,000 and formed the Kimberley Central Diamond Mining company, which controlled the core of the Kimberley mine. Cecil Rhodes and his partner Charles Rudd had concentrated their attention on the De Beers mine, buying up as many claims as they could. In 1880 the De Beers mining company was formed with a capital of £200,000 and with Rhodes as company secretary. In the crash of 1881, shares fell to less than half of their nominal value. Rhodes increased his shareholding and became chairman of De Beers.

The new companies were making other changes. The introduction of the iniquitous pass system was an ominous portent for the developing social organization of South Africa. Any black servant or mineworker had to produce a certificate proving the registration of his labour contract. This certificate was endorsed when he was discharged, and to leave the diggings lawfully, he had to produce the certificate and get a pass. Any person found wandering in a mining camp without a pass and unable to give a satisfactory account of himself ran the risk of summary arrest, a £5 fine, and three months' hard labour or 25 lashes. Either a policeman or an employer could search the servant's room, property or person without a warrant. In the next decade the closed compound, surrounded by a high fence and covered with wire netting, was introduced for black miners. The men lived twenty to a room and before their discharge were confined in detention rooms for several days, during which they wore only blankets and fingerless leather gloves padlocked to their wrists, swallowed purgatives and were examined for diamonds concealed in the anus, mouth, and any cuts, wounds, or swellings.[26] In contrast to this meticulous concern for illicit diamond buying, little attention was paid to safety. In 1879 the annual death rate of African mineworkers rose to 79 deaths per 1,000 workers.[27]

The financiers, diamond merchants and company promoters were not concerned. Their aim was to complete the process of consolidation begun by the revocation of the ten-claim clause in 1874. If the diamond fields were amalgamated, the deposits could be worked systematically at lower cost, and then production could be adjusted to maintain the price of diamonds on the world market. Only two men had either the capital or the ability to achieve this goal. Barney Barnato had an annual income of £200,000. Cecil Rhodes's income was only a quarter of this but he had forged a powerful alliance with Alfred Beit. A financial journal reported: 'It is well known that behind Mr Rhodes was a greater power and from whose fertile brain emanated most of the ideas which were finally adopted and carried out.'[28]

Falling demand and plummeting prices precipitated a fierce price-cutting war between Barnato and Rhodes. Barnato's production costs were lower; but while Rhodes had complete control of the De Beers mine, Barnato did not completely control the Kimberley one. A substantial part was controlled by the French Company, owned by Jules Porges and several other French financiers. Rhodes and Beit decided to buy out the French Company and force Barnato to amalgamate with De Beers. Beit organized a syndicate of French and German financiers (including his cousins the Lipperts) who offered to put up £750,000.

Porges and his colleagues had a shrewd idea of the importance of their shareholding and held out for £1,400,000. Rhodes and Beit went shopping for more finance. At this time the great French banking house of Rothschilds retained E. D. de Crano as their adviser on the South African mining industry. De Crano was a close friend of Rhodes's chief engineer, Gardner Williams. When Williams prepared a glowing account of the industry's prospects if Rhodes could raise the necessary capital to amalgamate the industry, de Crano passed the report on to the Rothschilds. Rhodes and Beit went to London to argue their case in person. At the interview Rhodes pressed his case forcibly, but Rothschild remained non-commital. Then, as Rhodes was about to leave, Rothschild, in the guarded language which is the special, though not exclusive, preserve of bankers, said: 'Well, Mr Rhodes, you go to Paris and see what you can do in reference to the purchase of the French Company, and in the meantime I shall see if I can raise the million pounds sterling you desire.'*[29]

At the general shareholders' meeting of the French Company, Barnato put in a bid for £1,700,000. This seemed to spell the end of Rhodes's carefully wrought plan to amalgamate the diamond industry under his control. The Rothschilds connection saved Rhodes: it persuaded Barnato to withdraw his bid for the French Company, and Rhodes bought the company for £1,400,000 and then handed it over to Barnato in return for shares in Barnato's Kimberley Central Company. Rhodes now had the stake in Kimberley Central that he had long sought. The Rothschilds collected £100,000 and the Lipperts 1 million francs as commission for their part in the deal.

As the price war continued unabated, Rhodes tried to persuade Barnato to agree to amalgamation. But as he was, by virtue of lower production costs, the stronger of the two, Barnato saw no reason why he should. At the end of February 1888, Rhodes summoned his allies to a meeting at the Poole Hotel in Capetown to plan his next step.

Starting with £250,000 from Beit, Rhodes and Beit began to

*Hardly a problem for Rothschilds: in 1875 the bank had loaned £4 million to the British prime minister, Benjamin Disraeli, to buy the Suez Canal Company.

buy Kimberley Central shares on the open market. When Barnato caught wind of this, he also plunged into the market, buying shares in London, Paris and Kimberley to strengthen his position. As the price of Kimberley Central shares soared from £14 to £49 apiece, Barnato put pressure on Rhodes by reducing the price of diamonds once again. The question was whether Rhodes would be able to buy enough shares in Kimberley Central before Barnato's price-cutting tactics forced him to surrender. But Rhodes was backed by those with the greater resources, and in March 1888 he emerged as the victor, with 60 per cent of the capital of Kimberley Central.

Rhodes immediately began reorganizing the industry. He amalgamated Kimberley Central and the French Company with his own holdings and formed 'De Beers Consolidated Mines Ltd'. The driving force behind the amalgamation had been Rhodes' perception that a diamond is bought because it is expensive, and that therefore the supply of rough diamonds should be restricted to that amount which could be sold on the market without affecting the price. Rhodes bought up the Dutoitspan and Bultfontein mines for £2½ million, and in 1889 De Beers reduced production by 40 per cent. This move was so successful that the price of diamonds rose by 50 per cent. But the control that Rhodes had achieved over South African diamond production was only a partial solution; because as long as there was unrestricted competition in the marketing of diamonds instability would remain. So Rhodes moved swiftly to centralize control of diamond marketing. In 1890, De Beers assigned the sole marketing rights for its rough diamonds to a group of London diamond merchants, most important of whom were Wernher Beit and Co., Barnato Brothers, Rosenthal & Sons Co., and A. Dunkelsbuhler & Co. De Beers' dominance of the world diamond industry gave Rhodes the funds to expand into Central Africa.* But he underestimated both the costs of this operation

---

*The objects of De Beers Consolidated were comprehensive: '. . . to acquire by purchase, amalgamation, grant, concession, lease . . . any houses . . . farms, mines . . . waterworks or other works . . . diamonds and other precious stones, gold and other minerals . . . machinery, plant . . . patents for invention . . . to carry on the business of miners in all its branches . . . To acquire

and the significance of recent mineral discoveries in the Transvaal.

THE DISCOVERY OF THE WITWATERSRAND GOLD FIELDS

With a white population of only 8,000 in 1877, the tax base of the Transvaal Republic was too small to support even a rudimentary structure of public administration. Unable to pay the salaries of public officials, or to meet interest payments on outstanding loans, President Burghers realized that mineral wealth could be the salvation of the Transvaal. His dilemma was acute. On the one hand the Republic was bankrupt and as a result stood in danger of being absorbed by the Cape Colony; on the other, if mineral wealth, such as that of Kimberley, was found, it might well save the financial situation, but the resulting influx of miners, speculators, traders and financiers would overwhelm the hard-won cultural identity of the Boer community.* President Burghers' successor, Paul Kruger, believed that if minerals were found the independence of the Republic could still be preserved, and he offered a reward of £5,000 to anyone discovering minerals in the Transvaal.

In Kimberley lucky prospectors had found the richest deposits right at the start. The discovery and development of the Witwatersrand gold deposits was a much longer process.

Gold was found in the early 1880s at Barberton and Lydenburg in the Transvaal. Several mines were developed with the same small-scale techniques as had been used in Africa for centuries, but the deposits were small and irregular. Nevertheless, these discoveries promoted widespread systematic and careful

---

any tract or tracts of country in Africa or elsewhere . . . To treat with rulers or governments of any country for the acquisition by the company of benefits or valuable rights . . .' See Paul Emden, *The Randlords*, London, Hodder & Stoughton, 1935, p. 260.

* So strong was the determination of the Republic to retain its homogeneity that there was a law on the statute book which prohibited prospecting and forbade anyone finding diamonds, gold or other precious metals from telling anyone except the government in Pretoria. This was strikingly similar to the injunction laid on the people of Mozambique by their leaders. (See page 32.)

prospecting; and in 1884, 1885 and 1886 several outcrops of the Witwatersrand gold field were found.

In most major gold fields, like those in California and Australia, the gold had been found in alluvial deposits; often in the form of solid nuggets. The Rand was different. It had extremely consistent but low-grade deposits of gold in ribbons of quartz (the 'reef') buried at varying depths under the earth's surface. The deposits were immense, but winning the gold from the quartz posed a problem. The breakthrough was made in 1886 by a wealthy Afrikaner farmer, Fred Struben. Using a five-stamp battery specially imported from Ipswich in England, Struben crushed the ore and extracted the gold by running it over copper plates coated with mercury, which amalgamated with the gold. He delivered the first 61 ounces of gold to the Standard Bank at Pretoria in February 1886.

Struben's achievement underlined the need for capital to develop the Rand. In Kimberley it had been possible, if somewhat improbable, for a man to become very rich after an initial investment of no more than a pick and a shovel. On the Rand it was not possible to develop a gold prospect without capital and financial backing. When a gold outcrop was discovered, the mineral rights had to be bought from farmers shrewdly aware of the worth of their land. Mine workings and a crushing mill had to be established before production could start. Later, as mining progressed, a shaft would have to be sunk. In addition the course of the reef was not easy to follow because of extensive faulting.* At an early stage, mining engineers had to sink test boreholes to pinpoint the course, depth and thickness of the gold-bearing reef. All these factors pushed out the independent prospectors, as well as men like Struben, and left the field open to those men who had, or could raise, the necessary capital.

In the first instance this meant the men of Kimberley.† They

---

*Faulting arises when a fracture in the rock strata displaces the strata relative to one another.

† In fact, Rhodes was slow to appreciate the size and richness of the Rand; and when he did move to buy claims, he bought lavishly and generally unsuccessfully. He did, however, make one significant intervention. In August 1886 during an interview with Rhodes, Kruger agreed to repeal the regula-

had the wealth and ability to develop the new mines; they had experience of large-scale organization and appreciated the importance of technology; but above all they had international prestige and connections with the great finance houses of Europe. So it was that many of the gold-mining companies formed between 1887 and 1892 were connected in some way with prominent figures in the diamond trade. Some of the thrusting entrepreneurs, like Barney Barnato and Joseph Robinson, who had been frozen out of Kimberley by Rhodes, now turned their eyes to the Transvaal. Barnato bought claims on a large scale.

The intense activity and high prices of Kimberley diamond shares during the great amalgamation battle had attracted stockbrokers on the London Stock Exchange, and Throgmorton Street had begun dealing in diamond shares; but now this trading was dwarfed by a spectacular surge of investment in gold-mining companies. Miners, mineowners and speculators floated some 400 companies, and in 1889 these reached a combined market value of £100 million.[30] Buying rose to fever pitch at Kimberley during the boom:

> News would come down of some rich strike on the Rand and at once the street would be crowded with brokers shouting out the prices like bookies on the rails before the start of a big race. In the evening business was transferred to the bars.[31]

The initial enthusiasm soon began to recede, however; partly in response to the activities of the speculators and partly because of the increasing technical difficulties encountered as the mines went deeper. Rising labour costs were already eroding profitability in 1889, when the mines struck pyritic ore. The existing process of separating gold from the quartz would not work with pyritic ore. Near panic ensued, share prices tumbled, mines closed, and men were thrown out of work.

Two important discoveries restored the flagging faith of investors in the South African gold fields. Two Edinburgh

---

tion which prohibited the sale or transfer of mining claims and another which prohibited claim-holders from holding more than a limited number of claims.• This repeal removed a major obstacle to the growth of large mining companies chemists, John Macarthur and William Forrest, researching into improved ways of separating the gold from the quartz, made a crucial breakthrough in 1887. They discovered that the crushed particles could be suspended in a cyanide solution. This led to a new and more profitable process, which was first tested at Robinson's mine in 1890. Up to 96 per cent of the gold in the pyritic ore could now be recovered; and because working costs fell dramatically in consequence, the reserves of payable ore were extended. At the same time, mining engineers began to suspect that the reef of gold extended much deeper and much farther than the outcrop mines could reach. They argued – accurately, as it turned out – that the Reef dipped from north to south; and that it would be more profitable to mine away from the outcrop and at greater depths because more of the Reef would be easily accessible (as Figure 2 shows). But they found it difficult to convince the industry. Rhodes, when asked by his engineer if he might peg deep-level claims on his own account, said: 'A fool and his money are soon parted. Peg if you want to.'[32] But Alfred Beit did not share Rhodes's scepticism and bought up 1,750 deep-level claims for half a million pounds. Bringing to development just ten of these claims, he turned his original investment into a group of companies worth more than £50 million.

Up to this time the mining companies had relied on the attraction of cash wages, recruiting teams, and the white traders of the Transkei and Natal to recruit mine labour. Advances made by the traders provided the crucial incentive for many Africans to enter the money economy and work on the mines.[33] But this was insufficient, and mine managers had begun using bribery to secure adequate supplies of labour.[34] Competition between mine managers pushed wages for black miners up to 63 shillings a month, and recruitment costs were double the wage bill. To meet this situation the mineowners established the Chamber of Mines in 1889. Its main aim was to reduce the industry's labour costs. It limited competition between the companies by standardizing wages and working conditions in the industry. By 1897 wages for black mineworkers were down to an average of only 40s.10d. a month.[35] The Chamber also significantly reduced the

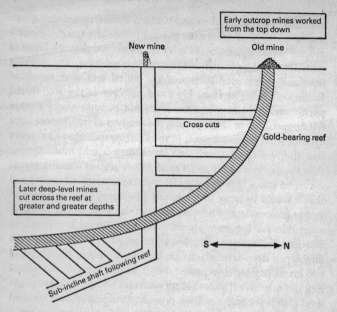

Fig. 2. The deep-level mines on the Rand

industry's costs by organizing the recruitment of labour from outside South Africa.*

Alfred Beit revolutionized South African gold mining by developing the group system of mining companies, which reduced costs and restored the confidence of foreign investors in the industry. Beit's vehicle for exploiting his own deep-level claims was Rand Mines Limited.† This was very different from other mining companies. It did not, in fact, operate any gold mines at all! Rand Mines was a holding company which bought goldmining properties before establishing a subsidiary to develop the prospect. Shares in this subsidiary company were not issued un-

---

*For more details on the black labour supply for the mines see Chapters 4, 6 and 7.

†In 1887 Hermann Eckstein had formed a company to handle the Johannesburg interests of Wernher and Beit. It was this company that became Rand Mines in 1893.

til Rand Mines became convinced that there was a viable mine. To develop these mines, Beit built up a strong team of engineering and financial experts. Because all services were centralized in Rand Mines, individual mines had access to more working capital, better engineers and cheaper supplies. The group could afford to pay the high salaries commanded by highly skilled American engineers like John Hays Hammond, who was paid more than £1,000 a month. When the potential mine had been thoroughly evaluated and was on the verge of production, the shares in the mining company were released to the public.

A mine developed by Rand Mines was considered a sound investment and not merely a speculative holding, since it was so much more likely to prove profitable. In addition, a share in Rand Mines itself offered investors a new and safer form of investment, because it offered a share in the prospects of not merely one mine but several. The element of speculation was much reduced. Although it was still possible for one of Beit's mines to fail completely, the return on the original investment was guaranteed by the remaining mines. Investors had the choice of investing either in the finance house itself or in one of its gold mines. The former offered more stability, and the latter the chance of more spectacular returns: but under Beit's group system, both were sound investments. The investors of Europe responded to the guarantees of the group system by providing £125 million between 1887 and 1913 to develop the deep-level mines:

> Largely as a result of the group system of finance on the Rand and its intimate overseas financial connections, the shares are dealt in as easily on the main capital markets of Europe as on the Johannesburg Stock Exchange.[36]

By 1895 most of the major mining groups had been created. Rand Mines grew into the largest mining company in the world, controlling companies worth £18 million. Charles Rudd and Cecil Rhodes had founded Gold Fields of South Africa,* which in 1887 had been the first company registered in Britain to bring

---

*The objects of the company were stated as being for the purpose of 'acquiring and dealing with certain auriferous and other mineral properties interests and rights in South Africa'. The first issue of 125,000 shares (100,000 in London and 25,000 in South Africa) was fully subscribed.

the Rand gold fields before the British investing public, and in 1892 this became Consolidated Gold Fields. In 1889 Barney Barnato established Johannesburg Consolidated Investment Co. Two Germans, George and Leopold Albu, formed the General Mining and Finance Co., while another German, Adolf Goerz, started in 1893 a group which eventually became the Union Corporation. The companies made spectacular profits. In 1895 Consolidated Gold Fields alone made a profit of £2,161,778 on a capital of £1,875,000. The founders of the mining groups were enormously rich and powerful. The British Press dubbed them the 'Randlords,' and the economist J. A. Hobson wrote that:

It would be safe to say that this tiny group of men hold in their control the financial, the industrial, and the political destinies of South Africa. Every important interest is directly managed by these men and their close business associates* . . . [they] directly control banks, railways, telegraphs, coal mines and through the finance and trust companies which they direct are able to control many other companies.[37]

The richest of the Randlords, and indisputably the most powerful man on the sub-continent, was Cecil Rhodes. Chairman of De Beers Consolidated and Consolidated Gold Fields, he had been premier of the Cape Colony since 1890. In 1895 his annual income was conservatively estimated at half a million pounds, but his ambitions were still not satisfied.

MINING COMPANIES IN CENTRAL AFRICA

Southern Rhodesia

Rhodes had a messianic belief in the British Empire. As leader of the Cape financial and mining interests, and as premier of the Colony, he pressed his expansionist policies on a reluctant British Treasury.† In 1889 he founded the British South Africa Company as the vehicle for the expansion of the British Empire into Mashonaland and Matabeleland, north of the gold-rich Transvaal. Shareholders' funds were attracted to the company by his extravagant promise of the 'gold of fifty Rands'. His first step

---

*Barney Barnato even owned the Johannesburg Stock Exchange.
†See below, Chapter 6.

was to obtain a concession from King Lobenguela of the Ndebele and a Royal Charter from the Queen of England. This he did by a combination of trickery and deceit, astute lobbying and brute force.*

Learning that he had been duped, Lobenguela wrote to Queen Victoria:

The white people are troubling me much about gold. If the queen hears that I have given away the whole country it is not so.[38]

Lobenguela thought that he was giving Rhodes permission to dig only one mine, but Rhodes was after the whole country and prepared an armed invasion force. In September 1890, his Pioneer Column raised the British flag at Salisbury.

The cost of the invasion and the other expenses of colonization exhausted the capital of the British South Africa Company and brought it to the verge of bankruptcy. Banks in London and South Africa refused to accept BSAC cheques unless they were guaranteed by Rhodes himself or De Beers. Shares in the company dropped from the previous year's high of £3 15s. to 12s. Rhodes ordered that all cheques made out to him by De Beers and Consolidated Gold Fields should be paid straight into BSAC.[39] Thus the profits of the diamond and gold fields of South Africa provided the essential funds for the colonization of Rhodesia.

Why did Rhodes continue to pour money into this venture at a rate that threatened even his vast financial resources? It was not just because of his imperial dreams. There were strong political and economic reasons. Rhodes aimed to encircle the gold-rich independent Transvaal and to drive it into closer cooperation with the Cape. He saw that

the political future would partly depend upon the terms of an economic unification already taking shape in the railway building and the commercial negotiations between the South African states. Matabeleland and the Bechuanaland railway were needed to strengthen the Cape Colony's hand in these negotiations, and to bring the Transvaal into a railway and customs union.[40]

*The story has been told many times. Perhaps the best account is that given by Patrick Keatley in *The Politics of Partnership*, Penguin Books, 1963.

Whatever the imperial ambitions of Rhodes, the British South Africa Company itself was a mining company, or more correctly a 'gigantic speculation in mineral futures over which the royal charter cast the mantle of empire'.[41] Notwithstanding Rhodes's extravagant claims, however, the gold in Southern Rhodesia proved to exist only in small scattered deposits; and, until the railway arrived in 1898, it was extremely costly to process and export. By that year 13,000 settlers had arrived, while the total gold *production* of the previous eight years stood at a mere £20,000, or less than one hundredth of the *profits* from the Rand gold mines in 1898 alone.[42] The railway facilitated the import of machinery; and gold production rose to £126,000 in 1899, £1 million in 1905 and £2 million in 1907. This was an improvement, but it was a far cry from the Rand. In 1910 the eleven leading Rhodesian gold mines made a profit of only £614,000; while the Rand gold-mining companies notched up profits of more than £7½ million.[43]

The British South Africa Company was dangerously over-extended. It had spent large sums on developing the railways, fighting wars, and establishing an administration. It was now clear that the minerals of the area were not going to yield the expected profits. To recover its heavy outlays, the company encouraged the settlement of Rhodesia by white immigrants who, by developing the country, would raise the value of BSAC's investment in the land and the railway.

Northern Rhodesia

Rhodes's northern thrust took him across the Zambezi in 1891. He immediately secured a concession from the Paramount Chief Lewanika of the powerful Barotse tribe, giving the BSAC absolute rights over the 'whole of the territory of the said [Barotse] nation* or any future extension thereof including all subject and dependent territory'.[44] A trader who was present

*Lewanika had neither the intention nor the authority to grant rights over the Lamba tribe, who lived to the north in the area where copper was later found. This was to prove of crucial significance in the pre-independence negotiations over the mineral rights, and fatally weakened BSAC's claim to he rights. See page 197.

when Lewanika signed the concession makes it clear that the company deliberately tricked the Chief, who was

> under the firm impression that [the concession] at once secured to him the personal protection of Her Majesty the Queen and Her government, never for a moment suspecting that the document was nothing less than a gigantic monopoly of the entire natural resources of his country as well as the cession of the administrative, commercial and industrial rights to a trading and commercial association and consequently quite at variance with his expressed desires and the wishes of his people.[45]

When he did discover the truth, Lewanika tried to repudiate the concession, but to no avail. The company kept its concession and reaped a bountiful financial harvest in the years to come.

The Belgian Congo

In 1889 the BSAC sent two expeditions into the Congo to find and annex the gold mines reputed to exist in the province of Katanga. But in the Congo Rhodes clashed with an imperialist every bit as aggressive as himself: King Leopold of the Belgians. Deft diplomacy at the Berlin conference of 1884–5 had secured international recognition of Leopold's African fiefdom, ironically called the Congo Free State.[46] The battle for control of this area was temporarily interrupted when the local chief, Msiri, was killed in a brawl with a Belgian officer. Leopold could not organize a full-scale military expedition himself, and so he 'sold' the area to a newly-formed concession company, the Compagnie du Katanga. In exchange for annexing, occupying and administering the area, the Compagnie du Katanga was given the title to one third of the land in the province. The other two thirds remained with the state. The concession was to last for ninety-nine years, and the company enjoyed an option on mineral rights throughout the province. This vast real estate deal was carried out without any reference to the views that may have been entertained by the inhabitants of the area. Rhodes still coveted Katanga. But the Berlin Conference had decided that the boundary of the competing imperialisms in Africa should be the watershed between the Congo and the Zambezi.

In 1900 the Comité Spécial du Katanga (CSK) was created by an agreement between the Congo Free State and the Compagnie du Katanga jointly to manage the assets of the two associates. Four members of the CSK's six-member board were appointed by the State, and two by the company. Shortly after its foundation, the CSK entered into negotiations with Robert Williams, the founder of a British company called Tanganyika Concessions Ltd (TANKS). Williams agreed to undertake prospecting in Katanga on behalf of the CSK. It was agreed that the CSK and TANKS would each put up half the necessary capital and name half the administrators in any subsidiaries to be established; while the profits would be split 60 per cent to the CSK and 40 per cent to TANKS. The parents soon produced offspring. In 1902 the Compagnie du Chemin de Fer au Katanga was created, and four years later the Union Minière du Haut Katanga came into existence. Prospecting and proving of the mineral deposits discovered in 1891 lasted from 1906 until 1911, when the copper mine came on stream. In 1912 production was 2,492 tons. Five years later production had reached 27,462 tons.[47]

During the first centuries of contact with Europe, Africa had defended her resources from outsiders, and her minerals were exploited at a rate commensurate with the continent's economic development. But fifty years after the discovery of diamonds at Kimberley, the picture had completely changed. Through a combination of force and trickery, the mining companies had broken down the earlier resistance of African rulers to the foreign exploitation of African minerals. The intensive exploitation of African mineral deposits by the mining companies perpetuated and increased the differential in wealth and power between Europe and Africa, established by the slave trade.

2 The Growth of the Mining Companies

Between 1867 and 1935, more than £1,200 million of public and private capital was invested in Africa. Most of this was invested directly or indirectly in the development and exploitation of Africa's mineral resources. Mineral production multiplied sixfold in forty years, while mineral exports rose from a value of £15·5 million in 1897[1] to one of £102·72 million in 1935,[2] as the mining companies expanded their operations in South and Central Africa and began to invest in West Africa.

SOUTH AFRICA

The rapid growth of the gold-mining industry in the Transvaal in the 1880s intensified the conflict between the white settlers of Dutch origin and the trading communities of largely English origin in Natal and the Cape. After some of the mining companies had backed an unsuccessful *coup d'état*, the situation deteriorated, and in 1898 war broke out.* The Anglo-Boer war lasted four years and brought the gold mines to a complete halt for two years.

Even before the war was over, Lord Milner, the British Commissioner at the Cape, was preparing for the reopening of the mines. He contracted with the Portuguese to send a minimum 50–55 per cent of the Rand traffic on the Delagoa railway, in return for a guaranteed amount of labour for the mines. Fearful that this would still not be sufficient, in 1904 he arranged for 50,000 Chinese labourers to be sent from northern China to work on the mines. But after vigorous protests from white miners in South Africa and the election of a Liberal government in England in 1906, recruitment was stopped. All the Chinese were repatriated by 1910.

* See Chapter 6 below.

The Chamber of Mines

The Chamber of Mines played a key role in the recovery of the gold mines by reducing working costs and centralizing the recruitment of labour for the industry. In the ten years following the establishment of the Chamber in 1889, the African labour force increased over 500 per cent, from 14,000 to 97,000 in 1899; with considerable impetus from the 1894 Glen Gray Act, sponsored by Cecil Rhodes when he was premier of the Cape Colony. This Act imposed a labour tax and forced Africans to look for work in the money economy. At the same time the Chamber succeeded in reducing the level of African wages from R78 (£39) per annum in 1887 to a mere R58 (£29) a year in 1897.[3] In 1902 the Chamber institutionalized the collusion among the companies by introducing the 'maximum average' agreement. Under this, the mineowners agreed that the average earnings of all African mineworkers on any mine should not exceed a stipulated maximum average agreed by the industry.

The experience of the industry with a single recruiting agency outside the country led the Chamber to seek a further rationalization of the recruiting system. In 1911, through the good offices of General Smuts, the Chamber secured the passage of a bill in the Union Parliament which gave legislative backing to the maximum average agreement.* The effect of the bill was to eliminate intra-industry competition for labour within South Africa. While recruitment outside the Union was carried out by the Witwatersrand Native Labour Association (WENELA), the Chamber's Native Recruiting Corporation (NRC) was established to recruit mine labour in South Africa, and the three High Commission Territories (Bechuanaland, now Botswana; Basutoland, now Lesotho; and Swaziland). By 1913 the Chamber of Mines had established its monopoly control over African mine labour. Recruitment was centralized and wages were standardized, along

---

*Clause 13(c) of The Native Labour Regulation Act of 1911 read: '. . . no person . . . shall by offering higher wages or greater benefits or other inducements, persuade or attempt to persuade any native who has been lawfully recruited to desert or repudiate any then existing and binding contract of service whether or not the contract be in writing . . .'

with working conditions and length of service. The effective elimination of inter-company competition over labour meant that the companies could concentrate their financial and engineering resources on the improvement of working methods. Average working costs dropped from 29s. 6d. per ton milled in 1897 to 18s. 11d. in 1937. Lower costs meant in turn that the grade of ore which could be mined economically dropped from 7·98 dwt (pennyweight per ton) in 1907 to 4·5 dwt in 1936.[4]

The cost of the high and continuing output from these marginal ore bodies was borne as always by the African mineworker. In 1910 his average cash wage was 48s. 7d. a month.[5] The wage per shift increased only fractionally from 1s. 11·7d. per shift in 1914 to 2s. 0·3d. per shift in 1920.[6] In real terms this represented a sharp reduction of income. The industry went from strength to strength.

Changes on the Rand

Throughout the first quarter of the twentieth century, the gold-mining industry continued to expand, and it would be hard to overestimate its importance to the South African economy. By 1913, more than £125 million had been invested in the mining companies, much of it from overseas.[7] The mines had crushed 207·5 million metric tons of ore, produced 2·94 million kilograms of gold worth £401·2 million, and distributed dividends of £101·8 million to South African and overseas shareholders.[8] Gold accounted for 67 per cent of South African exports in 1914[9] and 40·9 per cent of exports from the whole continent.[10]

At this time the major producing mines were still heavily concentrated on the Central Rand, which had produced 83·9 per cent of the Rand's total output from 1898 to 1911. In the same period the Far East Rand had produced a mere 6·4 per cent of the gold output, but it now became increasingly important, until in 1929 it was producing 80 per cent of the industry's profits.*[11]

One of the men who played an important part in this development was Ernest Oppenheimer, a well-respected figure in the diamond trade, who for many years had worked for Dunkels-

*See Figure 4 for a map of the gold fields.

buhler, members of the powerful London syndicate of diamond merchants. Oppenheimer had been many years in South Africa, and his aim was to build up a major *South African* mining house to compete in the gold industry. He prepared the ground carefully, recognizing the political benefits of registering the new company in South Africa at a time when all the major mining houses were registered in London. He discussed his project with General Smuts and reported that the General 'looks upon the formation of our company with considerable favour'.[12] Smuts also welcomed Oppenheimer's intention to involve American financiers in the new company. Finally in September 1917 Oppenheimer was ready. The Anglo American Corporation of South Africa was launched.*

Both William B. Thompson, founder of the Newmont Mining Corporation, and J. P. Morgan, of the New York banking group, took substantial portions of the equity. The London *Times* noted that this was the 'first occasion on which a definite arrangement has been made for the employment of American capital on the Rand'.[13] The company recorded the meagre profit of £11 13s. 8d. in its first year, on a capital of £2 million. Within a few years, however, Oppenheimer had merged his interest with two other mining houses established on the Far East Rand, Consolidated Mines Selection and Rand Selection, to become the most important gold group in Johannesburg. Not content with this meteoric progress, Oppenheimer was manoeuvring to gain complete control of the world diamond trade.

He outlined his ambitions for the new company in letters to his two main American backers. To Thompson he wrote that his aim in the gold industry was

to secure for our company a fair share in the business offering on the Far Eastern Rand . . . Then I shall steadily pursue the course of bringing about an amalgamation of [Consolidated] Mines Selection

---

*Oppenheimer had a problem with the title of the new company. Before settling on Anglo American Corporation, to signify that the capital came from both Britain and America, Oppenheimer had previously considered the title African-American, but decided against it on the grounds that 'African-American would suggest on this side our dark-skinned fellow countrymen and possibly result in ridicule'.

and Rand Selection with our own company . . . We shall [then] be able to bring about a willing combination of the three Eastern Rand holding companies which would straightaway make us the most important gold group in Johannesburg.

To Morgan he wrote that his other aim was

to create, step by step, a leading position in the diamond industry, thus concentrating by degrees in the corporation's hands the position which the pioneers of the diamond industry [the late Cecil Rhodes, Wernher, Beit, etc.] formerly occupied. Such a position is most difficult to attain requiring intimate knowledge of the diamond trade . . . but above all the support of powerful financial groups who would be prepared to play the part which Messrs Rothschilds played vis-à-vis the original leaders at the time of the De Beers amalgamation.[14]

The Diamond Industry

By 1901 the total value of diamonds produced at Kimberley had reached £100 million, but the monopoly enjoyed by Kimberley and De Beers was beginning to crumble. In 1899 the Transvaal government passed the Precious Stones Act, giving the State 60 per cent of all diamond deposits discovered thereafter. Three years later the Premier mine was discovered in the Transvaal, and in 1907 its production reached 90 per cent of the output from De Beers. A world recession in that year led to a sharp fall in the demand for diamonds. After some hesitation, Premier agreed with De Beers to a production cutback. The next threat to the De Beers' policy of orderly marketing came with the discovery in 1909 of rich alluvial diamond deposits in South West Africa. Although the situation was complicated, because South West Africa was then a German colony and the diamonds were being marketed by a company in Berlin, a conference of producers in 1914 established a fixed quota system to regulate production. Each producer was allocated a fixed percentage of the total supply, which was surrendered to a central marketing agency.*

*The quotas were: De Beers 48·5 per cent, South West Africa 21 per cent, Premier 19·5 per cent, New Jagersfontein Mine 11 per cent. The marketing agency was the same as 1890 (see page 41) except that Wernher Beit and Co. had been dissolved on the death of Wernher and Beit and replaced by Beitmeyer and Co.

Solly Joel, chairman of Barnato Brothers, observed that when it came to diamonds 'there is only one thing and that one thing is reduced production and higher prices'.[15] The extent of the producers' success in stabilizing the market and maintaining a high price for diamonds was remarkable. In 1888, before the amalgamation, the price of diamonds was 20s. 6d. per carat; while in 1920, despite much increased production, the price had risen to 113s. 11d. per carat.[16] This was a considerable achievement, because world production had reached 3,400,000 carats by 1919, with new diamond producers in the Kasai province of the Belgian Congo and in Angola.* Then, after the First World War, the market was flooded with cut diamonds from Russia, as the new revolutionary government sold confiscated jewellery to raise foreign exchange. The South African producers bought up the diamonds and cut their own output by 64 per cent. Market and price stability were preserved, but the existing marketing arrangements remained vulnerable.

Ernest Oppenheimer realized that if a new producer or group of producers, big enough to challenge De Beers, emerged it would be possible to overthrow the existing arrangement between the main producers and the London buying syndicate. Exploiting the opening, Oppenheimer began to buy up production outside South Africa and to form close associations with diamond producers in Angola, the Congo and British Guiana. His first coup was to win a contract for the mining and marketing of the South West African diamonds from under the nose of De Beers.† In 1919 Anglo American became a senior member of the London marketing agency. In 1923 in partnership with Barnato

---

* South Africa's production was 2,660,000 carats, of which De Beers, Premier and Jagersfontein accounted for 81 per cent; South West Africa 540,000 carats; Belgian Congo 100,000 carats; Angola 100,000 carats.

† In negotiations with the Union government, which now had a mandate for South West Africa, Oppenheimer emphasized his South African connections and pointed out that most of the capital for Consolidated Diamond Mines came from South African residents. He won the contract on condition that 'your corporation and those who are associated with you in this matter undertake to work the assets of the companies you are acquiring at all times, with due and proper regard to the interests of the Union government and of the Territory of South West Africa'.

Brothers, Oppenheimer won the rights to market Angolan diamonds; and next year he signed a similar contract with Chester Beatty's Selection Trust diamond interests in West Africa.

In 1925 Oppenheimer withdrew from the London marketing syndicate and concluded a five-year agreement with Consolidated Diamond Mines. De Beers' system of controlled world production and centralized marketing through a central channel was in disarray. At a Producers' Conference in 1926, the principle of centralized marketing was re-established; but marketing was now to be handled by a group of companies led by Anglo American.* Then Oppenheimer moved in on De Beers. He was in a powerful position. He controlled the buyers' syndicate; he had firm connections with diamond producers in Angola, the Congo, West Africa, British Guiana, South West Africa, Namaqualand; he had good political contacts with both government and opposition in South Africa; and finally he owned 25 per cent of De Beers. In 1926 Oppenheimer became a director of De Beers and in December 1929 was elected chairman, with the support of the Rothschild and Morgan banking groups.

He immediately began reorganizing the diamond trade. First he eliminated the possibility of future conflict by integrating both buyers and producers into one organization. South African diamond producers were integrated through a series of share swaps by which Anglo and Barnato's transferred their diamond interests to De Beers in return for a sizeable stake in De Beers itself. Oppenheimer then set up a new and enlarged syndicate. The Diamond Corporation, as it was called, came into existence in 1930, and it signed long-term contracts with diamond producers outside South Africa. The Diamond Corporation was registered in South Africa as a private company, free of any obligation to publish its accounts or to reveal its profits and losses, and De Beers was given the right to appoint the chairman.

Oppenheimer's new structure observed the principles of control over production and marketing through a single channel. To these well-established principles, however, Oppenheimer added

---

*The others were the Barnato Brothers, Johannesburg Consolidated Investment in which Oppenheimer had a share, and A. Dunkelsbuhler, in which Oppenheimer was a partner.

a new one: the producers should own the selling organization. To prevent future clashes with the South African government and the Administration of South West Africa, Oppenheimer persuaded the two governments to become members of the Diamond Producers Association in 1934. De Beers now increased its control by taking substantial equity stakes in all the major South African diamond producing companies, and, together with the Anglo American Investment Trust (ANAMINT),* it bought shares in major foreign producers. The design was complete. The resultant De Beers monopoly of world diamond production and marketing has survived with only minor alterations to the present day.†

SOUTHERN RHODESIA

The scale of mineral production in Southern Rhodesia was insufficient for the British South Africa Company to cover the costs of administering the territory. Indeed the company was saved from bankruptcy only by the revenue earned by the Rhodesian railway. This had been extended from Bulawayo to Broken Hill in Northern Rhodesia, to serve a small lead and zinc mine that had been started in 1906 by Sir Edmund Davis's Bechuanaland Exploration Company. Sir Edmund was also chairman of Wankie colliery, which had produced good-quality coking coal since 1902 and now expanded production to meet the needs of Union Minière. The railway line, which reached the Katanga copper mines in 1912, brought machinery and supplies from the Portuguese port of Beira, together with coal from Wankie, and returned with copper for shipment to Europe.

Southern Rhodesia stubbornly refused to yield the promised mineral riches, and in 1923 BSAC was at last relieved of its administrative responsibilities for the territory. The next year, thirty-five years after it had been established, the British South Africa Company declared its maiden dividend. The new government of Southern Rhodesia encouraged prospectors and small mines, and there was some increase in mineral production. But

*The vehicle for Anglo's diamond interests.
† See Chapter 17.

production remained small in comparison with South Africa's. By 1935 gold worth £131·5 million had been extracted: but of the 1,701 gold producers in 1936, only ten produced more than 10,000 ounces a year, while small producers working limited rich and scattered deposits accounted for 79 per cent of the country's gold.[17] Asbestos and coal were mined, and two American companies, Union Carbide and the Vanadium Corporation of America, had subsidiaries mining chrome. In 1935 minerals accounted for 79·9 per cent of Rhodesian exports and were worth £6·45 million.[18]

NORTHERN RHODESIA

In the nineteenth century Britain had been the world's largest producer of copper; but by the First World War the United States was producing, at 618,000 tons a year, some 60 per cent of the total world output. Within the British Empire there were only two sources of copper, Canada and Australia, which produced only 41,000 and 30,000 tons respectively in 1920. Total African production was a mere 31,000 tons.[19]

The explosive growth of the electrical and automobile industries in Europe and North America led to a rapid expansion of world copper production, which reached 21,100,000 tons in 1929. European copper fabricators and manufacturers were concerned that some 90 per cent of world copper production was under the control of a powerful American-dominated copper cartel, Copper Exporters Incorporated, established in 1926. All the leading US copper producers (Anaconda, Kennecott, Asarco, etc.) and the important European-controlled producers Union Minière and Rio Tinto were represented in the cartel, which was aggressively forcing up the price of copper. In 1928 production increased by only 13·6 per cent, but the cartel pushed up its income by 84·4 per cent. In the month of March 1929 alone, the price soared from 12 to 24 cents a pound. Major European copper consumers reacted sharply to this manipulation of the world market, refused to buy copper at these prices, and began using substitute metals. They pinned their hopes of escaping the cartel on the newly discovered Northern Rhodesian

Copperbelt. But the danger was that this, too, would come under American control.

In 1922 Copper Ventures Ltd, controlled by the American financier Chester Beatty, was granted exclusive prospecting rights to two major areas, the 50,000-square-mile Rhodesia–Congo Border concession and the 1,800-square-mile Nkana concession. Beatty hired an American engineer from Union Minière, Raymond Brooks, to carry out systematic exploration of the area. Within two years, Brooks had proved the existence of a large copper-bearing area and discovered the deposits at N'Changa, Roan Antelope, Mufulira and Bancroft, all of which were subsequently to become important mines.

By now Beatty was running out of money. He tried to interest the major American copper companies, but they did not recognize the importance of the finds. Beatty was forced to sell one concession to raise money for developing the other. He sold the smaller Nkana concession to the Bwana Mkubwa mining company controlled by Edmund Davis. Bwana Mkubwa was an opencast copper mine which had begun production in 1913 and had closed only eighteen months later, due to rising costs. But behind Bwana Mkubwa stood Ernest Oppenheimer's fast-growing Anglo American Corporation.

Oppenheimer had been watching developments in Northern Rhodesia closely for some time when Edmund Davis, who had acted as intermediary for Oppenheimer in negotiations with Belgian and Angolan diamond companies, asked for help in financing Bwana Mkubwa. Oppenheimer agreed on condition that Anglo was appointed consulting engineers. In 1926 Anglo was appointed consulting engineers to the British South Africa Company as well; and by the end of 1927 had interests in the Broken Hill and Bwana Mkubwa mines, and in both the Rhodesia–Congo Border and the Nkana concessions.

Meanwhile Beatty was ready to develop his most promising property, the Roan Antelope mine in the Nkana concession. Drilling had established the existence of 40 million tons of copper ore, grading 3·5 per cent. Since the concession was controlled by Bwana Mkubwa and Anglo, Beatty offered Anglo a 24 per cent stake in the new company. Roan Antelope Copper

Mines was established in 1927, with the American Metal Company also taking an important interest. The development of the Copperbelt was now moving so fast that both Beatty and Oppenheimer decided to establish new companies to handle their operation there. In 1928 the financial structure of the two rival groups crystallized. Beatty established his Rhodesian Selection Trust, backed by the American Metal Company. Anglo American took a 10 per cent interest in RST, and eight months later set up its own subsidiary, Rhodesian Anglo American (RHOANGLO). Several major mining companies loosely associated with Anglo took shares in the new company.* At Anglo's next annual general meeting, Oppenheimer told shareholders that the Northern Rhodesian Copperbelt was likely 'to become of greater importance than any other in the British Empire'.[20] Soon Rhoanglo began developing its Nkana mine.

The object of both RST and Rhoanglo was to bring their mines into production as quickly as possible and demonstrate that the Copperbelt was a large low-cost producer capable of withstanding a period of low prices should the copper cartel seek to drive competition off the world market. The danger was that shortage of capital would give the Americans a chance to gain control of the Copperbelt and leave European industry at the mercy of the cartel. In 1929 Beatty floated N'Changa Copper Mine Ltd, to develop a rich copper deposit in the Rhodesia–Congo Border concession. Once again short of capital, he approached the Guggenheim-controlled American Smelting and Refining Company (ASARCO)† with a complex deal that offered the Guggenheims control of N'Changa, whose concession area was to be greatly extended. With the American Metal

---

*The British South Africa Company, Johannesburg Consolidated Investment, Rand Selection and the Newmont Mining Corporation. The Board of Directors read like a Who's Who of the South African mining world. Edmund Davis was a director, so was Solly Joel of JCI, and Sir Henry Birchenough, President of BSAC. Another director of BSAC on the board was Sir Drummond Chaplin, former administrator of both Northern and Southern Rhodesia.

†The Guggenheims were one of the most powerful families of financier-industrialists in America at this time, and Asarco was one of the largest American copper companies.

Company's interest in RST, this would have meant American domination of almost the whole of the Copperbelt.

Immediately there was a British counter-bid. BSAC, Rhoanglo, Union Corporation, JCI, Rio Tinto and Rothschilds offered to finance N'Changa, and Beatty accepted the British offer. Rhoanglo was the biggest shareholder in N'Changa and was appointed consulting engineers. Attention now centred on the race between Rhoanglo and RST to bring their mines into production. RST's Roan Antelope was first, in October 1931, just beating Rhoanglo's Nkana mine. Jubilation was short-lived, however. The demand for copper collapsed in the worldwide industrial recession, and copper production ground to a halt.

BELGIAN CONGO

By 1932 the Belgian Congo had attracted more than £100 million of Belgian, British, German, American and South African capital; and the country was exporting a wide range of minerals. Copper production had begun in 1911; diamond mining in 1913; tin mining in 1918; and the mining of uranium and radium, on a small scale, in 1922. In Kasai province the Forminière company was exploiting huge deposits of lower-quality diamonds* from 50 mines in its 110 hectares† concession.

The economy of the Congo was dominated by four financial groups: Société Générale, Groupe Empain, Group Comminière, and Banque de Bruxelles; together controlling roughly 75 per cent of the capital in the Congo. Société Générale was by far the biggest of the groups and in 1932 controlled capital worth 4,852 million Belgian francs, or some 56 per cent of the total.[21] The group owned or controlled some forty-one companies in the transport, construction, trading, agricultural, financial and banking sectors. Through its companies and their subsidiaries, the

*The ubiquitous Ernest Oppenheimer had the marketing rights to Forminière's diamonds. Forminière in turn had acquired a 17-per-cent stake in Oppenheimer's Angolan Diamond Company, the Companhia de Diamantes de Angola. Oppenheimer also had a small stake in the other major Congolese diamond company, the Société Minière du Beceka, which in turn was a subsidiary of the Compagnie du Chemin de Fer du Bas-Congo au Katanga.

†One hectare is 10,000 square metres (approximately 2½ acres).

Société Générale commanded almost all the colony's copper, diamond, radium and cement production as well as much of the gold output. But undoubtedly the most important single company controlled by Société Générale and the largest mining company in Central Africa was Union Minière.

The Union Minière mines had been established on the basis of rich oxide copper ores found in surface deposits; but as the depth of the workings increased, the grade fell off and the oxide deposits gave way to sulphide ores. At first Union Minière lacked the capital to use the new electrolytic process for sulphide deposits developed by American companies in Arizona and Chile. But with income rising in the post-war boom, Union Minière could afford to bring its technology up to American levels, and by 1929 it was producing 140,000 tons annually. Copper now accounted for 50 per cent of the Congo's exports; and Union Minière had become the third largest copper producer in the world, with its Katanga mines accounting for seven per cent of total world copper production. The company was the largest single employer of labour in the Congo.

ANGOLA AND SOUTH WEST AFRICA

In both Angola and South West Africa, the discovery of rich diamond deposits led to a dramatic growth in exports. In 1907 South West Africa's mainly agricultural exports were worth £81,000. Only three years later, diamond exports alone reached £836,000; and by 1913, diamonds worth £7 million had been exported.[22] Other mineral production, mainly copper and lead, accounted for between 15 and 20 per cent of the territory's exports from 1925 until the slump of the early thirties brought production to a halt. Diamond production was controlled by Oppenheimer's Consolidated Diamond Mines. In Angola another Oppenheimer company, the Companhia de Diamantes de Angola (DIAMANG), led the expansion of Angola diamond exports from £250,000 and 11·8 per cent of Angolan exports in 1925 to £630,000 and 31·6 per cent of the country's exports in 1935.[23]

WEST AFRICA

Mineral exports became increasingly important to the palm-oil and cocoa exporting countries of West Africa. The Anglo-Oriental Tin Co. controlled six tin mines in Nigeria. Although the annual production of between ten and fifteen thousand tons was around 13 per cent of world production, tin exports never amounted to more than 15 per cent of Nigerian exports.[24] Neighbouring Gold Coast had weathered a Witwatersrand-style boom of mining-company floatations in 1901. Many of the companies were speculative ventures; but gold production expanded dramatically from £38,000 and 4·5 per cent of the colony's exports in 1900 to £597,000 and 41·2 per cent in 1905. Production increased to a value of £1,741,000 in 1917, but an even more spectacular increase in cocoa exports meant that gold now accounted for only 31·6 per cent of Gold Coast exports. Gold production then declined after the First World War, until the increased gold price of 1932 sparked a revival of the industry, and by 1936 gold production was worth £3,048,000.[25] The Gold Coast was also the second largest producer of manganese in the world, from the African Manganese Company's Nsuta mine thirty-nine miles from Takoradi. In 1922 Chester Beatty's Selection Trust group spun off a diamond-mining subsidiary, the Consolidated African Selection Trust (CAST), which began mining on a small scale at Akwatia in Ghana.

CAST was also prospecting for diamonds in other parts of West Africa. They were discovered in Sierra Leone; and in 1934 CAST established a wholly-owned subsidiary, Sierra Leone Selection Trust. Next year the new company obtained exclusive prospecting and mining rights over most of Sierra Leone. Mining began in Kono district, and the company established its headquarters in Yengema. The diamonds were of extremely high quality, and the company had no difficulty in gaining a satisfactory production quota from De Beers. Production continued steadily through the Second World War and the immediate post-war period.

The development and expansion of the African mining industry from 1870 to 1930 was spectacular. But it was inextricably linked to the state of the advanced capitalist economies in Europe and America. Before the large-scale exploitation of mineral wealth, Africa had been only marginally affected by world economic movements, but in 1930–31 it was to receive a severe buffeting. The mining companies had completely transformed the economic structure of the continent.

3 The Structural Transformation of the African Economy

The restructuring of Africa's economy by the mining companies, and the massive export of minerals and capital they initiated, largely destroyed the self-sufficiency of pre-capitalist agricultural economies, and transformed existing trade patterns. The metropolitan centres exercised total control of Africa's economy, and crippled any attempts at independent economic development, except in South Africa and Southern Rhodesia, where local white settlers were able to use the power of the state to encourage some local industrial development. Those African states under full colonial control had no such opportunity.

THE DEVELOPMENT OF FINANCIAL LINKS

The connections established in the last quarter of the nineteenth century by the South African diamond- and gold-mining companies were the conduits for the major proportion of the capital invested in Africa from 1867 to 1935. The development of Kimberley during the 1870s coincided with a period when the wealth of Britain and Europe began to grow at a faster rate than ever before. London developed its role as the hub of world trade, and European capital began to seek new outlets at the same time as Kimberley was looking for more money to develop its mines. The main market for diamonds was London. The leading Kimberley merchants opened offices there and as a natural extension of their diamond-selling business they began trading in diamond shares. Rhodes, Barnato, Beit, Wernher and the other diamond tycoons strengthened their links with the metropolitan capitals of Europe. Rhodes won the great amalgamation battle of 1886, not so much because of his own resources but because of his superior connections with the financial markets of London, Paris and

Berlin. His victory marked the first decisive intervention of European capital in the development of mining in Africa. Henceforth the development of Africa's mining industry would depend on the willingness of Western capital markets to make the funds available.

When the Kimberley tycoons began to switch their attention to the Witwatersrand gold fields, so too did the investors of Europe.* The size of the Rand gold field and the scale of resources required meant that European capitalists were much more important in the development of the Rand than they had been in the development of Kimberley. But in the 1880s South African gold-mining companies were regarded, and rightly so, as highly speculative ventures. The development costs of the new deep-level mining which soon followed meant that it could well be five or even ten years before a particular mine was brought to profitable production. Although a large sum of money came from Rhodes's 'patient and ever hopeful investors' buying easily handled £1 shares in England, the rising costs of secure development led to a shift towards bank finance.† Even in the early 1890s, it might cost £1 million to open up a single promising mine. Such sums could be provided only by the institutional investors. The strong personal links were not enough. The banks and institutional investors needed a greater degree of certainty before they would commit large funds to the gold-mining companies of the Rand. It was Alfred Beit's achievement to attract the institutional investors, looking for solid and stable investments, by his development of the group mining system.

More than 75 per cent of the capital invested in Africa came from British investors, large and small.[1] Most of this was invested in the British territories of Southern Africa, but much went also to non-British territories; so that, for example, more

---

* Gold shares were now being traded on the London Stock Exchange and the market immediately dubbed them 'Kaffirs', a tag they have retained to this day. *Kaffir* is an insulting term used by white South Africans to describe black South Africans.

† Rhodes's Consolidated Gold Fields remained heavily dependent on individual subscribers for many years, largely because of Rhodes's charismatic appeal. See A. P. Cartwright, *Gold Paved the Way*, London, Macmillan, 1967.

than half of the total capital invested in Portugal's African colonies originated in Britain. Not only was the British capital market then at its height, but at a time of rapidly expanding world trade, South Africa's gold mines produced the very means of financing that expansion. Yet despite the importance of this investment for Africa, most of the British capital invested overseas went to the United States, Canada, Australia, India and Latin America. In no year before 1914 did new capital issues for Africa in London exceed 10 per cent of total overseas issues.* The proportion increased after the First World War, but never reached beyond 30 per cent of all new overseas issues.[2]

Before the First World War, French and German investors were of some significance to the South African gold industry. Important links between South Africa and the European capital markets were forged by a small group of German and French traders and bankers who had learnt the skills of high finance in Hamburg, Frankfurt and Paris before coming to South Africa. Among the leading Randlords, Beit, Albu, Neumann and Goerz had all worked for merchants or banks in Germany; and Julius Wernher was sent to Kimberley by the leading Paris diamond merchant, Jules Porges. In France shares could be bought and sold over the counter of the Coulisse and the Crédit Lyonnais. In Germany the capacity of the public to invest in new issues was limited by a regulation requiring company shares to have a minimum nominal value of 1,000 marks (£50), but this was not a bar to institutional investors, and German banks and financiers were deeply involved in the development of South Africa's mining industry. Pressure from Hamburg merchants like the Rosenthals, Littkies and Lipperts pushed Bismarck to raise the flag over South West Africa. The leading German bank, the Deutsche Bank, had opened a branch in London in 1890. It was followed in London and then on the Rand by its great rival, the Dresdner Bank. Two of the major South African mining houses, Union Corporation and General Mining, were backed by these banks. Adolf Goerz, the founder of the Union Corporation, was the brother-in-law of the founder and manager of the

---

*With the exception of the period immediately after the Anglo-Boer War, when loans for reconstruction totalled some 40 per cent of all issues.

Deutsche Bank. The General Mining and Finance Company was formed in 1895 by the Dresdner Bank to take over the interests of the Albu brothers. Despite this German involvement, it seems unlikely that capital invested by continental investors amounted to more than 8 per cent of total private investment in South Africa.[3] Most of the investment capital of Germany, France and Belgium was invested in Europe, and the remainder was concentrated in their respective colonies.

THE PATTERN OF CAPITAL INVESTMENT IN AFRICA 1870–1936

In the period from 1870 to 1936 capital exceeding £1,127 million was invested in Africa,* with most of the £580 million in private capital attracted by the continent's mineral wealth.[4] Some 66 per cent of all capital invested in Africa before 1935 went to a small group of mineral-producing countries: South Africa, South West Africa, Southern Rhodesia, Northern Rhodesia, and the Belgian Congo.[5] And these few countries attracted an even higher proportion (71 per cent) of the £580 million of private capital invested.[6] Two thirds of the private capital invested in South Africa went into the mining industry. In South West Africa and Southern Rhodesia the proportion was 90 per cent. If one includes the private capital invested in essential railway and other transport systems, then some 61 per cent of the capital invested in the Belgian Congo was connected with the development of the country's mineral resources.[7]

The investment of £546 million in public capital was similarly concentrated in the mineral-producing countries: largely for building the administrative and transport infrastructure needed by the mines. Before the discovery of diamonds in South Africa, there were only 63 miles of railway throughout the continent; and even in 1872, there were no railways in Africa south of the Sahara apart from 152 miles in southern Africa. During the next sixty years, between 50 and 60 per cent of public capital went to

*This figure refers to listed capital. It is estimated that a further £94·5 million of non-listed capital was invested in the same period. 'Listed' and 'non-listed' are defined in the notes to Table 1.

Table 1: Foreign capital investment in Africa south of the Sahara, 1870–1936 (*a*)

Country	Total capital invested (listed and non-listed) £m.	Percentage of total capital invested in Africa	Total public listed capital £m.	Total private listed capital £m.	Percentage of private capital invested in mining (approx.)
South Africa(*b*)	523·0	42·81	224·5	250·8	66
S.W. Africa	31·7	2·59	21·6	7·2	90+
Southern and Northern Rhodesia	102·4	8·38	37·6	53·5	90
Belgian Congo(*c*)	143·3	11·73	35·8	100·7	30
Angola	31·9	2·62	10·1	19·5	
Gold Coast	35·3	2·89	13·5	20·2	
Sierra Leone	3·4	0·28	2·5	0·75	
Nigeria	75·1	6·15	34·7	36·8	20
Total British territories	941·3	77·05	448·8	413·5	
Total non-British territories	280·4	22·95	97·5	167·3	
Total Africa	1,221·7	100·00	546·3	580·8	

Notes: (*a*) All figures corrected to nearest £100,000; because of rounding, totals may not add up.

(*b*) Includes Basutoland and Swaziland.

(*c*) Includes Rwanda Urundi.

Definitions: Private listed capital: Equity and loan capital subscribed for non-government enterprise as listed on metropolitan stock markets or reported in financial press.

Public listed capital: Government investment by way of loans or grants.

Non-listed capital: Investment not disclosed to the public. This figure is thus an estimate.

Source: S. H. Frankel, *Capital Investment in Africa*, OUP, 1938, pp. 156–70, and particularly Table 28, p. 151.

the building of railways in South Africa, Rhodesia, Bechuanaland, Belgian Congo, Angola, and Portuguese East Africa (Mozambique): whose combined 21,000 miles in 1935 made up some 66 per cent of the continent's 32,000 miles of railway.[8]

THE GROWTH OF MINERAL EXPORTS

As a result of this massive capital investment, African mineral production for export expanded dramatically, from £15·5 million in 1897 to £102·72 million in 1935, when it accounted for 53·5 per cent of the continent's total exports. Gold exports worth £42·2 million in 1913 had increased to £83·5 million by 1935. Diamond production, after reaching £15·6 million in 1929, was badly hit by the world depression and fell back to £5·8 million in 1935. Copper exports increased from £870,000 in 1913 to £6·2 million in 1935. Table 2 shows the value and percentage of gold, diamond and copper exports for the years 1913, 1929, and 1935. Palm, cocoa and wool exports are included for comparison.

Table 2: Selected African exports, 1913, 1929, 1935

	1913		1929		1935	
	Value of African exports £m.	*Percentage of total African exports*	*Value of African exports £m.*	*Percentage of total African exports*	*Value of African exports £m.*	*Percentage of total African exports*
Mineral						
Gold	42·4	40·9	49·2	27·5	83·5	46·7
Diamonds	14·7	14·2	15·6	8·7	5·8	3·3
Copper	0·87	0·8	4·9	2·8	6·2	3·5
Wool	5·7	5·5	14·7	8·2	9·7	5·4
Palm	6·9	6·7	12·8	7·2	6·6	3·7
Cocoa	3·3	3·1	13·4	7·5	8·1	4·5

Source: S. H. Frankel, *Capital Investment in Africa*, O U P, 1938, Table 49, p. 208.

Minerals displaced agricultural products as the main exports from Africa to the industrialized world. In South Africa, before the discovery of diamonds, wool had accounted for 76 per cent of the exports from Cape Province: with exports also of hides, skins, ostrich feathers and mohair.[9] By 1880 diamonds worth £3·4 million accounted for 43·6 per cent of all Cape exports.[10] By 1910 minerals accounted for 81·1 per cent of South African exports, while agricultural and pastoral exports accounted for only 18·3 per cent.[11] Before the First World War, rubber and ivory constituted 96 per cent of exports from the Belgian Congo. As mineral production got under way this percentage dropped, until by 1926, when the country was producing copper, diamonds, tin, uranium and radium, mineral exports accounted for 61 per cent of the total.[12] In Sierra Leone, where the growth of the mining industry came much later, there was an equally spectacular transformation. In 1928 palm (78 per cent) and kola (17 per cent) nuts were the major exports. In 1936 minerals – diamonds (33 per cent), gold and iron ore – accounted for 57 per cent of Sierra Leone exports, with palm and kola nut exports dropping to 40 per cent of the total.[13]

The result of this transformation was that by 1935 most of the leading African economies were, as Table 3 shows, heavily dependent on one or two mineral exports. South Africa, Northern and Southern Rhodesia were dependent for more than 75 per cent of their respective export earnings on one or two minerals.* The Belgian Congo, Angola, the Gold Coast, and Sierra Leone all depended on minerals for at least 40 per cent of their export earnings. All of Africa was not, of course, affected to the same degree. For example, although Nigerian tin production accounted for 10–13 per cent of world tin production, the main exports remained palm products and cocoa.

Within Africa a small group of countries (South Africa, South West Africa, Northern and Southern Rhodesia, and the Belgian Congo) dominated the continent's trade with the metropolitan states. In 1935 the trade of these five mineral-producing countries constituted 67 per cent of the continent's trade. And the five territories together produced 92 per cent of Africa's minerals.[14] Within these five, South Africa was by far the most important. By 1935, South African mineral exports of £77·5 million were worth three times the mineral exports of the remaining African territories. Gold alone accounted for 46·1 per cent of the total domestic exports of Africa and represented a greater value than all the non-mineral exports provided by the rest of Africa.[15]

*Until 1929 South West Africa was similarly dependent on diamonds and copper exports, but the depression of that year led to a drastic cut in diamond production.

Table 3: Africa's mineral exports, 1935 (*a*)

Country	Percentage of total African exports (*1*)	Value of domestic exports £m. (*2*)	Value of mineral exports £m. (*3*)	Mineral exports as percentage of total exports (*4*)	Major minerals and percentage of exports (*5*)
South Africa	54·87	97·9	77·5	79·1	Gold (72%) Diamonds (3%)
South West Africa (*b*)	1·39	2·5	0·8	32·8	Diamonds (24%)
Southern Rhodesia	4·53	8·1	6·5	79·9	Gold (63%) Asbestos, Coal
Northern Rhodesia	2·62	4·7	4·5	96·0	Copper (72%) Lead, Zinc
Belgian Congo	5·07	9·1	5·6	62·4	Copper (29%) Diamonds (26·1%)
Angola	1·13	2·02	0·6	45·5	Diamonds (32%)
Gold Coast	5·18	9·2	3·8	41·0	Gold (28·5%) Diamonds (5·9%) Manganese (6·6%) Cocoa (56·3%)
Sierra Leone	0·87	1·6	0·81	52·1	Diamonds (33%) Gold, Iron Ore
Nigeria	6·27	11·19	1·8	15·7	Tin (13%) Palm (34·9%) Cocoa (14%)
Total Africa (*6*)	100·00	£178·5	£102·7	57·55	Gold (46·7%) Diamonds (3·3%) Copper (3·5%)

Notes: (*a*) Because of rounding, totals may not add up. Percentages are calculated from Frankel's original figures.

(*b*) Importance of mineral exports understated because of temporary cutback in diamond exports. For comparison, in 1929 diamonds worth £2·6 million accounted for 44·37 per cent of exports. Minerals accounted for 73·42 per cent of South West African exports, and South West Africa accounted for 3·4 per cent of Africa's total exports.

Source: S. H. Frankel, *Capital Investment in Africa*, OUP, 1938: (*1*) Table 46, p. 198; (*2*) calculated from Table 51, p. 212; (*3*) Table 50, p. 211; (*4*) calculated from Table 51, p. 212; (*5*) p. 213 and calculated; (*6*) Table 43, p. 193 and Table 51, p. 212.

Not all of the companies were successful. But enough of them were for enough of the time to ensure a continuing flow of minerals and capital surplus from Africa to the metropolitan centres. The metropolitan investors in the South African diamond- and gold-mining companies earned a handsome return on their investment. From 1868 to 1928, South and South West Africa together produced £340 million of diamonds,[16] while the total amount of foreign capital invested in the diamond industry was probably no more than £20 million. The dividends of the diamond-producing companies, excluding the profits made by the individual diggers, exceeded £80 million.[17]

The South African gold industry used more than £200 million capital in its development before 1932. Of this, roughly £120 million came from foreign investors, while £63 million were reinvested profits. Income from the sale of gold in the period totalled some £1,145 million; and no less than £255 million was distributed in dividends, with overseas investors receiving 75 per cent, or roughly £190 million.[18] Because mineral exploitation began there much later, the hey-day of mining companies in Africa above the Limpopo had to wait until after the Second World War. Nevertheless, some very useful profits were being made meanwhile. Thus in the Belgian Congo, for instance, Société Générale made profits of 4,151,214 Belgian francs on capital employed of 4,800,524 Belgian francs between 1920 and 1934, while heavily investing from income at the same time.[19]

Transformation of Trading Patterns

The incorporation of African mineral resources into the world capitalist economy led to a startling transformation of the continent's main trading routes. Previously, these had run across the continent, while the main export routes fed the Indian Ocean trade with Arabia, India and China (see Figure 1). The expansion of the mining industry warranted substantial investment in cheaper and more modern forms of transport such as railways and river barges. But the new trade routes established by mining companies and the colonial governments did not serve the main centres of population and economic activity in Africa; they were designed to link the mineral and agricultural resources of the continent to the metropolitan economies by providing the swiftest and cheapest route to the sea, for the passage to Europe. In the Belgian Congo, for example, the main route for Katangan copper ran not through the Congo, but through neighbouring Angola, so that it supplied no spin-off benefits to the Congolese economy. The copper mines of Northern Rhodesia exported most of their copper production and received most of their supplies through the railway network of Southern Rhodesia and South Africa. Figure 3 shows the railways and some important mining areas in Africa in 1935. It will be seen how close the coincidence is between railway construction and mineral development particularly in southern Africa where the bulk of the track was laid.

These changes in the African economy brought profound social and political changes in their wake. The two most important were the large influx of white settlers and the demand of mines for cheap unskilled black labour from the rural areas.

MINING COMPANIES AND WHITE MINORITY RULE

In southern Africa especially, the mining companies and the wealth they generated attracted European settlers and gave them the means to assert and entrench their dominance over the African inhabitants. The large settler populations were able to win the political leverage which the African population lacked, and they used this leverage to divert, through taxation, some of the immense profits from mining to build up white farming and lay the basis of an industrial economy.

In South Africa, the British-controlled mining companies at first allied themselves with British imperial interests, but following the Boer War had decided to realign themselves with the white settlers. Sharp clashes occurred between 1910 and 1930, when the demands of white miners threatened their level of profits, but on no occasion did the companies support the political demands of the African majority. In particular those companies now owned and controlled by South Africans enthusiastically backed the white settlers. But the others too,

Fig. 3. Principal trading routes in Africa in 1935
SOURCE: S. H. Frankel, *Capital Investment in Africa*, OUP, 1935.

recognizing that their prosperity depended on the continuing supply of cheap unskilled black labour, came to regard the surrender of high wages and political authority to the white settlers as an acceptable price to pay.

In Southern Rhodesia the policy of the British South Africa

Company led to the entrenchment of white minority rule. And ironically, indeed, this came about because the country failed to produce the expected mineral bonanza.

The most important single element determining the nature of the economic and political development in Southern Rhodesia was the British South Africa Company's overestimation at the end of the 19th century of its mineral resources and the persistence of this overestimation for roughly 15 years ... The costs incurred in the meantime increased the stake of the Company in the country and led to additional heavy development investment particularly in railways.[20]

When the mines failed to produce the expected results, the company, badly over-extended and short of money, encouraged immigrants from England and Europe, in the hope that, by developing Rhodesia's agriculture, they would increase the value of the company's land and railway holdings. The BSAC thus helped to create a white rural bourgeoisie, which consisted largely of farmers, together with those owning or working small and medium mines, and which was effectively to command the development of the country in the absence of control by international capital.

In both Northern Rhodesia and the Belgian Congo the mining companies and their white employees acted as independent entities only tenuously connected to the colonial administration. A colonial official in Northern Rhodesia wrote that owing to the shortage of staff

there has never been the necessary strength of experienced officers to deal with developments. In consequence the mine management has been compelled to undertake duties and responsibilities which should scarcely come within its sphere ... Such origin has tended to render the mining community somewhat independent in outlook and tardy establishment of the various functions of government has met with a moderate welcome.[21]

In the Belgian Congo, Union Minière was the virtual ruler of Katanga province, and the links with the Congolese capital of Leopoldville were extremely tenuous. The main route between Katanga and the coast for communication with the European metropolis was the Benguela railway, which ran through Angola.

Just how independent Katanga and Union Minière had become was not to emerge until an African government in Leopoldville tried to assert its authority in 1960.

The Demand for Labour

Foreign investment was instrumental in establishing the mining industries of central and southern Africa, but the mines depended for their operation and profitability on massive supplies of cheap unskilled migrant labour. Extensive and often brutal recruitment by the mining companies; the land, hut and poll taxes levied by the colonial authorities; and the expropriation of lands, precipitated an exodus of male workers from the rural areas to earn money in the burgeoning mining camps and towns.

In South Africa, as we have seen, the mineowners established the Chamber of Mines in 1889 to reduce the industry's labour costs.* It recruited labour from all over the sub-continent, and even set up recruiting stations as far north as Tanganyika. In Mozambique the Portuguese authorities used taxes and the force of arms to ensure that the companies secured the quota of labour that the colony had agreed to provide under the Delagoa Bay agreement. By 1910, around half of all black mine labour came from Portuguese East Africa.[22] By 1926 the South African gold mines employed 203,000 black mineworkers; and by 1936, the number had risen to 318,000, drawn from all over the sub-continent. Labour was available in large numbers in the 1930s because of a succession of severe droughts.[23]

To meet the demand from white settlers and officials for domestic and clerical labour in the Belgian Congo, the colonial government encouraged the growth of the population around the colony's administrative centres. The main demand for labour came from Union Minière and from the Lever Brothers' palm-oil-producing subsidiary, Société des Huileries du Congo. In the beginning, Union Minière recruited only from Katanga and neighbouring Kasai, but demand soon outstripped supply. Into the breach stepped the labour recruiters, who bought, or

*See Chapters 1, 2, 6, 7 and 12 for more on the role of the Chamber of Mines.

simply press-ganged, able-bodied men; leading them with ropes tied round their necks to Union Minière, which paid at the rate of 1,000 or 1,200 francs a man.[24] Despite these unsavoury methods, however, the critical shortage of labour for the mines continued: so that in 1926–7 Union Minière was forced to cut back production by 10 per cent.[25] The solution developed by the Société des Huileries and Union Minière was a division of the Congo into exclusive recruiting zones. The result was predictable. In those areas the companies recruited a staggeringly high proportion of the able-bodied male population. In some districts of Kivu, 54 per cent of the male population was recruited, while there were villages that lost as many as three quarters of their men. And all this affected a very high proportion of the total population, since it was the most heavily populated areas that suffered the greatest proportional losses.[26]

In Northern Rhodesia, the picture was similar. Even before the development of the Copperbelt, more than 20,000 men in the territory had been drawn away from their villages to work in Southern Rhodesia, while another 10,000 were working in Katanga. By 1930 the copper companies in Northern Rhodesia were employing 30,000 men, mostly from the Bemba, Bisa and related tribes. In 1936 at least 120,000 from a taxable population of 280,000 in the Bemba area of Northern Rhodesia were working away from their home villages.[27] Shortly before the Second World War, more than half the men were absent, and in some districts the proportion reached two thirds.

The mining companies in Southern and Central Africa continued to rely heavily on migrant labour. Only in the Belgian Congo was there any move to create a stabilized skilled black labour force for the mines. In 1928 Union Minière introduced a policy aimed at gradually increasing the percentage of workers on long-term contracts and allowed to live with their families. But most miners remained migrant labourers on short-term contracts. This had disastrous consequences for the men and the societies from which they came. The degradation of miners forbidden to bring their families to the mines was only matched by the misery in the rural areas caused by the loss and absence of so many men for so long.

The Destruction of the Traditional Society

Over large areas of Africa the voracious demand for both land and labour by the colonial authorities and the mining and concession companies destroyed the economic, social and political structures which had held African society together. In the absence of the able-bodied young men, the maintenance and development of the rural economy was left to the old, the sick, the women, and the children. In many tribes it was the men who were responsible for capital formation in the rural economy, through the improvement and extension of the community's farms.[28]

But then it was the policy of the mining companies and the colonial authorities to keep the rural areas unproductive, in order to provide a reliable flow of cheap unskilled labour for the mines and farms of colonial Africa. In South Africa and Rhodesia, where African farmers responded ably to the rising demand for agricultural produce, the governments moved swiftly to inhibit this response.[29] Africans were prohibited from buying land in the best farming areas and were crowded into scattered small areas of generally unproductive land.[30] Having prevented them from competing with the white settlers, the colonial authorities then withheld from African farmers the aid and education that they freely gave white farmers to encourage the adoption of more intensive and scientific methods of production. In the twenty-five years to 1936 South African government expenditure on white agriculture was £111·25 million, while African agriculture received only £0·75 million. The pattern was the same in Rhodesia.[31] The traditional growing of maize, millet, cassava and sweet potato by the *chitemene** method and heavy population pressure resulting from the various Land Area Acts further reduced the productivity of the land to which the African population was confined. Without the injection of capital and labour, and without a government-supported educational effort, the rural areas outside the white farms were condemned to backwardness and poverty. There was widespread malnutrition; many of the men who trekked to the mines were rejected as unfit for

*Slash and burn.

work,[32] victims of an economic system which required the decay of the pre-capitalist agricultural sector.*

The damage done to the traditional agricultural economy over wide areas of Central and Southern Africa was accompanied by a deep moral and social crisis, because the familial and tribal ties which sustained the traditional social structure were fatally undermined. In order to recruit labour, the mining companies exploited traditional leaders and customs. In the Congo, for example, the practice of demanding a dowry in cash began at the beginning of the twentieth century. The price was subject to continuing inflation and tended to be highest where the effects of colonialism were highest, as along the line of rail and near the mining companies' recruiting stations. On the order of the local chiefs, the strongest young men in a village were handed over to the recruiting agents against the provision of a marriage dowry. Since it would take several years' hard work in the mines to raise sufficient money for the dowry, and several more to pay off the debts incurred at the wedding, the mines were assured of a continued supply of labour.[33]

In the advanced capitalist nations, the exodus from the rural areas which accompanied the process of industralization was preceded by a dramatic increase in agricultural productivity. By contrast, industrialization in the underdeveloped countries of Africa was the *cause* of a massive decline in rural productivity. The rural migration in Africa was precipitated and its direction determined by the needs of satellite economies moving in step with the industrial economies of Europe and America. When demand for primary products was booming, the labour market expanded rapidly, drawing ever more workers into the cash economy. But falling industrial demand in the metropolitan centres halted this growth of the labour markets and sent surplus labour back into the rural areas.

*Any improvement in the agricultural productivity of the African farmer would tend to push up the price of labour needed in large quantities on the mines and farms because productive African farmers would not need to earn cash wages to pay the colonial taxes. The income from the sale of farm produce would be sufficient. To induce Africans to work in the mines in such a situation would require sharply increased taxes but also increased wages to meet those taxes.

The depression of the early thirties led to a collapse of industrial activity in the Western economies, with many millions of workers thrown into prolonged unemployment. But in Africa the effect was even more devastating. As African economies were built on a narrow undiversified base, to provide primary goods for export, they were particularly sensitive to setbacks in world trade and lacked a domestic industrial sector to cushion the effects of falling industrial demand in the metropolitan areas. Diamond mines in South and South West Africa, Angola and the Congo were closed down. In the Belgian Congo, copper production was drastically cut back from 138,000 tons in 1930 to only 50,000 by 1932; and an estimated 100,000 workers were forced back to the rural areas. In the copper mines and in many other sectors of the economy, food rations were substituted for cash wages.[34] In Northern Rhodesia the development of new mines was halted; existing mines were closed or cut down their production; and more than 15,000 Africans were dismissed, many of them with only 24 hours' notice.[35] But the rural areas to which all these men now returned had been crucially weakened by the earlier departure of so many young male workers and were no longer able to support them.

By 1935 viable social and economic systems in large areas of Southern and Central Africa had been destroyed or totally transformed. African manpower and mineral resources had been incorporated into the metropolitan-dominated world capitalist system. The result was decapitalization, structurally generated unproductiveness, and increasing misery for the indigenous inhabitants.

4 International Mining Companies and the Post-Colonial State 1935-70

During the depression, the collapse of industrial activity in the developed countries gave the underdeveloped countries a chance to correct the imbalance of their economies. While this happened to some extent in some South American countries,[1] in Africa it was only South Africa that had the necessary degree of political independence to take advantage of the situation and divert resources to build up her industry and agriculture.* In the rest of the continent, the shape and size of the growing African mineral industry was determined by the mining companies, their need for profits, and the need of the industrialized states for Africa's minerals.

EXPANSION OF THE AFRICAN MINING INDUSTRY

African mineral production began to expand again only as industrial activity in the metropolitan centres picked up in the mid-thirties.

In Northern Rhodesia, the mines and towns of the Copperbelt started to grow again. The Roan Antelope and Nkana mines increased production, while Rhodesian Selection Trust now opened a new mine at Mufulira. But the depression hit Beatty hard and he had been forced to trade his 46 per cent stake in RST for an 11·8 per cent stake in American Metal.† Rhoanglo lacked the capital to bring its N'Changa mine into production; and so Anglo American used some of the bumper profits from its South African gold mines to launch N'Changa Consolidated Mines in 1937, with an initial capital of £5 million.[2] By 1939 the

* See Chapter 6.
† Which joined with Climax Molybdenum to form American Metal Climax (AMAX) in 1957.

three producing Copperbelt mines (Roan Antelope, Nkana and Mufulira) had an annual output of 211,000 tons of copper.[3]

The diamond market took longer to revive but there was a cautious resumption of production. CDM resumed operations in 1935, Kimberley in 1935, Dutoitspan in 1936 and Bultfontein in 1937. In South Africa, the gold industry, which had escaped the effects of the depression, was enjoying the greatest boom in its history.

The outbreak of the Second World War in 1939 precipitated a rapid expansion of mining in Africa, to meet the demands of the Allied war machine. Copper from Northern Rhodesia, and later uranium from the Sengier mine in the Belgian Congo, were of immense strategic importance to the Allies (uranium from the Sengier mine was used on all American A-bombs until 1952). Plant in South Africa and Northern Rhodesia was run at levels far above its rated capacity to meet the demand from Europe. This exacted a heavy toll on machinery. After the war, it took several years for production levels to recover and once again reach those attained during the war.[4]

In the immediate post-war era, European nations engaged in rebuilding their shattered economies were perilously short of foreign exchange, particularly dollars and other 'hard' currencies. Unwilling or unable, therefore, to buy minerals and metals on the open market, France and Britain instead developed deposits in their African colonies which were within the sterling and franc monetary zones.* The outbreak of the Korean War in 1950 caused a worldwide shortage of minerals, as the American armament industries sucked up available supplies. Indeed, this shortage was such that the Americans set up the Paley Commission to determine the extent of domestic mineral resources and establish the country's current and future mineral requirements. Meanwhile US mining companies scoured the world for new sources of supply, and were especially attracted to Africa.

* Britain and France used the gold reserves and blocked sterling and franc deposits of their African colonies held in London and Paris to finance their own post-war economic recovery. In effect Africa was forced to make low-interest loans to rebuild European industry while the continent languished in poverty.

A great wave of exploration and prospecting swept across the continent in the 1950s to reveal far more of Africa's vast mineral wealth. Mining companies discovered huge deposits of bauxite, high-grade iron ore, copper, and other valuable raw materials. And, as ever, South Africa remained in the forefront of the African mining industry. Rich copper deposits were discovered in the Cape and the Transvaal, and the first important new diamond pipe since 1902 was found in the Northern Cape. There was a spectacular expansion of the gold industry when, at the end of the fifties, after a dozen years of development and a capital expenditure of £550 million, the giant Orange Free State gold mines came on stream. Copper production expanded in both Northern Rhodesia and the Belgian Congo. West Africa attracted a lot of attention, particularly from American mining companies. In Liberia the American-controlled Liberian Mining Company began mining iron ore, while in Ghana, Kaiser Aluminium was considering the exploitation of the country's bauxite and hydroelectric resources. Aluminium Ltd began to develop Guinea's extensive bauxite deposits. The French began mining uranium in Gabon for their nuclear programme. In Sierra Leone a diamond rush caused a rapid expansion of diamond production.

The fifteen years after the Second World War were the heyday of mining companies in Africa. New mines were developed in all corners of the continent, and existing mines were expanded. Under the benevolent eye of the various colonial or minority white governments, the companies achieved enormous profits. The exploitation and underdevelopment of Africa proceeded apace. If nationalist governments had been in control of Africa's mineral resources, they might have developed them at a pace more suited to indigenous needs and retained some of the capital surplus to build up productive, educational, managerial and industrial infrastructures. The foreign technology and capital could have been transferred to national control as the result of bargaining between trading partners. But the mineral exploitation was imposed by external financial and colonial powers, while the technology and capital remained firmly in the hands of foreign mining companies. The colonial powers diverted only enough of the mining receipts as was necessary to provide the essential transport infrastructure for the company mines, and to meet administrative costs. Little was spent on the development of the economic, educational and social base for well-balanced growth. The expenditure on African education and agriculture by the companies and the colonial authorities was pitifully small and uneven. The provision of educational facilities in Zambia at Independence in 1963 was at the same inadequate level as Ghana's had been in 1943.

In Northern Rhodesia, increases in output were achieved through higher productivity rather than an increase in the labour force, which remained relatively stable at around 230,000. In the Belgian Congo, Union Minière's stabilization policy had, by 1956, reduced the percentage of annually recruited workers from 63 to 8 per cent of the mine labour force, while the percentage of workers accompanied by their wives rose from 30 to 86 per cent over the same period. The company provided housing, security, higher wages, and training for skilled jobs. And by 1957, the productivity of African miners was equal to that of the European ones.[5] But Union Minière remained the exception. The South African gold mines' well-established network of recruiting stations drew men from all over the sub-continent. In 1956 the mines employed 305,000 black miners, of whom 63·7 per cent (200,000) came from outside South Africa.[6]

As the companies dramatically expanded the scale and scope of their activities, profound political changes shook the continent. The rise of African nationalism seemed to threaten the protection which the companies had enjoyed from colonial rule. When the white settlers of the Belgian Congo and Northern and Southern Rhodesia made their infamous attempt to create an enlarged white-dominated federation in Central Africa, mining companies lent their powerful support to the cause. The Union Minière-sponsored Katangan secession was ended only after a bitter civil war and many thousands of deaths. The late fifties and early sixties mark the high-water mark of direct political intervention by the mining companies in African affairs.

Majority rule came to Northern Rhodesia. But white regimes survived in Southern Rhodesia, South Africa, Namibia (South

West Africa) and the Portuguese colonies of Angola and Mozambique. The mining companies, enjoying a comfortable accommodation with these regimes, continued to build their production and profits on the exploitation of low-paid African labour.

When independence came to the majority of African states at the beginning of the sixties, the companies generally adopted a low political profile and concentrated on maintaining good relations with national governments. The new governments, heavily influenced by foreign advice, adopted a strategy of mobilizing foreign capital for economic development. Mineral production was encouraged; and with rising metal prices during the early sixties, mining companies expanded existing capacity and established new mines. Still further mineral deposits were discovered by the companies and the United Nations Development Programme, which launched a worldwide series of geological and mineral surveys in 1961. The mining industry boomed.

West Africa, aided by its proximity to US and European markets, emerged as a major mineral-producing area. The LAMCO iron-ore mine made Liberia the largest African, and the world's third largest, exporter of iron ore. There was an increasing flow of minerals from West Africa to the industrialized states: bauxite from Guinea; diamonds from Sierra Leone; iron ore and copper from Mauritania; uranium and manganese from Gabon; phosphates from Togo, Senegal, and Western Sahara; uranium from Niger; and gold, diamonds, manganese and bauxite from Ghana.

The mining companies were reluctant to invest in Central Africa, after the upheavals of the early sixties. But they showed no such reluctance in the white-ruled states of southern Africa. Iron ore and petroleum deposits were discovered and exploited in Angola. In Southern Rhodesia, despite the effects of United Nations' economic sanctions imposed after UDI, chrome production increased, while new nickel and copper mines were developed. In Namibia, De Beers began mining diamonds from the sea, and Rio Tinto Zinc discovered a huge deposit of uranium. In South Africa itself, the Palabora open-cast copper mine came into production, and the platinum mines in the Transvaal massively increased their production to meet the rising demand from the petro-chemical and automobile industries of the advanced capitalist states. Elsewhere in the sub-continent, a new mine was established in Swaziland, to supply iron ore to Japanese steel mills, while new copper-nickel and diamond mines came into production in Botswana.

As a result of this rapid expansion, the contribution of mining to the African economy rose from 5 per cent in 1960 to 10 per cent in 1968, making it one of the fastest growing sectors of the continental economy. Mineral products including petroleum now made up 56 per cent[7] and primary goods 92 per cent of Africa's total exports.[8] Impressive though this growth was, Africa's mining industry remained controlled by foreign mining companies, and by far the bulk of its production was exported to the major industrial nations of the world.

The economies of many African states were severely distorted and heavily dependent on the fluctuating income from mineral exports. Whereas in most industrial states the production of minerals accounts for between 1 and 3 per cent of the gross domestic product, in African mineral-producing countries the proportion is much higher. In 1970 in Namibia mining accounted for approximately 50 per cent of the GDP; in Zambia, 35 per cent; Gabon, 32 per cent; Liberia and Mauritania, 30 per cent; Sierra Leone and Swaziland about 12 per cent; and Guinea, about 9 per cent;[9] and 12 per cent of the GDP in South Africa.[10] As ever, the African mining industry was geared to supply the industrialized world. In 1970 minerals accounted for 95 per cent of total exports from Zambia; 90 per cent from Mauritania; 75 per cent from Sierra Leone; 69 per cent from Liberia; and 67 per cent from Zaire;[11] while even in South Africa, the most developed nation on the continent, minerals accounted for 58 per cent of total exports in 1970.[12]

The disastrous effects of this dependence were seen in 1974 when the economies of the industralized world went into recession Once again, as in the 1930s, the effects were exported to Africa. Copper-producing countries like Zambia and Zaire were particularly badly hit. All over Africa production was cut back, expansion plans put on ice, mines mothballed, investments cancelled and workers made redundant.

THE INTERNATIONAL MINING COMPANIES IN THE
WORLD ECONOMY

In the 1960s new machines and new productive methods began
to make radical changes in the way that goods and services were
produced, transported and marketed. The most important of
these changes involved the widespread adoption of computers;
of numerically controlled machine tools; of containerization; and
of giant oil and ore carriers. These techniques have made
possible a much larger scale of production, and as a consequence
smaller plants are becoming uneconomic and uncompetitive. A
distinguishing feature of nearly all these innovatory techniques is
a sharp reduction in the amount of labour required to operate
them and a sharp increase in the capital cost of new plant.
Computers can easily cost more than a million pounds each;
giant oil tankers, £7 million or more; an oil refinery will cost at
least £30 million; and a new steel plant as much as £200 million.
But none of these will require more than a handful of workers to
run them.[13] Part as cause and part in consequence of this second
industrial revolution, as it has been dubbed, larger companies
have emerged to exploit the economies of scale now made possible. As it develops the new technology promotes further concentration of capital into large multinational units. Small companies join together in ever-larger agglomerations of capital or
face being driven out of business completely. The result is that

the giant companies using the new technology available to them are
becoming the main accumulators and investors of capital, the determinants therefore of the growth path of the economy; the main employers of labour, the determinants therefore of remuneration and
conditions of labour; the main economic power base in the world, the
determinants therefore of political power.[14]

The mining companies in Africa have been profoundly affected
by this second industrial revolution. Technological innovations
such as the development of giant ore carriers, advances in blasting technology, heavy truck and tyre design, the development of
huge draglines, and an increasing use of computers in the design
and operation of mines have expanded the scale of modern

Table 4: The importance of mineral exports to African economies, 1972

Countries		(a) Total exports US $m.	(a) Value of mineral exports US $m.	Minerals as % of total exports	Main mineral exports and percentage of country's total exports	Other important exports and percentage of country's total exports
Algeria	(b)	905·9	678·1	74·9	oil and natural gas (74·9)	food stuffs (12·2)
Angola		515·4	227·0	44·1	petroleum (25·4) diamonds (11·4)	coffee (27·6)
Botswana	*					meat
Cameroon		42·0	16·4	7·6	diamonds copper-nickel	coffee (27·8) cocoa (18·1)
Central African Rep.	(b)	216·2	11·9		aluminium (7·6)	
Congo's People's Rep.	(b)	364	3·1	32·6	diamonds (32·6)	timber (55·9)
Egypt	(b)	45·2	9·4	6·8	diamonds (6·8)	raw cotton (51·0)
		788·9		1·2	fuels and mineral oils (0·8)	
Gabon		195·9	129·6	66·1	petroleum (43·0) manganese (19·9)	timber (29·9)
					uranium (3·2)	
Ghana	(b)	209·1	36·5	17·4	gold (10·1) diamonds (4·2)	
Guinea	(d)	51·0	33·0	65·0	manganese (2·3) bauxite (0·8)	coffee (10·0)
					alumina and bauxite (60·0)	
Kenya		267·4	30·2	11·3	iron ore (5·0)	coffee (25·9) tea (17·2)
					petroleum products (9·3)	
					soda ash (2·0)	
Liberia	(b)	224·0	166·3	74·3	iron ore (71·7) diamonds (2·5)	rubber (16·9)
Libya		2,938·0	2,938·0	100·0	petroleum (100)	
Malagasy	(c)	145·0	13·3	9·2	chromite (2·1) graphite	
Mauritania	(b)	99·9	77·0	77·0	iron ore (77·0) copper	fish (8·0)
Morocco		619·1	141·1	22·8	phosphates (22·8)	fruit and veg. (28·9)
Namibia	(d)	304·2	130·0	60·0	diamonds (32) copper lead (28)	fish (25) sheep
Niger		53·5	9·4	17·5	uranium (17·5)	ground nuts (33·6) cocoa (7·2)
Nigeria		4,293·1	3,575·9	83·3	petroleum (81·9) tin (1·4)	ground nuts (1·4)

S. Rhodesia	(e)			21·0	asbestos (6·8) gold (4·5) copper (4·1) iron (2·7) chromite (2·4)	tobacco (29·8)
Rwanda	(b)	24·1	8·9	36·9	tin ore (20·4) wolfram (16·5)	
Senegal		212·3	9·4	4·4	phosphates (4·4)	ground-nut oil (37·3)
Sierra Leone		107·2	78·3	73·0	diamonds (61·9) iron ore (11·1)	palm kernels (4·3)
South Africa		4,288·1	2,479·9	57·8	gold (34·5) copper (3·5) diamonds (2·7) asbestos (1·1) manganese (1·1)	food and livestock (17·1)
Swaziland		83·4	24·0	28·8	asbestos (14·6) iron ore (14·2)	sugar (29·3) wood pulp (16·9)
Tanzania		288·8	17·4	6·0	diamonds (6·0)	coffee (18·6) cotton (16·3)
Togo		48·8	18·3	37·6	phosphates (37·6)	cocoa (29·6) coffee (20·8)
Tunisia		310·5	123·3	39·7	oil (26·3) phosphates (13·4)	olive oil (26·7)
Uganda		220·9	15·8	7·2	copper (7·2)	coffee (71·5) cotton (23·3)
Zaire	(c)	13·0	623·0	76·6	copper (60·7) diamonds (5·7) cobalt (4·2) zinc (2·1) tin (2·4)	palm oil (5·0) coffee (4·8)
Zambia		758·5	748·4	98·7	copper (90·7) zinc (3·0) cobalt (1·6) lead (1·0)	tobacco (0·5)
1970 Africa (inc. SA) Total		14,460	6,640	45·9		
1970 Africa (exc. SA) Total		12,310	6,390	51·9		

Notes: All figures approximate. Export percentages change with production and price changes. Mineral exports from Ethiopia, Mozambique and other African states not listed here were not significant in 1972.

* indicates major change in pattern of exports since 1972.

(a) Figures converted to US $ at prevailing rates as given in *UN Statistical Yearbook 1975*, Table 190.

(b) Figures for 1971 (Algeria, CAR, CPR, Egypt, Ghana, Mauritania, Rwanda).

(c) Figures for 1970.

(d) Estimate for 1970.

(e) Figures for 1965 (no breakdown published after UDI).

Source: Africa 74/75, Africa Journal, 1974.

Percentage calculations by author.

mining operations enormously. Massive low-grade mineral deposits have supported viable mines, as larger and larger open-cast mines reduce unit production costs. With this technological revolution, the large companies have grown still larger, while the smaller ones have either been absorbed or gone to the wall. Roan Selection Trust, for example, has become a wholly-owned subsidiary of the American AMAX company, despite the fact that it was itself one of the largest copper producers in the world. In South Africa, Anglo American has absorbed many of the smaller mining houses and taken a significant stake in many of the remainder. The result of this centralization is that, while in the nineteenth and early twentieth centuries most of the mining in Africa was carried out by individual joint stock companies with operations in only one country, today most of the mines are being developed by the international corporations, operating in many countries around the world.

THE INTERNATIONAL MINING COMPANIES AND THE INDEPENDENT AFRICAN GOVERNMENTS

At first the new governments, ill equipped to tackle the complex issues of mining policy, were wary of challenging the immense power of the mining companies. Dependent in so many cases on mineral production and exports for so much of their revenue, African governments tended to give first priority to maintaining or increasing the production and export of minerals. Insofar as they interfered at all in the activities of the mining companies, it was to improve conditions of employment or to increase taxation: as, for instance, in Zambia. However, during the 1960s, African governments came to feel that

on the one hand in the eyes of the world, and of their people, they cannot claim to exercise sovereignty while outside interests appear to control the disposal of the most important of their wasting natural resources. On the other they feel that unless they are directly concerned with the management of these enterprises the governments cannot be sure that they are conducted in the national interest and not in a manner intended to benefit only their overseas principals.[15]

94

The first attempts to secure more control of the mining industry were not encouraging. In Ghana, the government of Kwame Nkrumah failed to get the mining companies to build an aluminium smelter as part of the great Volta Dam Project. In Guinea also the government wanted a smelter to augment the Aluminium Company's bauxite mine. The company ordered a go-slow and finally halted all work at the mine. The government cancelled the concession but was finally forced to sign an agreement with another American aluminium company, Harvey Aluminium, which also used foreign smelters.[16] Similarly in Zaire, General Mobutu's extended struggle with Union Minière suggested that such nationalization moves would have to be much better planned if they were to be really successful. But in 1967 President Nyerere issued his famous Arusha Declaration and later nationalized foreign-controlled companies. Tanzania's successful series of nationalization measures spurred similar action in Zambia. In 1968, under the Mulungushi Declaration, President Kaunda restricted the activities of foreign companies, including the two giant mining groups which controlled the Zambian Copperbelt. The Zambians watched the 51 per cent takeover of the copper mines in Chile in 1969 very closely; and this seemed to show that, contrary to Zaire's experience, an agreed takeover was possible. In 1969 Zambia 'invited' the copper companies to offer the government a 51 per cent stake in their interests. Zambia's nationalization moves had a powerful effect on other African governments. In Sierra Leone, President Siaka Stevens declared his government's intention to take a 51 per cent stake in the Sierra Leone Selection Trust operations. In Uganda, President Milton Obote announced that the government would take a 55 per cent stake in Falconbridge's Kilembe copper mine;* and in Ghana, when the government of Dr Busia was overthrown, the new military government ordered a commission of inquiry into aluminium operations and took a majority

---

*In 1970 General Amin's military government reversed the takeover, but in 1975 the General 'confiscated' Kilembe copper mines on the grounds that Uganda 'had never received the money from the copper exported' (*African Development*, May 1975, p. 47).

stake in Consolidated African Trust's Diamond Mine and Lonrho's Ashanti Gold Fields. By 1975 Zaire, Togo and Mauritania had also taken majority stakes in the mining company operations in their countries.

Political independence has undoubtedly changed the operating environment for the mining companies. But it has remained very much an open question whether the increased state participation in the African mining industry will promote economic development. The governing elites, inheriting an underdeveloped economy and the overdeveloped state apparatus of the colonial era, are unable to tackle the structural imbalance in their economies. They are merely intermediaries between Africa's resources and the international mining companies. The mining companies require political stability to ensure the continued operation of the mines. But Africa's ruling elites are inherently unstable. Their chronic political instability is rooted in the fundamental imbalance and irrationality of the economies of independent Africa. A rash of military coups has not removed the political instability, because military governments have not tackled the underlying structural imbalance. It is this contradiction between the companies' need for stability and the instability of the underlying economic structure that even yet threatens the position of the mining companies in Africa. But for the moment they remain firmly in control of Africa's mineral resources.

Although the mining companies have ceded majority ownership of many of their African mines, they have evolved a whole range of techniques to neutralize the effects of these takeovers. The most important element of their strategy is to cede *nominal* control to the country in the form of majority ownership while retaining as much *effective* control over the mines as possible through management, advisory and sales contracts, and by reinforcing the rights of minority shareholders. As long as day-to-day management remains the prerogative of the mining companies, much of the investable surplus needed in Africa for development continues to leave the continent. In the company accounts this surplus sometimes appears as profits, but often it is disguised as inflated 'head office charges', 'management and consultancy fees', 'machinery costs', 'shipping and handling charges', and 'marketing commission'. The paramount concern of the mining companies is to ensure the continuing flow of minerals and profits from Africa. The developmental needs of Africa are likely to be a long way down any company's list of priorities.

The second industrial revolution has increased the cost of entry for a late-comer into the select group of industrialized states. The world division of labour created in the nineteenth and early twentieth centuries has a tendency to keep on reproducing itself. Even if detailed knowledge of the new techniques were freely available to the underdeveloped countries, and it is not, they would still lack the enormous capital resources, the skilled manpower, the organizational and operational ability, to participate in this revolution. The truth is, of course, that the underdeveloped countries are in no position to compete. Weakened by the constant outflow of economic surplus, they do not even control their own resources. They remain in thrall to the international companies, whose monopoly of skills and information extends the frontier of technology still further to strengthen their own position.

5 African Minerals in the World Economy

By 1973 the African continent was one of the major mineral-producing areas of the world and accounted for 84 per cent of the world's cobalt; 80 per cent of the gold and diamonds; 46 per cent of the vanadium; 37 per cent of the platinum; 33 per cent of the chromite; 32 per cent of the manganese; 29 per cent of the phosphate; 24 per cent of the antimony; 20 per cent of the copper; 21 per cent of the uranium; and 10 per cent of the crude petroleum. Africa is also a significant producer of iron ore, bauxite, coal, asbestos; and, to a lesser extent of tin, lead, zinc, columbium, vermiculite, potash and fluorspan (see Table 5).

Quantity alone does not determine the importance of African mineral production. The metallurgical grade chrome produced in Southern Rhodesia, South African amosite asbestos, Gabonese manganese and Sierra Leonean gem diamonds are of major importance because of their high grade or special qualities. The importance of South Africa's gold, platinum, diamonds and antimony production is enhanced because the marketing is largely controlled by South African companies and, in the case of gold, by the South African Reserve Bank.

Despite the impressive scale of mineral production, however, most of Africa's mineral wealth remains unexploited. Africa has some of the world's largest deposits of iron ore, bauxite, phosphates, platinum, vermiculite and coal. New deposits are likely to be found as more of the continent is extensively prospected, and Africa's importance as a source of minerals for the advanced capitalist states is sure to increase significantly in the years to come because the industrialized nations have become heavily dependent on foreign sources of supply.

MINERALS IN THE INDUSTRIALIZED NATIONS

The whole structure of contemporary civilization in the industrialized world is dependent on minerals. Without them there would be no skyscrapers, no cars, no ships, no planes, no typewriters, no central heating, no air-conditioning and none of the provision of running water and disposal of sewage which an industrial society takes for granted. An average 1,000 c.c. motor car, for example, contains 686 kilos of steel, 75 kilos of cast iron, 25 kilos of light alloys, 4 kilos of copper, 4 kilos of brass and bronze, and 12 kilos of zinc, tin and lead alloys: a total of 806 kilos of metals. A 2,500 c.c. car will use 1,730 kilos of metal. In England car production utilizes approximately 20 per cent of the annual steel consumption, 10 per cent of the aluminium, 35 per cent of the zinc, 50 per cent of the lead, 13 per cent of the nickel and 7 per cent of the copper.[1]

When industry began, the necessary minerals were usually found locally, but as demand grew more and more had to be imported. The industrial revolutions in Europe and America were built around the fortunate juxtaposition of iron and coal deposits (for example, at Sheffield in England, the Ruhr in Germany, and Pittsburgh in the USA). As the local ore bodies became depleted, the developed nations increasingly turned to the rest of the world for their raw material needs. Imported ores were often of much better quality and almost invariably of higher grade than local deposits. In Britain, for example, the grade of iron ore in the main Frodingham and Northampton iron-ore fields is no more than 27 per cent. Imported Liberian ore grades at 67 per cent metal content. In the USA not a ton of chrome has been produced since 1962, largely because domestic low-grade chemical deposits cannot compete with high-quality metallurgical grade ore imported from Southern Rhodesia. The productive capacity of the developed nations is adapting to the new situation. New metal refineries and steel plants are being sited at the coast, where there are deep-water berths for the new giant ore carriers. The early self-sufficiency of the major industrial powers in essential raw materials has been dramatically transformed, and their con-

Table 5: African mineral production, 1973 (a)

Mineral	Unit	Total African production (inc. S A)	Most important African producing country (world rank in brackets)	Percentage of world production	Percentage of African production	Other important producing countries in Africa and percentage of African production
Steel industry metals						
Iron ore	metric tons	47,805,000	Liberia (7)	4·9	49·2	South Africa (14·5) Mauritania (14·2) Angola (7·8) Algeria (3·6) Sierra Leone (3·0) Guinea (2·2)
Nickel	"	31,626	South Africa (7)	2·8	61·4	Rhodesia (37·9) Morocco (0·6)
Manganese	"	2,963,600	South Africa (2)	14·9	46·4	Gabon (33·0) Ghana (10·6)
Chromium	"	1,078,000	South Africa (1)	22·0	67·2	Zaire (5·7) Morocco (4·1) Rhodesia (25·2) Malagasy (6·1) Sudan (1·5)
Cobalt	"	18,374	Zaire (1)	68·9	81·9	Zambia (10·6) Morocco (7·5)
Vanadium	"	8,893	South Africa (1)	42·4	91·8	Namibia (8·2)
Tungsten	"	1,047	Rwanda (15)	0·9	42·7	Zaire (27·9) Rhodesia (18·5) Uganda (10·7) Namibia (2·7)
Columbium	"	1,329	Nigeria (3)	4·0	94·1	Zaire (3·8) Mozambique (2·2)
Older major metals						
Copper	"	1,426,800	Zambia (5)	9·9	49·5	Zaire (32·4) South Africa (10·8) Rhodesia (2·2) Namibia (1·9) Mauritania (1·7)
Tin	"	15,745	Nigeria (6)	3·2	37·0	Zaire (32·6) South Africa (16·7) Rwanda (8·4) Namibia (4·6) Rhodesia (3·3)
Lead	"	212,100	Morocco (9)	3·0	49·6	Namibia (29·8) Zambia (11·9) Tunisia (7·4)
Zinc	"	290,400	Zaire (13)	2·1	40·6	Zambia (25·2) Namibia (18·1) Morocco (6·1) Algeria (1·0)

	Unit	Production	Country (rank)	%	%	Other producers
Light metals						
Bauxite	,,	4,068,000	Guinea (7)	4·5	74·9	Sierra Leone (16·3) Ghana (8·6)
Precious metals						
Gold	kilos	898,926	South Africa (1)	75·4	95·2	Ghana (2·5) Rhodesia (1·7) Ethiopia (0·7)
Platinum	ounces	1,785,000	South Africa (1)	36·8	100·0	
Fuel minerals						
Coal	metric tons	67,925,000	South Africa (8)	2·8	91·8	Rhodesia (4·5) Zambia (1·4) Nigeria (35·5) Algeria (17·3)
Crude petroleum	,,	286,505,000	Libya (6)	3·8	36·6	Egypt (2·9) Angola (2·9) Gabon (2·7)
Natural gas	mill. cu. metres	16,249	Libya (12)	0·9	67·1	Algeria (29·2) Nigeria (1·9) Tunisia (0·7)
Gemstones and abrasives and insulants (b)						
Diamonds (b)	met. carats	33,499,000	Zaire (1)	29·3	39·1	South Africa (22·6) Ghana (8·1) Botswana (7·3) Angola (6·3) Sierra Leone (4·9) Namibia (4·8)
Asbestos	metric tons	452,000	South Africa (3)	6·7	73·9	Rhodesia (17·7) Swaziland (8·2)
Nuclear and chemical						
Uranium	,,	4,080	South Africa (3)	13·7	66·1	Niger (24·5) Gabon (9·4)
Phosphates	,,	28,453,000	Morocco (3)	17·3	60·0	Tunisia (12·2) Togo (7·9) South Africa (7·3) Senegal (5·4) Spanish Sahara (2·4)
Antimony	,,	16,757	South Africa (1)	22·3	92·4	Morocco (7·2) Algeria (0·4)
Fluorspar	,,	357,324	South Africa (7)	4·7	58·9	Kenya (20·1) Tunisia (13·9) Namibia (6·9)

Notes: (a) All figures are approximate. Where 1973 figures not available, production estimated from 1972 or 1971 figures. Percentages calculated by author.
(b) Includes both gem and industrial diamonds measured by weight not quality or value. See Chapter 19 for further analysis. South African and Namibian production combined far exceeds the value of Zairean production.
Source: UN *Statistical Yearbook 1975*; *Mining Annual Review 1974*, *Mining Journal*.

tinued prosperity is becoming more and more dependent on foreign supplies.

The most striking case of such dependency is Japan. In 1970 it produced a mere 0·8 per cent of world minerals, yet imported 10 per cent of world production.[2] By 1980, according to a report prepared by the Japanese Ministry of International Trade and Industry, Japan will require 30 per cent of world mineral output.[3] In 1975, Japan imported 100 per cent of her bauxite and nickel, 91 per cent of her iron ore, 82 per cent of her copper, 57 per cent of her zinc, and 46 per cent of her lead requirements.[4] The great Japanese trading companies scour the world for long-term mineral contracts to ensure that Japan's smelters, refineries and steel mills will not run short of supplies. Although Japan gets most of its minerals from Asia and Australia,* it is turning its attention increasingly to Africa. Japan has long-term contracts for iron ore with companies in Angola, Liberia, Mauritania, Sierra Leone, Swaziland and South Africa; for copper, with Zaire, Zambia and Uganda; and for manganese, with Gabon, Angola and Ghana.[5]

The United States, in contrast to Japan, has large mineral resources; and this makes the transformation in her mineral position all the more remarkable. In the 1920s the US produced a surplus of around 15 per cent. But since the Second World War it has been a net importer of metals and their ores. By 1950, the surplus had become a deficit of 10 per cent. By 1971, domestic resources supplied 100 per cent of only three metals (molybdenum, vanadium and magnesium);† while the US imported 100 per cent of its chromite, manganese, rutile and tin; 87 per cent of its nickel, aluminium and bauxite; 82 per cent of its asbestos; 77 per cent of its gold; 60 per cent of its zinc and lead; 50 per cent of its antimony; 34 per cent of its iron ore; 33 per cent of its titanium; and 25 per cent of its copper requirements.[6]

* In 1970 Japan took 87 per cent of Australia's total iron ore export of 33 million metric tons (*Minerals Yearbook 1971*, Vol. III, US Bureau of Mines, 1973, p. 102).

† The US was self-sufficient in five other mineral commodities: coal, feldspar, phosphate, uranium and steel (although much of the iron ore to make the steel was imported).

The interim report of the National Materials Commission set up by President Nixon in 1969 stated that by the end of the century the US would be dependent on outside sources of supply for over 80 per cent of its mineral needs.[7] In 1970 US metal and mineral imports amounted to $9 billion, against exports of $5 billion. If the trend of the past twenty years persists, the report estimated, this annual $4 billion deficit will have grown to over $60 billion by the end of the century.[8] The chairman of the giant American Metal Climax company warned that by the year 2000 the US would face a chronic shortage of metals and minerals, and that the US would never again be self-sufficient in most of the metals it requires.[9]

Western Europe accounts for 43 per cent of world trade and 40 per cent of world mineral trade.[10] It is the world's largest importer of minerals; importing 37 per cent of its iron ore and 70 per cent of its non-ferrous metal needs. It imports 96 per cent of its tin, 95 per cent of its copper, 92 per cent of its nickel, 76 per cent of its lead, more than 30 per cent of its bauxite and 23 per cent of its aluminium.[11] Individual countries are even more dependent on imports. West Germany imports 100 per cent of its nickel and tin; 99 per cent of its copper and bauxite. The United Kingdom similarly imports 100 per cent of its bauxite, copper, zinc and nickel; over 99 per cent of its lead; and over 90 per cent of its tin requirements.[12]

The international mining companies have developed mineral production in the underdeveloped countries to a level far exceeding local needs, in order to satisfy the voracious demand of the advanced industrialized states for minerals. The result is a massive gap between the production and the consumption of minerals in the underdeveloped countries. Table 6 gives the consumption of seven major minerals as a percentage of production in Africa, the Third World, and the industrial states. It will readily be seen that the production deficit in the industrially advanced states is matched by the excess production in Africa and the Third World.

Table 6: The production and consumption of major minerals in the developed and underdeveloped nations in 1970 (thousand metric tons)

Metals	Western Industrialized Nations (inc. S. Africa)		Third World (inc. Africa)		Africa (exc. S. Africa)		South Africa	
	Prod.	Cons.	Prod.	Cons.	Prod.	Cons.	Prod.	Cons.
Aluminium	7,484	7,299	535	475	161	20		49
Copper	2,706	5,402	2,363	257	1,140	13	144	35
Lead	1,758	2,416	714	264	213	20		26
Nickel	348	426	204	8	11	2	12	4
Tin	14	161	168	18	18	1	1	2
Zinc	3,202	3,450	1,089	395	262	12		55
Iron ore	320,053	471,135	173,463	29,700	46,957	1,500	7,605	7,605

Source: Alexander Sutulov, *Minerals in World Affairs*, 2nd edition, University of Utah, Salt Lake City, 1973, Table XI, p. 52; Table XV, pp. 58–9.

TRADE

Africa's mineral exports generally follow the patterns of trade established by the companies in the colonial era, which have continued and even been reinforced subsequently. Table 7 shows the persistence of these colonial patterns of trade. Britain gets gold from Ghana and South Africa, bauxite from Ghana, copper from Zambia, iron and manganese from Sierra Leone, and diamonds from South Africa, Sierra Leone, Ghana, and Tanzania. France gets copper from Congo-Brazzaville and Mauritania, manganese from Gabon, bauxite from Cameroon and Guinea, uranium from the Central African Republic and Gabon. Perhaps the only exception to this pattern of trade is Guinea; with whom France broke off relations in 1958 when Guinea voted for independence, and which has since traded substantially with the socialist states. Even so, France remains the second largest supplier of imports to Guinea and the second largest buyer of Guinean exports.

Recent efforts to persuade African states to affiliate and associate themselves with the EEC may be seen partly as a continuation and reinforcement of the colonial pattern of trade and dependency, and partly as a defensive move against the incursions of the US into what had hitherto been regarded as the exclusive preserves of France and Britain.[13] The US in its worldwide quest for additional sources of minerals has invested in Zaire (ex-Belgian), Gabon (ex-French), Ghana (ex-British), Libya, Liberia and South Africa. Latin America remains the USA's main source of mineral imports, but African supplies are increasingly important. The association of African states with the EEC seems to presage the division of the world into major trading blocks dominated by developed states (EEC, USA, Japan), each with its attendant satellite continents or subcontinents (Africa, South America and South-east Asia respectively). The 1972 devaluation of the dollar and the accompanying demands for trading concessions from Europe and Japan represented in part a determined attempt by the USA to remain competitive and escape exclusion from important trading areas. Europe's riposte was to set up the STABEX scheme designed

Table 7: The direction of Africa's trade in 1971

Country	Colonial power	Main trading relationships	
		Percentage of imports from	Percentage of exports to
Algeria	France	(a) France (42·4) West Germany (10·0)	France (53·6) West Germany (12·9)
Angola	Portugal	Portugal (31·6) West Germany (11·4) USA (11·0)	Portugal (30·4) USA (19·6) Japan (10·7)
Botswana	UK		
Cameroon	France/UK	France (49·5) Other EEC (19·0)	France (27·6) Other EEC (39·7) US (9·0) UK (2·6)
Central African Republic	France	(a) France (57·8) Other EEC (19·9)	France (50·6) Israel (14·9)
Congo People's Republic	France	(a) France (67·5) Other EEC (24·6)	France (30·9) Other EEC (32·6)
Egypt	France/UK	USSR (13·5) West Germany (7·0) France (5·2)	USSR (39·7) India (6·1) Czechoslovakia (5·1)
Ethiopia	Indep. (Italy)	Italy (16·1) Japan (14·6) West Germany (11·0)	USA (43·9) West Germany (8·0) Japan (6·1) Italy (5·6)
Gabon	France	(b) France (56·6) USA (14·6)	France (34·5) USA (7·9)
Ghana	UK	UK (25·1) USA (15·0)	UK (21·3) US (23·8)
Guinea	France	(c) UK (30·6) USA (13·3)	USA (20·1) France (17·4) USSR
Kenya	UK	UK (30·7) EEC (20·4) Japan (10·9)	UK (19·7) West Germany (9·0) USA (7·2)
Liberia	Indep. (USA)	West Germany (31·5) Japan (26·2) Italy (16·8) USA (11·0)	West Germany (58·6) USA (17·0) Sweden (12·0)
Libya	Italy	(b) Italy (23·3) UK (10·0) West Germany (9·4)	Italy (24·0) West Germany (17·5) UK (16·4)
Malagasy	France	(b) France (46·4) West Germany (8·3) Japan (3·7)	France (29·6) USA (11·2) Japan (3·8)
Mauritania	France	USA (44·5) France (36·6)	France (20·7) UK (15·7) Other EEC (24·1)
Morocco	France	France (31·0) Other EEC (18) US and Canada (15)	France (36) UK (5) Other EEC (21)

Country	Principal partner	Imports	Exports
Mozambique	Portugal	Portugal (26·1) South Africa (14·9)	Portugal (38·3) South Africa (10·4)
Namibia	South Africa		
Niger	(b) France	France (46·4) West Germany (7·8)	France (38·7) Nigeria (27·7)
Nigeria	UK	UK (32) USA (14·0)	UK (22) USA (14) Other EEC (39)
Rhodesia	(d) UK	UK (30·4) South Africa (22·9)	Zambia (25·3) UK (21·9)
Rwanda	Belgium	Belgium (22·0) USA (14·0)	Belgium (23·0) Uganda (7·5)
Senegal	France	France (47·4) USA (5·8) West Germany (5·8)	France (51·9) Ivory Coast (6·9)
Sierra Leone	UK	UK (29·0) Japan (10·0)	UK (62·0) Other EEC (14)
South Africa	UK	UK (20·9) USA (16·5) Other EEC (26·5)	UK (26·4) Japan (12·9) Other EEC (19·3)
Spanish Sahara	(e) Spain		
Swaziland	UK		
Tanzania	UK	China (18) UK (14) Other EEC (14)	UK (25·0) Japan (24·1)
Togo	France	France (37·4) UK (12·8) Other EEC (16·2)	UK (24·0) Other EEC (11) USA and Canada (9)
Tunisia	France	France (36) USA (15) Italy (9)	France (28·3) Other EEC (34·9)
Uganda	UK	UK (32·3) Japan (13·5) Other EEC (23·2)	Italy (20) France (19) West Germany (13)
Zaire	(b) Belgium	Belgium (24·5) West Germany (10·4) US and Canada (12·0)	UK (24·2) USA (22·3) Japan (10·9) Other EEC (13·0)
Zambia	UK	UK (24·7) South Africa (14·8) USA (10·2)	Belgium (51·8) Italy (11·2) Other EEC (21·5) Japan (20·6) UK (16·3) West Germany (9·4)

Notes: UK is not included in EEC imports or exports. 'Other EEC' refers to those member countries not specifically mentioned.
(a) Figures for 1970. (b) Figures for 1972. (c) Figures for 1966. (d) Figures for 1974. (e) Now Western Sahara.

Source: Africa 74/75, Africa Journal 1974.
All figures approximate. Percentage calculations by author.

to try and secure the EEC's future supplies of raw materials. STABEX aims to stabilize the export revenues of African countries associated with the EEC. So far, STABEX, which was agreed at the Lome Convention in 1975 covers major agricultural commodities, such as coffee, cocoa, and cotton, but it does not cover any minerals apart from iron ore.[14]

These manoeuvres underline the importance to the advanced capitalist states of maintaining access to mineral supplies from Africa and the Third World. And it is this dependence on the mineral supplies of the Third World that offers the poor countries a chance to increase the price of their mineral exports. Their ability to do so depends in the first instance on the proportion of world mineral production that they control. To give some indication of the *potential* strength of the Third World's bargaining position, Table 8 gives, for the year 1973, a breakdown for each metal of the proportion of world production originating in the advanced capitalist states, the socialist states, the Third World in general and Africa in particular.

In interpreting these figures, one must remember that with the world supply and demand of many minerals so finely balanced, the withdrawal of even small quantities can have widespread effects on market prices and industrial activity. The USA imported only 3·6 per cent of her total oil requirements from the Middle East countries,[15] but their price rises and threats to withhold supplies had serious economic and political repercussions. Thus the specific relationships between the various metropolitan powers and their satellites may be more significant than the overall dependence of the industrialized nations on the underdeveloped nations. Table 9 indicates the importance of African minerals to selected industrialized states. From this we can see the importance of Zambian copper, South African gold, Namibian uranium, and Ghanaian manganese to the British economy; of Gabonese uranium, Guinean bauxite and Togolese phosphates to the French economy; and Rhodesian chrome and Liberian iron ore to the US economy. One can also see the particular importance of South African mineral production to the Western industrial nations. It would be virtually impossible for any other country to replace South Africa as a supplier of chrome, platinum group metals and gold even in the long term; and very difficult to find alternative supplies of manganese and uranium in the medium term. South Africa is estimated to have 48 per cent of the world's manganese reserves, 49 per cent of gold, 64 per cent of vanadium, 83 per cent of chrome and 86 per cent of platinum reserves.

The success of collective action by the Organization of Petroleum Exporting Countries (OPEC) in putting up prices has encouraged other mineral-producing countries to come together and press for higher prices. CIPEC, or the organization of copper-exporting countries (Zaire, Zambia, Chile, Peru), was already in existence. The IABPC, or International Association of Bauxite-Producing Countries (Guinea, Guyana, Jamaica, Surinam, Sierra Leone and Yugoslavia), was set up in 1974. A similar organization of iron-ore-exporting nations was established in March 1975. There was talk also of establishing a manganese-exporting group. But the situation is different for each metal, and the success of these groups will depend on such factors as the availability or cost of substitute sources; the degree of control that national governments can exercise over the mineral output of their countries; the political and economic solidarity of the mineral-producing countries; and above all the importance of those minerals to the developed world.

To meet the challenge of these groups, the industrialized nations have enormous financial and technical resources, which enable them to adopt a wide range of defensive measures. The rising cost of raw mineral imports is passed on in manufactured products at first, but further rises will promote the construction of new mines around the world in both underdeveloped and developed countries. The increase in world supplies will tend to hold prices down and weaken any cartel of developing countries. Higher prices will also stimulate greater production in the industrialized countries; the building-up of government stockpiles; and the reduction in quantity of imports needed, by developing new alloys that use different metals.

A more imminent and serious threat to the advanced capitalist nations may be that energy costs will limit production well before known mineral reserves run out. As lower and lower

Table 8: African mineral production in the world economy, 1973

Mineral	Unit	World 1973 production (a)	Developed capitalist (inc. S A) (b) %	Communist (c) %	Third world (excl. S A) (d) %	Africa (inc. S A) %	Africa (excl. S A) %	South Africa %	World's largest producer and percentage of world production
Steel Industry metals									
Iron ore (Fe content)	metric tons	482,600,000	39·4	26·2	28·1	9·9	8·5	1·4	USSR (24·5)
Nickel (Ni content)	" "	692,400	46·0	25·8	26·4	4·6	1·8	2·8	Canada (35·2)
Manganese (Mn content)	" "	9,200,000	22·8	34·6	36·4	32·2	17·3	14·9	USSR (30·9)
Chromium (Cr_2O_3 content)	" "	3,290,000	25·2	32·9	32·1	32·8	10·8	22·0	USSR (24·3)
Cobalt	" "	21,850(e)	15·1		84·1	84·1	84·1		Zaire (68·9)
Vanadium (V content)	" "	19,250	70·0	17·4	8·8	46·2	3·8	42·4	South Africa (42·4)
Tungsten (Wo_3 content)	" "	48,431	27·7	45·6	26·6	2·2	2·2	0·002	China (20·9)
Columbium	" "	31,040	64·0		29·3	4·3	4·3		Canada (64·0)
Older major metals									
Copper (Cu content)	" "	7,140,000	40·6	21·3	36·7	20·0	17·9	2·1	USA (21·8)
Tin (Sn content)	" "	185,000(e)	8·9	0·08(e)	89·5	8·5	7·1	1·4	Malaysia (39·1)
Lead (Pb content)	" "	3,410,000	48·5	25·5	22·5	6·2	6·2		USA (16·0)
Zinc (Zn content)	" "	5,670,000	53·6	20·5	22·7	5·1	5·1		Canada (21·8)
Light metals									
Bauxite	" "	68,410,000	33·8	15·4	50·8	5·9	5·9		Australia (21·5)

	Unit	World production	Developed capitalist (b) %	Communist (c) %	Third World (d) %				Leading producer
Precious metals									
Gold	kilos	1,135,000(e)	89·6	0·5(e)	9·9	79·2	3·8	75·4	South Africa (75·4)
Platinum	ounces	4,850,000	49·5	50·5		36·8	36·8		USSR (50·5)
Fuel minerals									
Coal	metric tons	2,206,800,000	43·9	50·7	5·2	3·1	0·3	2·8	USA (24·0)
Crude petroleum	,,	2,774,600,000	20·9	18·0	61·0	10·3	10·3		USA (16·4)
Natural gas	million cu. metres	1,278,280	62·0	22·5	15·0	1·3	1·3		USA (50·2)
Gems, abrasives and insulants									
Diamonds	metric carats	44,633,000(f)	16·9	21·3	60·1	75·1	58·1	16·9	Zaire (29·3)
Asbestos	metric tons	4,490,000	49·5	26·6	12·9	9·1	2·4	6·7	Canada (39·9)
Nuclear and Chemical									
Uranium (U)	,,	19,668	92·8		7·2	20·7	7·0	13·7	USA (51·7)
Phosphates	,,	98,500,000	41·8	25·0	32·7	28·9	26·8	2·1	USA (38·8)
Antimony (Sb content)	,,	69,400	6·0	14·9	39·6	24·1	1·8	22·3	South Africa (22·3)
Fluorspar	,,	4,700,000	42·1	22·2	35·6	7·9	3·3	4·7	Mexico (23·4)

Notes: (a) All figures are approximate. Where 1973 not available, figures are estimated from 1972 or 1971 production. Percentages calculated by author.

(b) Developed capitalist: Western Europe, North America, Oceania, Japan, Israel, Greece, Greenland, South Africa.

(c) Communist: USSR, Eastern Europe, China, North Korea, North Vietnam, Cuba.

(d) Third World: Africa (excludes South Africa), Asia, Middle East, Far East.

(e) Figures exclude USSR and China.

(f) Includes both gem and industrial diamonds, measured by weight not quality or value. See Chapter 19 for further analysis.

Sources: UN Statistical Year Book 1975, Mining Annual Review 1974.

Table 9: The dependence of industrialized nations on major minerals from Africa in 1970 (a)

Industrial nation	Mineral	Dependence on imports (percentage) approx.	Total imports from Africa (percentage)	Major African suppliers with percentage South Africa	Rest of Africa
United Kingdom	Iron ore	60	10·4		Liberia (10·4)
	Chromium (ore)	100	56·4	South Africa (56·4)	
	Manganese	100	28·9	South Africa (28·9)	
	Copper	100	31·2		Zambia (31·2)
	Bauxite	100	65·0		Ghana (65·0)
	Platinum	100	38·7	South Africa (38·7)	
	Crude petroleum	95	24·5		Libya (24·5)
	Natural gas	100	72·0		Algeria (72·0)
	Phosphates	78	77·0		Morocco (66·6) Senegal (10·4)
France	Iron ore	14·5	37·0		Mauritania (20·2) Liberia (16·8)
	Cobalt ore	100	95·5		Morocco (95·5) (b)
	Cobalt metal	80	14·3		Zaire (14·3) (b)
	Manganese	100	46·5		Gabon (44·3) Morocco (2·2)
	Copper	100	21·0		Zaire (1·8) Zambia (19·2) (c)
	Lead ore	85·0	35·3		Morocco (35·3) Algeria (26·9)
	Crude petroleum	98	44·5		Libya (17·6)
	Uranium ore	56	100·0		Gabon (100)
	Phosphate rock	100	78·2		Morocco (45·4) Togo (21·7) Tunisia (11·1)
	Antimony ore	100	30·6	South Africa (30·6)	
	Fluorspar	76	83·1	South Africa (9·3)	Tunisia (56·5) Mozambique (17·3) (d)

Country	Material				
West Germany	Iron ore	90	17·1		Liberia (17·1)
	Chromium ore	100	51·8	South Africa (51·8)	Gabon (20·8)
	Manganese ore	99	68·3	South Africa (47·5)	Zambia (13·6)
	Copper	95	25·9	South Africa (7·7)	Libya (41·4)
	Crude petroleum	100	41·4		
	Asbestos	99	15·1	South Africa (15·1)	
	Alumina		58·3		Guinea (58·3)
Japan	Chromium (ore)	97	61·7	South Africa (61·7)	Zaire (83·8)
	Cobalt (ore)	100	83·8		
	Manganese	90	27·0	South Africa (27·0)	
	Nickel	100	13·4	South Africa (13·4)	
	Vanadium	100	46·6	South Africa (46·6)	
	Phosphates	100	18·8		Morocco (18·8)
USA	Chromium	100	18·8	South Africa	Rhodesia (2·4)
	Cobalt	46	38·9		Zaire
	Columbium	20	24·7		Nigeria (13·8)
	Manganese	99	55·0	South Africa (8·8)	Gabon (46·6)
	Platinum	79	15·6	South Africa (15·6) (e)	
	Natural diamonds	100	24·9	South Africa (19·4) (f)	
	Antimony	49	55·0	South Africa (8·8)	Gabon (31·8)

Notes: (a) All figures are approximate and represent ore imports and not scrap, which is sometimes important.
(b) Belgium supplies 44·3 per cent of French imports and these are largely Zairean ore refined in Belgium.
(c) Belgium supplies 32·8 per cent of French imports largely from Zairean ore refined in Belgium.
(d) Mozambique given as source of origin but believed to be from Rhodesia.
(e) UK accounts for 47 per cent of US imports and most of this comes from South Africa.
(f) UK accounts for 26 per cent of US imports and these come mostly from Africa.
Source: UN Statistical Year Book 1975, Mining Annual Review 1974, Africa 74/75.

grades of ore are mined, greater and greater quantities of power are required to crush, process and smelt the small amounts of metal. Table 10 shows how much coal equivalent was required

Table 10: The energy cost of metal production, 1972

	Energy Required (measured in lb. of coal)	
To make 1 lb. of	From ore	From recycled material
steel	1·11 lb.	0·22 lb.
aluminium (a)	6·09 lb.	0·17–0·26 lb.
copper	1·98 lb.	0·11 lb.

Note: (a) Assumes that bauxite is reduced to alumina by hydroelectric power. If the whole process used coal then it would take 8·32 lb. of coal to produce 1 lb. of aluminium. Producers argue that the light weight and structural strength of aluminium produce great energy savings when in use, which counteract the high energy-cost of aluminium production.
Source: Fortune, October 1972, p. 110.

in 1972 to produce a pound of some common metals, assuming average grades. However at present most countries recycle very little of the metal that they manufacture and, if costs dictate it, the advanced countries would be able to recycle a lot more of their scrap metal. The US Bureau of Mines believes it quite likely that, if necessary, the US would be able to recycle three quarters of its metals in another ten or fifteen years.[16] The Western countries will continue to enjoy a very high standard of living, but they will cease to be 'throw-away' societies.

The major mining companies have stepped up the development of ocean-mining systems dramatically. American companies alone are expected to invest at least $6 billion in ocean-mining operations before 1990.[17] Although the African, Asian and South American countries have proposed an International Seabed Resources Authority with jurisdiction over the seabed, the US government has already set up the Ocean Mining Administration to license US firms unilaterally if need be.[18] The main attraction of ocean mining is the nodules containing nickel, manganese, copper and cobalt lying on the sea bed; nickel and cobalt are probably the most important. Multinational consortia have been established to exploit these minerals, and the companies involved include Union Minière, Rio Tinto Zinc, Consolidated Gold Fields, Metallgesellschaft, Kennecott Copper, International Nickel Co., Tenneco Corp, and several Japanese companies, including Itoh & Co., Mitsubishi, and Sumitomo.[19]

Mineral-exporting nations can also expect to encounter stiff economic, political and even military pressure from the industrialized nations if they threaten to withdraw mineral supplies, as the experience of Chile and Cuba demonstrates. When groups of mineral-exporting nations do form, the developed nations will try to split them, as they have set out to do in the case of OPEC and CIPEC.

Beyond the immediate conflicts over mineral supplies and prices lies the more fundamental question of whether the planet can sustain the present consumption rate of mineral resources. In the middle of the eighteenth century, Britain was the world's largest metal producer, with an annual total of 20,000 tons. By the middle of the nineteenth century, this had risen to $1\frac{1}{2}$ million tons a year; and by 1900, to 9 million tons. But in the first sixty years of the twentieth century more metal had been extracted from the earth than during the whole period of human existence down to 1900.[20] Of all the known gold, three quarters have been mined since 1900.[21] The United States consumes between a quarter and a half of the world's supply of metals, and its rate of demand is increasing at about 3 per cent a year.[22] Given that the world's mineral resources are finite, how long can this staggering increase in mineral production continue? Some recent studies have forecast the imminent exhaustion of world reserves of several minerals (see Table 11); but the truth is that we do not know how large the world's mineral reserves are.

The very concept of reserves is vague and requires careful use. The known 'reserves' of minerals give an impression of exact measurements, but in reality they are imprecise estimates. A number of factors enter into the evaluation of an orebody and the determination of its metal content; so that the estimates of mineral reserves should be treated with considerable caution.

Table 11: The exhaustion of world mineral resources

Metal	Exhaustion according to A	Exhaustion according to B
Lead	2036	1980
Mercury	2113	1980
Gold	2001	1985
Silver	2014	1985
Platinum	2057	1985
Zinc	2022	1985
Tin	2033	1990
Uranium		1990
Copper	2020	2000
Tungsten	2044	2000
Natural gas	2021	2000
Nickel	2068	2050
Oil	2022	2050
Cobalt	2120	2050
Molybdenum	2037	2050
Aluminium	2027	2200
Manganese	2066	2200
Iron	2145	2300
Magnesium		2300
Chromium	2126	2300
Coal	2122	3000

Key:
A = *The Limits to Growth*, Earth Island, London, 1972, pp. 56–8 (assumes five times known reserves and exponential growth).
B = P. R. and A. H. Ehrlich, *Population, Resources and Environment*, 1970, Figure 4.1, p. 60.

Reserve figures based on data released by the mining companies will tend to underestimate the true extent of reserves, because the company will be concerned only with that proportion of the deposit that can be developed economically at prevailing costs and with contemporary technology. Moreover, a mining company may wish to keep the true size of a deposit secret to help it bargain with the host government, to compete with other companies, or even to influence world metal prices.

Whatever the true extent of the world's mineral resources, the most important question for Africa and the Third World is whether the continuing high level of exports is compatible with economic development. The industrialization of the Third World would lead to a dramatic upsurge in the world demand for minerals and require the creation of enormous 'standing stocks'. Let us take steel as an example. In 1968 a UN study calculated that the *per capita* steel consumption for the whole world was 115–20 kilos a year. For the Third World, however, the figure was much lower (45 kilos per head); while Africa had the lowest *per capita* steel consumption in the world, at a mere 8 kilos a year.[23] Consumption in most African countries, indeed, did not exceed an annual 6 kilos per head. According to one calculation, a world population of 7 thousand million in the year 2,000, enjoying present European production and consumption standards, would require 60 billion* tons of steel per year; or 140 times as much as the entire globe produces in a year at present. Incredible as it may seem, such an increase is probably within reach for iron ore: but it is much less likely for other key metals such as copper, lead, zinc and tin. The world standing stock for tin would have to be some fifteen times as large as the total world reserves of tin at present known.[24]

There is little likelihood that such enormous reserves of the key industrial minerals will be found at prices anywhere near existing levels. And if they are not, then we can expect sharp conflicts between the underdeveloped and the industrialized states. For while underdeveloped countries become increasingly reluctant to export their valuable minerals, preferring to use them for their own development, it seems unlikely that the industrial states, with their superior economic and military power, will be content with a reduced share of world mineral consumption.

The pressure by producer countries for higher prices reflects at least in part this fundamental conflict of interests. But so far the producing countries have not moved from demanding a higher price for their exports to a determination permanently to reduce the quantity of those exports. The major tin- and copper-exporting countries have reduced exports from time to time, but only with the aim of holding or raising price levels. Nevertheless, the importance of mineral imports for the industrial nations does

* One billion = one thousand million.

give some economic power to the exporters. The question is: can the underdeveloped countries wield this power? At the moment they cannot for it is not they who control the mining, processing and marketing of their minerals. It is the international mining companies.

Part Two

Mining Companies in the
Political Economy of Africa

6 Gold, Nationalism, and Economic Development in South Africa, 1900–1948

At the beginning of the twentieth century, the South African economy showed the classic features of capitalist underdevelopment. It was heavily dependent on the income from a single primary commodity, produced almost entirely for export by foreign companies. These companies were controlled by overseas shareholders who demanded a large share of the investable surplus generated by the mines. The export of this surplus was crippling South Africa's economic development and reinforcing her dependence on gold. Today, seventy-five years later, South Africa has reduced its dependence on mineral exports, and mining accounts for only ten per cent of the gross national product. Many factors contributed to this transformation: the nature of gold as a commodity; the gold industry's group system; the exploitation of cheap unskilled black labour; the social base of the country's main leaders; and the alliance between a white rural bourgeoisie and the white working class. But the necessary precondition for South African economic development was political independence.

In 1795 Britain had annexed the Cape Colony to secure the sea route to India, the financial and military centrepiece of the British Empire.[1] By the second half of the nineteenth century the British had evolved a policy of self-government for 'responsible' colonies, which reduced the administrative and financial burdens on the British Treasury without inhibiting commercial expansion or endangering imperial supremacy. This policy had already been tried with success in Canada and Australia, but in South Africa it foundered. The British aim was to coax or coerce the two Boer republics of the Transvaal and the Orange Free State into a federation with the British colonies of the Cape and Natal. At the same time the Cape Colony would be built up to dominate the federation. As long as the poverty-stricken and fragile republics in the interior remained dependent on colonial ports they posed no threat to imperial security, which demanded only control of the coast. But the discovery of diamonds and gold altered the whole balance of power on the sub-continent. The British annexed the diamond fields at Kimberley and incorporated them in the Cape Colony, but when they attempted to annex the Transvaal in 1880 they were humiliatingly defeated at Majuba. Thereafter the British relied on the powerful mining and commercial interests of the Cape, led by Cecil Rhodes, to counter the strategic threat posed by the growing wealth of the Transvaal.

The revenue which the new gold mines generated for the Transvaal Treasury offered the Transvaal Republic the chance to escape the commercial monopoly of the Cape merchants. With a loan from Rothschilds, the republic began building a railway from the Transvaal to Delagoa Bay in Portuguese East Africa.* The railway made good economic sense, but much of the new revenue was used to pay high salaries to government officials. The Transvaal quickly became a high-wage, high-cost economy, with whites expecting, and getting, wages far in excess of their counterparts in Europe. Corruption was rife. On one occasion an investigation revealed that the whole Volksraad (the legislative assembly), up to and including President Paul Kruger's deputy, had been bribed!

The influx of miners, traders and speculators attracted by the new gold mines was causing internal political difficulties for the republic. The *uitlanders* (outsiders), as they were christened by the Boers, were demanding the vote. Their demands were resisted, to ensure that the Boer community kept political control of the republic. President Kruger said, 'If we grant them the franchise, we might as well pull down the flag.'

The British continued the pursuit of a Cape-dominated federation in South Africa. The simmering dispute between the Transvaal and the Cape Colony was intensified in October 1895, when Kruger forced rail traffic from the Cape to be transferred to ox

*Rhodes's characteristic counter was an offer to buy the railway. When this was rejected, he approached the Portuguese and offered to buy the whole of Portuguese East Africa (Mozambique). This offer was, in its turn, rejected.

wagons at the Transvaal border. The clash seemed to offer the Cape a chance to absorb the Transvaal. Cecil Rhodes, the British High Commissioner, and Joseph Chamberlain, the most powerful British Colonial Secretary of the century, favoured imperial expansion. Rhodes planned an uprising. Chamberlain wrote to Lord Salisbury, the British Prime Minister, that if the uprising were successful it 'ought to turn to our advantage'. But there was little he could do but watch because

by 1895 South Africa had passed beyond the British government's direct control. For six years the empire had ridden gratefully upon Rhodes' coat-tails. Power and initiative lay with Rhodes on the one hand and with Kruger on the other, not with the Colonial Office. Once the two South African rivals and their systems became irreconcilable, Chamberlain . . . had little choice but to follow and support Rhodes with whose financial and political empire British influence had become largely identified. Imperial supremacy had no other leg to stand on.[2]

Although the companies were united in their opposition to Kruger's policies, they did not all share Rhodes's fervent imperialism. They complained that the government of the Transvaal was failing to organize the supply of cheap African labour and that the republic's dynamite monopoly was costing them thousands of pounds a year. But these complaints could be overcome without embracing the British Empire. The threat to Britain's interests was recognized by Chamberlain:

Whatever defects may exist in the present form of government of the Transvaal, the substitution of an entirely independent Republic government by or for the capitalists of the Rand would be very much worse for British interests in the Transvaal itself and for British influence in South Africa.[3]

By moving swiftly, Rhodes and Chamberlain hoped to ensure that the Transvaal remained within the British sphere of influence. Rhodes and Beit financed and organized a group of conspirators who planned a dramatic *coup d'état*. The plan was for an armed rising which would encourage a popular rising among the discontented *uitlanders*. The gold houses of London did not want a rising.[4] Most of the mining companies opposed the scheme: of the ten major mining groups, only four – Wernher Beit, George

Farrar's Anglo-French group, the Abe Bailey syndicate, and Rhodes' own Gold Fields – supported the plan. The other six (the so-called cosmopolitans) – J. B. Robinson, Barnato, Neumann, Albu, Goerz, and Lewis and Marks – opposed the plan, favouring instead a new government subordinate to their interests and not those of the British Empire. In October 1895 Chamberlain handed over part of Bechuanaland to the British South Africa Company for the construction of a railway to Rhodesia. This gave Rhodes and his fellow conspirators the necessary base from which to launch their armed raiding party. Meanwhile De Beers smuggled arms into Johannesburg hidden amongst mining supplies.

Despite all the preparations, the raid led by Dr Starr Jameson was a total fiasco. The raiders did not succeed in taking the Rand towns, nor did the popular uprising materialize. Lionel Philips (President of the Chamber of Mines), Rhodes' brother Frank, and John Hammond (Beit's chief engineer) were all arrested, tried and sentenced to death. At this point Barney Barnato intervened and, by threatening to close down the mines and throw all the men out of work, persuaded Kruger to lift the death sentence. Kruger could afford this gesture because his own position was enormously strengthened, while both the British strategy of indirect supremacy and Rhodes's political career were in ruins.

The failure of the Jameson Raid did not resolve the battle for political control of the sub-continent; and while the financial strength of the Transvaal grew, powerful voices at the Cape and in Britain called for direct intervention. The development of the deep-level mines proved conclusively that the Transvaal would be the pivot of any South African Federation. Moreover the new Delagoa railway was already diverting revenue from the Cape. By 1898 the profits of the Cape railway had dwindled to almost nothing and the Colony's treasury had a deficit of more than half a million pounds. Sir Alfred Milner, the British High Commissioner in South Africa, added his voice to the Cape and Rhodesian trading, mining and railway interests which were calling for British intervention. The 'fear of British South Africans defecting from the imperial cause . . . drove the Cabinet to give way to their clamour for direct action against Kruger's regime'.[5] The

British were persuaded that in order to safeguard the strategically important Cape Colony, it was necessary to re-establish supremacy over the Transvaal by force of arms.

Late in 1899 the second Anglo-Boer war began. At first the British won a string of swift and spectacular victories, but the war turned into a succession of skirmishes with the mobile Boer guerrilla forces. The British adopted classic anti-guerrilla tactics, burning crops and farms and herding the Boer farming communities into camps. The war proved very costly; and when hostilities ceased in 1902, the defeat of the Boers was still incomplete.

The peace treaty that emerged from the subsequent negotiations was significantly favourable to the Boer republics in part because the victory was incomplete, and in part because the British and Cape interests had to recognize the vast wealth of the Transvaal. The governments of both Natal and the Cape had invested large sums to build the railways from the coast to the Transvaal. They needed a share of the business generated by the Rand in order to stave off bankruptcy. The mining companies and the commercial and manufacturing interests wanted a national government and an integrated market to ensure their further expansion. The mineral wealth of the Transvaal thus gave those defeated on the battlefield a trump card in their negotiations with the victors. The British sought and won from the Boer leadership a commitment to a Union of South Africa, but the dominant force in the Union was seen to be the Transvaal Republic.

THE UNION OF SOUTH AFRICA

The Union of South Africa, established in 1910, joined the Boer republics of Transvaal and the Orange Free State in a political union with the English-speaking provinces of Natal and the Cape. General Botha became premier of the Union, and with General Smuts was committed to the success of the experiment. They based their policies on a full integration of the two communities and the continuance of strong links with Britain.

Not all members of the new Cabinet were so enthusiastic.

General Hertzog, who had been reluctant to sign the peace treaty, argued instead for the separate development of the English and Boer communities. Even as the South African whites won a significant degree of political independence, there was evidence of a deep split between the rural, culturally separate, Boer community and the externally-oriented, largely English-speaking community. For the first two years of the Unionist Parliament, it seemed as if Botha and Smuts might bridge the gap between Hertzog and themselves, and successfully reconcile the competing demands of mine owners, the white miners and the white rural communities. The key to this political balancing act was a legislative programme acceptable to all three: involving the reinforced and extended exploitation of the black community in South Africa. The black community began organizing in self-defence and in 1912 formed the South African Native National Congress.

LABOUR AND THE GOLD MINES

New legislation reinforced customary labour practices in the mines. The Native Labour Regulation Act (1911) gave legislative effect to the maximum average agreement among the mining companies,* thus guaranteeing the coordinated control and recruitment of African labour exercised by the Chamber of Mines. The white miners had been profoundly disturbed by the importation of Chinese labour for the gold mines, because it showed how vulnerable they were to displacement. They therefore extended their traditional demand for a closed shop, to prevent any advance into skilled jobs by African mineworkers at lower wages. The answer to these demands was the Mines and Works Act (1911). Administrative regulations under this Act reinforced the customary bar against the employment of Africans for skilled or semi-skilled work on the mines.

The white farming communities were anxious to retain an adequate supply of cheap black labour to work on the farms and were also concerned by the increased level of land-purchases by Africans. Pass laws and the recruitment of foreign migrant

* See above, page 54.

labour by the Chamber of Mines at minimum rates of pay prevented any large-scale transfer of black labour from the farms to the mines. African competition in the agricultural sector was restricted by the Native Lands Act (1913), which prevented Africans from buying land outside a defined area, amounting to only 7·3 per cent of South Africa.*

By 1913 it was clear that, despite the government's legislative programme, a significant realignment of political forces was under way. General Hertzog left the Cabinet, declaring: 'The time has come when South Africa can no longer be ruled by non-Afrikaners, by people who have no real love for South Africa.' In 1914 he founded the National Party, which immediately began to erode the government's rural support. In September 1914, when South Africa declared war on Germany and began preparations to attack South West Africa, some Afrikaners in the Transvaal and Orange Free State rebelled and announced the establishment of a provisional government. Botha and Smuts declared martial law and crushed the rebellion. Meanwhile, the division between Smuts and the miners was growing. In June and July 1913, there was a large strike by white miners to secure recognition of their aims. To end the strike Smuts had to negotiate with four armed delegates, while an unruly crowd of several thousand miners jeered outside. The miners' union was recognized; but when the miners went on strike again in the following year, Smuts unhesitatingly declared martial law. In 1914 Colonel Creswell, well known for his outspoken support of the white miners, became the leader of the Labour Party, which over the next decade steadily detached the white working-class vote from the South Africa Party of Botha and Smuts. Creswell and Hertzog moved towards an alliance based on their separate but complementary political goals.

Creswell devoted his whole political life to ousting the black from the mines. Hertzog's party on the other hand wanted cheap and servile Africans on the farms . . . The exclusion of Africans dovetailed with

---

*In 1936 this was increased to 13·7 per cent but even today some of this land remains in white hands. Africans constitute 80 per cent of South Africa's population.

the farmers' insatiable demand for labour. This compatibility formed the economic basis of the partnership between white landowners and the labour aristocracy.[6]

Smuts was caught in a pincer movement; and in the general elections of 1913, 1920 and 1921, the electoral support for his South Africa Party ebbed, as the strength of Hertzog's National Party and Creswell's Labour Party grew. Smuts moved closer to the mineowners, with whom he had been identified since his ruthless use of military force in 1914, just at the time when the profit margins of the gold mines were under severe pressure.

LABOUR AND THE MINING COMPANIES

During and after the First World War, there was a massive increase in the cost of living in South Africa. Prices rose by almost 50 per cent between 1917 and 1920.[7] The white miners were quick to strike in support of their demands, and between 1913 and 1919 had won wage increases of more than 40 per cent, as well as a reduction in hours. This pressure, along with the rising cost of stores, was seriously cutting into mining-company profits. From 1914 to 1919 working costs rose from 17s. 5d. to 22s. 9d. per ton milled, and profits in 1919 were half the 1913 figure. Under this sort of pressure, the marginal or low-grade mines were likely to be closed down.* In March 1919 the President of the Chamber of Mines forecast that, if the gold premium† disappeared, 31 mines employing 14,400 whites would become unpayable. He reminded General Smuts that the gold-mining industry spent about £28 million a year within South Africa and supported over a quarter of a million whites and one million Africans.[8]

The government's Low Grade Mines Commission stated in its interim report that the marginal mines constituted 'from the

---

* It would, of course, be possible to raise the wages of black miners without threatening the existence of marginal mines, but only if the colour bar were lifted. (See below, page 157.)

† Gold was sold at a premium above the standard price of £4·248 per ounce from 24 July 1919 until Great Britain returned to the Gold Standard on 29 April 1925.

employment and expenditure point of view roughly one half of the Witwatersrand gold-mining industry'.[9] The marginal mines had been kept in production only because the mining companies held down the wages of African mineworkers, which in the six years from 1914 to 1920 had increased by only just over a half-penny to 2s.0.3d. per shift.[10] In real terms, black wages were 13 per cent lower in 1921 than they had been in 1916.[11]

To meet the crisis caused by the post-war inflation, the companies sought to increase the ratio of low-paid Africans to highly-paid white miners. In 1918, the Chamber of Mines had agreed with the white unions that the existing ratio of white to black miners would be maintained. But the price of gold fell from 130s. per ounce in February 1920 to 95s. per ounce in December 1921. The Chamber announced an increase in the ratio of African to white miners from 8·5:1 to 10·5:1. The white miners replied with the demand for one white miner to every 3·5 Africans. Negotiations failed, and the white miners went on strike in January 1922.

1922 RAND REBELLION

The Chamber tried to keep the mines going with African miners and white managerial staff. The Union responded by calling a general strike affecting the mining, power, light and transport industries. The mood of the white labour communities on the Witwatersrand was militant. A Reverend Osthuizen proclaimed from his pulpit that the miners' 'forefathers had fought for a white South Africa but upon the 15th of December the Chamber of Mines had declared that there should be a black South Africa'.[12] Although the National Party leadership stood aside, local leaders like Tielman Roos supported the strikers and their slogan: 'Workers of the world unite and fight for a white South Africa.' On 5 February the striking miners, at a meeting in Johannesburg Town Hall, went further and announced that

this mass meeting of citizens is of the opinion that the time has arrived when the domination of the Chamber of Mines and other financiers in South Africa should cease and to that end we and the members of the Parliament assemble in Pretoria tomorrow to proclaim a South African

Republic and immediately to form a Provisional Government for this country.[13]

The strike was now open rebellion. A coordinated series of strikes, marches and armed commando raids gave the miners control over most of the Rand towns. General Smuts reacted vigorously, declaring martial law for the fourth time in ten years and crushing the rebellion with a massive display of force. The toll at the end of the Rand revolt was 154 dead and 534 wounded.

Smuts' victory left the mining companies free to increase the proportion of cheap African labour. Technical advances enabled the Chamber of Mines to fragment some jobs and to reclassify others, previously considered skilled work, as unskilled. Company profits recovered dramatically. In 1924 working profits were the highest recorded at any time from 1911 to 1932.[14]

The bitterness of the white mineworkers and their desire to revenge themselves on Smuts and the mineowners pushed the Nationalists and the Labour Party into a formal alliance. Following the Wakkerstrom by-election defeat in 1924, Smuts called a general election. When the votes were counted, the Nationalists had 63 seats; the Labour Party, 18; and Smuts's South African Party, 53. In the new 'Pact' Government, Hertzog became Prime Minister and Creswell Minister of Labour.

THE PACT GOVERNMENT 1924–31

The presence of the Labour Party in the Pact Government was the political recognition that white miners and the white working class were considered a legitimate part of the ruling white power structure in South African society. The revolutionary and anti-capitalist aspirations of the white working class were headed off by an appeal to their racism. The threat of another Rand rebellion and the political power of the white workers determined the structure of labour relations on the mines and in South African industry for the next forty years.

The new government embarked on an ambitious legislative programme. Afrikaans was made an official language to rank alongside English; and Hertzog introduced four 'Native Bills', to remove Africans from the white electoral roll and limit African ownership of land. Colonel Creswell immediately appointed the Mining Regulations Commission to study the situation of white labour on the mines. The Mines and Works Amendment Act of 1926, based on the Commission's report, restored the statutory colour bar on the mines and reserved skilled or semi-skilled work for whites. The cost of the Pact Government's labour policy was borne by the black labour force.

Cheap African labour became even more essential to the profits of the gold-mining companies.

From 1924 onwards there is a virtual end to serious labour disputes in the Rand mining industry. In total contrast to the previous quarter century of almost continuous turbulence and frequent syndicalist violence on the Rand mines, the forty subsequent years have been marked by an industrial 'peace' probably unparalleled in the world's mining industry. The Chamber of Mines acquiesced in a collective bargaining agreement with the white trade unions that from 1924 onwards recognized the written and unwritten rules of white-black demarcations as simply not an Agenda item . . . Once the Chamber acknowledged that no South African government from 1924 onwards would regard the qualitative combinations of labour utilization as a subject for discussion, it concentrated its negotiating objectives on obtaining government authority for the employment of 'foreign' Africans – that is from outside the Union of South Africa and the British protectorates.[15]

The Chamber could not increase wages to attract more African labour from inside South Africa without threatening the life of the marginal mines, which provided such an important proportion of the industry's output and the country's foreign exchange earnings. The companies therefore recruited more labour at the same low price from outside the Union. But the supply of African mine labour was still not enough, and throughout the period 1924–30 the mines operated below capacity.

Creswell carried the earnings and related work patterns of the gold mines into the nascent manufacturing industry. His legislative and administrative programme for industry centred around the Industrial Conciliation Act (1924) and the Apprenticeship Act (1922) – both initiated by the Smuts government but given their essential administrative interpretation by Creswell – and the 1925 Wages Act. The Industrial Conciliation Act set up industrial councils to regulate wage rates and working conditions. Both employers and white employees were represented on the councils. Between them, they excluded Africans and prevented changes in the existing structure of wages and prices. As Africans were not employees within the terms of the Act, they could not benefit from negotiations over wage rates. The Apprenticeship Act opened skilled trades to white youth and excluded other races. Together these two Acts gave white workers the power to control access to all skilled and semi-skilled occupations in the developing South African economy. The 1925 Wages Act was specifically designed to help unorganized, low-paid workers, by setting up Wage Councils to set minimum wages.* Thus

artisans, like miners, obtained a permanent stake in the white power structure, while employers offset the cost of sheltered employment by paying Africans less than a living wage.[16]

Population pressure on the land and the industrialization of the Rand was producing a large influx of labour into the urban areas. From 1926 to 1936, more than 150,000 rural whites moved to the towns,[17] while the proportion of Afrikaners working on the land declined from 80 per cent in 1911 to 48 per cent in 1936.[18] At the time of the Rand Rebellion in 1922, 75 per cent of the mine-workers were Afrikaners. But the process which was urbanizing unskilled whites was also forcing Africans to move to the cities. There was a possibility that the unemployed whites might discover a common interest with the unskilled unemployed Africans. To meet this threat the Pact Government absorbed the unskilled white workers into the privileged sector of the economy. This was the so-called 'civilized labour policy'. In a letter of 31 October 1924, Hertzog instructed all government departments to substitute 'civilized' for 'uncivilized' labour wherever practical.

---

*Fearing perhaps that the Act might be applied to the Africans on the mines, the Chamber of Mines fought vigorously, but unsuccessfully, to gain exemption from the Wage Act. The Wage Board established by the Act had no authority to discriminate on grounds of race or colour and had the power to investigate the mining industry and fix colour-blind minimum wages in the mines. However, although the Wage Board has set minimum wages for many African workers, it has not so far investigated the mining industry.

Thus, between 1924 and 1933, the proportion of white labourers employed by the South African Railways and Harbours Board rose from 9·5 per cent to 39·9 per cent, while the proportion of Africans fell from 75 per cent to 48·8 per cent.[19]

The government's concern to create employment opportunities helped to build up the industrial sector of the economy. The state had already entered the field of private industry in 1922, when the Electricity Supply Commission (ESCOM) was established. The Pact Government established the strategically important Iron and Steel Corporation (ISCOR). In 1925 the Customs Tariff Amendment Act gave protection to secondary industry. Between 1925 and 1935 seven protected industries accounted for just over 50 per cent of the total increased employment of Europeans in the private sector.[20]

The government's diamond policy was also designed to maximize white employment opportunities. In 1925 rich alluvial deposits were discovered at Lichtenburg in the Transvaal. The Pact Government declared them to be state diggings. Within a year innumerable diggers were producing a greater quantity of rough diamonds from this one field than the whole De Beers group. In 1926 another rich alluvial deposit was discovered in Namaqualand, and the government decided to experiment with a state-run diamond enterprise. The government opened up new ground and, to protect the white diggers, banned the employment of Africans on the new field for five years. In September 1927 the government went a step further and concluded a contract with an Antwerp firm for the construction of a diamond-cutting factory at Kimberley. The government subsidized the South African diamond cutters by abolishing the export duty on cut stones, while retaining it for rough diamonds, and by allowing the South African cutters to buy only those stones they required. This violated the long-established practice in the diamond trade of selling a standard assortment and not just the stones in demand. Ernest Oppenheimer sharply criticized the government in Parliament and claimed that the world diamond trade was in complete disarray because of its policy. The government, however, considered that increased white employment took priority.

The political base of Hertzog's National Party was the white rural community, and the Pact Government intensified state support for white farmers. It enforced the Natives (Urban Areas) Act of 1923, modelled on mining-industry practices, whose aim was to control the influx of Africans into urban areas and at the same time ensure a continual supply of cheap labour for the white farmers. It transferred large sums of money to the agricultural sector, by imposing a high rate of direct and indirect taxation on the gold-mining industry and by subsidizing railway tariffs. Compared with other gold-mining countries, there was a high rate of tax on the South African gold industry (42 per cent of taxable profits).* From 1911 to 1936 the South African government received £148 million in taxes from the mining industry in South Africa – £106 million from the gold-mining industry alone[21] – and spent over £112 million building up white agriculture.[22] 65 per cent of the country's working population, both black and white, lived by farming, but, as was the pattern in South Africa, African agriculture received the grand total of £750,000 in these years.[23]

To support white agriculture the railways charged differential rates. All stores and supplies for the Rand mines were charged high rates, while supplies for and exports from the farming communities of the Orange Free State and the Transvaal were carried at low ones. The result was that by 1936 only 14·8 per cent of the traffic (largely for the mining industry) produced 58·36 per cent of the revenue; while 85·1 per cent of the traffic (mainly farmers' produce and supplies) produced only 41·64 per cent of the revenue.[24]

It is estimated that on average the state transferred more than £15 million a year from the mining industry and the rest of the community to the farmers in the form of subsidies and tariffs.[25] This sum was greater than the annual average influx of new capital to the gold fields from 1887 to 1932. Nevertheless, after twenty years of intensive state-directed effort and the elimination of the competition from African farmers, the white agricultural community was still responsible for only a small proportion of the South African gross domestic product. There was little net

* In Rhodesia, the tax on gold mining was 23 per cent, in Australia 18 per cent, and in the USA the figure varied from 14 to 18 per cent of profits.

capital formation within the agricultural sector, which relied heavily on long-term borrowing from the Government Land Bank and the commercial banks.[26] The agricultural community was particularly vulnerable to a downturn in world trade.

THE DEPRESSION

The world depression of 1929–33 had a powerful effect on all sectors of the South African economy. The diamond industry was the first casualty. As the stock of unsold diamonds grew, Ernest Oppenheimer argued vigorously that the mines should be closed down. But the government feared the effects of widespread European unemployment and refused permission. Oppenheimer declared that he was 'not going to be pointed to as the chairman of De Beers who saw it brought to bankruptcy and who kept Europeans employed to ruin the shareholders'.[27] The Minister of Mines announced an inquiry into the diamond industry to make sure that the industry was conducted in the best interests of the people of South Africa. The target of the inquiry was Oppenheimer.

There is one man who is chairman of all the producing companies in South Africa, the same man is chairman of the Diamond Corporation. He alone is the centre of the whole diamond industry and moreover he advocates his own case in this house. The fact is that the Honourable Member for Kimberley can juggle, manipulate and deal with all the diamonds as he pleases . . . It is necessary for the government to take this great industry under its protection and that the interests of the public in general should not be lost sight of. That is why the government must investigate all those contracts so closely to see that the interests of the country are not given away.[28]

But the Commission was abandoned when Oppenheimer refused to cooperate. The Kimberley, Jagersfontein, Premier and Consolidated Diamond mines were closed down, and thousands of miners were thrown out of work.

The agricultural sector was also in desperate straits. Demand for South Africa's agricultural products fell, and so did prices. Agricultural exports tumbled from £19·8 million in 1929 to £8·5 million in 1932. This collapse threatened not only the livelihood of South Africa's farmers, but also the Pact Government's electoral base.

The political battle to protect white living standards revolved around the gold standard. In 1923, Britain devalued sterling by abandoning the gold standard. Hertzog resisted going off the gold standard because he felt that such a move would detract from South Africa's independent status recognized by the 1926 Balfour Declaration. But Britain was South Africa's main market, taking 90 per cent of the country's exports; and unless South Africa devalued as well, the farmers were threatened with almost total exclusion from the British market by their high prices. The gold industry argued strongly that the South African pound should follow the British example and take advantage of the higher sterling price of gold, which had risen from 84s. to 125s. an ounce. While the arguments proceeded, the situation within the country deteriorated. Farmers were unable to find outlets for their products. Unemployment grew. The fiery Roos, former chairman of the Transvaal National Party, barnstormed the countryside, calling for South Africa to abandon the gold standard. The possible defection of his rural constituency shook Hertzog. Further, the flow of money out of the country was reaching dangerous proportions: between 19 and 22 December alone, more than £3 million left the country. Five days later South Africa abandoned the gold standard. Sir Abe Bailey and the Chamber of Mines played a key role in pressuring the government and then bringing about the coalition between General Hertzog and General Smuts which took power early in 1933.[29]

The major white parties had come together to deal with the economic problems of the depression and to settle the question of the 'Native Bills' pending since 1926 for lack of the necessary two-thirds majority. It was a condition of Smuts's participation in the coalition that the Nationalists' alliance with the Labour Party be dropped. In the 1933 elections the Nationalists won 75 seats, the South Africa Party 61, Labour 4, Roos 2, Home Rule 2, Independents 6. In December 1934 the followers of Smuts and Hertzog met in Bloemfontein and formed the United South Africa National Party, which became known as the United

Party. The jingo element in the SAP split away to form the Dominion Party, which supported the maintenance of close links with the British Empire. Much more important, though, was a hard core of Hertzog's National Party, which refused to follow Hertzog into fusion. Led by Dr D. F. Malan, nineteen MPs remained in opposition, as the Purified National Party.

GOLD-MINING BOOM 1933-40

All of South Africa's exports were severely affected by the world-wide depression except gold, which had continued to earn a steady £20 million a year in foreign exchange.[30] When South Africa abandoned the gold standard, the price of gold shot up from 84s. to 125s. A price increase of this magnitude relieved the pressure from rising working costs; and as the industry geared itself up to increase production, it received another boost when President Roosevelt devalued the US dollar in 1934 and set the dollar price of gold at $35 an ounce (about 140s.). The price of gold had risen by over 70 per cent in less than two years.

Foreign capital began to flow into the Rand once again. In the seven years from 1933, some £80 million of foreign capital were invested in the gold mines.[31] This compared with £140 million in the previous forty-five years and £23 million in the previous eighteen.[32] These funds were used to develop the Far West Rand and to expand existing mines. Company profits jumped from an average of £13·4 million a year for the period 1923–32 to an average of £36·48 million a year for the period 1933–40.[33] Government receipts from taxation rose from an average of £3·5 million to nearly £14 million a year.[34]

The booming gold industry was not held back by any shortage of labour, since South Africa was suffering from a succession of severe droughts, which pushed thousands of rural Africans on to the labour market. The mining companies were offered an almost unlimited labour supply at the unchanged low rates of pay. In 1936, the number of Africans employed on the mines reached 360,000, compared with 210,000 in 1930.

The new balance of power between the companies and the white miners was demonstrated in 1933, when the miners demanded wage increases ranging from 20 to 35 per cent and a reduction in working hours. The companies responded with the contemptuous offer of a provident fund.[35] Company profits were enormous. The working profits of the gold-mining industry in the seven years from 1933 to 1940 were £275·3 million. By comparison, the industry's profits in the previous twenty-one years (1911–33) had amounted to only £263·3 million.[36] It was the greatest boom in the industry's history.

The gold-mining companies were growing more independent of the metropolitan centres. There had always been a strong element of local participation in the Rand gold field. In fact, capital generated in Kimberley had established the first companies. Then the sheer size of the companies and the development of the unique group system had enabled the companies to reduce their dependence on metropolitan sources of capital. When interest rates in European markets were low, the mining companies borrowed capital from the metropolitan centres; but if interest rates were high, the companies supplied a much higher proportion of their own capital needs. Thus, from 1887 to 1913, when European interest rates were low ($3\frac{1}{2}$ per cent or less), capital expenditure funded by working profits totalled only £19 million; but in the much shorter period from 1914 to 1932, when interest rates varied from $4\frac{1}{2}$ to 6 per cent, the companies generated £31 million of their capital requirements internally.*[37]

The increasing capacity of the companies to raise their own capital was accompanied by a growth in South African ownership. Before 1914, South Africans held less than $14\frac{1}{2}$ per cent of the shares in the gold-mining companies. By 1935 this stake had risen to over 40 per cent.[38] One reason for the sharp rise was the establishment of two important mining groups, Anglo American in 1917 and Anglo-Transvaal Consolidated Investments in 1933, both of which were South-African-controlled. The proportion of South African shareholders was much higher in some mines. Sir Ernest Oppenheimer said in 1934 that 66 per cent of the shares in the rich Daggafontein mine and 75 per cent of those in the East

---

* Of course this did not mean that South African industry no longer needed foreign investment but rather that it had more choice over the terms of new investment and could even get along without it for short periods if necessary.

Daggafontein mine were held in South Africa, largely by small shareholders.[39] At the same time South African governments were exercising more and more supervision over the industry. From 1918, through the mining lease system* and other legislation, the government controlled the establishment of new mines and the mining policies of the companies.[40] In addition, the proportion of gold-mining profits taken by the state in taxation rose from 42 per cent in 1920 to 71 per cent in 1942.[41] The gold industry became more responsive to national development priorities.

THE RISE OF AFRIKANER NATIONALISM

The Purified National Party of Dr Malan, which had refused to join the United Party, was the spearhead of an increasingly assertive Afrikaans community. The party articulated a series of interrelated demands central to the Afrikaner community. It sought full and complete independence of a South African republic free from British interference; the ending of effective Afrikaans inferiority within South Africa; the separation of non-whites from white society to pursue their own separate development; the intensification of state support for white farmers in the rural areas and for the unskilled white workers in the urban areas; and the Afrikanerization of schools and public life.[42]

The Afrikaner community was also trying to build up its economic strength. It had already established two insurance companies, SANLAM and SANTAM in 1918. In 1934 the Afrikaner banking house VOLKSKAS was founded. The movement for economic assertiveness culminated in the 1939 National Economic Conference, when Afrikaners took stock of their economic position in South African society. The average annual income per head of Afrikaners was £86; while for non-Afrikaner whites, it was £142. Only 3 per cent of South Africa's

---

*Under the mining lease system, the Minister of Mines grants leases to applicants who satisfy the Minister that they have the technical and financial resources to develop the prospect. The government also controls the rate of exploitation of the gold deposits to prevent companies mining just the richest seams and leaving too much gold in the ground.

factories, building and construction firms were owned by Afrikaners. Although Afrikaners had traditionally been a rural community, 48 per cent now lived in the towns. Dr M. S. Louw, Managing Director of Sanlam, said:

'If we want to achieve success, we must make use of the technique of capitalism, as it is employed in the most important industry of our country, the gold-mining industry. We must establish a financial company which will function in commerce and industry like the so-called "finance houses" in Johannesburg.'[43]

As a result of the conference an investment company, Federale Volksbeleggings, was established as 'a people's institution to further the Afrikaner's drive for economic independence'.[44]

THE WARTIME ECONOMY

Weakening metropolitan control during the Second World War enabled South Africa to alter the structure of its economy. Manufactured imports were scarce, and South Africa was forced to develop its own resources. The growth of secondary industry was encouraged by government policies and by the lack of competition from abroad. In 1942 the Industrial Development Corporation was established to encourage industrial expansion. The government used cost-plus contracts when buying supplies from local companies and price-control legislation which allowed cost increases to be passed on to consumers. Tariff protection and import controls compelled foreign manufacturers to invest in South Africa or lose their markets. The government also promoted the expansion of heavy industry, for which South Africa was well placed, since coal, iron ore, limestone, chrome and manganese were all produced within the country.

Despite these developments, however, the gold industry continued to dominate the economy. By 1940 the Far West Rand mines pioneered by Consolidated Gold Fields[45] had been brought into production. The gold-mining industry accounted for 20 per cent of South Africa's net national income, 40 per cent of government revenue, and 75 per cent of South Africa's exports.[46]

THE AFRICAN MINEWORKERS UNION

African mineworkers made a sustained attempt to win better conditions during the war. They established the African Mine Workers Union in 1941. Both the companies and the government recognized that the union posed a serious threat to the structure of the gold-mining industry. Since 1922, black mineworkers had borne the cost of maintaining and expanding the industry. The AMWU demands for higher wages threatened company profits, marginal mines, gold production and foreign exchange earnings unless white miners allowed a relaxation of the colour bar. Unwilling to confront the white miners, the government outlawed all strikes by African miners in all circumstances. It appointed the Lansdowne Commission to investigate working conditions on the mines and then largely ignored the Commission's recommendations, meagre though they were.

The anger of the black miners exploded in 1945 when, after a poor maize harvest, the mining companies reduced their food and beer rations. Protests followed, and a police baton charge at one mine killed two men and seriously wounded a hundred others. In April 1946 the annual conference of the AMWU demanded that the Chamber of Mines and the government take 'immediate steps to provide adequate and suitable food for workers' and that the minimum wage for all African miners should be raised to 10s. a day.[47] Later that year the union called a general strike in support of its demands; 74,000 workers stopped work, closing eight mines and affecting another five. The government arrested the strike leaders and used strong police action to quell the disturbances. Nine men were killed, more than twelve hundred were injured, and at least seventy men were dismissed. At no stage was the government or the Chamber even willing to discuss, let alone to grant, the demands of the strikers.[48] The strike lasted four days, but the AMWU never recovered from its defeat, and subsequent legislation prevented the union's re-emergence. The verdict of the Chamber of Mines was:

that trade unionism as practised by Europeans is still beyond the understanding of the tribal Native . . . A trade union organization would be outside the comprehension of all but a few educated Natives of the urban type; it would not only be useless, but detrimental to the ordinary mine Native in his present stage of development.[49]

The determination of the Chamber of Mines to hold down African wages on the mines was reinforced by the reviving strength of the white mineworkers. Afrikaner-dominated unions, closely linked to the National Party, had forced the Chamber of Mines in 1937 to reverse its open-shop policy and recognize seven unions on the mines. The predominantly Afrikaner white miners began to regain the power they had lost in the boom period of 1933–40.

THE TRIUMPH OF AFRIKANER NATIONALISM

The resurgence of the white miners was linked to the growing strength of the National Party. At the 1938 elections the United Party won 111 seats; but the Nationalists, with spreading support among Afrikaners, won 27. In 1940 at a conference in Bloemfontein, Hertzog finally and irrevocably severed his links with the Nationalists. In the 1943 elections the Nationalists under Malan increased their representation to 43 seats and again increased their proportion of the Afrikaner vote. Finally in 1948 the Nationalists won 70 seats and in alliance with the Afrikaner Party had 79 seats to the 74 won by their opponents. Dr Malan declared triumphantly: 'Today, South Africa belongs to us once more. For the first time since union, South Africa is our own.'

The political campaign of the Afrikaner community had triumphed, and the economic programme launched in 1939 and helped by the isolation of the wartime economy was already bringing results. By 1949 the proportion of factories owned by Afrikaners had risen to 6 per cent, and to 25 per cent of commerce from 8 per cent in 1939. Their total share of the ownership and control of the private economy had risen from 5 to 11 per cent in ten years.[50] Some members of the National Party argued that:

for all those who look to the future of South Africa there is only one solution and that is that, irrespective of any other key industries, the gold-mining industry should be nationalized by the State.[51]

But although the Nationalist leadership decided against this move, such statements contributed to a nervous mood among international investors. The flow of foreign capital into the country was reduced, and funds were diverted to Southern Rhodesia.

In power, the National Party was in a strong position to increase the relative independence of the South African economy. In the previous thirty years the South African economy had already become significantly more independent of metropolitan control. The major elements in this lengthy historical process were the increasing control of the South African economy by a nationalist bourgeoisie rooted in the rural areas; the encouragement and protection afforded local capitalists by successive governments; the growing concentration and localization of the gold-mining industry; and the continuing exploitation and suppression of cheap unskilled African labour in industry and the mines. Now the Nationalist government, uninhibited by political or ideological links with Britain and Europe, could use the power of the state to promote the economic development of South Africa in general and the Afrikaner community in particular.

7 The Gold Mines, Labour, and Economic Growth in South Africa, 1948-75

The immediate post-war period was an extremely favourable one for South African agricultural and mineral exports.[1] The gross value of agricultural production rose from £37 million in 1933 to £295 million in 1951.[2] The diamond industry was enjoying the greatest boom that the trade had ever known. The liquidation of huge pre-war diamond stocks and the devaluation of sterling had left De Beers flush with money, and the Diamond Corporation's cash reserves rose to £40 million. Part of the profits were used to expand the chemical and fertilizer output of the giant African Explosive and Chemical Industries owned by De Beers and I C I of England.

THE GOLD-MINING INDUSTRY

The profitability of the gold-mining industry was temporarily reduced by government import-control tariffs and other protectionist measures which increased the cost of mining stores; but the 1949 devaluation of sterling increased the sterling price of gold to 250s. an ounce and gave the industry a new lease of life. Then in the early fifties, it was realized that not only gold but also small quantities of uranium could be extracted from the ore. The first uranium treatment plant was opened in 1952. Uranium generated profits of £1·8 million for the gold industry in 1953, rising to £37·75 million in 1958 as South Africa signed long-term contracts with the US Atomic Energy Commission and the British nuclear authorities. The additional revenue from uranium helped to keep many marginal mines in production, and boost foreign exchange earnings.

The most important growth in the gold-mining industry came from the opening of huge new mines. The rich Orange Free

State gold fields were discovered in 1946 (see Figure 4). Anglo American pioneered them; controlled most of the successful new Orange Free State mines; became the banker to the industry; and, forging strong links with other groups, bound the industry

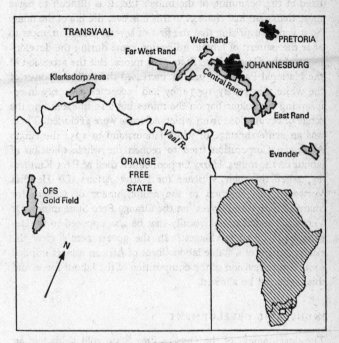

Fig. 4. The South African gold fields

together under its leadership.[3] Through its control of the diamond industry and from its own massive financial resources, the Anglo group provided more than £80 million* towards the development of the gold fields at a time when the London market was not open for new issues. The development of the Orange Free State gold fields cost over £350 million. By 1959, the OFS

*Including £18 million provided by De Beers over the protests of many shareholders.

mines were contributing 28 per cent of South African gold production and 37 per cent of the industry's working profits.[4]

The nature and cost of gold mining mean that working techniques and the balance between labour and capital intensity are fixed at the beginning of the mine's life. It is difficult to make more than marginal changes to this mix over the life of the mine. So it is not surprising that the first of several recent attempts to alter the pattern of labour utilization came during the development of the Orange Free State gold mines. But the accession of the National Party had greatly increased the political power of the white miners. By 1953 they had succeeded not only in reinforcing the colour bar on the mines but also in extending the range of occupations from which Africans were excluded. There was an acute shortage of white labour, and in 1952 the Anglo American Corporation tried to reopen the whole question of labour on the mines. Harry Oppenheimer, then MP for Kimberley, asked the then Minister for Native Affairs, Dr Hendrik Verwoerd, his reaction to the establishment of villages for 'married native employees' on the Orange Free State mines. Dr Verwoerd stated unequivocally that he was opposed to the development of such villages.[5] In the government's view the establishment of a stable labour force of African miners implied some future revision of the composition of the labour force, and this could not be allowed.

INDUSTRIAL DEVELOPMENT

The development of the Orange Free State gold fields had an important multiplier effect on the South African economy; helping to prolong the post-war boom and leading to the establishment of a local machine tool industry, a crucial sector in any developing economy. The government pursued an active and interventionist economic policy, protecting local manufacturing industry by tariffs and import controls. It established new state corporations and expanded existing ones, becoming an important producer of heavy engineering goods (VECOR), iron and steel (ISCOR), oil, gas and chemicals from coal (SASOL), fertilizers (FOSKOR), insecticides (Klipfontein Organic Products), and arms and amunition (ARMCOR). The role of the Industrial Development Corporation was expanded. It invested in mining (Palabora), finance (Central Accepting Bank), aircraft manufacture (Atlas), oil (SOEKOR), chemicals (Sentrachem) and shipping (Safmarine). The success of the government's nationalist economic policy was remarkable. In 1945 the market value of mining companies was R972 million,* while that of non-mining companies was R754 million. By 1965, the value of mining companies had risen to R3,664 million; while that of non-mining companies had risen to R5,399 million.[6]

AFRIKANER ECONOMIC INTERESTS

The Afrikaner-controlled sector of the South African economy consisted of the greater share of the farming capital, a complete monopoly of state capital, and an expanding group of industrial and commercial interests. The number of Afrikaners living in the rural areas fell from 48 per cent in 1936 to 31 per cent in 1951; and the contribution of farming to the national income, from 22 per cent in 1925 to 9 per cent in 1964.[7] But 80 per cent of South Africa's white farmers were Afrikaans-speaking, and the government supported farmers with loans, subsidies and grants. Tariffs kept out low-cost food imports. Farm production was controlled, priced and distributed by a series of control boards, which stabilized prices of domestic agricultural products above world prices, while exporting surpluses at a loss. As a result, while white Afrikaner farmers prospered, millions of black South Africans were unable to afford a balanced diet and suffered from malnutrition.

The Afrikaner share of industry and commerce was growing. In 1948–9 the Afrikaner share of the total private economy was 11 per cent, compared with 5 per cent in 1938. Afrikaner interests owned 25 per cent of commerce, 6 per cent of industry, and 6 per cent of finance, but only 1 per cent of mining.[8] The savings of the Afrikaner community continued to be channelled into Afrikaner financial institutions, such as the Volkskas Bank

* In 1960 the South African pound was replaced by a new decimal currency (one Rand = 100 cents).

and the Sanlam life insurance company. The Nationalist government used the power of the state to promote the growth of Afrikaner economic power. State corporations were largely staffed and managed by Afrikaners, and government investment and contracts were directed to strengthening and expanding Afrikaner-controlled firms and financial interests.[9] In 1953 the two Afrikaner investment companies, Federale Volksbeleggings and Bonuskor, formed the first major Afrikaner-controlled mining company, Federale Mynbou, which made steady progress in the fifties, helped by the siting of two of Escom's biggest power stations next to its coal mines.

ECONOMIC CRISIS

The demand by the black majority for political rights intensified in the post-war period but were vigorously resisted by the government. The struggle reached a climax at the end of the 1950s and the political crisis brought on an economic crisis, as investors lost confidence in South Africa. When the Anglo American Corporation offered the public £8·4 million of shares to finance the new Western Deep Levels mine, only £350,000 worth was subscribed, and the offer had to be underwritten by Anglo American and other group companies.[10] The South African stock market went into a sharp decline, wiping £100 million off the market value of Anglo American alone between 1959 and the end of 1960. South Africa's gold and foreign exchange reserves dwindled. The net outflow of foreign capital in 1959 turned into a flood after the Sharpeville massacre in March 1960* and the subsequent government state of emergency. About R200 million in private capital left the country in 1960. The Reserve Bank estimated that at least R148 million of this was repatriated foreign capital; and a further R28 million, previously resident South African capital placed abroad.[11] Foreign exchange reserves fell from R303·8 million in December 1959 to R135 million in June 1961.[12] As always when foreign capital was scarce, the mining houses appropriated working profits to finance capital

---

*At Sharpeville police opened fire on Africans demonstrating against the pass laws, killing sixty-nin e.

expenditure, but the crisis of confidence among foreign investors led to a dangerous reliance on internal funds. A total of £139 million was appropriated between 1955 and 1960, and in 1960 almost a quarter of working profits was appropriated to finance capital expenditure. This massive sum excludes loans made available by the mining houses and represents 38 per cent of the total capital and loans raised between 1946 and 1959.[13] The authoritative *Mining Journal* wondered how long the mining houses could keep up these rates of transfers 'in what can only be described as a siege economy'.[14]

The South African government and mining companies moved together to stem the flow of funds. As Anglo American's annual report for 1961 described it:

In June 1961 the authorities imposed stringent exchange control regulations which, *inter alia*, prevented the repatriation by non-residents of the proceeds of securities sold in South Africa and prohibited South African residents from remitting funds abroad for the purchase of South African or Rhodesian securities in other markets. These measures together with the raising abroad of a number of loans by private companies resulted in a severe curtailment in the net outflow of private capital.[15]

Elsewhere in the report Anglo revealed that in the middle of 1961, when the gold and currency reserves were at their lowest, Rand Selection Corporation (controlled by Anglo) raised loans totalling $30 million to be used 'in the general business of Rand Selection of South Africa'. The main function of the loan was to benefit the South African balance of payments, as Rand Selection did not need *dollars* to carry on its 'general business' in South Africa. Rand Selection was reorganized to make it more attractive to foreign investors, and at the same time, Oppenheimer's American associate, Charles Engelhard,* launched the American-South African Investment Corporation. Its aim was to attract American capital back into South Africa. The government itself raised a large loan from the Chase Manhattan Bank (with which Anglo also had connections).

Having staunched the flow of funds and bolstered the balance

---

*Reputedly Ian Fleming's model for Goldfinger in the James Bond book.

of payments, the government put its foot on the economic accelerator, while launching a savage repression of African political activity. The loans and investments from the mining companies and their friends, with a loan from the International Monetary Fund, saw South Africa through its most dangerous capital and foreign exchange crisis of the post-war era. As the country's gold and foreign exchange reserves began to recover, so also did share prices. The government swung the economy into a heavily promoted boom, 'instrumented by a cheap money, liberal credit, capital expansionist, public expenditure, forced industrialization programme unparalleled in South African history'.[16] Foreign investment began to flow back into South Africa. Part of this investment developed South Africa's base-metal mining industry, but most of it went into the manufacturing sector. Government policy promoted industrial self-sufficiency. It forced the major car producers to manufacture a higher percentage of the cars within South Africa, instead of merely assembling imported kits. Central bank controls prevented the major finance houses from investing in mining ventures overseas and encouraged them to invest in manufacturing and heavy industry within South Africa. Anglo American's investment in industry rose from R40 million in 1960 to R283 million in 1969 and R640 million in 1974.[17]

THE GOLD INDUSTRY

The trend towards concentration and local control of the gold-mining companies became more marked. In part this was due to the increasing power of the Anglo American Corporation, which acquired a substantial stake in many of the other mining houses. (See Table 12.) The revenue from the Orange Free State established Anglo American as the unquestioned leader of the South African gold industry, and the group acquired a majority stake in both Johannesburg Consolidated Investment and the Rand Mines group. By 1958 the assets of the Anglo group were greater than those of all the other South African finance houses put together.[18] The political and economic crisis of 1959–60 precipitated large-scale overseas selling of gold shares, which

Table 12: The concentration of the South African gold industry

Original company and founding date	Founders	Remarks
Consolidated Gold Fields (1887)	Cecil Rhodes	Owns 49 per cent of Gold Fields of South Africa
Union Corporation (1895)	Adolf Goerz	Until 1974 Charter was largest single shareholder with 10 per cent, now General Mining Group holds 50·1 per cent
Anglo–Transvaal Consolidated Investment (1933)	A. S. Hersov and S. G. (Slip) Menell E. Oppenheimer	General Mining has 17 per cent in holding company which controls Anglovaal
Anglo American Corporation (1917)		
Rand Mines (1893)	Julius Wernher Alfred Beit	Anglo group controlling 30 per cent interest in 1954–72, then control passed to Barlows
General Mining and Finance Corporation (1895)	George Albu	Anglo took substantial stake in 1950 and in 1964 assisted Afrikaner company, Federale Mynbou, to take over General Mining
Johannesburg Consolidated Investment (1899)	Barney Barnato	Anglo acquired Joel family holdings in 1940 and increased stake to 50 per cent in early 1960s to prevent takeover by Afrikaner interests
Rand Selection (1889)		Now Anglo American subsidiary
Consolidated Mines Selection (1897)		Now part of Charter Consolidated
Central Mining & Investment Corporation (1905)	Julius Wernher Alfred Beit	Now part of Charter Consolidated
South African Townships (1896)	Abe Bailey	Taken over by Anglo in 1942
African & European Investment Co. (1904)	Lewis and Marks	Anglo gained control in 1945

were taken up in considerable quantities by South African insurance companies, pension funds and similar institutions.[19] Not all the foreign investors were frightened away, however; because, as the proportion of shares held by British and Continental investors declined, American investment in the gold-mining industry increased.[20] But the most significant development was the entrance of Afrikaner capital into the gold-mining industry. In the 1950s Anglo American had blocked the efforts of Afrikaner financial interests to take over Rand Mines and JCI, because these mining houses held important strategic shares in De Beers and Anglo.[21] But in 1963 Anglo helped Afrikaner capital to acquire an important stake in the industry. Anglo and Federale Mynbou, an Afrikaner mining company, formed a joint company, Mainstraat Beleggings. The aim of the new company was to 'develop the common interests of Federale Mynbou and Anglo American'.

Mainstraat Beleggings became the largest shareholder in General Mining & Finance. The managing director of Federale Mynbou, Mr T. F. Müller, brother of South Africa's Foreign Minister, Dr Hilgard Müller, became managing director of General Mining. In 1964, Federale Mynbou took over General Mining;* the company's assets jumped from R60 million to around R300 million, and the Afrikaner stake in South African gold mining increased from 1 to nearly 10 per cent.[22] Mr Müller said that the takeover probably would not have come about but for the assistance of Mr Harry Oppenheimer (who had succeeded his father at Anglo in 1957). The Johannesburg *Sunday Times* called the deal a 'personal triumph for Mr Harry Oppenheimer' and 'an important step forward in his proposals for closer business cooperation across the South African language barrier'.[23] Afrikaner capital had finally become a significant force in the South African industry, but the timing and size of that entry had

* Federale Mynbou bought a 28 per cent direct holding in General Mining, and Mainstraat Beleggings' interests were transferred to Hollardstraat Beleggings (in which Federale Mynbou held 51 per cent and Anglo American 49 per cent). Hollardstraat Beleggings held 28 per cent of General Mining; this indirect stake together with its direct stake gave Federale Mynbou undisputed control of General Mining.

been determined by the mining houses. By 1974 Federale Mynbou controlled 37 per cent of South Africa's uranium, 20 per cent of its coal, and 32 per cent of its asbestos production, and was the main producer and exporter of chrome in South Africa.

The value of South Africa's gold output rose dramatically from R294 million in 1952 to R731 million in 1964, largely due to production from the Orange Free State gold mines. However, inflation and falling productivity due to shortages of white labour were eroding mining-company profits, reducing the amount of payable ore, and threatening the lives of several marginal mines. The government and the companies lobbied vigorously for an increase in the official price of gold, fixed since 1934 at $35 an ounce.

Once a mine has been closed, it cannot be easily reopened; and so in 1963 the government began subsidizing marginal mines to keep them operating until a rise in the price of gold made them viable once more. Although the devaluation of sterling in 1967 gave some relief to South African producers, the government had to introduce a more comprehensive scheme to assist all mines likely to close down before 1975 without subsidies. By June 1969, rising costs meant that nineteen of the country's forty-eight producing mines were being assisted by the state.

Inflationary pressures led the companies to try and change the pattern of labour utilization on the mines, where the bar on Africans filling certain occupations had not only been reinforced but even extended since the 1940s.[24] In the 1960s a shortage of white supervisors underground meant that African miners were waiting around for as much as one third of the working shift. The companies won support from the official leadership of the Mineworkers Union for changes to increase black productivity. In return, salaries and fringe benefits for *white* miners would be increased. New working regulations were introduced on an experimental basis at twelve mines in 1962. However, some of the miners were unhappy at these developments, and so were some members of the National Party in parliament. A group of dissidents broke away from the Mineworkers Union and threatened the official leadership with strikes and personal violence if the experiment continued.[25] The government, union and companies called off the experiment 'in view of the detrimental implications involved'.

GOLD PRICE INCREASES

A fundamental change in the world monetary system occurred in 1968, when a two-tier market for gold was established. The purchase and transfer of gold between central banks continued at the official gold price of $35 an ounce, but the free market price of gold was permitted to find its own level. The mining companies received revenue from the gold sold at a fixed price to the Reserve Bank of South Africa (to which all gold was sold) plus a proportion of the revenue gained by the Reserve Bank from free market sales. At the beginning of 1972, the free market price of gold was $44 an ounce. By the end of the year, it had reached $66 an ounce. As South Africa's foreign exchange position improved, the Reserve Bank began to hold back supplies from the free market, thus encouraging further dramatic rises in the price of gold.* By 1975 the price had reached very close to $200 an ounce. Spurred on by the rising price, the mining companies launched ambitious expansion schemes and began planning new mines. It was estimated that the Anglo American prospect at Elandsrand, the Union Corporation Unisel mine, and the Gold Fields Deelkraal mine would require an investment of R300 million before they came on stream in 1981. But the industry was suffering from a shortage of black miners.

LABOUR AND THE GOLD INDUSTRY

The uniformity and low grade of the Witwatersrand and Orange Free State gold deposits mean that working costs are the key factor in determining the amount of payable ore. The demand for gold is virtually unlimited; and provided, therefore, that working costs remain below the ruling market price, it is production and not demand which will determine the level of company profits.[26] The cost of labour is the largest single component of working

*See page 381 and Figure 19.

costs, and the main objective of the companies is accordingly to hold down or reduce the cost of labour. This will expand reserves, increase production and maximize profits. But the political power of the white mineworkers, their insistence on retaining a rigid colour bar on the mines, the group system of mining, and the elimination of competition between the companies have meant that large supplies of cheap unskilled black mineworkers have been crucial for the mining companies' profits and for the continuing existence of marginal mines.

CHAMBER OF MINES

The main function of the Chamber of Mines ever since its formation in 1889 has been to recruit this large black labour force at the lowest possible cost. By eliminating competition among the mining companies through the maximum average agreement, and by centralizing recruiting under WNLA and NRC,* the Chamber has reduced the cost of recruiting and kept black wages at an extremely low level. Table 13 shows how successful the Chamber has been. In real terms black earnings in 1969 were no higher and possibly even lower than they had been in 1911, while over the same period real cash earnings of whites had risen by over 70 per cent.[27] Even this overestimates the true level of black wages because, if we take into account that between 1899 and 1911 cash wages for black mineworkers fell by more than 25 per cent,[28] it is clear that the wages of black miners have not risen in real terms since the Chamber of Mines was founded. In the last few years black wages have been rising considerably faster in percentage terms than those of white workers; but because of the wide historical wage gap, an increase of, say, 50 per cent in black wages and 10 per cent in white wages means that in absolute terms the gap actually widens. The increases granted to black miners of 22 per cent in 1972 and 26 per cent in 1973 did not keep up with inflation, and amounted to less than 10 per cent of the increase in mining company profits in those years.[29] Even in 1974 the basic rate for black underground miners was a mere R57·20 per month or 220 cents per eight-hour shift.

* Since 1975 MLO (Wenela) Ltd and MLO (NRC) Ltd respectively.

Table 13: Wages on the South African gold mines, 1911–69

Date	Current Rands W.	Current Rands B.	Annual Cash Earnings (a) Index of Real Earnings W. (1936 = 100)	Annual Cash Earnings (a) Index of Real Earnings B. (1936 = 100)	Earnings Gap Ratio W:B	Employment (b) B:W
1911	666	57	102	100	11·7:1	7·7:1
1916	709	59	94	90	12·0:1	9·1:1
1921	992	66	90	69	15·0:1	8·2:1
1926	753	67	85	88	11·2:1	9·2:1
1931	753	66	90	92	11·3:1	9·3:1
1936	786	68	100	100	11·5:1	8·5:1
1941	848	70	94	89	12·1:1	9·0:1
1946	1,106	87	99	92	12·7:1	7·7:1
1951	1,607	109	113	89	14·7:1	6·9:1
1956	2,046	132	119	89	15·5:1	6·8:1
1961	2,478	146	129	89	17·0:1	8·1:1
1966	3,216	183	149	99	17·6:1	8·5:1
1969	4,006	199	172	99	20·1:1	9·2:1

Notes: (a) This table includes none of the substantial wages in kind that are provided to both black *and* white workers on the mines.

(b) In 1922 after the Rand Rebellion the black/white employment ratio rose to 11·4:1; in 1923 it was 10·0:1; in 1924 it was 9·7:1; in 1925 9·1:1.

Source: Transvaal Chamber of Mines & Government, *Mining Engineer Annual* reports, quoted in Francis Wilson, *Labour in the South African Gold Mines 1911–1969*, Cambridge University Press, 1972, Table 5, p. 46, and Appendix 3.

Black labour may be cheap for the mining companies, but the human costs of the migrant labour system are high and most of them fall on the black miners and their home communities. Migrant labourers are separated from their families and work in hazardous conditions on the mines. Between 1903 and 1973 almost 42,000 men died on the gold mines, and more than 90 per cent of these were Africans.[30] The companies

employ indentured, migrant peasants; pay them less than a living wage; house them in compounds; repatriate the diseased, crippled and enfeebled to their villages; and renew the supply of able-bodied men by drawing on rural communities throughout the continent.[31]

The colour bar operated by the white miners and the companies prevents blacks from moving into the higher jobs which require training and the creation of a stable skilled labour force. It does this in two ways: through job reservation, which defines the jobs which may not be performed by African miners; and through maintaining a maximum ratio of blacks to whites in employment on the mines.

The ratio element of the colour bar ensures that the industry does not alter its techniques so as to use more unskilled workers, while the reservation element prevents management from training blacks as skilled workers.[32]

The group system increases the need to keep black wages low. Individual mines would have been forced to maintain the profitability of each mine. In those circumstances mines would have either closed down or whites been forced to allow the colour bar at least as much flexibility as in other South African industries. But under the group system the companies balance the product of the marginal mines against the profits of the richer ones. Black wages are kept at the level that enables the marginal mines to keep in production, even if it means some reduction in the profitability of the richer mines because of labour shortages, and the low productivity of unskilled labour.

Although most of the cost of the migrant labour system falls on the black communities, it is not without its cost for the companies. They lose potential profits through the low productivity of unskilled miners.

The limited time horizon [of the migrant labour system] prevents the industry from ever developing the full skill potential of its labour force because it severely restricts the period in which the industry would otherwise have been able to reap the returns of greater specific investment in it. However, so long as the colour bar exists to prevent blacks from moving into more skilled jobs, so long will the cost of the limited time horizon be obscured. This loss can only be redeemed by the relaxation of the colour bar, together with the adoption of a policy of stabilization which minimizes labour turnover.[33]

Until the colour bar is relaxed, however, the gold-mining industry is dependent on adequate supplies of cheap, unskilled black labour.

THE SUPPLY OF BLACK LABOUR

As the industry's investment, engineering, design and production techniques are all based on large numbers of unskilled mine-workers, the availability of black labour has always been a major determinant of the South African gold-mining industry's output. In 1966, some 76 per cent of the variations in output from mine to mine could be attributed to variations in the numbers of Africans employed in each.[34] It is not just output but total profit levels reached by each mine that are affected. A shortage of black labour

is likely to cause not only a temporary reduction in output but an overall loss to the mine, because the inflationary trend has the effect of transposing some of the payable ore reserves not mined on one day into the unpayable range of the next – unless the price of gold is rising as fast as the cost of production.[35]

Over long periods the terms of trade have moved against gold. For example, from 1936 to 1969 the South African retail price index rose by 195 per cent, while the average price received per fine ounce of gold rose by only 86 per cent.[36] This makes the supply of black labour a crucial factor in determining the total profits of a mine over its life, and also therefore the industry's total gold output.

To meet the shortages of black miners, the government has tightened up influx control measures to deny black South Africans residence in the cities and force them to seek employment on the farms or on the mines.[37] But influx control has never ensured a sufficient supply of black labour on the mines, as South African black workers have consistently preferred the more congenial work and higher pay offered by manufacturing industry to the poor working conditions and low pay on the gold mines. To prevent too great a drain on farm labour supplies, the mining companies were allowed to recruit foreign labour, and the Chamber of Mines set up recruiting stations throughout Southern and Central Africa.* As neighbouring countries gained political independence, these supplies have become less secure. For a

---

*In 1973 there were 132 recruiting stations over the sub-continent.

long time, however, they were still generally sufficient to keep the mines running at or near their full capacity. Both Tanzania and Zambia banned further recruitment, but increases in recruitment from Malawi and Mozambique compensated for these losses. Throughout the sixties, indeed, the proportion of South African black mineworkers fell; and, as Table 14 shows, by 1966 nearly 65 per cent of black miners came from outside the Republic. By 1973 the percentage of foreign miners had risen to 79 per cent.

The most serious disruption of supplies in recent years came in April 1974. A WNLA plane crashed at Francistown killing 77 Malawian miners. President Banda immediately banned WNLA recruiting, and Malawian miners began returning from South Africa by a special VC10 shuttle service. The number of Malawian miners on the gold mines fell by 30,000 in 1974;[38] and at the beginning of 1975 they were leaving South Africa at the rate of 1,600 a week, without being replaced. This had a severe effect on levels of production, which higher wages and a recruiting drive in Rhodesia and South Africa could only partially counteract. The ban was motivated not just by outrage at the low level of safety procedures, but also by President Banda's desire to reduce his dependence on South Africa in view of Mozambique's imminent independence. Fears that the important labour supplies from Mozambique might be interrupted were one of the major reasons for Prime Minister Vorster's celebrated moves towards detente in southern Africa. In November 1975, President Banda lifted the ban on the recruitment of Malawian miners, and this, together with the new supplies from Rhodesia and South Africa attracted in part by the higher wage levels, meant that the immediate crisis on the mines had passed. But the fundamental dependence on foreign miners remained.

MINING HOUSES AND THE LABOUR SHORTAGE

As foreign labour supplies have become increasingly vulnerable to disruption and as white labour becomes relatively more expensive than black labour, the mining companies have sought to increase the productivity not of the white, but of the black labour force.[39] In 1968, the number of black mineworkers em-

Table 14: The geographical origins of black mineworkers employed by the Chamber of Mines, 1896–1974 (a)

Geographical Area (b)	1896–8 (%)	1906 (%)	1916 (%)	1926 (%)	1936 (%)	1946 (%)	1956 (%)	1966 (%)	1969 (%)	1973 (%)	1974 (%)
Transvaal	23·4 (c)	4·0	10·3	8·4	7·0	7·6	5·5	4·8	3·8		
Cape Province	11·1	13·7	33·0	29·8	39·2	27·8	24·4	24·8	23·6		
Natal and Zululand	1·0 (d)	4·8	5·3	2·6	4·9	4·4	3·8	2·4	1·9		
Orange Free State		0·3	0·6	0·5	1·1	1·5	1·0	2·1	2·1		
South Africa Total	35·5	22·8	49·2	41·3	52·2	41·3	34·7	34·1	31·4	21·0	24·0
Swaziland		0·7	1·9	2·1	2·2	1·8	1·6	1·1	1·4	1·0	2·0
Lesotho		2·6	7·9	10·9	14·5	12·5	11·9	16·8	17·5	20·0	21·0
Botswana	3·9	0·4	1·8	1·0	2·3	2·3	3·1	5·0	4·0	5·0	4·0
Mozambique	60·2	65·4	38·1	44·5	27·8	31·5	30·8	28·4	26·9	23·0	25·0
North of Latitude 22°S (mostly Malawi)	0·5	8·0	1·1	0·2	1·1	10·6	17·9	14·7	18·8	30·0	24·0
Total Foreign %	64·6	69·1	50·8	58·7	47·9	58·7	65·3	66·0	68·6	79·0	76·0
Total S.A. and Foreign (thousands)	54	81	219	203	318	305	334	383	371	372	328

Notes: Totals may not add up to 100 per cent because of rounding.
(a) 1896–1969 as at 31 December 1973; and 1974 as at 31 October. All figures include employment on Transvaal coal mines.
(b) Apart from 1896–8 the Mozambique figures exclude men from north of latitude 22°S.
(c) Includes Lesotho and Orange Free State.
(d) Includes Swaziland.

Source: 1896–1969, from Francis Wilson, *Labour in the South African Gold Mines 1911–1969*, CUP, 1972; 1973 and 1974 from South African Chamber of Mines.

ployed on the mines was 368,000, the same number as in 1941, although output has more than doubled.[40] This has been achieved partly because of higher grade ore in the new mines but also through greater mechanization, more efficient management and better training of the labour force.

Nevertheless, all the gains won by the workers from this improved productivity have gone to the white miners. Table 13 shows the extent of wage rises for white miners in recent years. The earnings ratio between white and black miners remained fairly constant from 1911 until 1945, at around 12 to 1; but since then white miners' wages have shot up to more than twenty times the average black wage. Nothing more clearly indicates the increased political strength of the Afrikaner trade unions, especially after the National Party came to power, and more closely reflects the growing shortage of white skilled labour in South Africa. The bargaining power of the white miners was shown in 1972, when a wave of strikes by African workers in all sectors of the economy seemed to herald a more difficult period for labour relations that might spill over into political action by the black majority. Mining magnates were loud in their calls for a more efficient use of labour; but when in 1973 the companies negotiated a slightly more efficient use of labour, they offered the white miners a 20 per cent wage rise without any change in the pattern of job reservation on the mines.

As the economy expands this shortage of white skilled labour grows more acute; and whereas previously the mining companies were able to compensate for the higher costs of white labour by holding down black labour costs, the vulnerability of foreign labour supplies to disruption has encouraged the mining companies to seek a relaxation of the colour bar. Such a relaxation would not only reduce company costs,* it would, by raising the wages of those black miners who were promoted and to a lesser extent the wages of unskilled black miners, enable the companies to attract more South African blacks to work on the

*At the end of 1968 the former chairman of the Board of Trade and Industries, Dr A. J. Norval, estimated that replacing 70 per cent of the white labour force would save the mining industry R30m. a year (*Star*, 22 November 1968).

mines and reduce the dependence on vulnerable foreign supplies.

In all these moves Anglo American has been the pacemaker for the mining companies. As a result it has attracted a lot of favourable publicity for its 'liberal' attitudes and political courage. But Anglo's pressure for higher black wages reflects not so much political liberalism as good economics. To understand this we must ask why Anglo has not simply broken ranks and already offered money to alleviate its labour shortage. The answer lies partly in the collusion of the mining companies through the Chamber of Mines and partly in the nature of the group system. Under the group system the major finance houses, Gold Fields, Union Corporation, Anglo American, Anglovaal, and so on, own and manage a large number of mines. At any time some of these mines will be rich mines which can afford such payments, while others will be marginal ones which cannot afford to pay more for their labour. In addition the older mines can less easily change their production methods to use fewer but better paid black mineworkers; partly because the design of a mine cannot easily be adapted after it is in production, and partly because the scale of investment required is too great for the likely return. Thus a group with a higher proportion of older and more marginal mines will oppose a solution to the labour shortage which increases black wages. By contrast a group with a higher proportion of richer, newer and more efficient mines will be able to afford higher black wages. Table 15 shows why Anglo American has been the prime mover for higher black wages in the gold-mining industry and Consolidated Gold Fields the most reluctant.[41] In 1961 the majority of Anglo American's poor mines were old, while the three new rich mines were all in the Orange Free State and employing up to 85 per cent foreign labour. Anglo could therefore afford to increase black wages in the hope of lessening its reliance on foreign labour and increasing the proportion of South African labour. Consolidated Gold Fields and Rand Mines could not afford such gestures. Throughout the sixties and early seventies Anglo continued to press for higher wages for black miners but without going so far as to challenge the colour bar or to leave the Chamber of Mines.

Table 15: The distribution of profitable gold mines among the major mining groups in 1961 and 1974

Group	No. of producing gold mines		Rich		Average		Poor		No. of poor mines more than 30 years old	
	1961	1974	1961	1974	1961	1974	1961	1974	1961	1974
Anglo American	12	9	3	4	3	3	6	2	5	1
Anglovaal	4	2		2	1	2	3		1	1
Rand Mines/Central (Barrand)	8	4		1	1	1	6	3	6	2
General Mining	3	4			1	2	2	2		
Gold Fields	11	7	1	3	2	2	8	2	5	2
Union Corporation	7	7		1	5	4	2	2	2	2
Johannesburg Cons. Inv.	2	2				1	2			1

Note: Mines are graded according to their wealth, measured by the working profit per ton milled in current cents (1961) and current Rand (1974).

Poor = 0–19·9 cents; Average = 20–59·9 cents; Rich = more than 60 cents.

Poor = 0–10·0 Rands; Average = 10–25 Rands; Rich = more than R 25.

Source: 1961 figures F. Wilson, *Labour in the South African Gold Mines 1911–1969*, CUP, 1972, p. 108; *Mining Journal*, 2 August 1974, 'Analysis of Rand and O.F.S. Quarterlies', p. 3.

What seems to be evolving is a system where mines pay wages above the basic according to their capacity to pay. A rich mine like Free State Geduld is clearly better able to pay more per shift to its Blacks than can East Dagga. If these differentials widen too much there is a probability that the whole system will be subject to strain with consequences that cannot be foreseen. However, while the other houses may not like Anglo's plans, nothing so drastic as a breach of traditional Chamber solidarity seems likely to occur.[42]

Anglo's strategy has been to pay fractionally more than the Chamber of Mines minima, and because most of its mines are newer and offer better working conditions Anglo has been able to maintain higher manning levels than the other groups. It was also able to reduce its dependence on foreign sources of labour. The result was that by 1973 Anglo took only 34 per cent of its black miners from Mozambique and Malawi, while Anglovaal took 75 per cent, Gold Fields 69 per cent, and Rand Mines 60 per cent.

The more conservative mining houses attacked Anglo for its policy and argued that it was moving too quickly. They felt that the deaths at Anglo's Western Deep Level Mines at Carletonville in September 1973, when police shot twelve miners protesting over regrading and the erosion of differentials, confirmed their point of view.

Carletonville proved to be the harbinger of a wave of unrest and strikes which resulted in the deaths of eighty black miners in a series of incidents over the following eighteen months as the migrant labour force responded to rapid inflation, political unrest in Lesotho and Mozambique, and a wave of strikes by black industrial workers in South Africa. But the quadrupling of the world price of gold eased the pressure on the marginal mines and black wages were increased by all the mining houses. Anglo executives were now anxious to reaffirm their solidarity with the other mining houses.

We attach the greatest importance to the Chamber. We moved out of line on black wages a few years ago . . . [We've] got no reason to think that Anglo American will move out of line again.[43]

THE INDUSTRY IN THE MID-SEVENTIES

Ever since 1890, analysts have forecast the closure of the South African gold fields. And yet in the mid-1970s the industry was earning record profits and was still the most important single sector of the economy, accounting for 56 per cent of South African exports.* The concentration of the industry under South African control has continued in the 1970s. Gold Fields of South Africa, previously 51 per cent owned by London-based Consolidated Gold Fields, has now a majority South African ownership. In 1974 an epic takeover battle between Gold Fields and General Mining for control of Union Corporation, which is estimated to have cost the companies more than £1 million, left neither side with absolute control. But when its offer failed, Gold Fields withdrew, leaving the General Mining group, including Sentrust Ltd, with 29·1 per cent of Union Corporation. A year later they increased their stake to 50 per cent. The new group became the largest mining house after Anglo American.[44]

As ever, the gold industry's fortunes depended on a continual supply of cheap black migrant labour, but these were threatened by political unrest in Lesotho and political developments in Mozambique and Rhodesia. The political uncertainty and inflationary pressures posed a serious threat to the gold industry; and because gold is still so important to the South African economy and balance of payments, the government and the mining companies both wanted to reduce the reliance on foreign labour. To do this, the companies had to increase the wages of black miners to a level which would attract South African blacks.

It gives some indication of how far mine wages lagged behind even the low rates blacks were paid in other areas of South African industry, in that it took wage rises of 455 per cent from 1971 to 1976, as well as a black unemployment rate of over 25 per cent to force any significant number of South African blacks to work on gold mines. In 1973 only 21 per cent of the black miners came

*In 1977 the Central East and West Rand produced 7·6 per cent, the Far West Rand 34·6 per cent, Klerksdorp 20·3 per cent, Orange Free State 30·7 per cent, Evander 5·3 per cent and others 1·5 per cent of South Africa's gold.

from South Africa and Transkei. By 1977 this had risen to 53 per cent. But if foreign supplies continue to be disrupted, and cost inflation continues to erode mine profits, the government and companies may be forced to re-examine the political bargain struck by the Pact Government after the 1922 Rand revolt. Under that, the companies kept the marginal mines going, maintained white employment, and upheld the colour bar; while, in return, the legislative policy of successive South African governments has isolated the labour supplies of the gold-mining industry from the competition of manufacturing industry, by influx controls within South Africa and by allowing the mining companies to recruit labour outside South Africa. But any revision of this *quid pro quo* must confront the political power of the white miners, who will strongly resist any change in the pattern of labour utilization on the mines. There were no signs of an immediate confrontation, but the balance of forces may not be the same as in 1922. Then an English-speaking government confronted the largely Afrikaner white miners at a time of economic decline. In the seventies the South African economy has remained relatively healthy despite inflationary pressures, while the National Party has come to identify more closely with industry. Nevertheless, tension within the Nationalist ranks has produced another split in the party, led by Dr Albert Hertzog, and recalling that of 1934; while a strong current of anti-capitalist, anti-semitic sentiment runs not far beneath the surface. As a leader of the discontented miners put it in 1969:

If the government now intends to become the lackeys of the Anglo-Jewish capitalists, it had better get used to the idea of being rejected by the miners.[45]

It remains to be seen whether this current of Nationalist opinion will prevent a change in the use of labour on the mines. But in contrast to 1922 one of the major mining houses is Afrikaner-controlled, and the companies see the outlines of an alternative solution which would protect the position of whites, while increasing the productivity of black miners. The Chamber of Mines has launched a massive R150 million programme of research into rock-cutting and mechanization on the mines.[46] If successful it may well offer the companies an occasion to do away with the blasting certificate, which is the cornerstone of job reservation on the mines, and enable great increases in the productivity of black miners, while avoiding a direct challenge to the white miners. It was reported in 1974 that some of the mining houses intended to cut their black labour force by 40 per cent in four years simply by introducing new technology and increasing productivity.[47] But the pace of these changes will depend very much on political factors, and the growing power of South Africa's industrial black labour force may itself force changes in the use of black labour on the mines.

8 From Primitive Accumulation to Boom: the Mining Companies in Southern Rhodesia

Apologists for white minority rule in southern Africa have argued that the racial discrimination and the reliance on cheap migrant labour in the mining industry is a historical aberration brought about by a particular combination of unfortunate circumstances;[1] that the migrant labour system and the mine compound are a barrier to economic growth; and that, if only the companies and the white workers would abandon the 'irrational' colour bar, the benevolent operation of market forces under capitalism would ensure full economic development for black and white alike. In fact, however, the experience of Southern Rhodesia shows that it was precisely this systematic and coercive exploitation of the black labour force which laid the foundation of the mining industry in Rhodesia, and which remains fundamental to the structure of the economy and to the maintenance of white minority rule.

1890–1903*

At the end of the nineteenth century, white settlers backed by Cecil Rhodes invaded the area since known as Rhodesia, and despite a furious and prolonged resistance smashed the military power of the local African population. The early growth of the mining industry was fuelled by wild promises of another Rand, but the companies soon found they faced severe problems. The small and irregular mineral deposits which were subject to frequent faulting; the lack of a stable labour force; shortages of skilled manpower, machinery and fuel supplies, taken together with the British South Africa Company's insistence on a 50-percent share in all new mining ventures, meant that the Rhodesian

* See also above pages 48–50 and pages 60–61.

mining companies could not compete with the profits being produced on the Rand. Finally, in 1903 the confidence of the foreign investors, which had been sustained for over ten years by extravagant claims and baseless promises, collapsed, almost completely destroying the industry.

The BSAC and the mining companies were hopelessly overextended, and to ensure their survival they developed new strategies. The BSAC encouraged immigration of white settlers whose presence and activities would increase the value of the company's railway and vast stock of land. By 1902 more than three quarters of all the land in the country had been expropriated from the Africans.[2] In order to remain on their land, they were forced to pay rent or to provide labour for the whites now flooding into the country. The number of settlers grew from 11,000 in 1901 to 22,000 in 1912.[3] For the mining companies, the greater size, regularity, and profitability of the Witwatersrand gold deposits meant that they could not expect any major supplies of foreign capital to reconstruct the Rhodesian industry. Their strategy for survival was to reduce the working costs of their mines drastically, particularly the cost of black mineworkers.

SUPPLY OF LABOUR, 1903–33

From the first, the mining companies and the new settlers had faced severe problems in securing the supply of cheap black labour they sought. When the first settlers had arrived and the mines were established, the local population responded quickly to the opportunities they provided to sell their labour and agricultural produce.[4] They were so successful that on the mines they won successive sharp increases in their real wages, and their strong competition forced the settlers to demand protection from African producers.[5] This situation was unsatisfactory for the farmers and for the mining companies, who both wanted regular supplies of cheap labour and not a shifting, independent labour force entering wage employment from time to time in response to its own needs and largely in the agricultural off-season. At the instigation of the settlers and the mining companies, the BSAC introduced a series of measures to force African peasants to work in the white economy.

The companies and other employers of black labour urged the British Secretary of State for the Colonies to introduce a new labour tax in addition to the existing hut tax and thereby force the Africans to seek work. This was refused, but the hut tax was doubled and additional payments were levied. This apparently small and limited concession to local pressure created a major shift in the burden of taxation, from the settlers and companies to the African population.[6] The rate of taxation for Africans in Southern Rhodesia had now increased to a level 20 to 30 per cent higher than that levied on Africans elsewhere in the region.[7] In addition the B S A C steadily restricted the access of Africans to the land which they had previously occupied. Over the next twenty years Africans were forced into less productive areas, which were unable to support the population imposed on them. This led to steadily falling yields[8] and coupled with the inroads made by a protected and increasingly competitive white agricultural sector, it became impossible for African farmers to produce a marketable surplus.[9]

The expropriation of the land and the imposition of heavier taxes were insufficient for the mining companies, however, because although they forced Africans to work in the money economy, they did not direct that labour to work on the Rhodesian mines. The companies needed a more permanent labour force, but conditions on the Rhodesian mines were so poor that few black workers stayed very long. The level of desertions was a constant problem to the companies, as the workers either returned to their villages within a few weeks, or moved swiftly on to the relatively better conditions and pay of the South African gold mines. The companies' first solution had been to draft a Pass Law, which the Chamber of Mines presented to the administration in 1901 and which came into effect the following year.[10] The Pass Law, however, was not a complete solution, because the Rhodesian mining companies still had to compete for their supplies of labour with the South African mines. Moreover the British Colonial Office was determined that the reconstruction of the Rhodesian industry should not interfere with the more important reconstruction of the South African gold-mining industry after the Anglo–Boer War. In particular the Colonial Office was anxious to ensure that such supplies of cheap labour as were available within the region should go to South Africa,[11] especially as the scandal of Chinese labour had almost jeopardized the use of cheap labour on the Rand.*

In an attempt to stabilize the labour force, the Rhodesian companies imported some Arab, Somali, and Abyssinian workers, but the experiment failed, as workers who had not directly experienced the traumatic effects of colonialism were too 'difficult' for the companies and those who had not already deserted were soon returned to Aden.[12] This experience showed the mine-owners the importance of restricting the bargaining effect that mobility gave to the labour force. So in order to force Rhodesian blacks to sell their labour to Rhodesian mines, at the price the mines were now prepared to pay, the companies introduced a system of forced labour which the Africans came to call *Chibaro*, or slavery.

CHIBARO

Within three months of the collapse of the industry in 1903, the mineowners had set up the Rhodesia Native Labour Bureau (RNLB). The object of the bureau was to secure for the mines 'a nucleus of natives contracted to work for twelve months at a definite minimum wage'. This would have great advantages because these workers

form the guarantee that certain work can be carried on . . . tide employers over the wet season when independent labour is scarce and . . . make employers to a large extent independent of the vagaries of the casual labourer.[13]

In other words the task of the RNLB was to secure for the mines a supply of African labourers who were not otherwise prepared to volunteer their labour because wages had been so sharply cut. It also had to frustrate their attempts to work in South Africa. Beyond this the function of the RNLB was to distribute the

* See above, page 53.

available supply of labour evenly among the mines and so eliminate the damaging competition between the richer mines offering better conditions and the more marginal mines.[14]

Despite a near monopoly of recruitment within Northern and Southern Rhodesia, the RNLB found it difficult to supply its quota of labour. In general, the Bureau secured its supplies around the periphery of Rhodesia, farthest from the mines and those peasants with a detailed knowledge of the working conditions in them, because

no central African peasant would, voluntarily, seek out conditions of employment where he was to be paid the lowest wages, obligated by the longest contracts, and sent to the mines with the worst health and labour management records in Southern Rhodesia. To avoid *Chibaro* labour, however, a peasant had to be fit to walk the hundreds of miles to the labour markets, have the necessary cash with which to provide himself with food and clothing for the journey and not to have left home while he had important obligations to his kinsmen unfulfilled. The normal vicissitudes in the agricultural cycles, sheer distance from the labour markets and new burdens such as tax, all made inroads into the bargaining power of the 'independent' work seeker.[15]

In some areas the District Commissioners would issue passes for those wishing to travel only if they were willing to serve with the RNLB. In others the Bureau advanced credit, which then had to be worked off.

When these pressures were insufficient, the RNLB relied on force. Peasants were simply rounded up by agents of the Native Commissioner, handed over to the RNLB and then marched to the mines. Those who refused to go were sometimes whipped, or in other cases had their grain stores burnt down.[16] The BSAC applied similar pressures on the peasantry to pay tax. In 1904, for example, the police raided the villages of tax-defaulters in Northern Rhodesia, burning homes, crops and grain stores of those Africans who did not have the necessary cash.[17] For those who still escaped the RNLB's net, several well-positioned outposts intercepted Africans making their way to South Africa.

THE CLOSED COMPOUND

When the unfortunate black worker reached the mines, he was housed in a compound. The closed mine compound of southern Africa is unique in capitalist development. It is not an archaic institution simply reflecting the racist attitudes of the whites towards the blacks, which has now been rendered obsolete by the passage of time. The compound was, and remains, primarily an instrument of coercion, the foundation on which the mining industry and indeed the whole fabric of white minority rule in Rhodesia (and the rest of southern Africa) is built.

The closed compound offers the employers a means to the total control of the worker both during and outside working hours.[18] In the compounds, black miners were isolated as far as possible from the local economy and population. Living conditions were appalling, the food inadequate, safety provisions casual, health care almost non-existent, and the discipline brutal. Within the compound, any shortage offered the management a potential lever for control. Supplies of food, tobacco, *dagga* (marijuana) and alcohol were closely regulated. The companies also restricted the miners' access to their families, to local women, to education and to religion. In short it was the compound which provided the framework for the total exploitation of the black workers and, with the Pass laws, denied them the chance to respond to 'market forces' by selling their labour in the best market. It was the compound with its state-sanctioned system of industrial violence which converted reluctant and forced labour into forced production. It was the compound that did so much to prevent the emergence of black working-class movements which could have improved the lot of African miners.* And finally it is

the unique and powerful social, political and economic cutting edge that the compound system represents both for the state and employers that accounts for its continued prominence in central African industry seventy-five years after it was first introduced.[19]

* Nevertheless African workers did resist this degradation in many ways. See C. van Onselen, *Chibaro – African Mine Labour in Southern Rhodesia 1900–1933*, Pluto Press, 1976, and T. O. Ranger, *The African Voice in Southern Rhodesia*, Heinemann, 1970.

The combination of the pressure on the land, the heavy taxation, and the powerful system of coercion developed by the mining industry finally secured the necessary supplies of cheap black labour. So savage and successful was this process that black mine wages in 1922 were lower than they had been in 1904 when *Chibaro* was being introduced.[20] Some of the base-metal mines did not even pay the meagre RNLB rates. In many mica and asbestos mines half the labour force were children and at least one mine was wholly staffed by children, while the Wankie Colliery consistently used convict labour throughout the first twenty years of its life.[21] But in general it was the RNLB which, throughout the period of reconstruction,

ensured the industry its share of labour drawn from within a regional economic system in which it could not offer competitive wages. It was the supply of *Chibaro* labour that ensured that mines who could not attract a supply of 'voluntary' labour remained in continuous production. It was the bureau that systematically extracted the longest contracts from the poorest peasants, which in turn ensured that the mines could develop ore reserves and continue milling during the Rhodesian wet season. Above all, it was *Chibaro* that bridged the gap between the labour supply and demand during the years when the industry's requirements for black workers expanded while at the same time it reduced wages for African miners.[22]

STRUCTURAL CHANGE

The mining industry was aided by the continuing proletarianization of the Rhodesian peasantry, which was making cheap labour available and at rates that in the 1920s came to undercut even *Chibaro* rates. The participation of African labour in wage employment increased continuously, because the cumulative effect of the assault on the peasant economy by the mining companies, the settlers and the BSAC administration was such that a growing proportion of peasants could no longer obtain the means of subsistence in any other way.[23] This was an irreversible process which continued irrespective of whether wages rose or fell, and which the cyclical boosts in the local economy could not reverse, so complete had been the destruction of the once competitive peasant economy. Whereas the sale of produce had accounted for some 70 per cent of the cash earnings of the African population in 1900 it accounted for less than 20 per cent of such earnings in 1932.[24]

This structural change in the economy was now accompanied by an important political change. In 1923 the British government removed responsibility for the administration of the territory from the B S A C and handed it over to the settlers. By now there were five clearly distinguishable social groups in Southern Rhodesia: the white farmers and owners of small mines; the white wage-earners; white shopkeepers and traders; the larger mining and trading companies, many of them foreign owned; and lastly the African peasantry and wage-earners who constituted the majority of the population.[25] It is the shifting relationships between these groups that determined the political and social evolution of the country over the next fifty years.

Throughout the nineteen-twenties and thirties the existing alliance between the larger mining companies and the white rural bourgeoisie of farmers and owners of the smaller mines continued to strengthen its position at the expense of the black majority. Legislation was introduced to assist the white farmers and wage-earners. The Land Apportionment Act (1930) not only prevented competition from African farmers, but ensured that the European farmers were given better farming land and the poorer land was allocated to the Africans. Without any investment in teaching new methods of cultivation this poor-quality land deteriorated further under the traditional extensive farming methods of the African peasants. Land apportionment also made it possible to direct capital expenditure, such as on roads and dams, into European areas, so widening the differential in overall productivity between European and African farmers.[26] The Native Registration Act of 1936 tightened up the Pass Law and reinforced the wage structure which enabled white farmers to pay consistently lower wage rates than other employers for unskilled black labour.[27] The government introduced legislation to strengthen the position of the white workers in the face of African competition. The Industrial Conciliation Act of 1936 established Industrial Councils on the South African pattern to arbitrate in industrial disputes and determine wage rates. As in South Africa, the definition of employee specifically excluded Africans from the ambit of the Act. Through this Act the white workers also gained the power to control the entrance of apprentices to the skilled trades, a power which they used to exclude Africans as far as possible.

The government strengthened the position of the white community against the international companies. In 1933 it bought the mineral rights from the British South Africa Company for £2 million. The state helped to establish the small mine owners with loans and a government drilling programme,[28] and it laid the foundations for future growth of a manufacturing and industrial sector by setting up state enterprises to supply electricity, to establish iron and steel mills and to build cotton mills. The Tobacco Marketing Act of 1936 was designed to help the tobacco growers compete with the United Tobacco Company. Finally, in 1948 the government bought the railway from the British South Africa Company.

Despite this government intervention to foster economic development and white supremacy, at the end of the thirties Southern Rhodesia still had a typical colonial economy, heavily dependent on primary goods produced for export and with an almost non-existent industrial sector. The progressive decrease in the productivity of the African peasant farmers presented a serious obstacle to industrialization, given the small size of the European population, because of the reduced demand for the goods and services of the domestic economy, until the Second World War and the post-war demand for Rhodesian primary exports provided an external stimulus to the process of economic development.

The Second World War produced an explosion in international demand as the metropolitan economies switched increasingly to production of war materials. In most African countries this led merely to inflation as the supply of imported goods dwindled and the prices rose. Higher prices were met by the higher export prices. But in Southern Rhodesia, as in South Africa, the government was able to intervene with direct anti-inflationary controls and encourage the growth of secondary industry. The government established and strengthened the infrastructure for the industrial sector of the economy. But above all it was exports which led the way to growth. Rhodesia was helped by the booming demand for her chrome and asbestos, which Britain needed to save dollar purchases. There was a switch from maize to tobacco as the main crop for Rhodesian farmers. The growth of the agricultural sector was no longer limited by the limited internal market, but depended increasingly on the external demand for its high-quality tobacco.

Now also, for the first time, a substantial manufacturing sector emerged. The contribution of manufacturing to national income rose from 9 per cent in the late 1930s to 15 per cent in the early 1950s. Significantly this growth was accompanied by a concentration of production into larger units. The labour requirements of the new sector differed sharply both quantitatively and qualitatively from those of the pre-war manufacturing and also of the mining and agricultural sectors. The growing industrial sector concentrated on construction, especially of houses, food processing and consumer goods. All of these, but particularly the production and consumption of low-price consumer goods, came to depend on the upgrading of a section of the African labour force and the general growth of the purchasing power of the African peasants and wage-earners.[29] By the end of the 1940s African wages began to rise in real terms.

With the exceptionally rapid growth of demand the manufacturing classes temporarily eclipsed the traditionally dominant mining and agricultural sectors of Rhodesian society.[30] The secondary and tertiary industries became the leading sectors of the Rhodesian economy and they needed a larger market and a more stabilized labour force to continue their growth.[31]

The government encouraged white immigration from Europe, and the new arrivals created an increased demand for goods and services which, in turn, drew more Africans into the wage-earning sector of the economy. The internal demand for manufactured and agricultural products sustained the economic growth of the Southern Rhodesian economy. Foreign capital was attracted to the country, especially after 1948 when there was an outflow of capital from London in the wake of the new Labour government's policies. This capital would normally have been more attracted to South Africa, but when the Nationalists gained power 'the City . . . was increasingly inclined to channel money directly into Rhodesia instead of routing funds via Johannesburg'.[32] The economy surged ahead, but the problem of a limited domestic market for manufactured goods led many people to revive the idea of a Federation of Central African States.

THE FEDERATION CAMPAIGN

The campaign for a federation between the two Rhodesias and Nyasaland had been pursued intermittently over the years, but now a new campaign was launched. The aim of this new federation campaign, led by the Southern Rhodesian premier Sir Godfrey Huggins (later Lord Malvern), and Roy Welensky in Northern Rhodesia, was to create a large white-dominated state in Central Africa underpinned by the revenue from the Northern Rhodesian copper mines. The settlers of Southern Rhodesia needed the revenue from the copper mines to provide the essential capital to build up Southern Rhodesia's infrastructure and industry. To the Europeans in the north, who were in a much smaller minority, the federation offered the guarantee of continued white domination. But even they were aware of the motives of the south. After the key Victoria Falls Conference of 1949, the *Central African Post* editorialized:

> It is our money that Southern Rhodesia is after. Does anyone believe for a moment that she would have the slightest desire to federate with us if we had not very profitable copper mines.[33]

The African majority in both territories were excluded from the discussions, but they made it clear, especially in Northern Rhodesia, that they did not support a white-dominated federation, concocted by white politicians and white civil servants without their participation.[34]

As the Huggins–Welensky bandwagon gained momentum, big business and the international mining groups clambered eagerly on board. They were naturally sympathetic to the prospect of a large, stable, and potentially very profitable economic and political grouping. As early as 1941 Ernest Oppenheimer had decided that if the amalgamation of the two Rhodesias came about Anglo should have an office in Salisbury to be in close contact with the government.[35] In 1950, three years before the Federation, Anglo transferred the headquarters of Rhoanglo, Rhokana, Nchanga and Broken Hill to Salisbury and built up a major office there. Oppenheimer explained to the shareholders that

the transfer was effected with the two main objectives of obtaining administrative efficiency and of reducing United Kingdom tax liabilities of the companies concerned.[36]

Oppenheimer's commitment to the idea of a federation was stronger than is apparent from this statement. Both Rhoanglo and Rhodesian Selection Trust, the other major copper-mining company in Northern Rhodesia, supported the federationists' London pressure group, the United Central Africa Association.[37]

THE FEDERATION, 1953–63

In 1953 the combination of astute lobbying, settler pressure, and a Conservative administration in Britain joined Nyasaland, Southern and Northern Rhodesia together in the Central African Federation. The new government declared the start of a new era of partnership between the three territories and between the white minority and African majority. But throughout its ten-year existence the Federation never bridged the enormous gap between the rhetoric of partnership so freely employed by the Federationists and the reality of its persistent discrimination in favour of the white population of Southern Rhodesia at the expense of the economic development of the other two territories, and of the African majority in all three territories. The all-white, six-man Federal Cabinet embodied the inequitable nature of the partnership. Four of its members were from Southern Rhodesia.* The capital of the Federation was, of course, Salisbury – the Southern Rhodesian capital. But if the structure of the Federation was biased in favour of the Southern Rhodesian settlers, it was the experience of ten years of Federation which

* The other two members represented Northern Rhodesia and Nyasaland respectively.

really undermined the rhetoric of partnership and brought about its decay.

When the Federation was established the revenue from the copper mines was diverted from Northern Rhodesia and constituted the most important single source of revenue for the Federal Treasury in Salisbury. But although the North provided a large percentage of the Federal government revenue, only a small part returned there in the form of development expenditure. In 1960, the *Central African Mail* accused the Federal government of siphoning off a total of £63 million from the North. The paper said this was the difference between the revenue collected and the funds spent in Northern Rhodesia.[38] In addition, the mining companies, out of their income and capital reserves created by the copper-mining operations, lent the Federal government large sums for the development of the transport and power infrastructure of the Federation.[39]

A disproportionate part of the Federal government's capital expenditure was allocated to the South. One example of this was the decision to build the Kariba dam. Even the mining companies who were strong supporters of the Federal government felt compelled to protest. On 3 September 1953 Southern Rhodesia and Northern Rhodesia had signed an agreement that the Federal government would construct a dam to generate the extra electric power needed to meet the increasing demands of the copper industry and the developing secondary industries of the South. The agreement laid down that the dam was to be built at Kafue in Northern Rhodesia. However, later the Federal Cabinet (with its built-in Southern Rhodesian majority) unilaterally decided to build the dam at Kariba on the Zambezi River, which marked the border between the two Rhodesias. Both Anglo American, who had been the consulting engineers for the Kafue project, and RST strongly favoured Kafue. One senior RST director went so far as to criticize the Federal decision to build the dam at Kariba publicly.[40] Apart from the merits of Kafue on technical grounds, the Kafue scheme had the advantage that it offered considerable potential for irrigation schemes. But for the Southern Rhodesians the main argument for Kariba was that the power station would be on the Southern bank, and therefore under their control. The Federal prime minister, Lord Malvern, reacted strongly to the mining companies' opposition. He called the company chairmen to his office in Salisbury and told them that if they refused to support Kariba he would impose an export tax of £50 a ton on their copper.[41] This would have cost the companies nearly £20 million a year. They withdrew their opposition and subsequently provided £20 million in loans for Kariba. Was this the 'inspiring statesmanship which is creating the great new Federation in the heart of Central Africa' of which Sir Ernest Oppenheimer had so eloquently spoken?

The mining companies supported and profited from the Federation. For Anglo, which already had substantial interests there, the Rhodesian economy offered an outlet for the profits it reaped from its Northern Rhodesian copper mines (and to a certain extent and for certain periods profits from South Africa).[42] These profits enabled the group to acquire Wankie Colliery in 1953; to create Rhodesian Alloys (a joint interest with British steel-makers John Brown) in the same year; to build up a dominant position in the cement industry; and to acquire important citrus and sugar estates. In 1957 Anglo, together with RST, took over the state-owned Rhodesian Iron and Steel Corporation, the sole producer in the Federation.* In 1956, Rhoanglo's annual report announced that, as part of the development of a sound money market in the Federation, the company had established Rhodesian Acceptances Ltd, to 'finance the export of Rhodesian manufactured goods, the import of goods to the Federation and the purchase of raw materials for local manufacturers'. The mining companies backed their investment programmes with cash contributions to the major white Federationist party, Roy Welensky's United Federal Party. Anglo, RST and the BSAC all gave money to the party. Anglo's direct contribution was £5,000 a year.[43] Anglo and RST jointly paid the salary of the UFP's secretary for several years, and, together with Imperial Tobacco and the BSAC, they operated a company

---

*Apart from this investment in iron and steel RST did not develop extensive interests in Southern Rhodesia, presumably because its American control dictated that funds were repatriated rather than reinvested in the area.

called the Kachalola Corporation, which owned and operated a string of African newspapers in Southern Rhodesia and the only regular newspaper in Nyasaland.[44] The strongest supporter of Federation was the BSAC, which gave £60,000 a year to the UFP.[45] The BSAC, with its traditional insensitivity to local political aspirations, continued subsidizing the UFP until 1962. As one writer put it, the company was 'the last institution in Central Africa to notice that the Federation was finished'.[46]

A growing spirit of African nationalism in all three territories led to the appointment of the Monckton Commission by the British Government in late 1959 to review the constitutional arrangements for the Federation. The response of the Southern Rhodesians was to launch a furious public relations campaign to save the Federation which was so beneficial to them. At Westminster a strong and well-organized Rhodesia lobby emerged, which overlapped to a large extent with the Katanga lobby which emerged soon after Congolese independence in 1960.* Money from the BSAC, Tanganyika Concessions and Union Minière directly funded many of the activities of both lobbies. Indirectly, the tax revenue from all the mining companies financed the Federationists' campaign which was organized by the Federal government. It was the Federal government which decided to open an account with the advertising agency, Colman Prentice and Varley, and their wholly-owned subsidiary Voice and Vision Ltd. The company had handled the Conservative party General Election campaign in 1959, and one of the directors was Brigadier Terence Clarke, a Conservative MP, so the company was well connected in the Tory Party at all levels up to and including the Cabinet. The campaign is estimated to have cost around £160,000 a year,[47] and used full-page advertisements in the British Press as well as sponsoring the visits of some forty MPs to the Federation. To build up a favourable image of the Federation, Voice and Vision usually chose MPs who had no specialist knowledge of the area. Of the twenty Labour MPs who went to the Federation, none was a specialist in colonial affairs – and of the Conservative MPs virtually all were known to be sympathetic to Welensky.[48] The campaign succeeded in getting some Labour

*See page 241 below.

MPs to abstain from a Labour motion criticizing the Federation.

According to Ian Waller, a well-respected political journalist, the companies financed another publicity campaign, separate from that of the UFP and Federal government. The companies' campaign was handled by the 'doyen of political PROs,' Mr Toby O'Brien, of the E.D. O'Brien Organization and a former head of Conservative Central Office publicity. Mr O'Brien took on only those campaigns he believed in. Mr Waller commented:

> His choice is not, perhaps, to everyone's taste. It includes Katanga and President Tshombe through his representation of Union Minière and Tanganyika Concessions; he is PRO here for the Portuguese Government with special reference to what he calls 'one-sided views on Angola in Britain'; he also handles the Spanish Government's tourist campaign here.[49]

But the most important ingredient of the Rhodesian and Katangan lobbies in Westminster was the hard core of Tory MPs who formed the core of both groups. Many of them had business interests in Central Africa. They saw the Federation as the best way to preserve those interests, and felt that the Federation should even be expanded to include Katanga. Table 16 lists the most important members of the 'Rho-Kat' lobby. The central figure was Lord Salisbury, the 'king-maker' of the Conservative Party and until mid 1961 a director of the British South Africa Company. The Chairman of BSAC, Lord Robins (of 'Rhodesia and Chelsea'!), was a member of the House of Lords, as was another company director, Lord Malvern – previously Sir Godfrey Huggins and prime minister of Southern Rhodesia for twenty-five years. Lord Malvern explained the Rhodesian political situation to the House of Lords:

> 'Now this may shock your Lordships. These Africans, until they are very much advanced, are all liars. I can explain that: it is not anything wrong in their world, it is one of the defensive mechanisms provided by their Creator.'

But, Lord Malvern assured the House of Lords, 'We were not brought up like that.'[50]

Many of the members of the Rho–Kat lobby were also among those who rebelled over the Suez affair in 1956 and felt that the

Table 16: The leading members of the Rhodesia–Katanga lobby

Name	Principal Interests	Remarks
Lord Salisbury	Director, BSAC, 1957–61	'King-maker' of Tory Party
Lord Robins	Chairman, BSAC; Director, Tanganyika Concessions	Close friend of Welensky
Lord Malvern	Resident Director, BSAC	Ex-PM of Southern Rhodesia
Lord Selborne	Director, Tanganyika Concessions and Union Minière	Personally lobbied British PM, Harold Macmillan
Lord Clitheroe	Director, Tanganyika Concessions	Ex-Chairman, Tory Party
Captain Waterhouse	Chairman, Tanganyika Concessions	Ex-MP Suez rebel
Brigadier Clarke	Director, Voice and Vision	MP
Julian Amery	Ex-Director, BSAC, Daggafontein Mines Ltd, Western Deep Levels	MP, Cabinet Minister
Paul Williams	—	MP, Chairman of Monday Club
John Biggs-Davison	⎤	MPs and well-known apologists for Portuguese and South
Patrick Wall	⎦	African governments

Other Prominent Members of Lobby

MPs: Robin Turton, Anthony Fell, Captain Henry Kerby, Dr Donald Johnson, F. M. Bennett, Philip Goodhart, Colonel Neil McClean

Others: Lord Lansdowne, Patrick MacDonagh (stockbroker), Geoffrey Kitchen (Pearl Assurance) and Lords Chandos, Balniel, Coleraine and Hinchingbrooke

Note: BSAC = British South Africa Company.

Voice and Vision handled the Central African Federation's public relations campaign and was a subsidiary of the Colman, Prentice and Varley advertising agency.

government should have ignored the United Nations resolution and United States pressure and completed the military action against the Egyptians. Their hatred of UN interference automatically put them on the side of Tshombe in the Katanga breakaway and on the side of Welensky against the African Nationalists. Captain Charles Waterhouse had been an MP at the time of Suez, but had resigned to take up the Chairmanship of Tanganyika Concessions Ltd. Waterhouse was against African majority rule and declared in Salisbury that 'there is never going to be any question of ruling this country by counting heads'.[51]

The aim of the Rho–Kat MPs was not just to lobby for the protection of white settler interests in Central Africa, but more ambitiously

to bring down the existing leadership of the Conservative Party and replace it with a Cabinet of 'Empire' men who would order a standstill in Africa, back Tshombe and Welensky to the hilt and defy the UN.[52]

Despite the strenuous efforts of the mining companies and the Rho-Kats their attempt to reverse the tide of history failed. The dream of a white-dominated Central African Federation stretching from Beit Bridge in the South to Katanga in the North in which whites would rule in perpetuity on the rich foundation of Northern Rhodesian and Congolese copper faded away in the face of an increasingly militant African nationalism in the Federation.

The mining companies and the other foreign companies, though more interested in safeguarding their profits than in African advancement, did not fight these developments once they saw their inevitability. They concentrated on adapting themselves to the new situation. RST and Anglo stopped their payments to the UFP in July 1959 when they sensed the growing strength of the African nationalist movements in Northern Rhodesia.[53] But the situation was different in the South and there the mining companies felt no need to detach themselves from the ruling white party.

FROM FEDERATION TO UDI*

In the expansionist atmosphere of the Federation, and under the pressure of industrialization, the leading Federationists

> deliberately thought in terms of social class, and aimed at a working alliance between the European ruling strata and the more prosperous Africans, bus-owners and master builders, building contractors and senior employees.[54]

The strategy of the government was to encourage more inter-racial competition while at the same time creating a black middle class to keep the lid on the rising expectations of the African nationalists.

Under first Garfield Todd and then Edgar Whitehead, a series of reforms was initiated. But the attempted development of an African middle class provoked a strong reaction from the white farming community. The switch from maize to tobacco as the main crop of white agriculture had shifted the emphasis from the internal to the external market for its produce, thus reducing the agrarian bourgeoisie's dependence on, and interest in, the industrialization of Rhodesia. In addition, as tobacco was more labour-intensive than maize production, the farmers remained on the whole more dependent on unskilled labour than did the mining and manufacturing sectors of the economy.[55]

In the 1962 General Election, the reaction of the white rural communities and the white wage-earners defeated the United Federal Party and ensured the victory of the Rhodesian Front party. The policy of the new government was to ensure that the supply of cheap labour to the white farmers and small mines was not disrupted by the demands of the manufacturing sector.[56] The break-up of the Federation, and the suppression of the African Nationalist parties by the new government, deprived the British government of the chance of following the, by then, well-established pattern of decolonization, a process by which power was handed over to a black middle class.[57] The Rhodesian Front government demanded independence; and, when negotiations

*Unilateral Declaration of Independence.

finally broke down, Premier Ian Smith declared independence unilaterally.

The international mining companies quickly adapted themselves to the new situation and the change of direction. In the post-war period the increased concentration and improved mechanization of the mining industry had removed the need for a constantly increasing supply of labour. By and large, the growth and profitability of the companies, with the partial exception of the Anglo group, were not dependent on the development of the local industry.[58] What companies like Turner & Newall and Union Carbide needed was a 'stable environment' which would enable them to continue producing and exporting minerals for sale on world markets. In the new conditions created by UDI the mining industry quickly became even more essential to the maintenance of white minority rule.

SANCTIONS AND THE MINING COMPANIES

Britain's response to UDI was to forswear the use of force and institute economic sanctions, partial at first and later more complete. In 1966 sanctions were made mandatory on all UN members. The Rhodesian economy was transformed into a siege economy. Selective sanctions were imposed by the UN in 1966, and then a total trade boycott was declared in 1968.

The effect of sanctions on the Rhodesian economy has been mixed. The country certainly did not crumble in a matter of weeks rather than months, as Mr Harold Wilson promised.* Different sectors of the economy were affected to varying degrees. Agricultural exports were hit hardest by the lack of markets, and although some tobacco continued to be exported, many farmers were forced to switch over to other crops. In manufacturing, the imposition of sanctions produced an import substitution boom, as local manufacturers began to produce goods which had previously been imported. However, after a while industry began to suffer from the country's lack of foreign exchange, which prevented the purchase of new capital equipment. The condition of

*A key factor in the country's survival was the continuing supply of oil from BP and Shell (*Sunday Times*, 27 August 1978).

the railways deteriorated badly under this constraint. When Zambian copper was re-routed the railway's revenue fell and the amount of capital available for replacement of ageing rolling stock was further reduced. The overall picture was of an economy booming in the first phase of isolation, but when all the slack was taken up the economy began to feel more of the adverse effects of isolation, while the country's stock of capital equipment aged and became obsolescent.

The survival of minority rule depended on Rhodesian mineral exports continuing to find their way through South Africa and Mozambique to world markets.* To boost production, the government imposed controls on the export of capital to encourage the mining companies to expand their investment within Rhodesia. In 1965 the mining industry accounted for only about 5 per cent of the gross domestic product, but, more important, mineral exports accounted for about 20 per cent of Rhodesia's foreign exchange earnings and were worth R$65 million.[59] The most important mineral export was asbestos, produced by Turner and Newall's Rhodesian subsidiary, Rhodesian and General Asbestos Corporation, worth R$21·6 million in 1965. Gold produced by a large number of small producers was worth R$13·8 million.[60] Copper exports were worth R$13 million and were produced largely by the Messina (Transvaal) Co., but Lonrho's Inyati mine was about to increase its production dramatically. Chrome was produced by the Union-Carbide-controlled Rhodesian Chrome Mines and its wholly-owned subsidiary, African Chrome Mines, producing 490,000 of the 650,000 tons mined in Rhodesia that year. Of Union Carbide's production, the company stated that more than 50 per cent was shipped to Union Carbide plants in the US and another 25 per cent to company plants in Canada, Norway and the United Kingdom, while the remainder was sold either to other US companies or to foreign companies.[61]

---

*It was of course equally important for the crucial oil imports to continue. The manoeuvrings of the oil companies BP, Shell, and Total, to deliver oil to Rhodesia have been widely reported. (See for example, *Sunday Times*, 3 and 10 September 1978.) The company through which the oil was transferred to Rhodesia was Freight Services Ltd, controlled by the Anglo American Corporation.

Anglo American's Wankie Colliery produced most of the country's coal, with exports worth R$4·8 million in 1965.[62]

The Rhodesian government backed the expansion of minerals as the main foreign-exchange earner during sanctions. It set up a separate Ministry of Mines and an Institute of Mining Research to promote the country's mining industry. The Rhodesian subsidiaries of the mining companies, though legally separated from their international parents after UDI, continued operations much as before. As Union Carbide's Mining and Metals division President explained it:

'On February 8 1966, the de facto Rhodesian government directed our local management, pursuant to the Emergency Power Regulations, to continue to produce, sell and export chrome and appointed the then serving Managing Director of both companies its agent to effect this purpose. As a result, the local management of our Rhodesian affiliates continued to operate the mines and ship ore to ports in Mozambique.'[63]

When the US State Department requested the company to stop shipments to Mozambique, the Rhodesian government directed the company to sell all its chrome production to a state-controlled trading corporation. The British companies responded in similar fashion to Union Carbide. Companies like Rio Tinto Zinc and Turner and Newall made their Rhodesian subsidiaries legally independent, but mining operations continued as before.

Faced with the government's stringent controls on capital movement and dividend remittance, Rio Tinto Zinc, Anglo American and Lonrho all announced plans at various times in the next five years to expand existing mines or develop new ones. Anglo American's Rhodesian Nickel Corporation developed its Trojan nickel mine at Bindura to produce 630,000 tons of nickel ore by 1971.[64] Rio Tinto Zinc opened the Empress Nickel mine, producing 720,000 tons of nickel and copper ore per year. By 1969 this mine alone was estimated to be earning £3½ million a year in foreign exchange for Rhodesia.[65] In 1971 RTZ was bringing another nickel mine, the Perseverance, into production. Lonrho-controlled Coronation Syndicate's Inyati copper mine began to expand production quite dramatically and the first stage of a refinery at the mine was commissioned in late 1970.[66]

Turner and Newall brought the new King asbestos mine into operation at Mashaba. MTD (Mangula) Ltd, the subsidiary of Messina (Transvaal) Development Ltd, opened a new mine at Shackleton and Rhodesia's first tungsten mine at Beardmore near Fort Victoria. The result of the mining companies' investments was that fixed investment in mining increased by 80 per cent, compared with 1965 – much of this coming in 1969–71 when at least ten new mines were opened, involving a capital expenditure estimated at $8 million. Mineral output increased dramatically after UDI, reaching an estimated R$105 million in 1970 (R$65 million in 1965).

Most of this mineral production has been exported despite sanctions. How ? A survey of the mining industry in Rhodesia in 1972 published by the British Sulphur Corporation stated that the

facts surrounding the export of Rhodesian minerals since UDI will probably never be published because too many examples of sanctions breaking would be thrown up which would be traceable to individuals and companies and trade statistics are likely to remain forever an un-disclosed mystery to avoid embarrassment internally and overseas.[67]

Despite this, it is still possible to describe the general pattern of events. For South-African-controlled companies, the main importance of sanctions was the Rhodesian government's imposition of controls on the export of capital, and the problem of marketing their Rhodesian output was considerably simplified by the existence of South African parent companies who could sell Rhodesian metals on their own account.

UDI affected the activities of several foreign mining companies including Lonrho and the American Chrome companies. At the UN Sanctions Committee it was alleged that Lonrho's South African subsidiary, Coronation Syndicate, was exporting copper from its Inyati mine in Rhodesia contrary to the Sanction regulations. The methods used were revealed in 1973, when the former company secretary of a Johannesburg firm, Hochmetals, explained how the sanction-busting was carried out. Hochmetals had been the agents for the export of the copper from the Inyati mine. To begin with, there was little difficulty in exporting the copper with South African certificates of origin. When the enforcement of UN sanctions was tightened, the company had to think of a new device. Just ninety miles from Inyati and conveniently over the border in Mozambique, there was the abandoned Edmundian mine. The idea was to use Edmundian as a 'front' for Inyati's copper and to ship the copper from Beira or Lourenço Marques accompanied by false documents claiming the copper originated from the Edmundian mine in Mozambique. The scheme went ahead. The Edmundian mine was reopened and small-scale production started up to offer some semblance of credibility to the fiction. It is not clear how much Rhodesian copper was exported in this way, but the Japanese authorities sent one shipment of ore supposedly originating at Edmundian back to Beira in July 1969.[68]

Union Carbide also actively tried to avoid sanctions. In November 1966 the company transferred some \$2 million to its South African subsidiary, Ruighoek Chrome Mines. On 16 December, the day the United Nations adopted mandatory selective sanctions (which included chrome), Union Carbide sent another \$1 million to Ruighoek. Five days later Ruighoek sent \$2·68 million to Rhodesian Chrome Mines (Union Carbide's Rhodesian subsidiary) as advance payment on shipments of chrome ore.[69] The company applied to the Johnson administration for a licence to import 150,000 tons of chrome ore on the grounds that it was purchased before sanctions were enacted! In 1967 the Vanadium Corporation of America had merged with Foote Minerals (in which Newmont Mining had a 33 per cent stake), and now Foote Minerals applied for similar licences in 1967 and 1968 to import respectively 40,000 and 56,000 tons of ore which had already been 'mined and paid for' according to the company. The Johnson administration refused the applications of both companies.

Union Carbide and Foote Minerals then went into action lobbying in the US Senate, working in close cooperation with the Rhodesia Information Services office in Washington. The operating expenses of the office were \$100,000 a year.[70] *Newsweek* called the campaign, and the resultant Byrd amendment allowing chrome imports into the United States, 'the neatest lobbying job in recent memory'.[71] Although the output from the companies' Rhodesian mines had been successfully marketed through a top-secret organization called UNIVEX,[72] the companies were losing some $28 million a year in potential return on their investment and when the possibility of legislation removing the ban on chrome imports arose the two companies 'immediately went to work with the hard sell', as *Newsweek* put it.

First they helped move the legislation through the conservative Armed Services Committees of both the House and the Senate, arguing that chrome was vital to national security. The bill was based on an ingenious ploy forbidding the President to ban the import of any strategic commodity which the US was also buying from a Communist country. In the case of chrome the US had been getting about one third of its supply from Russia in 1965, the year the official sanctions took effect, and subsequently had to boost its orders to more than 50 per cent because of the embargo.[73]

The lobbying in Washington was led by Representative James Collins and Senator Harry Byrd, and by a vote of 46 to 36 the Senate added a proviso to the Military Procurement Act of 1971, allowing the import of Rhodesian chrome. The main argument used by the lobby was that of 'national security' but as a high State Department official told *Newsweek*: 'It was a powerful but essentially phony argument, because we have all kinds of short-term supply; there just wasn't any national security element to the argument.'[74] The reason was simple: there were already 5·5 million tons of chromium ore in the national stockpile, and the Office of Emergency Preparedness declared that 2·2 million tons were in excess of national foreseeable strategic needs. In addition, the Nixon administration had already submitted legislation to authorize the government to dispose of some 1·3 million tons of excess metallurgical chrome from national stocks. As the *Wall Street Journal* pointed out in March 1972, there was no ready market for the stockpile excess so there could not possibly be a need for Rhodesian chrome. The paper also reported that 'one Union Carbide official admitted the "strategic" label was simply camouflage to get Congress to authorize US companies to break UN sanctions'.[75] The *Washington Post* commented that

Although they complained strenuously about sanctions' violations by other nations, nowhere in the two firms' testimony did they suggest the United States begin by blowing the whistle on violators – a step that would have made life rougher for the white minority government but more equitable for the world's chrome users in sharing the burden of the loss of Rhodesian ore.[76]

The vote in Congress had another detrimental effect because, as the London *Sunday Times* pointed out:

Coming as it did just four days before Sir Alec Douglas-Home left to negotiate with Ian Smith, [the vote] was the death knell of Britain's non-violent 'solution' of the Rhodesian problem.[77]

One reason the Byrd Amendment was passed by the Senate, according to the *New York Times*, was the 'climate of ignorance, cynicism and anger at the UN for ousting Taiwan'.[78] The main reason, however, was the reluctance of the Nixon administration to oppose the Byrd Amendment which had been originally blocked by the Foreign Affairs and Foreign Relations Committees of the Congress. Senator McGee declared that the Administration's blind-eye policy was deliberate, and evidence of the Administration's true position on Rhodesia. Whereas the Johnson Administration had refused to allow the import of Union Carbide's Rhodesian chrome into the US, in September 1970 the Nixon Administration granted the company's request. Despite the action of some longshoremen in refusing to handle Rhodesian chrome, Union Carbide managed to take delivery of its chrome, so making one of the largest breaches in UN mandatory sanctions. For six years Rhodesian chrome was imported into the USA until the Byrd Amendment was finally repealed in 1977.

Despite the success of Rhodesia in evading sanctions and maintaining its illegal independence there remained pressure for economic and political reasons to reach a settlement with Britain. While all the mining companies exploited the situation created by UDI they did not all have identical interests. Anglo American and Lonrho, which have extensive interests in both black Africa and the white-ruled South, played a discreet supporting role in the various diplomatic initiatives and public manoeuvrings.

With its copper interests in Zambia, Anglo American was well placed to act as a 'bridge' between the white and black politicians of Africa. In 1970 Harry Oppenheimer flew Mrs Helen Suzman, the Progressive Party MP, to Zambia to see President Kaunda in a meeting which he had arranged.[79] He appointed Dr Zac de Beer as Anglo's chairman in Zambia. De Beer was not a mining man, but was a long-standing political companion of Oppenheimer and a prominent supporter of the Progressive Party which advocated dialogue between white and black Africa.* Later Oppenheimer supported the South African policy of detente, because in his experience 'isolation is a continual trouble and can cause severe difficulties in financing companies and selling goods'.

A flurry of diplomatic activity surrounded South Africa's diplomatic offensive in 1975, and the mining companies played their part. As President Kaunda and Prime Minister Vorster manoeuvred the African Nationalists and Premier Ian Smith towards the Victoria Falls Agreement of 1974, Oppenheimer and the Anglo group played an important role behind the scenes and at a practical level. The African National Council members flew from Salisbury to Lusaka in an Anglo jet which was specially laid on. In the company's annual report, Oppenheimer explained that Anglo American backed the moves because 'if the policy of detente succeeds . . . the economic benefits to the whole area would be incalculable'.[80] The benefits to Anglo, with interests throughout the region, would also be not inconsiderable.

Lonrho was also deeply involved with the negotiations over the future of Rhodesia. A Lonrho economist, Tim Curtin, advised the African National Council in its talks with Ian Smith in 1976. One of the leaders of the ANC was Joshua Nkomo, and his legal adviser was Mr R. A. K. Wright, who had also represented Lonrho during the famous boardroom row of 1973 and during the subsequent inquiry held by the Department of Trade and Industry. In fact, so assiduous was Lonrho's wooing of the Nationalists that Rhodesia's minister of information accused the

*The Progressive Party was founded, and funded, by Oppenheimer. See page 461 ff.

company of spreading panic stories about Rhodesia in the South African press in a deliberate attempt to undermine the morale of white Rhodesians. Lonrho denied the allegation.

For the last eighty years the balance of power has shifted between the various social groups in Rhodesia. But from the start the companies have constantly supported the white minority, and exploited the black majority. It remains to be seen how that majority will react to the companies when black independence finally arrives.

9 Copper, Labour, and Underdevelopment in Zambia

Zambia is a small, sparsely populated African state. Some two thirds of its four million people live in the poverty-stricken rural areas. What distinguishes Zambia from so many other African states is that in one part of the country foreign capital has established one of the largest industries in Africa north of the Zambezi. In 1977 Zambia was the third largest producer and second largest exporter of copper in the world. The copper-mining industry has made Zambia one of the richest countries on the continent but it has also severely distorted the country's economic and social status.

BEFORE INDEPENDENCE*

After the Second World War the two mining groups Rhoanglo and RST, which controlled the industry, steadily expanded production. From 250,000 tons in 1943, production had reached 594,000 tons a year by 1959, and the Northern Rhodesian Copperbelt was responsible for more than one seventh of the non-Communist world's total copper production. In the halcyon days of the Federation, tax was levied on the companies at a generous rate, and profits were high.[1] The companies were enthusiastic supporters of Federation and gave large sums to the United Federal Party.† As Independence approached, the companies began to reduce the rate of expansion and increase the repatriation of profits and capital. Most post-Second-World-War mine development was financed out of the industry's own reserves, but by the early 1960s the percentage of profits being invested was

* See Chapters 1, 2 and 3, above for the early history of copper mining in Zambia.
† See pages 178–86 above for more about the Central African Federation.

falling fast, dividends were increased, development expansion reduced, and more loan finance was being raised.[2]

MINERAL RIGHTS

On the eve of Independence, the Zambians did not even control the mining rights over their own minerals. These were controlled by the British South Africa Company, in which Anglo had a share. Africans were not even allowed to dig sand from the river bank without making a payment to the company.[3] The legality of the company's mineral rights had been challenged many times. Chief Lewanika, who signed the original agreement, claimed that he had been tricked by Rhodes's agents; and subsequently Chief Yeta of the Barotse had persistently demanded that the company relinquish its rights, because the company was not carrying out its obligations under the treaty. In 1934 the Governor of Northern Rhodesia suggested that the company's claim to the mineral rights in the Copperbelt was extremely tenuous, since Lewanika's rule did not extend to that area. But the company blocked this challenge and kept its lucrative mineral rights, until on the eve of Independence nationalist politicians launched a determined attack on the company's claim. They had commissioned detailed research, which demonstrated that this claim to the mineral rights was founded on a fiction. Negotiations continued up until the last minute, as the company held out for substantial compensation. The Zambians offered £2 million for goodwill, which the British government would match, but these payments would be liable to tax. Anglo American also put pressure on BSAC to settle, because a public wrangle over the mineral rights might endanger its important copper-mine interests. Finally, with only a few hours to Independence, BSAC accepted the Zambian and British offers.[4] Soon after, Anglo merged BSAC with Central Mining and Consolidated Mines to create a new London-based mining house, Charter Consolidated.

THE EXPLOITATION OF ZAMBIA

In the forty years before Independence, over £400 million generated in Zambia, largely by the copper mines, was exported to the developed world and Rhodesia. In the ten years before independence alone, the two copper-mining groups, Rhodesian Selection Trust and Anglo American, sent £260 million in dividends, interest and royalty payments out of the country.* In the period from 1923 to 1964 the British South Africa Company received more than £160 million gross and £82 million net from the mineral royalties,[5] while the British Treasury collected approximately another £40 million in taxes from Northern Rhodesia and spent only £5 million on development.[6] When the colonial administration's income from the mines rose in the early 1940s, it had no development plans worthy of the name, and so passed the accumulating funds over to the British government in the form of interest-free loans. Moreover, because the mining companies were domiciled in London until 1950, they paid their income taxes to the British government and not to the colonial administration. The British Treasury also benefited because the copper mines were within the sterling area and so Britain did not have to use up scarce foreign exchange to buy the copper it needed.

In 1951, Northern Rhodesia joined the Central African Federation. In the years from 1953 to 1963 the Federal government drained nearly £100 million from the country, most of which was used to promote industrial development in Southern Rhodesia.[7] At the beginning of the Federation, the Northern Rhodesian debt was less than £20 million. When the Federation collapsed, and the £280 million debt it had incurred was divided up in 1963, Zambia was saddled with £96 million, for which it had little, if anything, to show.[8] These figures do not include the transfer of funds by the many expatriate staff working on the mines and in government service. Of course, they are a crude measure of the capital flow from Zambia, but they do indicate the extent to which Zambia's underdevelopment is due to the massive exploitation of its mineral resources by foreign mining companies and governments. In a country where only 1,000 children had completed secondary school education by independence,[9] this was an appalling loss of investable surplus needed for development.

*This figure includes payments between companies.

DEPENDENCE ON COPPER

As a result of the mining companies' activities, the Zambian economy is totally dependent on the copper industry, which usually accounts for about 40 per cent of the gross domestic product, 15 per cent of employment, 25 per cent of the country's wage bill, between 49 and 70 per cent of government revenue (according to the price of copper), and about 93 per cent of the country's exports (again, according to the price of copper on the world markets). Even among the world's major copper exporters, this dependence on copper is extreme, as Table 17 shows.

Table 17: The dependence on copper of the world's major copper exporters in 1965 (percentages)

Country	GDP	GNP	Exports	Revenue	Employment
Zambia	40	34*	93	68	15
Zaire	18	23*	51	45*	2*
Chile	4	3*	65	14	3
Peru	2	1·5*	18	12	1

*Estimated

Source: A. M. J. De Swardt and A. R. Drysdall, 'Mining and Prospecting in Zambia', quoted in M. Bostock and C. Harvey, *Economic Independence and Zambian Copper*, Praeger, 1972, p. 4.

This heavy dependence is made more serious by the violent price fluctuations to which copper is liable. The constant fluctuation of the copper price, and therefore of government revenue, makes coherent long-term planning an exceedingly difficult, if not impossible, task. This is true whether the price is above or below the minimum that the government has assumed for the plan period. It is almost as difficult to accelerate government spending when income rises as it is to curtail it when income falls; though, of course, the consequences are less disastrous in the former case. The fluctuations of the copper price on the London Metal Exchange are dramatic. From the low price of £234 per ton in 1963, prices fluctuated erratically, to reach a peak of over £1,400 per ton in April 1974, before falling steeply in 1975 to less than £500, which was below RCM's cost of production.*

INTEGRATION WITH THE ECONOMY OF SOUTHERN AFRICA

The Copperbelt was developed by the companies as an integral part of the southern African economy and transport system. Nearly all supplies and essential mine machinery passed through the South African and Southern Rhodesian rail network linking Zambia with Cape Town, Durban and Beira. Most of the copper was exported to Europe along the same routes, but some went through Angola. In 1964 Zambian imports from Rhodesia were running at around £30 million a year. Coal supplies for the mines came from Anglo's Wankie Colliery in Southern Rhodesia. Electrical power came from Kariba South Power Station, and imports from South Africa were about £16 million.[10]

INDEPENDENCE – 1964

The demand for independence had united all Zambians, but it concealed the varying interests of the different groups in Zambian society. Zambian workers believed that independence would bring them higher wages, better working conditions, better housing, and rapid promotion to the jobs and salaries previously held by Europeans. In 1964 the majority of the population lived at subsistence levels in the rural areas but the average Zambian miner earned Kwacha 648 (£324) a year and the average wage of the Europeans on the mines was K4,578 (£2,289).[11] The political elite lacked a social or economic base to underpin its political ascendancy, while its claim to national leadership was undermined by the foreign interests which owned and controlled the copper industry, and most of the other companies in Zambia. It had, however, by virtue of the Independence struggle, inherited the administration and the economic orientation of the colonial authorities. It began to consolidate its own position by building up the power and patronage of the state. Membership

*See Figure 20.

of UNIP* was the key to advancement. In 1965 its slogan was 'It pays to belong to UNIP.'[12]

MINERS' DEMANDS

The demands of Zambian miners for more rapid African advancement on the Copperbelt became one of the most contentious issues in the political, social and economic life of the country. The miners had played an important part in the struggle of Independence and formed the hard core of UNIP's urban support. After Independence, the Copperbelt remained a UNIP stronghold; and of all Zambian workers, the miners were the best organized, the most militant, and politically the most powerful. They demanded advancement and a reduction in the enormous gap between their wages and those of the European miners. The government argued that higher wages for the miners would only increase the disparity of incomes between miners and the rural population. The miners pressed their demands and in March 1966 they went on strike, bringing the Copperbelt to a complete halt. The stoppage lasted for a fortnight before President Kaunda intervened to secure a return to work with the promise of a commission of inquiry. Slowly the miners returned to work, and a short while later the Brown Commission began its investigation.

THE BROWN REPORT

The 1966 Brown Report graphically explained the militant mood of the miners, who had participated in the Independence struggle and yet still met clear evidence of racial discrimination every day at work. They naturally looked to the new government to put matters right:

With their own Government at last in power, the African miners thought they were setting out on a journey to the celestial city, but the first steps they undertook under the guidance of the mining companies seemed to lead unmistakably into the Slough of Despond.[13]

*UNIP: United National Independence Party – Zambia's ruling party.

The pace of Zambianization was too slow for the miners. The report recommended a 22 per cent increase in miners' wages and argued:

> With independence a major reorganisation of the labour structure in the mining industry was necessary. The manner in which the companies set about this task took full account of the need for wage restraint, but produced a result which is unacceptable to the workers in the industry. This is a situation which must be put right if there is to be any chance of industrial peace. Weighing in the balance the importance of the industry on which the development of Zambia ultimately depends, we have felt justified in recommending, as part of a new settlement, a general increase in wages which might otherwise be regarded as excessive in terms of the growth rate of the economy as a whole.[14]

The government accepted the Brown Report recommendations not just because of these cogent arguments but also because, as Richard Hall says:

> The Copperbelt was the citadel of UNIP power and it had to be guarded against penetration by opponents who might exploit the miners' discontent.[15]

THE EFFECTS OF RHODESIAN UDI 1965-7

The Rhodesian government's Unilateral Declaration of Independence in 1965 precipitated a reorientation of the Zambian economy away from Rhodesia, and started a chain of events which led to a progressive takeover of the copper companies. Zambia had to finance an oil pipeline from Tanzania, open up new coal mines to replace the 1 million tons of coal from Wankie, and finance – with Chinese aid – the new railway from Zambia to the Tanzanian port of Dar-es-Salaam. The Zambians bore the brunt of these costs* despite promises of assistance from Britain.[16] As Rhodesian imports were restricted and import-substituting enterprises were encouraged, Zambia's economy

---

*The UN estimated the cost of sanctions to Zambia from 1965 to 1977 at between $750 and $800 m. To offset this Zambia received aid of only $100 m. in the same period.

boomed. But most of the profits generated by this boom were flowing out of the country, together with large amounts of capital.[17] Many of the companies in Zambia were either subsidiaries or closely linked to Rhodesian and South African companies; and their policy was to remit as much profit and capital as quickly as they could. Estimates show that remittances by non-mining companies increased by 84 per cent in 1966 and a further 15 per cent in 1967.[18] The mining companies were earning massive profits because of the high price of copper and declared large dividends (see Table 18). The Zambians clawed back some of the profits by levying an export tax.* But because both mining and non-mining companies were considered 'good risks' by the commercial banks, they could obtain substantial local loans, and repatriate a large proportion of their capital reserves. The Bank of Zambia's annual reports show that commercial bank advances increased by 94 per cent in December 1965, a further 16 per cent in 1966, and 76 per cent in 1967.[19]

MULUNGUSHI

At the 1968 conference of UNIP at Mulungushi, President Kaunda declared it unacceptable that the Zambian economy should continue to be directed by foreign companies.

In the last three years, Zambia has in spite of intractable problems experienced an economic boom and growth unprecedented elsewhere on the continent, which brought considerable financial benefits and profits to expatriate enterprise. Instead of the expatriate enterprise accepting their profits and at the same time ploughing as much as possible into the development and redevelopment of their businesses, it became evident that they were obsessed with 'making hay while the sun shines' and expatriated increasingly large portions of their profits.[20]

He criticized the mining and other foreign-controlled companies for their gross under-capitalization, excessive local borrowing, and intolerably high level of dividend remittance.

*The export tax was set at 40 per cent of the amount by which the price of copper on the London Metal Exchange exceeded £300 per long ton.

To correct the situation, the President limited both borrowing by foreign companies from the banks, and the remittance of profits abroad. In future no more than 50 per cent of profits could be exported, and then only if the remittances did not exceed 30 per cent of the equity capital of the company. The President then invited twenty-seven companies in the construction, transport, retail and brewing industries to offer the government a 51 per cent stake in their enterprises. Expatriates would be granted retail trading licences only in selected urban centres. Finally the President turned to the mining companies. He criticized their high level of dividend remittance and the virtual lack of mine development.* Zambian output had increased at only half the pre-Independence rate of expansion, and Anglo's output had fallen by 2·4 per cent. The President quoted the profit and dividend figures for Roan Selection Trust† (see Table 18) and went on to tell both Anglo and RST:

'I am very disappointed at the virtual lack of mining development since Independence . . . The companies claim the royalty system has been against new development. Nevertheless I think they have not done enough towards further development of the country in which they make their great profits. Let me also say that I do not agree with the mining companies that royalties have been the obstacle to the development of the industry. I have been following their accounts and I know very well that they could have embarked upon further expansion if they chose to devote part of their profits for this purpose. Instead of reinvesting they have been distributing over 60 per cent of their profits every year as dividends . . . As from today the maximum that the mining companies will be allowed to remit abroad in dividends is only half of their profits. The other half they must utilise for further development.'[21]

AFTER MULUNGUSHI

The mining companies' response to the Mulungushi Declaration only increased Zambian suspicions. They rejected the President's

*The 1965 level of copper exports (680,000 tons) was not exceeded until 1969.

†Although he did not mention it by name.

Table 18: Net profits and dividend distribution of Roan
Selection Trust, 1960–67

Year	Net Profits *Km.	Retained in Business – Km.	Dividends Km.
1960	9·4	5·1	4·2
1961	6·6	3·5	3·2
1962	11·2	2·6	8·6
1963	11·9	2·3	9·5
1964	11·8	2·3	9·5
1965	17·4	3·9	13·5
1966	20·5	3·1	15·3
1967	20·7	5·3	15·4

*One Kwacha = $1.40 = £0.50, until 1967. See the note on currencies, page 18.

Source: Introduction to the Mulungushi Declaration.

criticisms, said that they had large investment programmes, and
waited for the revision of the tax arrangements he had promised.
They continued their policy of raising loans, repatriating capital,
and declaring high dividends. Anglo invited the Japanese to
provide capital for expansion at the Nchanga mine. Ian Mac-
Gregor, Chairman of AMAX, the American company with a
43 per cent stake in RST, insisted that RST keep its investment
in Zambia to a minimum until the Zambians altered the royalty
tax. Both copper companies kept the grades of ore milled high
and ran plant far above its rated capacity, smashing production
records and boosting profits; measures which reduced the life
expectancy of both the mine and its machinery.[22] As for the
restriction on dividend remittances, both RST and Zamanglo
increased their capital and reorganized their accounts so that
dividends could be substantially raised without remitting more
than 50 per cent of total profits. Zamanglo increased its capital
from K15·38 million to K30·24 million in December 1968. RST
increased its issued share capital from K43·69 million to K87
million by a bonus issue of shares. Both companies revised their
accounts, so that instead of showing 'non-expansion' capital

investment* as a pre-tax charge, they now showed it as an appropriation against profits – thus increasing substantially the size of profits. Expenditure on plant and equipment and other deductable items was treated in a new way which also improved the shareholders' position. The companies continued to remit large sums of money to overseas shareholders (only six per cent of the shares were held in Zambia). Anglo and RST distributed dividends overseas of £29 million in 1964, £22 million in 1965, £24 million in 1966, £25 million in 1967, and £25 million in 1968.[23] It was as if there had been no Mulungushi Declaration at all.

THE MATERO DECLARATION – 1969

The political elite was consolidating its position as a ruling class by progressively bringing more and more foreign companies into state ownership;† but now its dominance was threatened by internal divisions within UNIP.[24] The balance in the Cabinet had always been carefully composed from among three major groups, the Lozis of the West, the Bemba from the Copperbelt and the North, and the Chinyanja-speakers of Eastern Province. But at the 1967 UNIP conference, Simon Kapwepwe, the leading Bemba politician, was elected to the post of Party Vice-President. This upset the delicate political balance, especially as the Bemba and their allies displaced several Western and Eastern Province leaders in the same Central Committee elections. In subsequent parliamentary elections at the end of 1968, there was a resurgence of support for Harry Nkumbula's African National Congress party, which won several seats from Lozi UNIP ministers in Western Province, as well as displaying expected strength in the south. In 1969 the balance of internal

* 'Non-expansion' capital expenditure is designed to maintain existing production levels, as opposed to expenditure designed to increase the mining companies' production capacity. If it is charged before tax, profits are reduced; while, correspondingly, if it is charged after tax, profits are increased.

† The proliferation of state corporations: Mindeco, Indeco, Findeco, etc., led to the suggestion that the government would soon be taking over all the bars and night-clubs. The new Corporation would be called Sindeco (Anthony Martin, *Minding Their Own Business*, Hutchinson, 1972, p. 251).

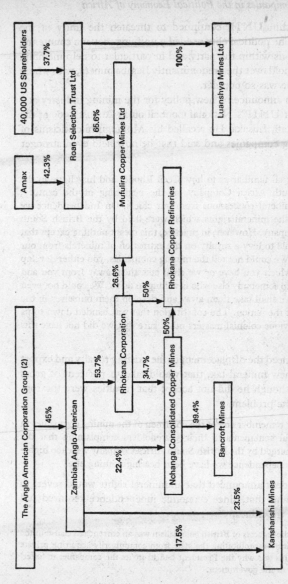

Fig. 5. The structure and ownership of the Zambian copper industry in 1969 (I)

NOTES: (I) Chart does not include Baluba, Chisengwa and Mwinilungwa.

(2) Anglo American (30%), Rand Selection (15%).

SOURCE: Adapted from M. Bostock and C. Harvey, *Economic Independence and Zambian Copper*, Praeger, New York, 1972, p. 260.

forces within UNIP continued to threaten the unity of the party.[25] The political elite needed a unifying move to counteract the divisions within the party and in particular to help maintain UNIP's hold over the predominantly Bemba miners, with whom Kapwepwe was so popular.

Kaunda announced a new policy for the mining industry at a meeting of UNIP's National Council on 11 August 1969 at the Matero Hall, Lusaka. He recalled his Mulungushi criticisms of the mining companies and said that he now held even stronger views:

'You are all familiar as to how Cecil Rhodes and his clique in the British South Africa Company, at the beginning of the century, acquired mineral concessions from our chiefs. On Independence we took over the mineral rights which were held by the British South Africa Company. However, in practice, this meant nothing except that we were able to levy a royalty on the extraction of minerals from our own soils. We could not tell the mining companies, you either develop the areas which you have or we shall take them away from you and give them to somebody else who is willing to do so. We could not even tell them we shall take them away and develop them ourselves in the interests of the nation. The constitution that was handed down to us by our previous colonial masters made sure that we did not have this power.'*

He announced the displacement of the existing royalty and export tax by a new mineral tax, that would take 51 per cent of gross profits, although he did not accept that royalties were the root cause of the problem.

'I do not remember any of the chairmen of the mining companies in their annual statements to their shareholders complaining that the royalties charged by the British South Africa Company were too high – but after Independence we have been hearing nothing else.'

The President announced that all mineral rights would revert to the state and that, since economic independence required full control of the mines,

* One of the legacies of British colonialism was an entrenched clause in the 1964 Constitution prohibiting the state from compulsorily acquiring private property. This was why the President had to invite the companies to 'offer' 51 per cent to the government.

'I shall ask the owners of the mines to invite the government to join their mining enterprises. I am asking the owners of the mines to give 51 per cent of their shares to the state.'

The announcement was a well-kept surprise and the President sat down to tumultuous applause. The next day he sent National Council delegates home to assess support for the new reforms in the country, thus preventing any prolonged struggle within UNIP. The companies and the government prepared to negotiate the terms of the government's 51 per cent stake.

THE AGREEMENT

The essential strength of the companies' bargaining position

lay in the fact that Zambia still needed them to run the mines, [while] the strength of the Zambian position was that in the last analysis the companies had only two alternatives: to do business on Zambian terms and make the best of a bad job, or to pull out of the country altogether and lose their whole investment and prospects of future income. Put like that there was no real choice.[26]

The Zambians had three main aims in negotiating the takeover: to acquire significant control over the activities of the companies; to increase the productive capacity of the mines; and to retain the companies' management and technical expertise until enough Zambians could be trained to take over these functions themselves.

The basic restructuring of the copper companies was settled quite quickly. (See Figures 5 and 6.) The Anglo mining assets would go into a new company called Nchanga Consolidated Copper Mines (NCCM); the RST assets into Roan Consolidated Mines. In each of the two new companies, the shares would be split into two groups. 'A' shares making up 51 per cent of the capital would be held by the new state corporation MINDECO; and the 'B' shares, composed of the remainder, would be held by the companies.

Detailed negotiations centred around four crucial points: the method of valuing assets; the terms of repayment; the future management fee for the companies; and guarantees that the

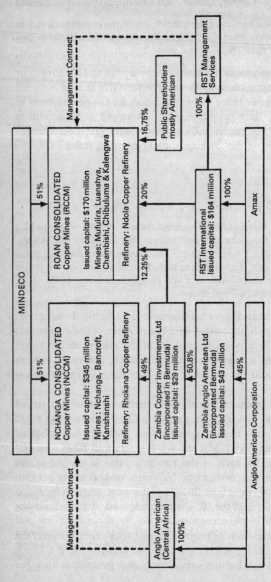

Fig. 6. The structure and ownership of the Zambian copper industry in 1970

NOTE: Chart does not include non-operating mines, Baluba (RST 42%, ZCI 34%), Chisengwa (RST 42%, ZCI 58%) and Mwinilungwa (RST 53%, ZCI 46%), which remained outside the new structure.

SOURCE: Adapted from M. Bostock and C. Harvey, *Economic Independence and Zambian Copper*, Praeger, New York, 1972, p. 261, Appendix Chart 2.

agreement would be honoured.[27] RST's assets were valued at K165 million, and Anglo American's at K240 million. The Zambians would pay 51 per cent of these valuations plus interest, K84 million (£49 million) and K125 million (£73 million) respectively, for 51 per cent of the assets.* Compensation would take the form of Zambian government bonds to be repaid over twelve years for Anglo and eight years for RST, beginning in 1970. Interest on the bonds was set at six per cent. The management contracts, covering a whole range of services from the hire of staff, engineering design and consultancy, to the purchasing of supplies, and the marketing of copper, constituted another contentious issue. The companies wanted lucrative management contracts to compensate for the sale of 51 per cent of the mines to the government. The management fee was eventually set at 0·75 per cent of turnover, plus 2 per cent of profits after mineral tax and before income tax. The sales service provided by Anglo and RST were to be paid for at the rate of 0·75 per cent of turnover. Service charges, management fees and bond repayments were all exempted from Zambian exchange control.[28] Disputes would be referred to the International Centre for the Settlement of Investment Disputes.

THE COMPANIES AFTER THE TAKEOVER

The foreign companies kept effective control of the mines through the many provisions designed to safeguard their position as minority shareholders. Indeed, they retained a veto power over wide areas of mining activity. These included the winding-up of operations; disposal of assets; grant of any retained concessions or mining rights to others; new financial commitments; borrowing powers; appropriation for capital expenditure; exploration and prospecting.[29]

*The government was satisfied that the capacity had been bought much more cheaply than new capacity could have been created. The Zambians paid K550 per ton of operating capacity, the Chileans at the same time paid K650 per ton and expansion schemes throughout the world were costing around K1,400 per ton at the end of the sixties. Of course one might argue that the companies had already received more than adequate compensation for their investment in the massive profits they had taken out of Zambia.

To induce the companies to increase the productive capacity of the mines, the government agreed that taxes would no longer be levied as flat rate taxes on exports, but would be linked to profits. Basing the tax on profits also meant that the companies paid no tax on an unprofitable mine; a concession for which the companies had long been pressing. Companies were also allowed to write off 100 per cent of capital expenditure as a pre-tax charge in the year in which the costs were actually incurred. (Previously, capital investment was depreciated over the life of the mine.) In addition, the repayment terms of the new government bonds were extremely favourable. The bonds were to be free of Zambian taxes; payable in US dollars; and freely remittable anywhere in the world designated by the companies.

With negotiations between the companies and the government concluded the new structure came into effect on 1 January 1970. RST and Zamanglo were both reorganized by their corporate parents. Amax made an offer for the shares in RST which it did not own and established a new, completely owned subsidiary, RST International.* The headquarters of Zamanglo were transferred to Bermuda. Anglo set up a new company, Zambia Copper Investments, to receive the bond repayments. Apart from the benefits of low taxes in Bermuda, Anglo now had large sums of capital available for its worldwide investment programme which were not subject to South African exchange control. Zamanglo became a major international finance house, investing its funds in Australia, Canada, and the United States. In 1974 it was renamed the Mineral and Resources Corporation (MINORCO).

MINDECO

The Zambians' lack of expertise had significantly weakened their bargaining position in the 1969 negotiations, and the government's strategy was to build up Mindeco as a counterweight of information and expertise to the companies. As Mindeco ex-

---

*Some disgruntled RST shareholders brought legal action against Amax on the grounds that Amax's offer undervalued RST's worth. The court upheld the shareholders and Amax revised the offer. In 1974 RST International was renamed Amax International Ltd.

panded its staff and expertise, it began to exercise more influence over copper policy. But it was a slow process. The Mindeco staff, generally less experienced and less well qualified than their mining company counterparts, were also handicapped by Mindeco's lack of resources, compared with the vast technical resources of Anglo and Amax. Nevertheless, steps were taken to establish reporting procedures, so that there was a constant flow of information from the companies to Mindeco headquarters in Lusaka. But Mindeco did not build up staff on the Copperbelt.* The general feeling at Mindeco seems to have been that the companies could be trusted over routine matters, and that what counted was to influence long-term policy.[30] Mindeco began negotiating with Amax and Anglo to rationalize the industry and whittle away some of the fringe benefits awarded the companies in the original agreement. It was agreed that the research and development units of RCM and NCCM should be merged and that the recruitment of expatriate staff would be handled by Mindeco. Discussions began on the establishment of a new sales company, owned 51 per cent by Mindeco, to take over the copper sales service provided by subsidiaries of RST and Anglo.

ZAMBIANIZATION

The demand for African advancement on the copper mines had long been an important issue in Zambia. Yet there remained a marked contrast in the pace and direction of Zambianization in the mining industry and in the government. In government Zambianization proceeded both from the top down and bottom up; whereas on the mines, until 1975 at least, it had only been introduced from the bottom up. The result was that the structure of the industry had not really changed since colonial times. The lines of authority still ran from white to black, in contrast to

---

*For a while they positioned an accountant in the companies' Copperbelt offices to check on accounting procedures, but after a short period he was withdrawn with the rather unconvincing excuse that he was costing Mindeco more than he was saving the government. One would have thought that his presence served as a useful deterrent to company attempts to export profits by juggling with the accounts.

government, where expatriates were only in advisory, technical and generally subordinate positions. It is true that there was a continuing shortage of high-level Zambian manpower to take over responsible positions in the government structure and the mines, and the government had clearly decided to concentrate on the displacement of expatriates in the public sector rather than in the mining industry; but this does not fully explain the relaxed attitude to Zambianization on the mines. In fact the government, the union leadership, and UNIP rarely referred to the problems of Zambianization. The government-controlled media largely avoided the issue. Even in the 1969 takeover, when almost every other aspect of the country's relationship with the mining companies was being examined and renegotiated, the issue of Zambianization was not seriously discussed. In June 1973 it was estimated that, at existing rates, Zambianization on the mines would not be complete until the year 2085.[31]

The reason for the government's relaxed attitude may well lie in the threat posed by the miners and rival political groups to the existing elite's control. Indeed, after the implementation of the Brown Commission recommendations, the government began a systematic attempt to weaken and control the powerful Mineworkers' Union of Zambia (MUZ).* The government changed the union's function from protecting and improving the welfare of its members to promoting improved productivity and increased production.[32] By exerting political pressure and manipulating union elections, the government succeeded in installing a tame leadership at the upper levels of the MUZ. This leadership constantly urged its union members to exercise greater discipline and was totally opposed to strikes. It did not need to reflect the views of its members, as it had been financed since 1964 by a compulsory deduction from monthly wage packets. Leaders genuinely representative of the miners could only emerge in the union's lower ranks or outside the union structure altogether.[33] The government's reaction was to draft some of these new leaders into government posts outside the mining industry and send others into restriction. In the circumstances it was not

* Successor to pre-independence Northern Rhodesian African Mineworkers Union (NRAMWU).

surprising that the great majority of mineworkers were found in a 1969 survey to be deeply alienated from the union. As one, fairly typical, miner put it: 'The government has now come in in a big way, stamping its foot on any active trade unionist. They have all been deprived of their powers.'[34] The miners saw a growing convergence of views and policies between the government, the union leadership and the companies; and the 51 per cent takeover as merely the formal expression of this convergence.

The centrality of the copper industry to the economic, political and social life of Zambia means that Zambians in high and powerful positions on the mines must always seem a potential threat to the ruling political elite. Expatriates, working at the mines on short-term contracts, have no political base in the country and are vulnerable to governmental pressure. They pose no political threat to the elite. As long as foreign managers are visibly in control of the mining industry, conflicts with the national government can be presented in terms of a continuing struggle for national independence, and the central questions of class interest and distribution of wealth within the country can be disguised and avoided.

The Zambian government has developed a marked capitalist orientation towards the miners, an orientation symbolized by the banning of strikes, the incessant hammering of the workers for greater discipline, and the insistence that wage increases must be linked to increases in productivity.[35]

The 1969 agreement expressly forbade the Zambian government to hire outside consultants to advise on management or technical matters. The management contracts merely stipulated that RST and Anglo were to run the mines in such a manner that the standard of management did not fall below that previously provided by the companies. To achieve this, the companies demanded and got an undertaking from the Zambian government not to interfere.* The 1969 agreements, therefore, contained no specific provisions governing the rate of training

---

* Zambian demands for increased Zambianization might even have been considered inimical to maintaining the standards stipulated in the contract and in breach of the management contracts, giving the companies the right to ask for immediate redemption of the bonds.

and Zambianization. The companies retained their exclusive right to hire and fire. By controlling both the intake of Zambians and their advancement, the companies restricted the privilege of gaining more experience to expatriates or those Zambians who share the values of the existing management. The only Zambian departmental heads in the mining companies were in the personnel divisions; the highest posts to have been Zambianized outside personnel were at mine captain level. All posts above that level (i.e. underground managers, mine superintendents, sectional and divisional engineers, and engineering superintendents) have remained the exclusive preserve of expatriate staff. Where Zambians had been promoted, the mines created new supervisory or advisory posts which were filled by the expatriates, and authority remained with the expatriate whatever nominal authority had been conferred on his Zambian superiors.*[36] The Zambianization process was monitored and evaluated according to purely statistical criteria. Since the number of posts agreed by the companies for Zambianization regulated not just the minimum, but effectively the maximum, number of posts available for Zambianization, many qualified graduates found themselves forced from the industry through the lack of career prospects and the different treatment that they received compared to their white equivalents.

The companies claimed that the level of knowledge and experience required to run the mines is such that Zambianization could only take place slowly. But their actions showed that they were determined to maintain their monopoly control of information and decision-making as long as possible. In July 1973 RST hired three Zambian assistant general managers, one of whom was a personnel superintendent and two of whom came from outside the industry.[37] It was hard not to suspect window-dressing since, if these men – lacking technical qualifications and

---

*The satirical Zambian columnist, Kapelwa Musonda, quoted an imaginary conversation with an employer who claimed to have achieved 100 per cent Zambianization without firing a single expatriate. The employer explained: 'The post of Sales Manager was Zambianized, so we made the expatriate Sales Adviser. As you know no Zambian can ever qualify as an adviser in anything . . .' (Kapelwa Musonda (pseudonym), *The Kapelwa Musonda File*, Lusaka, Neczam, 1973, p. 40).

working experience on the mines – could be appointed to such senior posts, why could the appointments not have been made from within the mines.[38] Some observers have also noticed a singular lack of effort by the companies to retain those Zambian graduates and engineers they do recruit. The companies claimed that they could not afford to compete with other sectors of Zambian industry, which needed fewer graduates and engineers and could therefore pay more. But the companies were already paying high salaries and fringe benefits to the often inexperienced expatriate staff who filled these posts.[39]

The priorities of the companies are revealed in other ways: for example, although Anglo established the Oppenheimer School of Social Work some years before Independence, it was only in 1973, ten years after Independence and seven years after the foundation of the University of Zambia, that a School of Mining Engineering was established by the government and the mining companies.

POLITICAL AND ECONOMIC DIFFICULTIES

The tensions within UNIP that had been headed off by the Matero Declaration of 1969 soon returned.[40] On 22 August 1971, Kapwepwe left UNIP and formed the United Progressive Party (UPP), the most potent threat to the ruling political elite since Independence. The reluctance of Harry Nkumbula's ANC party to join UNIP was troublesome, but its appeal was limited to the south and west of Zambia. The UPP was much more serious: after all, Kapwepwe and the Bemba had helped create UNIP. The ruling elite reacted vigorously. UNIP launched an all-out campaign against suspected UPP supporters. On 20 September, 120 UPP officials were detained, including ex-ministers, district governors, mayors and UNIP regional officials. By-elections were ordered in the six seats where MPs had changed their allegiance. For a while Kapwepwe seemed to be trying to ally UPP with Nkumbula and the ANC, but nothing came of it. In the elections UNIP won five seats back, but Kapwepwe won the Mufulira constituency. He remained a powerful focus for discontent and the only national leader to be compared with President Kaunda. In February 1972 the UPP was outlawed and Kapwepwe detained. The UNIP leadership now proceeded with its plans to make Zambia a one-party state.[41]

While the political elite was grappling with the UPP challenge, it was also hit by the sharply falling tax revenue from the copper industry, which underpinned all government expenditure. Government revenue from mining had fallen from its 1969 peak of K234 million to an average of only K42 million in 1971 and 1972. Although in theory the total tax take was 73·05 per cent of profits, the tax concession in the 1969 agreement had reduced the government's effective tax rate in 1971 and 1972 to 28 per cent of profits.[42] The companies' production costs were rising, but the government suspected that the companies were artificially inflating costs as a hidden way of exporting profits and reducing tax payments.

Various provisions of the 1969 agreement were putting a strain on Zambia's balance of payments. As part of the agreement the government allowed the mining companies to repatriate the capital repayments, and also lifted the Mulungushi restrictions on dividend remittances. (The companies, of course, still received their share of the dividends.) This led to a much higher leakage of foreign exchange. (See Table 19.) The net foreign exchange cost of the management fees ran between K2 million and K6 million a year, depending on copper prices and profits.*

The danger for the Zambians was that while there was provision for the capital repayments to be accelerated if the copper price and profits rose, there was no agreement for payments to be deferred if the price dropped. The Zambian negotiators had taken a calculated risk that the price of copper would not drop below K800 per ton over the repayment period. If it did, the government would be forced to dip into foreign exchange reserves to meet its contractual obligations. The copper price fell from K1,252 in March 1970 to K721 at the year end. The average price for copper was K750 in 1971 and K796 in 1972 (see Figure 20). The balance of payments on the current account deteriorated from a surplus of K77 million in 1970 to a deficit of

---

*The management fees worked out at K8 million a year if the average copper price was around K850 per ton. Not all of this fee left the country.

Table 19: The declared income of Anglo American Corporation and RST from Zambia, 1970–75 (£m.)

	six months 1970		1971		1972		1973		1974		1975	
	Anglo	RST	Anglo	RST	Anglo	RST	Anglo	RST	Anglo	RST	Anglo	RST
Repayment on ZIMCO bonds issued for 51 per cent of assets	4·39	2·38	8·29	2·38	9·09	1·89	8·88	12·74	33·5	—	—	—
Interest on outstanding bonds	1·25	n.a.	5·22	n.a.	4·39	0·49	4·19	0·51	—	—	—	—
Dividends RCM on assets	0·80	7·59	1·70	2·63	1·01	2·45	1·67	4·12	3·37	6·72	—	—
Dividends NCCM on assets	3·43	—	11·25	—	9·99	—	10·50	—	18·09	—	—	—
Management fees (¾ per cent of gross sales and 2 per cent of profit before inc. tax)	—	—	12·84	4·53	8·35	4·15	8·55	4·93	16·17	4·45	8·42	3·81
Sales fees: ¾ per cent of gross sales proceeds	—	—	6·11	2·97	4·50	2·47	4·53	2·97	6·40	2·71	5·52	2·89
Compensation for loss of sales and management contract	—	—	—	—	—	—	—	—	22	14·2	—	—
TOTALS	9·87	9·97	45·26	12·51	37·33	11·45	38·32	25·28	99·53	28·08	13·94	6·70

Total 1970–75 RST = 93·99   Anglo = 244·25

Note that funds were also transferred in other ways, e.g. fees (engineering fees at 3 per cent of constructed project, recruiting fees at 15 per cent of gross salary for first year), head office charges, etc.
All figures approximate. Currencies converted at prevailing rates of exchange.
Source: Annual reports RCM, NCCM, RST, ZCI, AMAX, Anglo American.

K176·5 million in 1971 and another one of K97·5 million in 1972.[43] The drastic fall in government revenue and the low copper prices were threatening to embarrass the Zambians, particularly as production had been severely cut by the Mufulira Mine disaster in 1970.* But under the 1969 agreements the government could not increase the mineral, export, income or withholding taxes nor the royalty payment or any other revenue measures as long as the bonds remained outstanding. Then in January 1973 Rhodesia closed the border with Zambia. At this time about 50 per cent of Zambian copper (some 440,000 tons) were being exported via Rhodesia and Beira (see Figure 7). The copper was re-routed, but imports of coke, sulphuric acid, chlorine for water purification and explosives and mine machinery for the mines were often in short supply and some materials had to be airlifted into Zambia;[44] although there were complaints that the mining companies were importing supplies which could and should have been obtained locally.[45]

THE 1973 REORGANIZATION

By mid-1973 the price of copper on the world market was moving sharply upwards. President Kaunda took advantage of the rising prices and on 31 August he announced that, although working relations with the mining companies since the takeover had been satisfactory, certain provisions in the agreements had proved to be detrimental to the interests of Zambia. The President explained that, although the companies were minority shareholders, they retained effective control of the industry through their power of veto, their control of management, and their resistance to Zambianization. The President complained particularly that despite the generous tax provisions, and the relaxation of foreign-exchange controls, the companies were no

---

*There was a massive cave-in, and extensive flooding. Some 89 lives were lost, and it was 3 years before production reached normal levels again. The loss of production was estimated at 200,000 tons. The official inquiry did not rule whether or not the companies were irresponsible in using the caving method of mining and in placing the mine tailings directly on top of the mine.

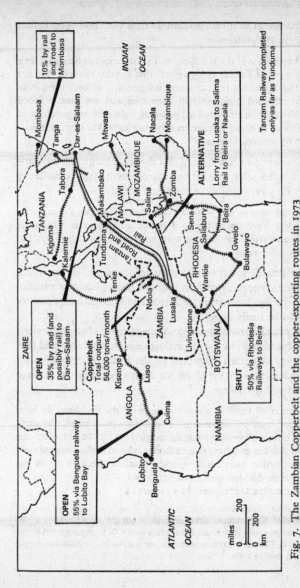

Fig. 7. The Zambian Copperbelt and the copper-exporting routes in 1973
NOTE: The Tanzam railway was completed in 1975, but the Benguela railway was closed from 1975, because of the fighting in Angola. The road link to Mombasa was closed in 1977 due to a dispute between Kenya and Tanzania.

SOURCE: *African Development*, October 1973, Zambian supplement, p. 225.

Labels within map:

10% by rail and road to Mombasa

Tanzam Railway completed only as far as Tunduma

ALTERNATIVE
Lorry from Lusaka to Salima
Rail to Beira or Nacala

OPEN
35% by road (and possibly rail) to Dar-es-Salaam

Copperbelt:
Total output: 56,000 tons/month

SHUT
50% via Rhodesia Railways to Beira

OPEN
55% via Benguela railway to Lobito Bay

INDIAN OCEAN

ATLANTIC OCEAN

ZAIRE

TANZANIA

MALAWI

MOZAMBIQUE

RHODESIA

ZAMBIA

BOTSWANA

ANGOLA

NAMIBIA

Mombasa, Tanga, Dar-es-Salaam, Mtwara, Nacala, Mombasa, Tabora, Kigoma, Kalemie, Makambako, Salima, Zomba, Sena, Beira, Tunduma, Tenke, Ndola, Lusaka, Salisbury, Gwelo, Wankie, Bulawayo, Livingstone, Kisenge, Luso, Cuima, Lobito, Benguela

Tanzam Road and Rail

miles 0 — 200
km 0 — 200

more concerned to invest in Zambia than they had been before the Matero announcement.

'Our experience in the last three and a half years has been that they have taken out of Zambia every ngwee* that was due to them. A major part of the capital for the expansion programmes of both companies has been obtained from external borrowing and not from retained profits. You may be interested to know that, right now, my government is being asked to approve an external borrowing by the two companies of about 65 million Kwacha.'[46]

The President also commented that the fees charged by the companies for the sales, marketing, management, and consultancy services they provided were high, and added:

'Although most of this work is performed in Zambia, the minority shareholders have entered into separate arrangements with non-resident companies for reasons best known to themselves but not comprehensible to us.'

Here the President was being a little disingenuous. He knew that the mining companies preferred to use non-resident companies because the fees were exempted from Zambian exchange control and could be easily exported.

Finally the President pointed out the absence of any provisions for Zambianization in the original agreement, and observed that recruitment decisions remained in the hands of the minority shareholders, again at a high fee for themselves. Then he came to the heart of his address:

'I mention all these to show you some of the problems we have experienced with the agreements as presently constituted. Countrymen, we cannot allow this situation to continue . . . In order that the people of Zambia may have more effective control of the affairs of their economy [and] in accordance with the mandate given to me by the nation, I have decided with immediate effect:

1. Outstanding bonds should be redeemed.†

* 100 ngwee = one Kwacha.
† Note that the Zambians have not bought out the whole holding of the companies; they merely redeemed the bonds with which they acquired 51 per cent control. The companies retained the same stake in the Zambian copper mines they had in 1969.

2. Steps should be taken to revert to the old system of providing for themselves all the management and technical services which are now being provided by the minority shareholders.

3. A new copper company, wholly owned by the government, should be established here in Zambia.'

The outstanding bonds were redeemed partly out of buoyant foreign exchange reserves due to the temporary high price of copper, which reached K1,500 (over £1,000) in November 1973, and partly with the proceeds from a \$115 million Eurodollar loan raised earlier that year.* The President announced that henceforth the copper companies would be subject to normal taxation and exchange control regulations. (This was possible under the agreement once the bonds had been repaid.) The declaration that RCM and NCCM should provide their own technical and management services meant that technicians and managers were now to be hired directly by RCM and NCCM and not seconded from either Anglo or RST. The copper mines employed some 5,000 expatriates: 3,000 were actively engaged in technical mining operations, and some 800 had permanent and pensionable contracts with the mining companies on secondment to the Zambian operating companies.

The President's statement did not complete the reorganization, because the Zambians also wanted to terminate the management and the sales contracts between Mindeco, Anglo and Amax. However, these contracts were not part of the 1970 master agreement, and were covered by entirely separate contracts. Prolonged negotiations with the companies lasted over a year, before agreement was reached, first with Anglo in 1974 and then with

---

*The repayment of the bonds was criticized on the grounds that the government borrowed money at 12 per cent on the Eurodollar market to redeem Zimco bonds which carried interest at only 6 per cent. In addition, the government redeemed the bonds at face value when they were being sold at a discount on the London Stock Exchange. One commentator suggested, with tongue only half in cheek, that the best and cheapest course for the government would have been to buy out Zamanglo and sell off its non-Zambian assets (*African Development*, October 1973, Zambian supplement, p. 55). Whether Anglo would have allowed this to happen is another matter!

Amax in January 1975.* The government paid Anglo K33 million (£22 million) and Amax K22 million (£14·2 million) in compensation. At NCCM, the Managing Director, replaced by a Zambian, stayed on as Deputy Managing Director. Amax and Anglo agreed to second staff to RCM and NCCM if they could not recruit enough to run the mines. To market the copper from RCM and NCCM, a new government-controlled company called the Metal Marketing Corporation of Zambia (MEMACO), based in Zambia, was established.[47]

MINDECO AND THE MINISTRY OF MINES

The President also restructured the relationship between Mindeco, RCM, NCCM and the Ministry of Mines to prevent Mindeco or the management of NCCM and RCM becoming a rival centre of power. Mindeco ceased to be the holding company for RCM and NCCM, the government's shares were transferred to the Ministry of Finance, and the Minister of Mines was made chairman of RCM and NCCM. Mindeco, once responsible for the whole Zambian mining industry, would in future be responsible for only the coal mine at Maamba, a gypsum mine in Mazumbuka, a few miscellaneous small mines and some prospecting.

Under the new arrangement, day-to-day control and monitoring will be much weakened, since the only obligation on the companies is to report to the Minister of Mines. The Minister, as a political appointee, will lack the detailed grasp of the copper industry that the chairman of Mindeco, Dominic Mulaisho, and the Mindeco staff, had acquired. Mulaisho himself was transferred to another post. The new head of Mindeco was a former special assistant to the President.

* Amax held out for better compensation in both 1969 and 1973. This was partly because of the company's hard-line policy directed by the chairman, Ian MacGregor, but in 1973 it was partly also because of fear that the company would be sued by disgruntled shareholders as it had been over the 1969 agreement. It is also possibly significant that although the articles of association governing the relationship between the companies and the Zambian government have been changed the details were not released.

COPPER – BOOM AND SLUMP

As the companies stalled the negotiations, and Mindeco was re-organized, there was no effective Zambian control of companies during the great commodity boom which sent copper prices soaring.[48] But the boom was short-lived, and after reaching a peak of over K2,800 (£1,400) a ton in April 1974, the price of copper on the London Metal Exchange fell dramatically as world demand slackened. In November the CIPEC countries (Zambia, Zaire, Chile and Peru) agreed on a ten per cent cutback in exports.[49] In early 1975 the price of copper fell below Zambia's cost of production, reducing the government's tax revenue to zero, and forced NCCM and RCM to borrow from international banking consortia to ease their liquidity problems and raise fresh capital.[50] In April the CIPEC countries cut back their exports by another five per cent, and in August NCCM announced a net loss of K8·5 million for the quarter ending in June.[51] By 1977 the price of copper on the LME had reached its lowest level in real terms for over twenty years. As during the 1930s, Zambia bore the brunt of a slump in the industrialized nations; unemployment reached 25 per cent; there was no government revenue from copper; NCCM and RCM declared a loss for the third year running; and despite production cutbacks there seemed to be no prospect of improvement while the world price was so far below Zambia's cost of production. Moreover, sanctions were estimated by the UN to have cost Zambia between $750 and $800 million between 1965 and 1977. To offset this, Zambia had received many promises but aid of only $100 million. The economic crisis was grave and the recession prolonged.

THE UNDERDEVELOPMENT OF ZAMBIA

After fifteen years of political independence Zambia had taken a few tentative steps towards economic independence. It had grown more independent of the southern African economy but it remained totally dependent on copper, and the mining companies retained day-to-day control of the industry, ensuring a constant flow of copper and investable surplus to the industrialized centres of the world economy. The close integration of the Zambian mining industry with the world economic system had intensified rather than diminished in the post-independence era.

The consequence was a continuing decline in the agricultural sector and a growing cleavage between the rural and urban areas. Despite its agricultural resources Zambia had become a net importer of food, and approximately 50 per cent of its annual food requirements were imported.[52] The income gap between the rural and urban populations had widened dangerously since independence. The real increase in *per capita* income in the employment sector during the period 1964-8 was approximately 35 per cent, while the increase in rural subsistence incomes during the same period was only 3 per cent.[53] But aggregating urban and rural incomes for comparison in this way conceals the more significant fact: the biggest gap in incomes is between the high-salaried and profit-making class based in the copper industry, its associated services, and in the government, on the one hand; and, on the other, the rural peasants and urban low-income wage-earners. The top ten per cent of employees in Zambia receive approximately 45 per cent of all wages and salaries. A 1969 survey reported that the top salaries in public posts reached K18,500, which was more than 25 times the estimated minimum subsistence wage of K60 a month. But 90 per cent of Zambian workers earned barely enough for subsistence.[54]

In the years since independence, the political elite, using the state as its economic base, has striven to establish itself as Zambia's ruling class, and as the intermediary between the international mining companies and Zambia's mineral resources. The effect of the Mulungushi, Matero and 1973 reforms has been to transfer ownership of Zambia's major industrial, commercial and financial enterprises from foreign interests to the state.[55] The proliferating state corporations reinforce the economic power of the elite, because their very size blocks the emergence of local businesses unless they are supported by the state or have close connections with state employees. The overwhelming dependence of the political elite and of the mushrooming government bureaucracy established in the post-independence era on a continuing flow of copper revenues led the government, in the absence of an alternative development strategy, to place supreme importance on the continuing profitability of the copper mines. This in turn has led the government to identify more and more closely with the goals of the existing mine management. For Zambian politicians, the maintenance of current levels of productivity and profits is essential to the economic and political survival of the government.

A series of nationalist economic measures have been presented in terms of a continuing struggle for national independence, but the gains are accruing to a small privileged section of the Zambian population. The widening gap between the elite and the majority of the population undermines political stability. When copper revenues decline the capacity of the elite to satisfy the demands of an expectant population is also reduced, and the danger of political unrest increases. Following the Matero measures in 1969, the tax revenue from copper dropped sharply, and foreign investors withheld their funds. The growth in employment opportunities through import substitution declined.[56] But although capital expenditure by the government fell, recurrent expenditure continued to rise[57] as the number of civil servants rose from 22,000 in 1963 to 54,000 in 1970.[58] Pressed to expand government services, but with copper revenues declining, the elite made more low-income groups liable for income tax in 1969, and then in 1970 limited wage increases to five per cent.[59] Opposition from the politically and economically powerful miners was largely neutralized by a judicious mixture of wage increases, controlled Zambianization, and the emasculation of their top-level union leadership. Declining popular support for UNIP led to the proscription of the UPP, the detention of the UPP leadership, the incorporation of the ANC into UNIP and the establishment of a one-party state. But sectional conflict has continued,[60] and the 1973 elections showed widespread disenchantment with the elite, especially in the rural areas. Only 39 per cent of the registered voters bothered to vote and nine government ministers were defeated in the poll.[61]

The root of the political problems facing Zambia's emergent ruling class lies in its continuing dependence on copper and in the growing disparity in wealth within the country. It is the

government employees and the political elite who have appropriated most of the economic benefits that have accrued to
Zambia in the post-independence era. It is they who would have
to bear the cost of a diversion of resources from the urban to the
rural areas and down-grading in the relative importance of the
mining industry. But the power of the elite depends on its role as
an intermediary between the mining companies and Zambia's
copper; the state machine is the base of the elite's power within
Zambia and is dependent on copper taxes and revenues. So the
elite has left day-to-day control of the mining industry in the
hands of the companies and sought to prevent any disruption in
the flow of minerals. The dependence on copper ensures Zambia's continuing underdevelopment, and consequent social tensions and political conflict. In an attempt to head off these tensions, President Kaunda has promulgated a series of economic
reforms[62] and taken more and more power into his own hands,
but the fundamental problems and hence the fundamental
instability remain.

The companies for their part have ceded ownership and some
control over the mines in order to protect their long-term interests. But they need political stability to ensure a continuing flow
of minerals and profits to the industrialized centres of the world.
Should the elite show signs of disintegrating or losing its grip on
the country then the mining companies will doubtless transfer
their support to another political or military group which promises greater stability, such as the army. But there can be no
lasting economic or political stability while Zambia's dependence
on the mining companies, and on copper exports to the industrialized nations, remains.

10 The Mining Company and the State in Zaire

In the sixty years after the completion of the Congo railway in 1898, the pre-capitalist Congolese economy became a satellite of the Belgian metropolis.* The export of primary goods was encouraged to meet the needs of Europe, and the Congolese economy became dependent on a small group of primary exports, rubber, copper, tin and diamonds, whose production was controlled by foreign companies and whose prices were liable to fluctuate violently.[1]

The Congolese economy was dominated by the companies of the Belgian Société Générale group. On the eve of independence the Société Générale was generally estimated to control 70 per cent of the Congolese economy outside the subsistence sector.[2] It controlled the copper, cobalt, diamond, and uranium mines and had a virtual monopoly over water and rail transportation in the Congo basin. This vast empire was controlled through two main channels. The Belgian parent Société Générale had direct shareholdings in all the most important companies (Union Minière, Forminière, Minière du Beceka, Chemin de Fer du Bas Congo au Katanga, etc.) and indirect stakes through two Congolese holding companies. The Compagnie du Congo pour le Commerce et l'Industrie (CCCI) held stocks in some fifty Congolese companies and more than twenty Belgian and foreign ones. The other holding company, Compagnie du Katanga, had a large investment in Union Minière. The colonial government had a substantial stake in the private sector of the economy, through direct investment in the big trusts, and a 50 per cent share or more in twenty companies. This portfolio

* See Chapters 1–4 for more on the early underdevelopment of Zaire. In 1959 the population of the Congo was 14 million, of whom 3 million lived in the urban areas.

was valued at more than $640 million in 1960 and produced an income for the government of $24 million in 1959.[3] The most important investment was the government's two-thirds stake in the Comité Spécial du Katanga (CSK), whose main holding was its stake in Union Minière. Yet although the colonial government controlled these companies, it regularly yielded that control to private interests. Thus: although it was entitled to appoint the President of the Board of Directors of Union Minière, through its control of CSK, the post always went to a director of Société Générale, which owned a fraction of the voting shares (see Figure 8). The same applied to Forminière, the Kasai diamond-mining company, in which the government had a 55 per cent share, but over which Société Générale exercised unfettered managerial command, with a stake of only 5 per cent.

Union Minière du Haut Katanga

The most important company in the Société Générale's Congolese portfolio and in the Congolese economy itself was undoubtedly Union Minière du Haut Katanga. In 1953, the company's output of copper totalled 200,000 tons, or 7 per cent of world production. Union Minière also produced 80 per cent of the world's cobalt, and 5 per cent of its zinc, as well as substantial quantities of cadmium, silver, platinum, columbium, and tungsten. In 1953 its net profits exceeded £20 million. By 1960 copper production had risen to 300,704 tons; and profits in 1959 were 3,535 million Belgian francs ($70·7 million).[4] The total net profits made by Union Minière from 1950 to 1959 are estimated at 31,000 million Belgian francs ($620 million).[5] It is, therefore, not surprising that the future control of such a profitable and powerful mining company was a vital issue in the pre-independence negotiations, and of great concern to overseas investors, particularly in Belgium.

THE STRUGGLE FOR THE CONTROL OF UNION MINIÈRE

In 1959, there were 414,000 issued voting shares in Union Minière; 134,016 of these were held by Tanganyika Concessions

(TANKS). The Comité Spécial du Katanga (CSK) held 248,000. And the six-member board was made up of four representatives appointed by the Congolese government and two by the Compagnie du Katanga. Société Générale controlled the Compagnie du Katanga through its Congolese holding company, the Compagnie du Congo pour le Commerce et l'Industrie (CCCI). It also had a direct stake of 33,584 voting

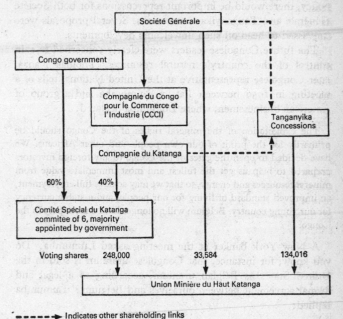

Fig. 8. The distribution of voting shares in Union Minière in 1960
SOURCE: J. Gerard-Libois, *Katangese Secession*, University of Wisconsin, 1966, p. 320.

shares in Union Minière (UMHK) and close ties with Tanganyika Concessions (see Figure 8).

The problem worrying European financiers and Belgian company directors was this. In theory, Union Minière was controlled by the six-member Comité Spécial du Katanga (CSK).

Four of CSK's directors were appointed by the Congolese government. Suppose that the government which came to power at independence was inclined to apply different economic and managerial criteria from those of the colonial administration and Société Générale. Through its majority on the CSK, such a government would be able to implement changes in company policy. If the Congolese government adopted an interventionist policy, there would be important repercussions for both Société Générale and Tanganyika Concessions. Several proposals were canvassed to head off such unwelcome developments.

The future Congolese leaders were clearly concerned to gain control of the country's natural resources. Thomas Kanza, later Congolese representative at the United Nations, tells of a meeting in 1959 between Patrice Lumumba and a group of American businessmen, where Lumumba declared:

The exploitation of the mineral riches of the Congo should be primarily for the profit of our own people and other Africans. We have decided to open the gates of the Congo to any foreign investors prepared to help us get the fullest and most immediate value from mineral resources and energy, so that we may achieve full employment, an improved standard of living for our people, and a stable currency for our young country. Belgium will no longer have a monopoly in the Congo.

A New York banker at the meeting asked Lumumba: 'Do you know, for instance, that Congolese uranium is sold in the United States as Belgian uranium, according to a legal and formal agreement between ourselves and Belgium?' Lumumba replied:

As I have said, Belgium won't have a monopoly in the Congo now. From now on we are an independent and sovereign state. Belgium doesn't produce any uranium; it would be to the advantage of both our countries if the Congo and the US worked out their own agreements in future.

Kanza noted that the Americans, 'all of whom represented powerful financial interests, looked at one another and exchanged meaningful smiles'.[6]

As the negotiations over Union Minière continued, overseas

investors – particularly in Belgium – withdrew their capital from the Congo. Union Minière declared a particularly high dividend in 1959, and demanded that the sixty-year-old agreement establishing the Comité Spécial du Katanga be reviewed. Finally, at a constitutional conference three days before independence, the CSK was dissolved, and the Compagnie du Katanga's 33 per cent direct stake in Union Minière reverted to the Compagnie, which was controlled by Société Générale. Although the Congolese government was still the largest individual shareholder in Union Minière, it was now in a minority faced by a strong coalition of private interests. The Société Générale, the Compagnie du Katanga and Tanganyika Concessions together had an absolute majority on the board of Union Minière. On the reconstituted board, Tanganyika Concessions theoretically held the balance of power between the Belgian interests and the Congolese government. In practice, however, there was never any doubt where they would lend their support. TANKS and Société Générale had been partners for sixty years, and natural identity of interests was cemented by strong boardroom links (shown in Table 20).

THE SEEDS OF KATANGAN SECESSION

The Union Minière copper mines in Katanga constituted an independent centre of economic activity totally separate from the Lower Congo River Basin economic system dominated by Leopoldville. Katangan copper was exported along a different transport route, outside the control of the central government (see Figure 9). The Benguela railway meant that the majority of Katanga's economic relations with the metropolitan economies, its copper exports and its essential imports followed this route, by-passing the administrative capital of Leopoldville. For the burgeoning industrial producers of Southern Rhodesia and South Africa, Katanga already represented an important market.

As political parties proliferated in the eighteen months before independence, the Confédération des Associations Tribales du Katanga (CONAKAT) emerged as the main party in the province, with most of its support in the south. The first

Table 20: Interlocking directorships of Société Générale, Union Minière and Tanganyika Concessions in 1962

Société Générale de Belgique	Union Minière du Haut Katanga	Tanganyika Concessions
Gillet	Gillet (Chairman)	H. Oppenheimer (Anglo)
Van der Straeten	Van der Straeten	Van der Straeten
Devillez	Waterhouse	Waterhouse (Chairman)
Bonvoisin	Selborne	Selborne
Robiliart	Robiliart	Robiliart
Dubois-Pelerin	Guilaume	Guilaume
de Spirlet		de Spirlet
Marthoz	Marthoz	
Wallef (Chairman)	Wallef	
Lampert	Alexander	Alexander
De Meere	Paulus	Hutchison
Smits	Blaise	Cochran
Nokin	Terwagne	Dickinson
Renders	Sengier (Vice Chairman)	Pinto Basto
	Cousin	Turner (Rio Tinto)

president of the party was Godefroid Munungo; and the second Moise Tshombe.* Conakat was strongly influenced by European settlers;[7] and there were widespread reports in Elizabethville that it was being financed by Union Minière. The company was also reported to be covering its bets by slipping a little money to the rival BALUBAKAT party.†

Plans for the secession of Katanga were openly discussed. In December 1959 Tshombe declared 'that a federal Congo

*Tshombe's father had amassed a fortune of several million francs by collaborating with the occupying Belgians and selling workers to the mining companies. Tshombe's family owned plantations, several shops and a hotel in Elizabethville. Tshombe first went into the family business, but later forsook business for the equally lucrative realm of politics.

†In these matters proof is not easy to come by, but in 1960 the Union Minière accounts list $2·5 million under the heading 'exceptional expenses' and the explanation for these expenses was unconvincing.

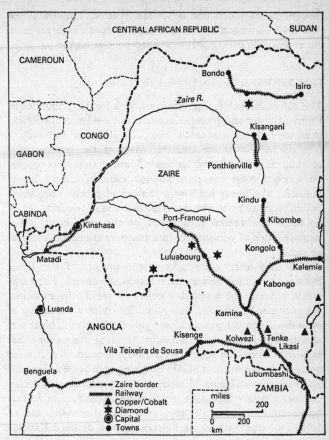

Fig. 9. The Katangan copper mines and export routes

including a Katangese state might or might not be possible, but that in either case Katanga would work for real community with Belgium'.[8] Some employees of Union Minière wrote to the Prime Minister of the Central African Federation, Roy Welensky, proposing a link.[9] Their idea was that Tshombe should take Katanga out of the Congo when it became independent at the beginning of July and declare a republic. Although the proposed link never materialized, throughout the period of Katanga's secession Welensky gave much material, moral and political support to the secessionist regime.

INDEPENDENCE – 30 JUNE 1960

The newly independent government, with Patrice Lumumba as Prime Minister and Joseph Kasavubu as President, inheriting a weak central administration from the Belgians, had only a tenuous hold over the country. Most of the government's revenue came from the tax on Union Minière. Control of copper, the Congo's most important natural resource, and its largest industry, was firmly held by a phalanx of private companies, bound together by an identity of outlook and interlocking shareholdings. The central government, on the other hand, was a weak coalition of personal rivalries based on ethnic and regional groups.

Five days after Independence, the soldiers of the Force Publique mutinied against their European officers. The Congolese government adopted a policy of rapid Africanization. Kasavubu and Lumumba flew round the country attempting to calm the troops. At 9.00 a.m. on 9 July the Belgian Cabinet met and discussed the Katanga situation. It was at this meeting that Belgian intervention seems to have been decided. Was it mere coincidence that at 10.05 M. Gillet, governor of Société Générale and President of Union Minière, was seen in discussion with a Cabinet official?[10] Belgian troops were dispatched to Luluabourg and Elizabethville 'to protect their nationals'. On 11 July, Tshombe, with strong Belgian support, declared Katanga independent in these equivocal terms:

This independence is total. None the less, conscious of the imperious necessity of an economic collaboration with Belgium, the government of Katanga to which Belgium, in order to protect human lives, has just granted the assistance of its own troops, asks Belgium to join with Katanga in a close economic community.

Lumumba and Kasavubu flew to Elizabethville, but Belgian troops at the airport refused them permission to land. Convinced that the Belgians were attempting to seize control of the Congo, Lumumba and the Congolese leaders appealed to the United Nations for assistance against this aggression. A few days later UN troops began to arrive.[11]

The secession of Katanga received widespread public support in Belgium, but the government, aware of the international repercussions, did not grant diplomatic recognition to the secessionist regime.* It continued, however, to provide it with all possible military and administrative assistance. 'Without this his government would be quickly pulled down from within and without' it was reported in the London *Daily Telegraph*; which added that 'the outline of Belgium's emergency policy for Katanga is to protect the great Belgian financial stake here and hold a political bridgehead in the hope of a Congolese union amenable to Belgium and the West'.[12]

Despite the Belgian government's strong support, the key to the survival of Tshombe's breakaway state was the revenue provided by Union Minière. These payments amounted to about £15 million a year and met over 70 per cent of Katanga's budget.[13] Union Minière's decision to make over to the secessionist government all taxes legally due to the central government was the key factor in prolonging the secession. While the Congolese government was short of funds, Tshombe was able to buy arms and a fleet of jet aircraft and to maintain a militia of 12,000 men. The white mercenaries who controlled the militia were paid £300 a month.[14]

Clearly those who directed company policy were convinced that Union Minière's continued prosperity depended on an independent Katanga. They argued, with tongues firmly in their corporate cheeks, that the existence of an independent Katanga was a vital fact, and since 'we are not in politics we have to pay taxes to whoever is in power'.[15] This sidestepped, of course, the question of who had put Tshombe in power in the first place. In the annual report of Tanganyika Concessions, the

---

*Thomas Kanza says that the Belgians sent diplomatic messages to other states recommending that they should not recognize Katanga because, while it might call itself independent, it had in fact merely reverted to the status of a colony (T. Kanza, *Conflict in the Congo*, Penguin Books, 1972, p. 201).

chairman, Captain Waterhouse, boasted that Union Minière and TANKS had 'played no small part in enabling the independent African government of the province (i.e. Katanga) to establish itself'.[16] Union Minière gave Tshombe its powerful radio transmitter, and Radio Katanga was to play an important part in the struggle with the UN in 1960–61.*[17]

The day-to-day relationship of the company with the Tshombe regime is more difficult to assess. Some of the company's Elizabethville employees undoubtedly had close contacts with Tshombe's circle in their private capacity, but it would seem that the main aim of the company was to ensure the continued export of the profitable copper production. It was Union Minière's proud boast in 1963 that only one full month of copper production had been lost during the whole of the troubles. Conor Cruise O'Brien, the UN representative in the Congo, makes this assessment of the situation in 1960–61:

> Tshombe was likely to be aware, through intermediaries, if not directly, of Union Minière thinking, but, if he chose to disregard their opinions, or one of their opinions, *while leaving their interests intact*, there was probably indeed little enough in normal circumstances that Union Minière could, or at least would, do about it. Companies like the Union Minière may perhaps engineer a coup d'état against a Government which directly threatens their interests. They are not likely to use any sanctions against a Government which, on the whole, defends these interests, even if it is doing so by means which may be in the long run dangerous and unwise. (*Emphasis added.*)[18]

UN INTERVENTION AND THE ENDING OF SECESSION

In the early stages of the secession, the Belgian government, the controllers of Union Minière, and the European population of Elizabethville all gave complete support to Tshombe. But the involvement of the UN created new pressures which eventually brought secession to an end.

---

*Although it was perhaps not as important as the transmitter in Leopoldville in the early days of independence, which the UN prevented Lumumba from using. There was also a transmitter in Congo-Brazzaville, just across the river from Leopoldville.

At first the UN mandate merely instructed UN security forces to maintain law and order. But the death of Lumumba in January 1961 at the hands of the Tshombe regime provoked a much stronger Security Council resolution and gave the UN forces greater powers to end secession. In this the attitude of the US government was crucial, and it is important to establish the basis of US intervention. Although the powerful Rockefeller and Guggenheim-Ryan groups had a stake in Tanganyika Concessions and a share in Forminière, the United States did not intervene primarily because of its *immediate* economic interests. The total American investment amounted to only $20 million, while Belgian investment was $2,000 million. At first the United States was prepared to lend the support of its benign neglect to the mining companies and the Katangan secessionists. As the Congo crisis dragged on without any sign of a successful conclusion, however, the Americans became increasingly anxious. President Eisenhower had originally agreed to support the UN operation; but the State Department itself was split between those who felt that the US should support the nationalists in Africa, and those who could not bring themselves to attack a Nato ally.[19] Lumumba's appeal for aid and the response of the Soviet Union in supplying transport planes changed the situation. When Kennedy came to power, the US and the USSR were in open diplomatic conflict over the Congo. The Kennedy administration felt that the US would lose all credibility in African eyes if it did not back strong UN action. Above all, the US was afraid that the country would fall into 'communist' hands.[20] So the UN action in the Congo came to depend on a working alliance between the US and the Afro-Asian bloc at the UN. Conor Cruise O'Brien describes the basis of this accommodation:

The vital principle for the US was keeping the Communists out of the Congo; this involved opposing the secession of Katanga, which if condoned would be a precedent valid in Afro-Asian eyes, for another secession round Stanleyville leading to 'a central African Cuba'. The vital principle for the Afro-Asians was to stop the European-instigated Katanga breakaway, with the deadly precedent of disintegration which it represented for so many of the new and vulnerable states. Few

239

Afro-Asian Governments were genuinely preoccupied by the need to keep Communism out of the Congo, and many Americans had considerable misgivings about ending the secession of Katanga; yet neither side could get what it wanted without the help of the other, and so the unspoken bargain came into being.[21]

With the US firmly committed to the UN intervention in the Congo, the crushing of the secessionist movement was only a matter of time. However, Tshombe's secessionist state proved to be an 'unconscionable time a-dying', due to the powerful influence of Union Minière and its associated companies.

In August 1961 Cyrille Adoula had become the premier of a new national government. Throughout the autumn O'Brien, as the UN representative in the Congo, negotiated with Tshombe to end secession, but without success. Fighting broke out between UN forces and Tshombe's gendarmerie, which was now some 15,000 strong. UN Secretary-General Dag Hammarskjöld was killed in a plane crash, as he was on his way to negotiate personally with Tshombe in Katanga. There was more fighting in December before Tshombe finally agreed in principle to end secession. This proved to be a tactical manoeuvre. Bolstered by the support of Union Minière, Tshombe spun out the negotiations with the Adoula government throughout 1962. At one point the Adoula–Tshombe talks broke down completely. Tshombe could not have engaged in this long series of delays and evasions without the financial support of Union Minière and the refusal of the British and Belgian governments to back the UN economic sanctions.[22]

Union Minière's reaction to renewed UN pressure was to strengthen Tshombe's position. A new agreement concluded between the company and the Katanga Central Bank provided that the Union Minière would no longer wait until the sales of copper were completed before paying tax to Katanga; indeed, the company would supply funds to the Katanga Central Bank in convertible currency and accept repayment in Katangan francs. This gave Tshombe's financial resources a powerful boost for the continuing struggle with the central government. The UN recognized that the crux of the problem was the big mining companies,[23] and planned to break Tshombe's intransigence by attacking his financial support. The aim was to freeze Union Minière's assets and divert the taxes paid by the company from Katanga to the central government. The American government was in favour of this plan but the British and Belgian governments held back. The British government's reluctance was due, as *The Times* said, 'to the interests which Britain has in Katanga, particularly in the Union Minière and in some of the railways'.

Meanwhile, Union Minière and Tanganyika Concessions were supporting a vigorous lobbying campaign on behalf of Katangan secession. In America, New York-based Belgian publicist Michel Stuelens spent $140,000 in fifteen months promoting the Tshombe viewpoint for Union Minière.[24] In Belgium, Société Générale was the largest industrial and financial group; 30 per cent of its profits came from Union Minière, and it used all of its political muscle to influence Belgian government policy. The new Belgian foreign minister, Henri Spaak, was unable to achieve a public reversal of his country's Congolese policy because of Société Générale's campaign. In England the lobby was powerful and ambitious.* Mr Toby O'Brien of the E. D. O'Brien Organization, and a former head of Conservative Central Office publicity, represented both Union Minière and Tanganyika Concessions. Captain Waterhouse, the chairman of Tanganyika Concessions, and himself a former Conservative MP, was one of the key figures in the Rhodesia–Katanga lobby, which supported the interests of the white settlers in Central Africa.[25]

Although Union Minière was still giving its support to Tshombe, the Belgian directors of the company, if not the Elizabethville employees, could read the writing on the wall. The determination of the US and the UN to end Katangan secession was no longer in any doubt. Most important of all, the fighting in Katanga had caused production to cease in January and February 1962. Union Minière, anticipating a third and perhaps a final UN attack on Katanga, had sent its own negotiating team to Leopoldville for discussions with Prime Minister Cyrille Adoula.

*See above, page 182 and Table 16.

The main aim of Union Minière in the Congo was to preserve its investment; and in pursuing this aim, it adopted the various strategies that situations demanded. At independence, Union Minière was not prepared to trust control of its investment to the new Lumumba government and so promoted a smaller and more pliable political framework in Tshombe's State of Katanga. Throughout 1960 and 1961 this continued to be the prevailing view in the higher echelons of Union Minière. It was only at the beginning of 1962 that the company recognized that secession had aroused too powerful an opposition abroad.

Evidence for this interpretation of Union Minière's strategy comes from the actions of its sister company, the diamond-producing Forminière. Following Tshombe's declaration of independence, Albert Kalonji in Kasai Province had also seceded. Although Forminière and Union Minière were both controlled by Société Générale, the diamond-mining company did not go to such lengths to support Kalonji as Union Minière did to support Tshombe. This is because Forminière has interests in other parts of the Congo besides Kasai, while Union Minière's activities are largely confined to Katanga. There is also a powerful American stake in Forminière. Elizabethville, the centre of Union Minière's operations, had a large European population and is far from Leopoldville. Forminière's operations are closer to Leopoldville, and the European population in Kasai was very much smaller. Moreover, while the Northern Rhodesians could give substantial support to the Katanga secessionists, the Portuguese authorities in Angola were not in a position to offer similar support to Kasai.

In the light, as they say at shareholders' meetings, of these considerations it would have been possible for a prudent man, even having investments in both areas, and a seat on both boards, to consider that the arrangements which best suited his interests would be different in the two areas. Kalonji, in ending his secession, and Tshombe in maintaining his, both acted in a manner which is consistent with the hypothesis that they were working in concert with such prudent men and serving essentially the same interests in the different ways which fitted different situations.[26]

Despite Union Minière's change of policy it was not until January 1963 that the secession of Katanga ended, Tshombe retreated into exile, and Union Minière agreed once more to pay its taxes to the central government.

1963–6

The authority of the central government was still fragile. At the time of its appointment in 1961, the Adoula government had represented a genuine balance between the Lumumbist forces and the Leopoldville groups, but as time went on the Lumumbists grew more and more dissatisfied with Adoula. The crisis came in October 1964, when a state of emergency was declared in Leopoldville and a number of opposition members were arrested. Christopher Gbenye fled to Brazzaville and established the Committee of National Liberation, while Pierre Mulele's rebellion in Kwilu province spread to Orientale and Kivu provinces. The Congo seemed on the verge of disintegration once again.

Tshombe returned from exile in Spain and announced that he could restore national unity. President Kasavubu agreed to give him the chance. As Conor Cruise O'Brien put it:

> Political circles in Leopoldville purged, corrupted and intimidated, became more representative of opinions in boardrooms in Brussels, London, Paris and New York than of any real currents of opinion in the Congo. So Tshombe, the tried and tested friend of such boardrooms, became prime minister of the Congo.[27]

As a shrewd politician, Tshombe recognized that his most damaging political liability was his reputation as the friend of the mining companies. A public move against the companies, Tshombe reasoned, would put him in a much stronger position to deal with internal opposition. In November 1964 he issued a decree taking over the rights of the Belgian Chartered companies. Under the decree, the entire portfolio of the CSK was allocated to the government. The effect was to reduce the voting strength of the Société Générale and TANKS in Union Minière from 40 to less than 29 per cent. Correspondingly, the Congolese government's share rose from 24 to 36 per cent. In February 1965, Tshombe went to Brussels. After the negotiations, he returned to Leopoldville with 150 letters, authorizing him to collect the Congo's portfolio of shares and titles worth £120 million. In return for 17 per cent of the worldwide interests of Union Minière, Tshombe agreed that the Congolese government would not unilaterally alter existing arrangements with the company.

But Tshombe was unable to achieve the internal stability which he had promised. Fighting continued throughout 1965. The most powerful of the external influences in the Congo was still the US government, and their main interest in the Congo was stability. When Tshombe could no longer deliver this, he lost the vital support of the US. New presidential elections were due in January 1966. In October 1965 Kasavubu dismissed Tshombe and appointed Everiste Kimba as caretaker prime minister. But on 24 November Joseph Mobutu, Commander-in-Chief of the Congolese army, seized power and deposed both Kimba and Kasavubu.[28] He had held power for a brief period in 1960, but this time he was determined to hold it for much longer; he announced that he would stay in control for five years, after which there would be a presidential election.

The problems which had plagued the Congo since Independence, now exacerbated by the bitterness of the civil strife, remained unresolved. There was no sense of national unity; the country was riven by regional, ethnic and political divisions; and the central government had not been able to impose effective administrative control over the country. Finally, the country's most important mineral resource was still controlled by Union Minière in accordance with the requirements not of the Congolese people but of the overseas shareholders. Mobutu used the army to end the rebellions and curb secessionist tendencies. He then united the fractious Congolese ruling class behind his policy of 'authentification' and economic nationalism. In the furtherance of authentification, the Congo changed its name to Zaire, and Joseph-Désiré Mobutu became Mobutu-Sese Seko; while the policy of economic nationalism brought Mobutu into sharp conflict with Union Minière.

THE 'NATIONALIZATION' OF UNION MINIÈRE[29]

On 6 May 1966 it was reported from Brussels that Union Minière had decided to raise the price of copper. The company had not consulted the Congolese government before making the announcement. The Congolese cabinet responded by raising the export tax on copper from 17 to 30 per cent.* It was announced that as from 1 January 1967 all companies legally constituted in the Congo would have to move their headquarters there. Two weeks later, Mobutu announced that from 30 June all copper exports through Angola would be stopped. The aim, he said, was to increase the Congo's share of the revenue.

Union Minière was reluctant to comply with the government's request. According to Union Minière's chairman, M. Louis Wallef, a move to Kinshasa (ex-Leopoldville) would be 'fraught with great difficulties'. He feared higher taxes if the company's headquarters moved there. He announced that a new building would be constructed in Kinshasa to house Union Minière's administrative headquarters. Mobutu was not satisfied and ten days later issued the Bakajika Bill, which provided for the Congo to take back all the rights granted before independence over any part of its lands, forests, or mineral resources. The choice before Union Minière was whether to move to Kinshasa and be subject to higher taxes; or to remain in Brussels and risk losing its valuable mineral rights. The company, however, was in an immensely strong position, since the Congolese government was still heavily dependent on the revenue provided by the company's copper. The various taxes on Union Minière and its copper provided over half the government's revenue and more than 70 per cent of its foreign exchange earnings. Without this revenue, the business of the central government would soon grind to a halt.

Negotiations began between the company and the government, and by November it seemed that agreement in principle had been reached. Congolese radio announced that Union

---

*In this the Congolese were probably influenced by the successful Zambian export tax in 1966 which clawed back some of the profits accruing to the companies from copper prices on the London Metal Exchange.

Minière du Haut Katanga would cease to exist as from 1 January 1967 and would be replaced by a new company, the Union Minière du Congo, in which the government held 50 per cent of the shares. But Union Minière insisted that it should retain control of copper marketing, and the agreement collapsed. On 22 December Wallef repeated that Union Minière would not move its headquarters to Kinshasa. The Congolese government suspended all shipments of copper from the Congo and announced the formation of a new company to take over Union Minière's assets. The French newspaper *Le Monde* speculated that Mobutu might have already reached an agreement with other mining companies to participate in the new venture. This proved to be premature.

Mobutu's first strategy was to split off Tanganyika Concessions from the Belgian companies, by offering it a 15 per cent stake in the new company. This was equal to TANKS' stake in Union Minière. The Congolese government would hold 55 per cent of the shares, and the remaining 30 per cent would be offered to private investors either in the Congo or abroad. But the financial and personal links between the directors of TANKS, Union Minière, and Société Générale were too close for this manoeuvre to succeed, and on 30 December the board of Tanganyika Concessions predictably announced its refusal of Mobutu's offer. Mobutu expropriated Union Minière's Congolese assets. These assets were fed into a new company, in which the government had a 60 per cent share; the rest would be offered to the public. The new company was to be called the Société Générale Congolaise des Minerais (GEOCOMIN). The era of Union Minière du Haut Katanga in the Congo was now over, but the battle between Mobutu and the Belgian board of Union Minière had barely begun.

On 24 December Mobutu had accused the company of selling copper and other minerals clandestinely and of supporting Moise Tshombe. He also claimed the 4,000 million Belgian francs that the company had diverted from the central government during 1960, 1961 and 1962; demanded payment for the Congolese copper *en route* to the Belgian refinery; and sought repayment of the Congolese government's investment in Union

Minière's worldwide operations. Union Minière went on to the offensive, rejecting Mobutu's demands, cancelling the Congo government's 17 per cent stake in the company's overseas operations, and threatening legal action against anyone who bought Katangan copper. President Mobutu replied by threatening to expropriate all the Congolese assets of the Société Générale de Belgique. The Belgian Ambassador to the Congo intervened, and Mobutu announced that he would not confiscate Union Minière's assets but merely its investments in other Congolese companies. At the same time, he appointed President Kennedy's former aide, Ted Sorensen, and the French lawyer René Floriot as advisers.

The struggle took another twist, however, when Mobutu announced that all Belgian technicians whose continued presence was essential to the maintenance of copper production must give a year's notice before they left the Congo. Union Minière announced that 1,000 technicians had asked to leave and, notwithstanding its record in the Congo, coolly proclaimed that the Congolese were infringing the Declaration of Human Rights by not allowing the technicians to leave!

The Congolese mood was now militantly nationalist. On 22 January a crowd marched through Kinshasa with an enormous coffin containing the 'mortal remains of the Union Misère'. The final interment of these remains took place some 150 yards from the Belgian embassy. It proved, however, much harder to bury the company.

Mobutu's next move was to encourage the creation of an alternative grouping of financial interests who could keep the copper moving. The 40 per cent share of GEOCOMIN offered to the public remained unsubscribed, and the President asked the Banque Lambert of Brussels to organize a consortium. The Bank approached the Newmont Mining Corporation, Roan Selection Trust, and the Penarroya Company. As soon as wind of this move reached Union Minière, the company issued a strongly worded communiqué threatening legal action against anyone who acquired an interest in GEOCOMIN. The mining companies approached by Banque Lambert withdrew because the proposed

consortium 'could hardly hope to operate in the teeth of opposition from the Union Minière. Refining of the Congolese
copper without the Union Minière refinery at Hoboken would
be virtually impossible, as would marketing it without the
company's enormous worldwide selling operation.'[30] Union
Minière also threatened to withhold the map of the Katangan
subsoil, which provided the key to the mineral deposits of
all Katanga and had been composed over a period of sixty years
by the company. Ted Sorensen advised Mobutu to discuss compensation with Union Minière. Negotiations were restarted.

If Union Minière were to recover its position in the Congo, it
would have to do so in a new guise. Mobutu was publicly committed to the Company's removal, and the nationalism that the
struggle had aroused was running strong. When agreement was
finally reached in February 1967, Union Minière had in fact
disappeared, but Société Générale retained its powerful grip on
Katanga's copper. Instead of Union Minière, three firms which
were part of the Société Générale were to provide GEOCOMIN
with a number of services. These services would cover 'all the
data . . . required for the proper functioning of the company and
its development, for the employment of personnel and for the
mining, industrial and commercial management of the company'.[31] The Société Générale des Minerais, on whose board
sat M. Louis Wallef of Union Minière, would execute the service agreement and would also look after the marketing of
GEOCOMIN minerals. In the end, Mobutu had had to settle
with Union Minière and 'le petit club', as the Société Générale
group of directors was known as. He gave them a five-year
management contract while he cast around for alternatives.

ENTER LONRHO

Around the middle of 1968, close observers of the London Stock
Exchange noticed that the shares of Tanganyika Concessions
were rising sharply. They moved from 30s. to 40s. and reached
as high as 60s. apiece. Clearly something was disturbing the
corporate undergrowth. What was going on? Not for the first
time, the intruder ruffling the composure of mining company

boardrooms was Lonrho, the aggressive British conglomerate founded by Roland 'Tiny' Rowland. Lonrho had a plan to build a new railway across the Congo from Luluabourg to Banana on the Atlantic seaboard and cut out the long haul through Port Franqui. With this railway, all of the Congo's production could be exported without passing through Angola along the Benguela railway owned by Tanganyika Concessions. But Lonrho was not only seeking to secure the copper for its new railway. Rowland had his eyes on an even bigger prize. Throughout the sixties, Lonrho had tried to join the league of big mining companies.* Now Rowland saw a chance to achieve this ambition by winning the Union Minière contract.

One of the problems which had faced the earlier Banque Lambert consortium dominated by American companies was that the Belgian miners would have left the Congo. The Americans would then be faced with the problem of providing French-speaking replacements to maintain relations with Congolese miners. Lonrho had a solution to this problem:

> If some outsider had wanted to keep the Belgian miners at their places while ousting Union Minière, it would have seemed quite logical to operate through a Belgian company in which the miners would have confidence. They could then feel sure that the money was safely piling up at home. It would also need to be a company with Congo experience and good contacts in Kinshasa; a company more-over not afraid of taking on the club. If there was such a company, there was only one: Comminière.[32]

Comminière had been in the Congo since the beginning of the century, and the chairman, M. Martin Thèves, sat on Lonrho's board.

Lonrho attacked the Union Minière contract on several fronts. The first step was to win control of Tanganyika Concessions, and Lonrho began buying TANKS shares on the London Stock Exchange. The chairman of Comminière, M. Thèves, was a powerful shareholder in TANKS, and he was involved in a complicated dispute over a situation that had arisen in 1967 when

*See Chapter 12. See also Suzanne Cronje, Margaret Ling and Gillian Cronje, *Lonrho: Portrait of a Multinational*, Penguin Books, 1976.

TANKS had briefly held a majority shareholding in Union Minière. Thèves alleged that TANKS' action in giving up this control was improper, and he was seeking to have this action reversed. If Thèves succeeded in this, then TANKS would have control of Union Minière. If Lonrho had meanwhile bought enough shares in Tanganyika Concessions, Rowland would be able to switch the copper contract from the Benguela to the new Lonrho railway.

In Kinshasa, Thèves and Rowland lobbied for government approval of the new railway scheme. Since Congolese copper was transported in the ships of the Maritime Belge, which was controlled by Société Générale, it was clearly prudent to ensure alternative shipping facilities. The final element in Lonrho's complex scheme was the purchase of the Watergate Shipping Co., which was capable of carrying Congolese blister copper to Europe and Japan. The Lonrho scheme was a brilliantly imaginative idea, which would have met both Mobutu's desire to escape from the Belgian company and given Rowland his opportunity to join the big mining companies on an equal footing.

But Lonrho's careful jigsaw fell apart. Thèves failed in his attempt to reverse TANKS' action. Anglo American got wind of Lonrho's attempt to buy into Tanganyika Concessions and started buying shares on the London market to prevent the takeover. Lonrho had to drop out of the bidding; it lacked the financial strength to match Anglo American. Then Mobutu was upset by a premature leak in the London *Daily Telegraph*, that the railway deal with Lonrho was all sewn up, and broke off negotiations. The final blow came when a dispute broke out between Martin Thèves and Lonrho, coinciding with a massive cabinet reshuffle in the Congo. Lonrho was left without contacts in the Congolese government. Mobutu seized Lonrho's Congolese assets worth $20 million on the grounds that national economic security was threatened. He had, it seems, decided that the Lonrho deal was just a little too shaky. His ability to pay the army and the government bureaucracy, the twin bases of his regime, depended on the continuing flow of copper revenues. He could not afford to do without that income for long.

Mobutu had failed to find a way out of his dependence on Société Générale. Without an agreement to compensate Union Minière, the Congo could not raise from the World Bank the finance needed for various development projects. The only way out of the impasse that Mobutu could see was to sign a management contract with Société Générale. The contract ran for twenty-five years. Fifteen years of the contract were computed as compensation for the seized assets, and by 1994 Union Minière could expect to receive some £250 million. Previously Mobutu had indicated that the most he would pay in compensation was £80 million, and most observers had predicted a figure of £150 million. That Mobutu settled in the end for so much more showed the weakness of his position. He had explored all the possibilities open to him and could find no viable alternative to Société Générale.

The compensation payments worked out very favourably for the successor to Union Minière, Société Générale des Minerais, which was part of the Société Générale group. SGM was paid 6 per cent of the value of the price that Zaire's copper exports fetched on world markets. One per cent of this was to pay for the management and sales contract under which SGM provided technical assistance, planning and various other services and in return had exclusive rights to sell all Zaire's copper, cobalt and other metals. The remaining 5 per cent was 'compensation' for loss of Union Minière's Zairean copper assets. By 1973 SGM had received over 88 million zaires,* which was more than half of the book value of its assets.[33] The contract had only run seven years and it had another fifteen years to run. Moreover Zaire was planning to expand capacity to 600,000 tonnes in 1977.

As SGM's income soared on the back of high copper prices in 1974 it was clear that the agreement would have to be revised. In March 1974 it was agreed that Zaire would pay a total of 4,000 million Belgian francs in complete and final settlement of the compensation due to Union Minière.

*One Zaire = US $2·00 = £0·86 from 1961 to 1971. The Zaire is pegged to the dollar. The payments were: 1967, Z0·9m.; 1968, Z8·9m.; 1969, Z11·5m.; 1970, Z17·7m.; 1971, Z14·5m.; 1972 Z14·4m.; 1973, Z20·4m. (*African Development*, March 1974, p.27).

This was a very satisfactory result for Union Minière. Its main aim all along had been to preserve its investment. In 1967 the company had written off all its assets in Zaire, and thus gained complete exemption from Belgian income tax until 1974. The compensation was used to develop new mines and extend the company's operations in Canada, Australia, Spain and Mexico.[34]

Mobutu encouraged other international mining companies to invest in Zaire and so lessen his dependence on Société Générale. A consortium of Japanese companies formed the SODIMIZA company, which is mining six copper deposits at Musoshi. Another international consortium, led by Anglo's Charter Consolidated, formed the Société Minière de Tenke-Fungurume, to develop a massive high-grade copper-cobalt deposit there. Lonrho has also returned to Zaire. All its nationalized subsidiaries, with the exception of Comectrick which supplies electricity to Kinshasa, were handed back in May 1973. In 1975 it was announced that Lonrho would build the new railway from the Shaba copperbelt to Kinshasa.

A massive investment programme was launched by the government, financed largely by foreign borrowing; contractor finance was used for many projects and suppliers' credit helped to meet the trade deficit. The programme was rudely shattered by the collapse of the copper price and the closure of the Benguela railway due to the civil war in Angola. The budgetary deficit rose 60 per cent a year from Z107.4 million in 1973 to Z779.9 million in 1976, foreign debt soared from Z857 million in 1973 to Z2,800 million at the end of 1977. The interest alone was Z500 million. Not surprisingly the fissiparous tendencies of Zaire were again revealed as Katangan ex-gendarmes invaded Shaba from Angola. They retreated but returned in May 1978 and seized Kolwezi. Belgian and French troops with US logistical support were parachuted into the province. The insurgents once again retreated, but the damage had been done as the mines were closed for a considerable time due to the evacuation of expatriate mine personnel.

The Zaireanization policy of 1973 had already been reversed and now the US, West Germany, Libya and Canada as well as many international organizations including the IMF and the World Bank, granted Zaire loans to ease the country's chronic debt burden. Temporarily secure, a grateful Mobutu launched a 'national recovery plan' designed to encourage foreign investment.

THE MINING COMPANIES AND THE STATE IN ZAIRE

Zaire's encouragement of further foreign investment after the bitter clashes of the 1960s seems at first sight surprising, but the explanation lies in the symbiotic relationship of the state and the mining companies in Zaire.

The exploitation of Zaire by international capital distorted the country's social structure. Powerful foreign companies expropriated large areas of land and pauperized the peasantry, while their monopoly of commerce and industry blocked the emergence of a genuine national bourgeoisie in either the urban or rural areas. The prevalence of wages in kind restricted the growth of the domestic economy outside the company sector. But while the economy was closed to local participation, the limited immigration of whites to fill lower level administrative posts ensured the early Africanization of the government bureaucracy. These salaried employees were quick to awake to the importance of their position. They were urbanized, educated and working close to the white rulers in key sectors of the colonial system, albeit in subordinate positions. It was this salaried middle class whose political and economic aspirations progressively clarified as it took control of the nationalist movement and later the state apparatus.

As independence approached, the Belgians concluded agreements for the future organization of the country with the small Congolese political elite (the '*évolués*'). This small group of *évolués* ensured their own careers in governmental and parliamentary institutions. In the struggle for power, their main rivals were the lower-level officials who had always been prevented from rising in the administrative hierarchy by the presence of white officials. One estimate of the size of this group at independence is 162,000: of whom 112,000 were in the administration; 22,000 in the army; 8,000 in the police; and more than 20,000 in various forms of teaching.[35] The rivalry between the two groups – the *évolué* political superstars and the majority of clerks, soldiers and teachers unable to achieve promotion at independence because of the continuing presence of Belgian officials – broke out into the open with the soldiers' mutiny in July 1960.

The mutiny threatened to sweep away the politicians who had signed the pre-Independence agreements with the colonial authorities, providing for the majority of Belgians in the Congo to stay on in their posts under contract to the new independent government. The mutiny, the Belgian intervention, and Katangan secession forced the Congolese politicians to undertake an immediate and total Africanization of all functions hitherto assumed by whites, in the army and civil service. Thus in Leopoldville and the various political centres, there occurred a fusion of interests between the privileged elite and the clerks and soldiers.

They awarded themselves large wage increases and increased the number of available jobs in the state sector. Between Independence and the end of 1961, it was estimated that salaries in the army rose by 450 per cent; those of the politicians by 380 per cent; and those of the teachers by 96 per cent. Out of a total budget in 1962 of 17 milliard francs, 14 milliards went on salary payments.[36] But more significant was the increase in the number of provinces from six to twenty-one, plus the federal district of Leopoldville. Each of these provinces had a government of seven members, with its own administrative and political clientele and an assembly of about seven hundred members.

This process of Balkanization was of no benefit whatever to the populations themselves and merely entailed a tremendous increase in the cost of administration, without any improvement in services. For their part, foreign interests and enterprises encouraged this political and administrative inflation and the strengthening of the new class. . .[37]

This new class was caught in the contradiction between its role as a nationalist ruling class and its continuing dependence on the revenue provided by the mining companies. To the extent that the Congolese government was dependent on popular support, it could not move too far from expressing the views of the people. On the other hand, so long as it remained dependent on the mineral revenues, mining companies, and other foreign investors for its revenues, it could not move too far from a position that supported their interests. The various political groupings represented different solutions to this fundamental contradiction. Personal and tribal linkages made the situation more complex. Behind Kasavubu were those ready to cooperate fully with the external forces. Behind Lumumba and Gizenga, one section took tentative steps towards radical reforms, while Cyrille Adoula marshalled a majority seeking a compromise. And in Katanga, Tshombe represented the interests of the Belgians and Union Minière. For five years this divisiveness prevented the consolidation of the power of the new rulers. If stable leadership was to emerge, then it had to pay attention to the interests and demands of the Congolese bourgeoisie and unite it behind a strong national identity, with which the workers on the mines and the rural peasants could also identify.

It was Mobutu's achievement to recognize this fundamental fact and to use the army, the revenues by the copper-mining companies, and support from the USA to consolidate the ruling position of the petty bourgeoisie. The policy of 'authentification', with the new party created by Mobutu, the Mouvement Populaire de Révolution (MPR), strengthened the tight central control of the ruling elite. But the expanded state needed an expanding revenue to underpin it; and after Mobutu had established a firm grip on the country, he was in a position to renegotiate the terms of Zaire's insertion into the world capitalist economy. He did not seek to realign the dependent structures of the Zairean economy; merely to force the mining companies and others to accept the Zairean bourgeoisie as intermediaries between foreign investors and Zaire's rich natural resources. The battle with Union Minière in 1967 won this recognition. There is no fundamental objection to the continuing exploitation of Zaire by the mining companies, as long as the Zairean rulers get a sufficient share of the surplus generated by the mines.

In a petition presented by a group of soldiers during the mutiny in 1960, there was a prophecy that in the Congo

there will be two branches of Congolese independence. First there will be . . . the class of the great Congolese leaders and their white counsellors. These will benefit from all the advantages of the new independent state . . . a second dishonoured wing which will include the inferiors, the criers of 'vive l'indépendance' will be, and remain the servants of the first branch.[38]

In the years after Independence the ruling class of salaried officials and the armed forces benefited from its control of the state apparatus while the majority of the population living in the rural areas were neglected. Copper production was expanded to service the urbanized elite while the rural sector decayed. Internal wages and salaries rose by 20 per cent in 1970, a further 20 per cent in January 1971 and another 10 per cent in October that year. Meanwhile, according to the Banque du Zaire, 'the incomes of rural workers, peasants and agricultural companies have deteriorated . . . The result is that the agricultural sector is not ready to respond to the local growth in demand for agricultural products, especially foodstuffs. As a result there has been a growth in imports of agricultural products.'[39] Between 70 and 80 per cent of the population live by agriculture and are suffering a continual decline in their standard of living. By 1975 Zaire was spending 30 per cent of its foreign exchange on food imports; local foodstuffs were in short supply, while meat for the elite was imported by air from Rhodesia.[40] Kinshasa had become a byword for corruption and graft.[41] Mobutu had become one of the richest men in the world and when he travelled to Peking in 1973 *Newsweek* reported that his Belgian advisers travelled with him and even took their pet dogs with them![42] The continuing ascendancy of the elite is buttressed by the international mining companies and their metropolitan backers, but the heavy dependence on copper and the switchbacks of the world copper price ensures that the fundamental instability remained.

11 Liberia and the Mining Companies

In the first half of the twentieth century, Liberia was so dependent on the Firestone Rubber Company that the country was known as the 'Firestone Republic'. Now, in the second half of the century, apparently unheedful of its experience with Firestone, Liberia is giving up its rich mineral deposits to the mining companies with a profligacy unequalled anywhere in Africa.

The first indication of Liberia's rich iron-ore deposits came at the beginning of the century when ships passing along the northern coast of Liberia reported the erratic behaviour of their magnetic compasses. In 1930 a team of Dutch geologists found ore in the Bomi Hills, about forty-five miles from the Liberian capital of Monrovia. The American company US Steel investigated the site in 1938 and decided that, largely because of the lack of transport, the mine was not viable, despite the high grade of iron ore (Fe 66–68 per cent). But after the Second World War, when the US needed new sources of iron ore, it began to look to Liberia once again.

The US had always had a close relationship with Liberia. The country's political structure originates in the American missionary-sponsored 'back to Africa' movement of the nineteenth century. The first settlement for returned American slaves was established on the coast near the present site of Monrovia in 1822. In defending their claims to rule Liberia, the Americo-Liberian elite have faced the twin threats of tribal uprising and external intervention. Out of this need for solidarity emerged a single dominant party, the True Whig party, which has remained the vehicle of Americo-Liberian supremacy until the present day. Tribal resistance to Americo-Liberian rule continued well into the twentieth century. In 1915 a rebellion among the Kru people was put down with American military assistance.

Another rising was defeated in 1931–2. But a more serious threat to the supremacy of the Americo-Liberian elite has always come from their corrupt and inept financial management, which has frequently led to foreign intervention in the country's financial affairs. In 1871, to avoid financial breakdown, Liberia had raised a loan of £100,000 from London bankers; but the rate of interest was so high that by the time the bankers had deducted their interest charges in advance, there was less than £50,000 left. For a while the country was put into international receivership. In 1926 the Firestone Rubber Company signed a concession for one million acres at a rate of $0·04 cents per acre developed. Firestone brought 80,000 acres into production, to form the largest single rubber plantation in the world. In 1927, to pay off Liberia's existing debts, the government concluded the infamous loan agreement with a Firestone subsidiary, the Finance Corporation of America. Only half the loan, for up to $5 million over forty years at 7 per cent interest, was ever issued; but service charges and advisers' salaries cost $270,000 a year, which was 20 per cent of government revenues in 1928 and 50 per cent in 1931. Thus a loan intended to relieve the government of its previous indebtedness became a greater burden than the original debt. In 1943 the seal was set on American domination when the US dollar became the Liberian currency.

The following year President William Shadrack Tubman became President of Liberia and in his inauguration speech announced an 'Open Door' policy, to encourage the investment of foreign capital in Liberia. An American colonel, previously on service with the US army in Liberia, established the Liberian Mining Company with a concession to exploit the Bomi Hill deposits. At first Colonel Christie had difficulty raising funds, but in 1949 the Republic Steel Corporation of America agreed to put up some money, and the US Export-Import Bank followed with a $4 million loan. Development of the mine proceeded quickly, and the first shipment of ore passed along the company's railway through the port of Monrovia to the United States in June 1951.[1]

Between 1950 and 1968 more than fifty foreign companies invested over $800 million, mainly to exploit Liberia's rich mineral resources. There were five iron-ore concessions in Liberia (see Figure 10). Four large-scale open-cast mining operations were put into production. The fifth has yet to commence operations. Mining came to account for 32 per cent of the gross domestic product, over 70 per cent of exports, and approximately a third of government revenue. Liberia became the

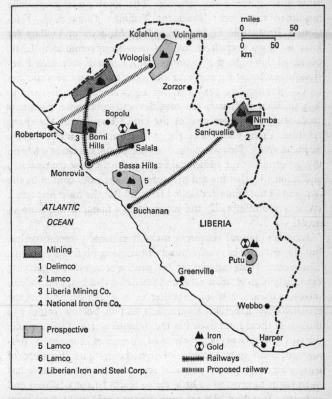

Fig. 10. The iron-ore mines and their export routes in Liberia
SOURCE: Adapted from *African Development*, July 1974, Liberian supplement, p. L.28, based on information from the Liberian Ministry of Lands and Mines.

largest iron-ore exporter in Africa and, after Sweden and Venezuela, the third largest in the world; exporting 20 million tons of iron ore a year.[2]

Government revenue has risen spectacularly since 1940, when it was only $800,000. By 1950 revenues had risen to $3·9 million, and in 1951 Tubman was able to repay the Firestone loan and make a new agreement with Firestone that added more than $7 million to government revenue. The local press graphically headlined the event: 'President Tubman Tears down Firestone's Irresistible Defence ... Bags Millions of Dollars for Liberia.' Two years later the first iron-ore revenue from LMC began to flow into the Treasury, and Tubman increased Firestone's tax from a meagre 12 per cent to a more realistic but hardly punitive 25 per cent. By 1960 revenues had risen to $33 million, with iron-ore royalties and rubber-tax payments accounting for 40 per cent of the total.[3] But despite the rising revenue, three years later the government ran into a severe financial crisis. This was caused in part by the demands made on the government for additional services by the new concessions, and in part by the upward pressure on wage rates caused by the demand of the mines for skilled labour.[4] But the most important cause was undoubtedly the government's financial mismanagement.

Liberia's natural resources make it extremely creditworthy; but the government came to rely heavily on prefinanced loans. These are loans advanced by private contractors carrying extremely high interest rates and financing charges, plus hidden interest charges of at least another 15 or 30 per cent.[5] That the creditworthy Liberian government had to borrow some $50 million at these rates indicates the dubious worth of the projects for which the money was borrowed. A team of economists commented, with only a touch of hyperbole: 'The literature of economic development provides few examples where more has been spent to provide so little for so few.'[6] In 1963 Liberia had to repay $86 million of short-term debt incurred in the three years 1959–62. The situation was made worse by Liberia's overwhelming dependence on iron and rubber exports.

Virtually all foreign concessions produce for export, and

foreign firms accounted for more than 80 per cent of all exports from Liberia. As a result of this heavy dependence on foreign trade, any fall in the price of iron ore or rubber causes immediate problems for the Liberian economy. The price of rubber fell from 37 cents a pound in 1960 to 26 cents a pound in 1963, and iron fell from $11·90 a ton to $7·03 per ton in the same period. Unable to meet the scheduled repayments, Liberia appealed to the International Monetary Fund for financial assistance to re-schedule the debts, and a programme of budgetary austerity was introduced in accordance with the IMF's usual policy.

But only four years later, Liberia ran into another financial crisis. The cause this time was the enormous outflow of resources to the mining companies. The authoritative business magazine *African Development* analysed the situation. Liberia, it said,

is a country exceptionally well endowed with natural resources, of iron ore as well as diamonds and other minerals, with good soil, a huge potential in forestry and a booming export trade, yet it is unable to make ends meet. In 1968 exports were worth $169 million while imports amounted to $108·5 million and yet there was a serious deficit in the balance of payments.

This was due partly to the high level of debt servicing, but

much more important was the outflow of cash to foreign interests. This totalled $93·6 million in 1968 or nearly a third of the GNP of the monetary sector of the economy ... Clearly the door is open wide – but much of what comes in also flows out.[7]

The most important of these foreign interests were the mining companies.

THE IRON-ORE CONCESSIONS

The iron-ore concession agreements were very generous to the operating companies. Most concessions had a life of seventy years (see Table 21). The agreements laid down no clear definitions of the procedures to be adopted for accounting and financial reporting, and government supervision was very lax.

Table 21: The principal mining concessions in Liberia, 1973

Company	Date of Agreement	Terms of Agreement (years)	Major Tax Provisions
Liberia Mining Co. (LMC)	1946	30	25% net profits to Govt 1952–9 35% „ „ „ „ 1960–8 50% „ „ „ „ 1969+
National Iron Ore Company (NIOC)	1958	80	Dividends on 50% of common stock purchased by government
Deutsche-Liberian Mining Co. (DELIMCO)	1958	70	50% of net profits to government
LAMCO Joint Venture(a) (Liberian American Swedish Minerals Co. & Bethlehem Steel Corp.)	1953/ 1960	70	Bethlehem Steel Corp. pays 50% of its net profit LAMCO pays 50 cents per ton royalty in 1963-4 and 50% of net profits thereafter
Liberian Iron & Steel Corporation (LISCO)	1967	70	Liberian government to receive 50% of net profits

Note: The Concession agreements were renegotiated by a Government Commission 1973–5 but the changes were not fundamental.

(a) LAMCO signed the original concession agreement in 1953. The expanded enterprise, known as the LAMCO Joint Venture, was formed in 1960.

Source: R. U. McLaughlin, *Foreign Investment and Development in Liberia*, Praeger, New York, 1966, p. 201, and *African Development*, July 1972.

A team of economists from Northwestern University summed up the situation: 'Most concessionaires are free to vary their tax liability within fairly wide limits without doing violence to either the letter of the law or their sense of business ethics.'[8] The economists calculated that the concession payments, including the company tax of $13·4 million, amounted to only 27 per cent of the mining company's net profit: while, at the time, the legal rate of taxation for concessions was 35 per cent.

This discrepancy is the result of a difference of about $10 million between declared and actual concession net profits, representing depletion, contingency, development and other before-tax reserve fund deductions made by foreign concessions and allowed to pass unexamined by the Liberian government.[9]

One reason for this laxity (and the generous length of the concession agreements) was the ease with which the concessionaires bought off government officials with stock options.

LIBERIAN MINING COMPANY (LMC)

Colonel Christie's company was the first iron-ore mine to come into operation and by 1970 had an annual production of about 4 million tons. The original agreement stipulated a royalty of five US cents per ton of ore: with the ore expected to fetch around $4 a ton. There was provision for payment of an excess royalty, to be calculated; but this proved to be inadequate when the price of iron ore rose rapidly to $15 per ton as a result of the Korean War, and LMC's profits were running at $10 per ton. Under government pressure LMC agreed to revise its agreement, and taxes rose on a sliding scale until in 1965 the government received 50 per cent of company profits. In that year LMC paid $3·75 million in taxes and another $600,000 in port dues, petrol and employees' taxes.[10] Although this made the LMC Liberia's largest taxpayer, the Liberian Treasury Department's supervision of LMC was somewhat lax. It is perhaps worth noting the fact that the Secretary of the Treasury was also a director of LMC. The company was given generous allowances for stripping, selling, and general expenses and contingencies. The contingency funds, for example, were built up from tax-deductible receipts, and the interest on the fund was also tax free. The level of tax payments is important because for LMC, as for most of the mining companies, this is the main linkage with the Liberian economy. The company generates little local wage employment or income. The mine employs only 2,700 workers, of whom 2,500 are Liberian; but 60 per cent of these are unskilled workers. The supervisory and managerial grades are largely filled with expatriates and non-Liberian Africans. The company has few links with the local economy as all its supplies come in by rail from the port of Monrovia and most of them are imported duty-free.

THE NATIONAL IRON ORE COMPANY (NIOC)

This company operates the Mano River concession, some thirty-six miles north of the Bomi Hills deposit. The original exploration work was carried out by the LMC, which waived its rights to the deposit under government pressure. In the 1957 Statement of Understanding between LMC and the government, LMC was offered a 15 per cent share of the equity of NIOC, free of all taxes both at source in NIOC and on receipt at LMC. The government took a 50 per cent stake in NIOC, and the remaining 35 per cent went to private Liberian investors under an interesting scheme. Colonel Christie (of LMC) offered to put up $80, interest free, to Liberians putting up $20 for each $100 of the NIOC equity. Christie was to be repaid his $80 out of dividends at a rate of half each year's dividends. A government commission allocated the stock by area and limited the number of shares which could be held by any one family, with the aim of ensuring wider participation and avoiding the concentration of holdings. Given the prevalence of corruption in the Liberian government, it was not surprising that the majority of the 1,600 shareholders were closely connected with members of the government and their families.

The company has a very low equity base in relation to the capital cost of the mine; it amounts to only $3·5 million, of which Christie and his associates put up some $1·2 million. The $40 million required to develop the mine was raised by loans from the First National City Bank of New York and the Export-Import Bank of Washington. Annual sales are around $20 million and gross profits around $13 million a year. After loan repayments, the government's share was estimated at a mere $1 million in 1965.[11] Colonel Christie and his associates get 15 per cent of the dividends tax free, plus the repayments on the loan to Liberian shareholders, also free of tax; freely remittable to the haven of their choice.

Production began in 1961 and has reached an annual rate of

approximately 5 million tons. But the mine has proved to be the least successful of all the Liberian iron-ore projects. Due to the erratic quality of the Mano river deposit, it is blended with the higher grade ore from Bomi Hills to assure the guaranteed grade necessary to meet contracts. The government's share of the revenue is small, due to the low equity base of the company. The only satisfied party may be Colonel Christie, who has been able to repatriate more of the LMC profits through the NIOC shareholder scheme.

THE LIBERIAN AMERICAN SWEDISH MINERALS COMPANY (LAMCO)

The LAMCO mine is the biggest iron-ore mine in Africa, producing some 4 million tons of ore for export in 1974. The massive Mount Nimba deposits are estimated at 250 million tons of high-grade haematite, grading 67 per cent iron content. To bring the mine into operation required a capital expenditure of $285 million, the construction of a new port at Buchanan, a 170-mile rail link from the mine to the port, and the first pelletization plant in Africa.

LAMCO has a complicated financial structure which is outlined in Figure 11. The original concession was owned by Edward Detweiler. Swedish iron interests led by Gränges A. G. bought the concession in 1956 through a Canadian-registered company, the Liberian Iron Ore Company, which four years later came to an agreement with Bethlehem Steel Corporation of America. The LAMCO Joint Venture was established in which Bethlehem took a 25 per cent stake and LAMCO 75 per cent. The Swedish syndicate owns 50 per cent of LAMCO and the Liberian government owns the other 50 per cent. The project is managed on behalf of the LAMCO Joint Venture by the Grangeberg Company of Sweden.

The financial arrangements, like those of the NIOC, show a high proportion of loan to equity capital. Since much of the ore was destined for the United States and Germany, LAMCO secured a $30 million loan from the Export-Import Bank, and a $52 million loan from the West German export-import bank,

Kreditanstalt für Wiederaufbau. The Swedish syndicate loaned LAMCO some $38 million, and a further $5·7 million loan was raised from the First National City Bank of New York. Bethlehem's entrance fee to the Joint Venture was a mere $4·5 million, which demonstrates the strong bargaining position enjoyed by

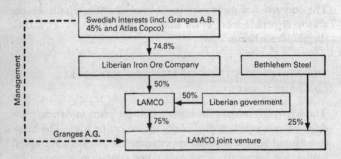

Fig. 11. The ownership of the LAMCO iron-ore mine

the major industrial consumers of African minerals.* A further $2 million was raised by the issue of 2 million shares in LAMCO; one million to the Liberian government and one million to the Swedish syndicate (LIOC). The rest of the capital expenditure was provided out of revenues. The mine's output goes to various steel producers in the industrialized world. Bethlehem is contracted to buy at least one quarter of the mine's output, up to a maximum of $2\frac{1}{2}$ million tons. German buyers have contracted for some 2 million tons annually until 1984; while French, Belgian and Italian interests have signed shorter contracts for a total of $1\frac{1}{2}$ million tons a year.

The company pays a small fixed annual rental of US 6 cents an acre on its concession, but the government's revenue comes mainly from its stake in LAMCO, giving it half of LAMCO's share of the net profits from the LAMCO Joint Venture. However this dividend received by the government is in lieu of any

* Shown also by the experience of the Selebi-Pikwe mine in Botswana: see Chapter 18.

royalties, export and import duties, or income taxes of any kind. In effect, the government has exempted LAMCO or any of its agents and sub-contractors from all tax liabilities in return for dividends. But because of the heavy reliance on loan finance by LAMCO, dividends are low. For the first ten years of the mine's operations, repayments of loans and interest charges together averaged more than $15 million a year. Not only were the dividends for distribution accordingly reduced, but as a condition of the Export-Import Bank loan, $25 million in profits had to be set aside in a special reserve fund. Other allowable deductions from gross profits include an equipment replacement allowance of $0·30 per ton. As LAMCO shipped 14 million tons in 1974, this is a sizeable allowance; especially since it is additional to the provisions for depreciation which are also tax deductible.

As in the other mining companies, the important technical and managerial posts are held by expatriates – in LAMCO's case, by Swedes. The company town of Yekepa is the second largest town in Liberia, but according to one visitor it is not so much a Liberian town as a Swedish town transplanted to Africa. It has 'Swedish shops, with Swedish sales girls, Swedish bankers and banks, Swedish schools and a Swedish arts centre'.[12] Liberians fill only the unskilled jobs, and most of the more skilled manual jobs are filled by Africans from the neighbouring states of Guinea, Senegal and Sierra Leone.[13] Nevertheless, LAMCO has hired a higher proportion of Liberian personnel for staff jobs than have the other iron-ore concessions. 'Undoubtedly a large proportion of LAMCO's Liberian staff has been hired on the basis of considerations other than merit.'[14] President Tubman's son was hired as a public relations consultant to LAMCO.

THE DEUTSCHE LIBERIAN MINING COMPANY
(DELIMCO)

The DELIMCO operation, which owns a seventy-year concession to mine iron ore in the Bong Hills, is a very clear example of vertical integration. Thirteen West German producers of pig iron banded together to form DELIMCO, and the directors of the company include Dr Hans-Günther Sohl, president of West Germany's biggest steel company, August Thyssen A.G. The government has a 50 per cent share in DELIMCO, but the mine is operated by the Bong Mining Company, which is owned 67·5 per cent by German and 32·5 per cent by Italian steel interests. Production in 1973 reached 5 million tons,[15] and the company's pelletizing plant is the largest in Africa.[16] DELIMCO, which is the biggest overseas venture of the German and Italian steel industries, with a capital investment of $150 million, was made possible, according to Dr Sohl himself, by the favourable investment climate that prevails in Liberia.[17]

The agreement with DELIMCO provides that the government will receive 50 per cent of the net profits as a tax rather than as dividends on the stock. Although the government has the right to elect five of the eleven members of DELIMCO's board of directors, the German shareholders have complete responsibility for financing and managing the company. Like LAMCO, DELIMCO is exempt from paying royalty or export tax, and also enjoys duty-free privileges on imports needed for construction and operation. Again like LAMCO, the company took out the necessary political insurance. The directors of Bong Mining Co. have included Stephen Tolbert,* brother of President Tolbert, who succeeded President Tubman, and Arthur Sherman, former head of the Liberian Bureau of National Resources, which was responsible for supervising mining operations. (It has now been superseded by the Ministry of Mines and Land.)

LIBERIAN IRON AND STEEL CORPORATION (LISCO)

The latest of the Liberian iron-ore concessions was granted in 1967 to LISCO and is controlled by the Liberian International American Corporation (LIAC), which is owned by Edward Detweiler, original holder of the LAMCO concession. The concession area is in the Wologosi range of hills, about 134 miles from the coast, where a new harbour will have to be constructed to take vessels of 150,000 tons capacity. When it gets under way,

*Until his death in a plane crash in April 1975.

the LISCO operation will be the largest in Liberia, requiring an investment of some $550 million. A down-turn in world iron-ore prices at the end of the sixties led to the withdrawal of the Japanese interests and delayed the whole project,[18] but in 1975 the project was revived as Amax joined the consortium, and production of 10 million tons of iron ore was projected for the early 1980s.[19]

MINING AND THE LIBERIAN ECONOMY

Mining in Liberia consists largely in scraping the tops off a series of iron mountains and shipping the ore along the companies' railways, down to the companies' ports, for speedy shipment to the companies' steel mills in Europe and America. It is a highly capital intensive transport operation, in which the most important investments are the scrapers, large trucks, railway rolling stock and port facilities. The mines are unconnected enclaves and have few linkages with the Liberian economy. They purchase few local goods and services (apart from fresh food), because each of the mines has its own railway lines to the most convenient port, along which it can easily import both the machinery for the mine and the consumer goods for the expatriate staff (see Figure 10). The mining industry's contribution to the employment sector of the Liberian economy is relatively small. Because of the capital intensive nature of the mines, the companies do not need to develop a skilled local labour force, and so most members of the workforce are unskilled. Moreover the companies employ a large number of expatriates, whose annual cost is as much as ten times that of their Liberian counterparts.[20]

The capital intensity of the mines, coupled with the government's loose supervision of the concession agreements, means that Liberia's share of the surplus generated by the mines is very low. A government study in 1967 established that the total value added by the Liberian iron-ore mines was over $84 million that year. In other words, the difference between the inputs and costs of the mining companies and the revenue from the sale of the iron ore was $84 million. Liberia's share of this figure, in the form of dividends, interest, wages, salaries, rent royalties, company tax and profit-sharing, came to less than $23 million.[21] Compared with the labour-intensive rubber plantations, which employ 24,000 workers, the iron-ore mines give a very much lower return to Liberia in wages, return on capital, and government revenue. 'The percentage of returns to Liberian factors of value added in rubber is about 65 per cent to 70 per cent as against about 30 per cent in the iron-ore industry.'[22]

GROWTH WITHOUT DEVELOPMENT

It was clear by the end of the 1960s that, despite its impressive economic growth, Liberia was not developing. A detailed study of the Liberian economy in the early sixties concluded:

Liberia's present material prosperity rests on extremely narrow social and economic foundations. Continued growth in aggregate income and government revenue is assured by prospective increases in the production of iron ore and rubber and in rising financial support from friendly foreign governments. The difficulty is that few Liberians will derive substantial benefits from continued expansion along present lines. Approximately half of Liberia's national income accrues directly to foreign households and business firms. Another quarter accrues directly or indirectly to a small and privileged group of Liberian households – probably no more than 3 per cent of the total – one or more members of which hold political office or salaried positions in government. The great mass of Liberian households and business firms – approximately 97 per cent – receive the remaining quarter of national income.[23]

In 1960 the total cash income of the tribal households, who make up 75 per cent of the working population, was $12 million, alongside the $35 million paid overseas in the same year by foreign companies operating in Liberia.[24] The government has invested comparatively little of these revenues in capital development projects. In fact during the early sixties, the country was the development disgrace of the continent. Government spending on cars, for example, was known to be nearly as large as total expenditure on schools and hospital facilities. Much of the government spending represented little more than a transfer of public funds to private purses. It was estimated that at least 15 per cent, and possibly as much as 35 per cent, of government expenditure took this form.[25] More than half the consumption expenditure in Liberia was accounted for by small groups of wealthy Americo-Liberians, government officials, politicians, landowners and businessmen – their income from the mines came from stock options and from additional government jobs – who do not generally invest their share of the national income productively; preferring to speculate in real estate, to invest overseas, or to import expensive consumer goods.

Since their arrival in the country, the Americo-Liberians have been intermediaries between the people and resources of Liberia and the external financial interests. The country is ruled by a small elite, who control the patronage of the government and the True Whig Party. Political solidarity is cemented by family ties (see Figure 12). For twenty-seven years, as managing director of their interests, President Tubman protected their position and enriched them beyond expectation, with the revenues provided by the foreign mining companies. The Americo-Liberians have kept a monopoly on economic activity in Liberia; leaving real control over most of the country's economy to foreigners. Expatriate professional managers run the mines, and Lebanese entrepreneurs run much of the country's trade and commerce, but both are in the country on sufferance and know it. The emergence of a genuine entrepreneurial Liberian middle class might threaten the political dominance of the True Whig leadership by challenging its inefficient economic management, corruption and lack of development.

Under President Tolbert, who succeeded President Tubman in 1971, some of the more obvious corruption has been tackled; tax collection has been more rigorously enforced, educational expenditure is increasing slowly, and more emphasis is being given to the rural areas and food production.[26] In 1973, the President's brother, Stephen Tolbert, as Minister of Finance announced that the iron-ore concession agreements were to be reviewed in the light of the government's policy of 'partnership' between foreign investors and Liberia.[27] But as the President categorically reasserted Liberia's open-door policy on a visit to

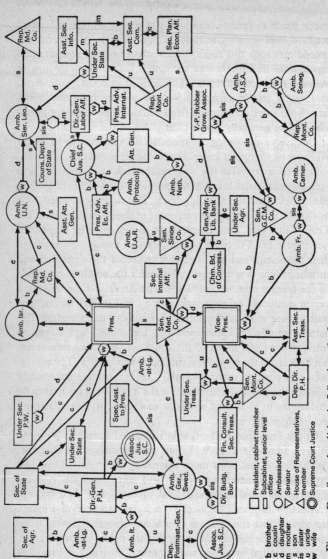

Fig. 12. Family and politics in Liberia 1967–8
SOURCE: J. Gus Liebenow, *Liberia: the Evolution of Privilege*, Cornell University Press, 1969, Chart 1, p. 139.

b brother
c cousin
d daughter
m mother
s son
sis sister
u uncle
w wife

☐ President, cabinet member
▭ Subcabinet, senior level officer
◯ Ambassador
▽ Senator
△ House of Representatives, member
◎ Supreme Court Justice

the DELIMCO mine in the Bong hills[28] and as Stephen Tolbert himself had extensive business interests, including the fast expanding Mesurado group of companies, few fundamental changes were expected.

And rightly, so it proved. Although the government's Commission on Concessions discussed many issues with the concessionaires, including debt-to-equity ratios, royalties and tax exemptions, the end result was a revision of agreements which were expected to increase government revenues by a mere $2·6 million.[29] But though in 1974 the iron-ore concessions accounted for 40 per cent of Liberia's gross domestic product, and 60 per cent of the country's exports, they accounted for only 12·9 per cent of government revenue.[30] The concession agreements remain among the most favourable in Africa, and Liberia was one of the few countries in the world still levying a fixed royalty which remained at 56 cents a ton when the price was $7·81 as it was in 1973 or $10·40 a ton as it was in 1974. The profits go, as ever, to the companies, and as Liberia shipped 25 million tons of iron ore in 1974 to the United States and to Europe, they are considerable. But after nearly 25 years of iron-ore mining in Liberia, the country still has no manufacturing industry based on iron and has to import all its steel. Since 1975 the world recession has led to a sharp fall in demand for iron ore and government income from mining was halved in 1977 to $14 million. In March 1977 the Liberian Mining Company closed down the Bomi Hill mine as reserves were exhausted.[31] When the other deposits are worked out, and the mining companies have moved on, one wonders if Liberia will have anything left apart from holes in the ground.

Part Three

**Mining Companies
in Africa Today**

12 The Major Mining Groups in Africa

Dependence is not the cause of Africa's underdevelopment; rather it is one facet of the totality of that underdevelopment. It is Africa's participation in the world capitalist economy, whose dominant units are the major international corporations, that causes and reproduces the continent's underdevelopment. In Part Three we examine the ways in which the international mining companies operate in Africa today, and explore the reasons why the aims, structures, and mode of operation of these companies produce dependence and underdevelopment.

In the mid-seventies, more than ten years after the majority of African states gained their political independence, economic independence from the mining companies remains as elusive as ever. At each stage in the mining process the technical, managerial and financial expertise of the mining companies, coupled with their economic and political power, ensures that the continent's mineral production remains firmly under company control, while the economic development of the host countries comes a long way down the list of priorities of these international groups.

In fact, although national and international statistics preserve the fiction, it is no longer true, if it ever was, that nations export their minerals to the world markets. When it is said that 'Liberia' is Africa's largest exporter of iron ore, this masks the reality that a small group of American and European steel producers are transferring iron ore from their mining subsidiaries in Liberia to their steel-making subsidiaries in America and Europe. Similarly, when 'Namibia' is described as having exported 1.69 million carats of diamonds in 1977, the reality is that one subsidiary of De Beers Consolidated (in this case Consolidated Diamond Mines) is transferring the diamonds it has mined to another De Beers subsidiary in London. It is therefore a real mystification to talk of country X or country Y exporting minerals, because these transfers are actually internal movements within international mining groups or transfers from a foreign mining company to a foreign mineral marketing group. These transfers should therefore be seen as part of the company economy rather than that of the host country.[1] To understand this fully, one must realize that the companies which control mining in Africa today are very different from their predecessors of a hundred years ago.

In the late nineteenth and early twentieth centuries, most of the mines in Africa were relatively small and controlled by British, French and Belgian companies operating in only one country. Today the majority of the mines in Africa are large and are controlled by giant international mining groups operating in all parts of the globe. The British, French and Belgian mining companies have lost their dominant position, as the decolonization of Africa allowed American and Japanese companies to expand their interests. The South African mining houses have expanded dramatically; but apart from the Anglo American Corporation, they have not developed their interests outside southern Africa. At the same time all major mining companies have taken care to reduce their reliance on individual African mines by developing new deposits in different parts of the world, particularly in Australia and Canada, financed by the profits from Africa. The companies can be broadly classified into three groups: the British and European mining companies; the North American and Japanese companies; and the South African mining houses. Table 22 lists the minerals and profits produced by twenty-one major international mining companies with significant operations in Africa in 1974, before the world recession began to bite.*

*A complete list of mines over 150,000 tons in Africa and the companies which control them is given in Appendix One.

Table 22: The major mining groups in Africa in 1974

	Mining group	Major investments in African minerals	Total assets	Total pre-tax profits 1974	Group assets in Africa Value	per cent	Group profits from Africa Value	per cent
British	Consolidated Gold Fields	South Africa: gold, tin, zinc, platinum Namibia: lead, zinc	£686m.	£66·24m.	£336·1m.	49	£36·9m.	46
	Selection Trust	South Africa: gold Namibia: copper, lead Ghana, Sierra Leone: diamonds	£145·8m.	9·8m.	£46·6m.	32	£23·3m.	16
	Rio Tinto Zinc	South Africa: copper, magnetite, vermiculite Namibia: uranium	£1,270·4m.	£279·1m.	£48·6m.	3·8	£47·0m.	16·8
	Lonrho	South Africa: platinum, coal Rhodesia: gold, copper Ghana: gold	£202·3m.	£46·5m.	n.a.	n.a.	£40·8m.	87·7
South African	Gold Fields of South Africa	South Africa: gold mines, tin, zinc Namibia: lead and zinc	R737·1m.	R38·3m.	R737·1m.	100	R38·3m.	100
	Union Corporation	South Africa: gold, platinum	R514·1m.	R42·83m.	R514·1m.	100	R42·83m.	100
	Barrand	South Africa: gold coal, chrome, lime, platinum	R563·5m.	R93·0m.	n.a.	95*	n.a.	95*

Table 22 – cont.

Mining group	Major investments in African minerals	Total assets	Total pre-tax profits 1974	Group assets in Africa Value	per cent	Group profits from Africa Value	per cent
Johannesburg Consolidated Investment	South Africa: gold, platinum, diamonds, antimony, copper, nickel	R370·6m.	R25·3m.	n.a.	80*	n.a.	80*
General Mining	South Africa: gold, coal, asbestos, chrome, uranium	R337·0m.	R34·5m.	R337·0m.	100	R34·5m.	100
Anglovaal	South Africa: gold, manganese, platinum, copper, antimony	R167·3m.	R35·5m.	R167·3m.	100	R167·3m.	100
Anglo American Group							
Anglo American Corporation	South Africa, Namibia, Zambia, Botswana, Rhodesia: gold, diamonds, copper, coal, uranium, nickel	R1,777·2m.	R83·86m.	R1,617·3m.	91	R77·99m.	93
De Beers Consolidated	South Africa, Namibia, Botswana, Lesotho, Angola, Tanzania: diamonds	R1,404·0m.	R312·9m.	n.a.	n.a.	R300·4m.	96
Charter Consolidated	South Africa: asbestos, diamonds, gold, Zambia, Mauritania: copper	£303·8m.	£27·94m.	£179·9m.	59·2	£17·97m.	64·3

Group	Company							
North American	Rand Selection Minerals and Resources Co	Same spread as Anglo Rhodesia : coal, nickel Zambia : copper						
	Amax	South Africa, Namibia, Botswana, Zambia: copper Namibia : lead Botswana : nickel	$1,767·8m.	$148·4m.	43·3	2·45	18·3	12·3
	Newmont	South Africa, Namibia: copper South Africa, Rhodesia: vanadium	$1,077·3m.	$113·6m.	n.a.	n.a.	$31·2	27·4
European	Imetal (Compagnie de Mokta)	Niger, Gabon, CAR: uranium Gabon : manganese Guinea : bauxite Malagasy: chrome	F2,855m.	F209m.	F142·75	5	F35·5	17
	Pechiney-Ugine-Kuhlmann	Niger, Gabon, CAR: uranium Gabon : manganese Cameroon : smelters	F13,545m.	F743m.	n.a.	n.a.	n.a.	n.a.

For Rand Selection Minerals and Resources Co: R1,31m. / $168·25m. | R48·1m. / $29·77m. | R1,206·1m. | 92·0 | R46·2m. | 96·0

Notes: All figures approximate, and refer to the whole mining group including its consolidated subsidiaries.

'Assets' are total assets as given in company reports.

Quoted investments are at market value at the end of company's financial year.

Unquoted investments are valued in company report.

n.a.: information not available. * Estimated.

Source: Company reports for 1974 calendar year, or 1974/5 financial year, according to company practice.

THE BRITISH COMPANIES*

Consolidated Gold Fields (CGF)

The oldest of the major British international mining companies, CGF, discovered and developed the Far West Rand gold fields. Today, CGF's 49-per-cent-owned associate, Gold Fields of South Africa, is a major South African finance house† that produced around 21 per cent of South Africa's annual gold production in 1977. Directly and indirectly the British company has a major interest in South Africa's zinc, platinum and tin production (see Table 23). CGF has an indirect stake in Tsumeb Mining and is prospecting for uranium around Rössing. Until 1977 CGF had a direct stake in the South West Africa Company which operates a lead and vanadium mine at Berg Aukas, employing one thousand Africans in conditions which were sharply criticized by the *Guardian* in 1974. This interest is now held via GFSA.

CGF's interests in southern Africa are still very important to the company's prosperity, but the emphasis has changed since the 1950s when the company set out on a worldwide expansion programme, using the massive profits from the South African gold mines to become a truly international group. In the mid-fifties South African interests accounted for 80 per cent of the company's profits, but by 1974 this percentage had fallen to 46. It fell still further to 26 per cent in 1977 as new ventures in (Australia (18 per cent of profits), North America (19 per cent) and the United Kingdom (37 per cent of profits) grew in importance.[2] The company has a reputation for shrewd share dealing on the London Stock Exchange, which generates a significant, if fluctuating, share of its annual profits.

Selection Trust Group

The Selection Trust group was founded in 1914 by an American mining engineer, A. Chester Beatty, who later became a natural-

*The British-based Charter Consolidated is considered together with other companies in the Anglo group.

†See below, pages 314–15 for more details.

ized Briton. Beatty built up substantial diamond interests in West Africa, in Sierra Leone and in Ghana. The company played an important role in the development of the Northern Rhodesian Copperbelt; but in the depression of the 1930s Beatty was forced to sell his shares in Rhodesian Selection Trust to the American Metal Company (now Amax). Subsequently there has been no direct link between Rhodesian Selection Trust (renamed Roan Selection Trust in 1965) and the Selection Trust group, except indirectly through Selection Trust's 8·6 per cent stake in the American company. In 1970, some 24 per cent of the group's assets were in Africa, and the continent produced some 49 per cent of the group's gross income. Through Amax, Selection Trust has indirect interests in the Zambian Copperbelt, the Botswana R S T copper-nickel mine and the Tsumeb lead and zinc mine in Namibia. Its interests in Central and Southern Africa are all minority financial investments; it does not manage any mines there. By contrast, Selection Trust used to manage both of its West African diamond companies in Ghana and Sierra Leone through Consolidated African Selection Trust, but in 1971 and 1972 the governments of Sierra Leone and Ghana took majority stakes in the mines, and this has hastened the group's diversification into Australia and Canada. In 1975 C A S T was merged with Selection Trust, which now concentrates its activities in Australia, Canada and South Africa, where it owns a large stake in an important new gold mine. By 1977 only 10 per cent of group assets were in Africa. Share-dealing produced 40 per cent of Selection Trust's earnings in 1973 and 25 per cent in 1974. Charter Consolidated* owned 27·25 per cent of Selection Trust in 1978.

Rio Tinto Zinc

Rio Tinto Zinc (R T Z) is the largest mining company in the United Kingdom.[3] The company is the product of a merger in 1962 between the Australian company, Consolidated Zinc, and Rio Tinto, a London company which owned a mine in Spain and had a small stake in the Northern Rhodesian Copperbelt. Under

* See below, page 317 for more details of Charter Consolidated.

Table 23: Major British mining companies and their investments in Africa, 1977

British company	Country	Local company	Percentage ownership	Managed by	Product	Remarks
Consolidated Gold Fields (a)	South Africa	Gold Fields of South Africa	49	GFSA		Mining finance house manages CGF interests in South Africa. Anglo American owns 11 per cent of GFSA
	South Africa	Doornfontein	10	GFSA	gold	GFSA 20 per cent
		East Driefontein	12	GFSA	gold	GFSA 29 per cent
		West Driefontein	11	GFSA	gold	GFSA 21 per cent
		Kloof	10	GFSA	gold	GFSA 30 per cent
		Deelkraal	25	GFSA	gold	GFSA 51 per cent
	South Africa	Waterval (Rustenburg) Platinum	100	CGF	gold	Holding Co. its 13 per cent stake in Rustenburg Platinum sold in 1977
Rio Tinto Zinc	South Africa	Palabora Mining Co.	38·9	RTZ	copper	48 per cent of South African production. Also vermiculite and magnetite
	Namibia	Rössing Uranium	46·5	RTZ	uranium	Production started in 1976
	Rhodesia	Rio Tinto Rhodesia (b)	90·0	RTZ Rhodesia	nickel	Operates Empress and Perseverance Mines
Selection Trust	South Africa	Vaal Reefs	10·0	Anglo	gold	
	South Africa	South Vaal Holdings	5·1	—	gold	New mine in development
	South Africa	UNISEL	35·4	Unicorp	gold	

Group	Country	Company	Direct interest (%)	Parent	Commodity	Notes
	South Africa	Palabora Mining	2·4	RTZ	copper	
	Namibia	Tsumeb Corp.	14·25		copper, lead	
	Sierra Leone	DIMINCO	49·0		diamonds	Held via Sierra Leone Selection Trust. Sierra Leone govt 51 per cent
	Ghana	Ghana Consolidated Diamonds	45·0	CAST	diamonds	Held via CAST
	UK	Consolidated African Selection Trust	100·0	CAST	—	Holds Ghanaian and Sierra Leone diamond interests
	USA	Amax	8·3	Amax	—	See Amax interests in Table 6
Lonrho	Ghana	Ashanti Gold Fields Corp. Ltd	45	—	gold	Ghana govt 55 per cent
	Rhodesia	Lonrho Investment Co.	100	Lonrho		
	Rhodesia	Nyaschere Copper (Private) Ltd	50	Lonrho	copper	35 per cent owned by R. ('Tiny') Rowland
	Rhodesia	Inyati Copper	100	Lonrho	copper	50 per cent owned by Coronation Syndicate; Bauxite prospect
	Malawi	Lonrho (Malawi) Ltd	100	Lonrho	coal	Inc. Tweefontein
	South Africa	Coronation Syndicate	66	Lonrho	coal	United collieries
	South Africa	Duiker Exploration Ltd	75	Lonrho		Falconbridge Nickel (25·0) Superior Oil (24·0)
	South Africa	Western Platinum	50	Lonrho	platinum	

Notes: (a) Direct interests only; for details of G F S A interests, see Table 29, pp. 306–13.
(b) Separately managed since Rhodesian U D I in 1965.
Source: Company reports for the financial year 1977.

the chairmanship of Sir Val Duncan,* the company grew spectacularly. Its assets jumped from £116·6 million in 1962 to £1,954 million in 1977. R T Z's stake in the Northern Rhodesian Copperbelt was quickly sold, and Duncan built up the company's assets in safer and more congenial investment climates: South Africa, Canada, Australia and New Guinea. R T Z is now a truly international group, specializing in massive operations where it believes its financial and large-scale project expertise give it an edge over competitors. Its mines are generally large-scale, low-grade and open-cast.

R T Z has three important mines in southern Africa. The Palabora Copper Mine in South Africa produces up to 110,000 tons of copper a year, about half of South Africa's total copper output, and was largely responsible for the dramatic expansion of South Africa's copper exports in the mid-sixties. Like R T Z's Bougainville mine, Palabora is one of the lowest cost copper producers in the world and extremely profitable. Indeed, though it accounted for a mere 7·7 per cent of the R T Z group's £905 million worth of assets, it produced a staggering 42 per cent of R T Z's profits in 1972. Its relative importance to the group has since declined, but over the five years 1966–71 Palabora made pre-tax profits of around £138 million. In the same period, it paid its African employees a mere £4·6 million. R T Z has been heavily criticized for low wages and conditions at Palabora.[4] R T Z Rhodesia has been separately managed since Rhodesia's UDI and has established the Empress nickel mine, which has been an important contributor to Rhodesia's booming mineral export earnings. R T Z's third project in Southern Africa is Rössing Uranium, an open-cast mine developed in Namibia in defiance of United Nations resolutions. From this unique low-grade orebody, which is visible from the air, the mine is supplying uranium to the British Nuclear Fuels Corporation on a £38 million seven-year contract from 1976 to 1982. Rössing is the United Kingdom's most important source of uranium, and the R T Z group also contracted to supply 43 per cent of Japan's uranium needs until 1985 from Canada and Rössing.[5] Total profits of the R T Z group from 1970 to 1974 before tax amounted

*He died in December 1975.

to £753·7 million and the group's African interests produced £161·9 million (or 21·5 per cent) of those profits. Due to the slump in copper prices RTZ's African investments contributed only 11·0 per cent of group profits in 1976 and a mere 6·92 per cent in 1977.

Lonrho

In 1959 Lonrho was the London and Rhodesian Mining company, a sleepy Rhodesian company registered in London with extensive interests in Rhodesian real estate. In that year, 'Tiny' Rowland became managing director and the company set out on a period of vertiginous growth, so that assets of £2·5 million and pre-tax profits of £158,000 in 1961 rocketed to £150·56 million and £19·3 million in 1972 and £325·63 million and £90·16 million in 1977. Lonrho has interests in 760 companies in forty-four countries.

This fast-growing and highly controversial conglomerate is not strictly speaking a mining company. Most of its activities are in agriculture (sugar, tea and cotton); secondary industries (brewing, printing); or service industries (car dealerships, newspapers). But we have included it in our survey of British mining companies because Lonrho has important mining interests in Ghana (gold), Rhodesia (copper) and South Africa (coal and platinum), and because Lonrho has ambitions to push its way into the first rank of international mining companies. Two major attempts in Zaire and Sierra Leone have failed,* but Rowland is an ambitious entrepreneur, and one of his future gambles may well come off.[6] At present the company is investigating a bauxite deposit in Malawi.

Lonrho has been heavily criticized in Africa because of its extensive interests in southern Africa, particularly the Rhodesian mines and oil pipeline. In 1974 the OAU Secretary-General, Nzo Ekankagi, signed a consultancy agreement with Lonrho. Criticism of this decision led to Ekankagi's resignation and the cancellation of the agreement. In Britain heavy criticism of Lonrho's business methods led to a spectacular boardroom row

*See Chapters 10 and 17.

in 1973, and the Department of Trade and Industry set up an inquiry into Lonrho.[7] Partly as a result of these criticisms Rowland began to rely more and more heavily on Arab money to buttress and expand his empire. His grandiose new strategy was to marry Western technology with Arab money and African resources to build an even larger and more profitable Lonrho. Not that Lonrho had being doing badly: its total pre-tax profits in 1970–74 were £125·65 million, and African mines provided approximately £32·45 million or 26·25 per cent of those profits. However, greatly increased investment in the UK and the decline in copper prices meant that the African mines only provided 12 per cent of Lonrho's total profits in 1977.

Other British companies with important mining interests in Africa include the London Tin Corporation, British Aluminium, British Steel, Turner and Newall, and the Commonwealth Development Corporation (see Table 24). But probably one of the most famous British companies in Africa did not itself manage a mine.

Tanganyika Concessions*

TANKS, as it was called, was founded in 1894 by Robert Williams. Despite its name Tanganyika Concessions has no interests in Tanganyika; its main interests are 17·6 per cent of Union Minière and 90 per cent of the Benguela Railway which carries Zambian and Zairean copper to the Angolan port of Lobito. In 1974 the railway carried 50 per cent of Zambia's imports and 52 per cent of its copper exports. It also carried 22 per cent of Zaire's copper exports. But in 1975 the railway was forced to close down as a result of the Angolan civil war. TANKS retains a 42 per cent interest in a timber company in Rhodesia, but is now registered in the Bahamas and its future is bound up with new ventures in North Sea oil and gas exploration, and new mines in Australia and Canada in partnership with Union Minière.

*In July 1977 the company was renamed Tanks Consolidated Investment.

288

Table 24: Some British mining interests in Africa, 1977

British Company	Country	Mining Company	Company Stake	Mineral Produced	Remarks
London Tin Corp.	Nigeria	Amalgamated Tin Mines	29·3%	Tin	83% of Nigerian output
British Aluminium*	Ghana	Ghana Bauxite Co.	45·0%	Bauxite	55% Ghana govt
	Guinea	Halco	10·0%	Bauxite	51% in mine, with Guinea govt 49%
British Steel	Mauritania	MIFERMA	9·5%	Iron ore	51% Mauritania govt
Turner & Newall	Swaziland	Havelock Asbestos	60·0%	Asbestos	40% Swazi govt
	Rhodesia	Rhodesian & General Asbestos Corp.	100·0%	Asbestos	Separate management since 1965 UDI
	South Africa	New Amianthus Mines	100·0%	Asbestos	
William Baird Ltd	Sierra Leone	Sierra Leone Dev. Co.	95·0%	Iron ore	Went into liquidation November 1975
Commonwealth Development Corp.	Swaziland	Swaziland Iron Ore Co.	5·7%	Iron ore	Anglo American 59%

* owned 48% by Reynolds Metals of USA
n.a. information not available.

EUROPEAN MINING COMPANIES

Union Minière was once the most notorious mining company in Africa but in 1969 its Zairean mining assets were nationalized and the company has used the compensation, revenue and tax benefits arising from the nationalization to develop new mines in Australia and Canada and to diversify into nuclear engineering and other industries in Belgium. Union Minière retains a few links with Africa, however. It still has a 5 per cent stake in the Anglo American Corporation's Wankie Colliery in Rhodesia, and Union Minière's Hoboken refinery in Belgium still refines Zairean copper.

Union Minière is part of the Société Générale de Belgique group, and compensation payments from Zaire pass through the group's copper-purchasing arm, the Société Générale des Minerais (SGM). The group's Zairean manganese and diamond interests are held largely through the Société d'Entreprise et d'Investissements (SIBEKA), which also owns a substantial part of the Angolan diamond company DIAMANG.

Probably the largest European mining company in Africa today is Pechiney-Ugine-Kuhlmann (PUK), the product of a 1971 merger between Pechiney, the leading French aluminium producer, and Ugine Kuhlmann, a German company. The group is the fourth largest aluminium producer in the world and manages a string of mines in West and Central Africa and Malagasy (see Table 25). The group also controls aluminium-fabricating plants in the Ivory Coast, Cameroun, Senegal, and Zaire.

Another major French mining group with extensive interests in Africa is the Rothschild's Imetal group, which was created after a major reorganization of the Société le Nickel company in 1974. The Imetal group consists of three major companies, Penarroya (58·5 per cent), le Nickel-SLN (50 per cent), and Mokta (93·8 per cent), which has extensive uranium interests in Africa. In 1974 only 5 per cent of the group's assets were in Africa, but they produced 17 per cent of the group's profits. But when the world nickel price collapsed in the wake of the world industrial recession, it was Imetal's African uranium mines

Table 25: Major French mining interests in Africa, 1977

Operating Company	Mineral	Mine	Country	Ownership				Remarks
				PUK %	MOKTA(a) %	CEA %	BRGM %	
Soc. d'Économie Mixte de FRIGUIA (COMINA)	Bauxite	FRIGUIA	Guinea	27				Guinea govt 49%
HALCO (Mining) Inc.	Bauxite	Boke	Guinea	10				Holds 51% of Cie Bauxite de Guinée which operates Boke
Cie Minière d'Andriamena (COMINA)	Chrome		Malagasy	65	5			Supplies 40% of PUK chrome
Soc. des Mines de l'Air (SOMAIR)	Uranium	Arlit	Niger	11·6*	24*	33·5		Niger govt 17%
Cie des Mines d'Uranium de Franceville (COMUF)	Uranium		Gabon	15·5*	39*	20		
Cie des Mines d'Uranium de Bakouma (URCA)	Uranium	Bakouma	CAR	2·5*	16·7*	n.a.		Alusuisse
Cie Minière d'Akouta (COMINAK)	Uranium		Niger		19·0*	44		31% by Niger, 25% by Japanese interests
Cie Minière de l'Ogooue (COMILOG)	Manganese	Moanda	Gabon		9·5*		22	US Steel 49%
Cie des Potasses du Congo (COMILOG)	Potash	St Paul	Congo				36	
Cie Sénégalaise des Phosphates de Taiba	Phosphate		Senegal				n.a.	
Syndicat des Bauxites du Cameroun (SEBACAU)	Bauxite		Cameroon	25·0			25·0	Cameroon 40%

Notes: *Interests held directly and indirectly through Compagnie Française des Minerais d'Uranium (PUK, 15% Mokta 57%) and Société Minière Pechiney-Mokta (PUK 50%, Mokta 50%).
(a) Part of Imetal group (Société le Nickel, Penarroya, Mokta).
(b) Niger Govt stake increased to 33%.
n.a. Information not available.

which kept it afloat. In 1976, only one per cent of the group's assets were in Africa but they produced 32·5 per cent of its total profits. In 1977 one per cent of assets produced a staggering 43 per cent of Imetal profits. In 1977 Amax had a 10·65 per cent stake in Imetal and H. F. Oppenheimer, another significant shareholder, was a director.

The French government has encouraged the development of uranium deposits in Gabon and Niger to provide the basis for its independent nuclear deterrent and nuclear power stations, and its Commissariat à l'Energie Atomique (CEA) has a substantial stake in uranium mines in Niger, Gabon and the Central African Empire. Through the Bureau de Recherches Géologiques et Minières (BRGM), the French government has extensive investments in manganese, potash and phosphates mines in former French colonies in Africa. The BRGM had a 23·9 per cent stake in the MIFERMA iron-ore mine in Mauritania until it was nationalized in 1975.

Although British, Belgian and French companies have long been mining in Africa they have been joined since the Second World War by other major European mining groups. Granges A.G., the largest Swedish iron ore and steel producer, leads a syndicate with a 37·5 per cent stake in the enormous LAMCO mine in Liberia, which Granges also manages. The Italian steel group FINSIDER has also invested in Liberia, in the DEL-IMCO mine with a group of major West German steel producers. Most important of these is Auguste Thyssen, which is also involved in a major new manganese mine to be developed at Tambao in Upper Volta. The giant Swiss aluminium company ALUSUISSE, has a 10 per cent stake in the FRIA bauxite complex in Guinea, and a fully owned subsidiary, the Sierra Leone Ore and Metal Company, mines bauxite for shipment to Europe. Alusuisse operates an aluminium smelter at Richards Bay in South Africa.

Colonial governments traditionally supported the mining companies in their mining endeavours, but sometimes they developed important mines themselves. In Angola the Portuguese state-owned Companhia Mineira do Lobita developed the massive Cassinga iron-ore mine, and in Spanish Sahara the

Fosfatos de Bu-Craa (FOSBUCRAA) high-grade phosphate mine was brought into production by the Spanish government agency Instituto Nacional de Industria. In 1975 Spanish Sahara became Western Sahara, and Spain ceded the country to Morocco and Mauritania. Spain retained a 35 per cent share in FOSBUCRAA, and the remaining 65 per cent is now held by the Moroccan state agency office Cherifien des Phosphates, the largest exporter of phosphates in the world.

NORTH AMERICAN MINING COMPANIES

The American mining groups with interests in Africa may be usefully divided into three groups: the base-metal mining companies with interests largely in southern Africa (Newmont Mining, Amax, Phelps Dodge and Falconbridge); the steel companies with interests mainly in West Africa (US Steel and Bethlehem Steel); and the aluminium companies in West Africa (ALCOA, Kaiser Aluminium, Reynolds, ALCAN, Olin Mathieson, Martin Marrietta) (see Table 26). Union Carbide, which does not come within these broad classifications, also has important interests in Africa.

Newmont Mining

In 1917, William Boyce Thompson organized an American syndicate which took a 25 per cent stake in Anglo American Corporation of South Africa. Later, when Thompson founded Newmont Mining Corporation* in 1921, he continued to invest in Africa.[8] Newmont took a 25 per cent stake in Rhoanglo but, strapped for cash, was unable to take up its options as Rhoanglo grew; and in 1953, when its stake had diminished to 5 per cent, Newmont sold out. But it was African minerals which provided Newmont with the resources to become an international mining company. In 1940 Newmont bought the O'Okiep copper mine in South Africa and the Tsumeb copper, lead and zinc mine in Namibia. Both mines, although presenting complex technical

*The Company was called Newmont Corporation until 1925, when 'Mining' was added.

Table 26: Major African mineral investments of North American companies, 1977

North American company	Country	Local company	Percentage ownership	Product	Remarks
Newmont	Namibia	Tsumeb Corporation	35·0	copper, lead	Held directly 29·6 per cent and indirectly 5·4 per cent (via O'Okiep) with Amax
	South Africa	O'Okiep Copper	57·5	copper	with Amax
	South Africa	Palabora Mining	28·6	copper	Managed by RTZ (38·9 per cent)
	South Africa	Highveld Steel & Vanadium	10·5	vanadium	Managed by Anglo (26·4 per cent)
Amax	Namibia	Tsumeb Corp.	29·6	copper, lead	with Newmont
	South Africa	O'Okiep Copper	17·3	copper	with Newmont
	Botswana	Botswana RST	29·8	copper, nickel	Anglo group 29·8 per cent, Botswana govt 15 per cent,
	Zambia	Roan Consolidated Mines	20·4	copper	Zambian govt 51 per cent, Anglo 12·25 per cent
Kaiser Aluminium	Ghana	Volta Aluminium Co. (VALCO)	90·0	aluminium	Smelter: see Reynolds Metals below, and also Chapter 16
Reynolds Aluminium	Ghana	BASCOL*	80·0	bauxite	Japanese interests 20 per cent
	Ghana	Volta Aluminium Co. (VALCO)	10·0	aluminium	Smelter: see Kaiser above, and Chapter 16
	Ghana	Ghana Bauxite Co.	45·0	bauxite	Held via British Aluminium (48 per cent owned)
	Guinea	FRIGUIA	10·0	bauxite	Held via British Aluminium (48 per cent owned)
Martin Marietta	Guinea	HALCO (Mining) Inc.	20·0	Bauxite	Holds 51 per cent of Cie Bauxite de Guinée mine and smelter at Boke
ALCOA	Guinea	HALCO (Mining) Inc.	27·0	bauxite	
ALCAN	Guinea	HALCO (Mining) Inc.	27·0	bauxite	
	Nigeria	Alcan Aluminium of Nigeria	72·8	aluminium	Fabricating plant
	Ghana	Ghana Aluminium Product	60·0	aluminium	Fabricating plant
	South Africa	Huletts Aluminium Co.	24·0	aluminium	Fabricating plant

* Project is at development stage only.

problems, proved extremely profitable; and in the early 1950s Newmont's income from Africa exceeded its income from North American sources. By 1971 O'Okiep and Tsumeb had paid out dividends of $530,698,000; of which Newmont's share was $215,762,000. This income was used partly to invest in the Palabora copper mine (28·6 per cent) and Anglo's Highveld Steel and Vanadium (10·4 per cent), but largely to finance new mines in Canada, Peru, Australia and Arizona. By 1973 three quarters of Newmont's income came from North America. But although only 12 per cent of the group's assets were in Africa, they produced a healthy 23 per cent of total profits, and of Newmont's total pre-tax profits from 1971 to 1974 of $315·9 million its African investments contributed $78·3 million or 24·8 per cent. Falling copper prices, however, led Tsumeb to cut back its development programme and led O'Okiep to declare a loss in 1975 and 1977.

Amax

The group's first investment in Africa was in 1930, when American Metal bought Chester Beatty's holdings in Rhodesian Selection Trust. As a result of the sale and share swop, Selection Trust acquired an 11·8 per cent stake in American Metal Corporation, and the American company gained a controlling 42 per cent stake in Rhodesian Selection Trust. Later, on the invitation of Newmont, American Metal took a 29·6 per cent stake in Tsumeb and a 17·3 per cent stake in O'Okiep. For a short while American Metal, which by this time had merged with Climax Molybdenum to become American Metal Climax (AMAX), had a 7·7 per cent stake in RTZ's Palabora mine, but this was sold in 1968. In 1970, Zambia acquired 50 per cent of RST's Zambian copper holdings. As a result, the Amax stake in the Zambian Copperbelt mines dropped from 40 to 20·4 per cent. RST became RST International, a wholly-owned subsidiary of Amax and responsible for the group's African interests and the Ametalco group of metal trading companies. In 1974 the American parent company changed its name to Amax, and today has a 29·8 per cent stake in the Botswana copper-nickel project at Selebi-Pikwe. Originally this was an RST (and hence Amax) project, but, because of Amax's reluctance to invest in Africa after the Zambian takeover, it is now controlled by Anglo. Amax total pre-tax profits from 1971 to 1974 were $371 million and its African investments contributed $50·8 million, or 13·7 per cent of the total,* but the industrial recession in the developed nations meant that all of Amax's African investments operated in 1977 at a loss. As a result of a series of takeovers and a consequent enlargement of Amax equity, Selection Trust's 11·8 per cent stake in Amax fell to 8·6 per cent in 1975.

Other American Mining Companies

Other important North American base-metal mining interests in Africa include Phelps Dodge's important Aggeneys copper deposit in Northern Cape being developed with GFSA, which is due to come on stream in 1980, and Falconbridge's Kilembe mine in Uganda, where production fell from an average of 16,000 tons to 10,000 tons in 1973 as a result of the political disturbances in that country, and was taken over by the Ugandan government in 1975.[9]

Aluminium Producers

The American aluminium companies have interests in major mining and smelting projects in Guinea and Ghana. In Guinea, the Boké bauxite mine is owned 49 per cent by the government of Guinea and 51 per cent by Halco consortium, which is owned by ALCAN, ALCOA, Martin Marrietta Aluminium,† and Pechiney. In Ghana, Kaiser Aluminium has a 90 per cent stake in the VALCO alumina smelter.‡ The other 10 per cent is held by Reynolds Metals. Kaiser and Japanese aluminium producers have formed the BASCOL consortium to investigate the Kibi bauxite deposits. ALCAN has fabricating plants in Ghana, Nigeria, and South Africa.

*But in the years 1966–70 Amax's African investments produced an average 32·4 per cent of the total pre-tax profits.

† Formerly Harvey Aluminium.   ‡ See Chapter 18.

Other North American companies with important interests in Africa include US Steel, which cooperated with Anglovaal to develop the Prieska copper mine in South Africa; Bethlehem Steel and Republic Steel, which both have substantial stakes in Liberian iron-ore production; and Union Carbide, the second largest chemical corporation in the United States. (See Table 27.) In Rhodesia, Union Carbide operates Rhodesian Chrome Mines, which accounts for more than 70 per cent of Rhodesia's chrome production. Union Carbide led the lobbying operation which lifted the US embargo on Rhodesian chrome in 1972.[10] Union Carbide partnered General Mining to build the Tubatse ferrochrome plant in South Africa, where the American company already controls three chrome mines including Ruighoek Chrome, in addition to manufacturing plants in various parts of Africa.

JAPANESE MINING COMPANIES

During the 1960s, Japanese trading companies signed long-term contracts with major iron-ore and copper mining companies throughout Africa, in order to secure metal supplies for Japan's rapid industrial expansion.* Zaire and Zambia are already major sources of copper, and Liberia of iron ore; and African minerals will become increasingly important in the 1970s. Japanese companies have taken minority stakes in several large projects, with the aim of getting a share in as many mining consortia as possible, to overcome their disadvantage compared with established French, Belgian, British and American corporations. The Nippon Mining Co. operates the Musoshi mine in Zaire and a small copper mine in Ethiopia. Sumitomo Metal Co. and Mitsubishi have a 76 per cent stake in Tin and Associated Minerals of Nigeria. Japanese aluminium producers have a 20 per cent stake in the BASCOL consortium in Ghana, and Japanese steel mills have investments in Liberian, Guinean, and Senegalese iron-ore projects, and in a manganese mine in Upper Volta. Japanese companies are searching for uranium in Gabon, Mauritania and Niger, and for chrome in Madagascar. Although investments

* See Chapter 5.

Table 27: Mineral investments in Africa by other North American mining groups, 1977

North American group	Country	Local company	Group ownership	Product	Remarks
Union Carbide	Ghana	African Manganese	45	manganese	Ghana govt. has 55 per cent stake
	Upper Volta	Tamboa Manganese Consortium*	7	manganese	Volta govt. 51 per cent, Auguste Thyssen (9 per cent) Tamco (30 per cent)
	Rhodesia	Rhodesia Chrome Mines	100	chrome	Major producer over 75 per cent of Rhodesian chrome
	South Africa	African Chrome Mines	100	chrome	
		Tubatse Ferrochrome	49	ferrochrome	with General Mining (51 per cent)
US Steel	Gabon	Cie Minière de l'Ogooue (COMILOG)	44	manganese	with French interests
	South Africa	Africa Triangle	30	development	Part of Anglovaal Group
		Prieska	46	copper	with Anglovaal (38 per cent)
		Atok Platinum	n.a.	platinum	with Anglovaal (59 per cent)†
		Zeerust Chrome	31	chrome	with Anglovaal
		Associated Manganese	20	manganese	
		Ferralloys	45	ferralloys	
Bethlehem Steel	Gabon	Somifer*	50	iron	
	Liberia	LAMCO Joint Venture	35	iron	Other shareholders Liberian govt. 37·5 per cent, Granges A.B. 37·5 per cent
	Sierra Leone	Sierra Rutile	85	rutile	with Nord Resources (15 per cent)

Company	Country	Operation	%	Minerals	Notes
Republic Steel Falconbridge Nickel	Liberia	Liberia Mining Co.	59.2	iron ore	
	Namibia	Oamites Mining Co.	74.9	copper, silver	
	Uganda	Kilembe Copper	72.8	copper	Taken over by Ugandan govt 1975
	South Africa	Western Platinum	25.0	platinum	with Lonrho (50 per cent) and Superior Oil (24 per cent)
Phelps Dodge	South Africa	Black Mt Mining	49	copper, lead	GFSA 51 per cent, Sold to Sumitomo Metals, and Mitsubishi Corp. (76 per cent) in 1974
Kennecott	Nigeria	Tin & Associated Minerals	49	columbium	
	South Africa	Union Platinum	n.a.	platinum	Holding Co. with interests in Rustenberg Platinum
	South Africa	Richards Bay Minerals	39.3	iron, titanium	Held through Quebec Iron & Titanium (66 per cent). RBM held with Union Corp. (25 per cent), IDC (25 per cent)
Nord Resources	Sierra Leone	Sierra Leone Rutile	15	rutile	with Bethlehem Steel (85 per cent)
	Namibia	Nord Mining & Exploration	100	tin, wolfram	
Foote Minerals	Rhodesia	Rhodesian Vanadium Corp.	100	vanadium	Sold to Rhoanglo in 1974

* Still being explored or developed.
† Sold to Rustenberg Platinum in 1977.
n.a. Information not available.

in Africa account for only just over 2 per cent of Japan's world investments, it is the most profitable area of Japanese foreign investment after West Asia.[11]

SOUTH AFRICAN MINING COMPANIES

The South African mining industry is dominated by the locally owned and managed mining finance houses which built their empires on the rich Witwatersrand gold field. There are a few smaller mining groups, such as the Messina group which mines copper in the Transvaal and Rhodesia, and there are some large state corporations including Iscor, which mines over 5 million tons of iron ore a year and produces over 76 per cent of South African steel, and Foskor, which produces phosphate. But the industry is dominated by the mining houses and the basis of their power remains the gold mines worked by cheap black labour.

The Gold Mines

Although foreign capital flowing from Europe built up the gold industry, today the industry is controlled by South African companies and investors. Table 28 shows the ownership of the gold mines in 1972, listed in order of gold output that year. Most foreign shareholdings are held through nominees. American shares are held through Barclays Bank GATR Depositary nominees, and Morgan Guaranty issues American Depositary Receipts against shares held by nominees. Other nominee companies are the French SICOVAM (Société Interprofessionelle pour la Compensation de Valeurs Mobilières) and the Belgian Soges SA. ASAIC is Charles Engelhard's American South African Investment Co. The date when each mine went into production is given in Table 28 in brackets after the name and shows that European investment is concentrated in the older, and American investment in the newer, mines.

The Chamber of Mines Today

The concentration and cooperation of the major mining groups in South Africa finds expression as ever in the Chamber of Mines. The close collaboration is based on the fact that the industry has always been able to sell unlimited quantities of gold at fixed or generally rising prices, so that there has been no need to limit output, or to compete over the price.[12] With the elimination of these two areas of competition, the industry works together to reduce costs, principally by eliminating competition among the companies for black mine labour, on which the industry depends.* But the significance of the Chamber of Mines as the representative and consultative body of the mining industry has grown, as the industry has become more concentrated, and the problems facing it more complex.[13] The Chamber acts as the coordinator of the industry's policy in such areas as state taxation, and legislation, and national monetary policy. About half the annual budget goes on research designed to reduce working costs in the gold mines. Another important function of the Chamber is the refining of all the gold produced in South Africa at its Rand Refinery in Germiston, outside Johannesburg. Finally, the Chamber acts as the industry's agent for the sale of gold to the Reserve Bank, which in turn sells the gold on the world market. There is close cooperation between the Reserve Bank and the Chamber over gold sales, and the Chamber distributes among the mines the income that is received from gold sold on the free market at prices above the official price. So at all stages in the mining, production and marketing of gold, the Chamber coordinates the industry's activities.

The ruling council of the Chamber is composed of the chairmen of the major mining finance houses: men like Harry Oppenheimer, Charles Barlow and Adriaan Louw. The President is usually appointed from among the members of the key Gold Producers Committee, which is the forum for discussion of all gold matters. Each mining house is represented on this seven-man committee, which meets once a fortnight. Its proceedings are secret. The central function of the Gold Producers Com-

*See Chapters 1, 2, 6, and 7 for the history of the Chamber of Mines.

Table 28: The ownership of the South African gold mines, 1972

Shareholdings — Percentage held

Mine	Managing house	Anglo Group (a)	Cons. Gold	GFSA Group	Union Corp.	Union Corp. Investments	Barvand	Anglovaal Group	JCI Group	General Mining/Sentrust	Asuc	Sicovam	Société Anonyme Soges	Barclays Bank	GATR	Others
West Driefontein (1952)	GFSA	14·2	12	20							3·3				9	
Western Holdings (1953)	Anglo	25			5							13			17	
Free State Geduld (1956)	Anglo	25									3·6	5			40	
Blyvooruitzicht (1942)	Barrand	15·6	7	11·9								11·6			11	
President Brand (1954)	GFSA	25		21·6			8				3	6·5	3		17	
Kloof (1968)	Anglovaal	13·3						8							27	
Harbeestonfontein (1955)	Gen. Min.	18·9						4								
Buffelsfontein (1957)	Anglo	25·2								17·5						
Western Deep Levels (1962)	Anglo	42·8		5·4								14·4			26	
Libanon (1949)	GFSA											5				
President Steyn (1954)	Anglo	36·4							5		3·2				21	
Vaal Reefs (1956)	Anglo	34·1	12	18·6							3·8				10·4	
Doornfontein (1953)	GFSA	6·6		5					5		10				11·5	
Harmony (1954)	Barrand	19					12					16				
Welkom (1951)	Anglo	30	10													
East Driefontein (1972)	GFSA	20		33·1											31	
Winkelhaak (1958)	Unicorp	8		3	20	22					8·6				2	
St Helena (1951)	Unicorp	20			22						5·2					
Ventersport (1939)	GFSA			13												
Kinross (1968)	Unicorp			3	37	28				5						

Mine (year)	Group							Holder
Bracken (1962)	Unicorp	5		35	27		18	13
Stilfontein (1952)	Gen. Min.			40	28			
Leslie (1962)	Unicorp	5			27		7	40 10
Loraine (1955)	Anglovaal	21			27			
Grootvlei (1938)	Unicorp	18	8					
Western Areas (1961)	JCI	12·1	17·5	3				12
Elsburg (1968)	JCI	12·3	34					5
Marievale (1939)	Unicorp		17					
East Daggafontein (1959)	Anglo	20	6					Unisec 10·8 per cent
ERPM (1894)	Barrand		7			63		
Vlakfontein (1942)	GFSA	12			15			
Durban Deep (1898)	Barand		9			25		24
SA Land (1938)	Anglo	15	26			25		10·5
South Roodepoort (1934)	Gen. Min.		6					
Virginia (1954) (b)	Anglovaal		6					Virginia-Merriespruit Inv. Trust 35 per cent; East Rand Cons. 6 per cent
Wit Nigel (1940)	Ind.							
West Rand Cons. (1908) (b)	Gen. Min.		11			16		
Merriespruit (1956) (b)	Barand		7			5		Virginia-Merriespruit Inv. Trust 22 per cent
Randfontein (1924)	JCI	19·7	32			20·6		
Zandpan (1964)	Anglovaal	19·7	4			17·7		

Notes: (a) 'Anglo Group' includes holdings through AMGOLD, the Anglo American Gold Investment Co, which is held, 70 per cent by the public, but controlled by Anglo.

(b) Virginia and Merriespruit were merged into Harmony Mines in 1973.

Source: Financial Mail supplement, 'Gold', Johannesburg, 17 November 1972, p. 84.

mittee, as indeed of the Chamber itself, is to determine the industry's labour recruitment policies and its wage rates. It also handles the delicate negotiations with the powerful white mine-workers' unions. Finally, research direction is handled by the Technical Advisory Committee, composed of the senior consulting engineers from each mining group. This committee reports to the Gold Producers Committee.

South African Mining Houses

There are seven major mining finance houses in South Africa today: Anglo American Corporation, Gold Fields of South Africa, Union Corporation, General Mining, Johannesburg Consolidated Investment, Barrand (successor to Rand Mines) and Anglovaal. They are all South African controlled, and in 1977 their assets amounted to over R7,300 million.* This understates the power of the mining groups as they *control* even greater assets. The Anglo group alone, for example, controls assets worth over R5,600 million. The finance houses are responsible for the bulk of South African platinum, vanadium, coal, asbestos, chrome, manganese, antimony, uranium, gold and diamond production. The three largest mining houses are Anglo American, General Mining,† and Gold Fields; between them they produced over 75 per cent of South Africa's gold‡ in 1977, which constituted more than three quarters of the Western world's gold production. In recent years the finance houses have moved some of their vast financial and managerial resources into other sectors of the South African economy, but they remain primarily mining companies, and together the seven groups account for a large proportion of African and world production of many important minerals. (See Table 29.) The mining houses represent by far the most powerful economic force in South Africa outside the state sector. They are all members of the Chamber of Mines, and interlocking directorships and share-

*Total assets as declared in the annual reports.

† Including Union Corporation.

‡ Total SA Production in 1977 was 687,773 kg, worth R2,809,106, approximately 70 per cent of world production.

holdings cement the close links between the companies. An example of this is Rustenburg Platinum, in which Anglo, JCI, GFSA, and General Mining all have an interest, but management is by JCI and control firmly in the hands of the Anglo group (see Figure 13). Mining houses may invest in a company

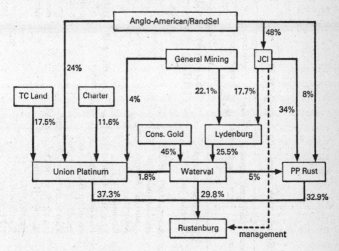

Fig. 13. The ownership of Rustenburg Platinum in 1975
SOURCE: *Financial Mail*, 27 March 1975, p. 1137. In 1976 a series of share swaps created a much simplified structure. A new holding company, Rustenburg Platinum Holding Co., is now the only vehicle for public participation, and is held JCI 28%, Anglo/RandSel 19·97%, General Mining 6·0%.

to generate income and capital appreciation and they will buy and sell stocks and shares in the light of the company's prospects, but if it is managed by the group then there will be a strategic stake which cannot be sold without endangering management control. The management of mines is an important source of income for mining houses. In 1974, for example, management fees and technical services accounted for R22 million of Anglo's R75 million profits.

Table 29: The major investments of the South African mining houses, 1977

Mining group	Category of investment	Percentage of assets (a)	Percentage of profits (a)	Companies managed by group (percentage owned) (b)	Important investments	Remarks
Anglo American Corporation	Mining financial			Rand Selection (100), Minorco (40)	GFSA (11) JCI (45)	Additional holdings by other group companies
	Investment vehicles			Amgold (48), Amcoal (49), Anamint (52), Amic (44), Amaprop (49), Austranglo (37), Amcan (29), Rhoanglo (17)		
	Gold	43	30	Free State Geduld (22·2), Free State Saaiplas (35·4), President Brand (31·0), President Steyn (36·6), Vaal Reefs (26·1), Welkom (29·7), Western Deeps (41·9), Western Holding (27·3) Developing: Elandsrand (72·7)	16 other gold mines	Held largely through AMGOLD, Anglo mines produce 40 per cent of South African production. Also 33 per cent of South African uranium
	Diamonds	19	32	De Beers (30)		Held 26 per cent via Anamint

Copper	1	ZCI (50) NCCM (Zambia) (49) Botswana RST (29·8)	1	RCM (Zambia) (12·25)	Held 49 per cent via Minorco
Platinum	2		1		
Coal	6	Arnot Colliery (100), Bank Colliery (100) Landau Colliery (100), Kriel (100) Wankie Colliery	8	Messina (10)	Held through AMCOAL. Anglo mines produce 33 per cent of SA output. Held via Rhoanglo
Other mining and oil	4	Rhodesian Nickel Corp. (34), Swaziland Iron Ore (59·4)	2	Hudson Bay Mining (29·5)	Canadian Co.
Industrial	17	Highveld Steel & Vanadium (26·4), LTA Ltd (31·3), Boart International	17		Held via AMIC
Property	1	Sorec Ltd (55)	1		
Finance	7	African Eagle Life (75)	8		Also Amaprop

Table 29 – cont.

Mining group	Category of investment	Percentage of assets (a)	Percentage of profits (a)	Companies managed by group (percentage owned) (b)	Important investments	Remarks
Gold Fields of South Africa	Mining financial			Gold Fields Mining & Dev. (100)		
	Gold and uranium	84·3	87·4	Doornfontein (20·1), East Driefontein (29), Kloof (29·9), Libanon (27), Venterspost (18), Vlakfontein (15), West Driefontein (20) Developing: Deelkraal (50)	10 other gold mines	GFSA mines produce 21 per cent of South African production
	Tin, zinc	5·2	4·2	Tin: Rooiberg Minerals (25), Union Tin (16), Zinc: Zinc Corporation of South Africa (39), South West Africa Co. (100)		Rooiberg is largest tin producer in SA Sole zinc producer in SA Held via Kiln Products
	Industrial and property	5·6	4·3			
	Finance	4·0	4·1			
Union Corporation	Mining financial			Geduld investment (100)		
	Investment vehicle			UC Investments (8·4)		

Gold	35·1	21·5	Bracken (23), Grootvlei (20·9), Kinross (33), Leslie (22), Marievale (16), St Helena (23), Winkelhaak (19)	10 per cent of South African production
			Developing: Unisel (29·6)	
Platinum	15·6	9·6	Impala Platinum (46·8)	30 per cent of South African production
Industrial	23·2	49·7	Sappi (5·0)	Over 50 per cent of South African paper
Finance/investment	15·8	14·8		
Property and other	10·3	4·4		
Barrand				
Mining financial			Transvaal Consolidated Land & Explor. (59), Rand Mines (100)	Holds gold, chrome and platinum interests
Gold and uranium Coal			Blyvooruicht, Durban Deep, ERPM, Harmony (17·2), Witbank Colliery (41)	
Chrome and platinum	32·7		Winterveld (59), Henry Gould (59), Milsell Chrome (59)	Largest chrome producer in South Africa
Other mining	11·6		Northern Lime (54)	Largest in South Africa
Industrial	55·7		Barlow's Tractor Div. (100)	Earth-moving equipment

Table 29 – cont.

Mining group	Category of investment	Percentage of profits (a)	Percentage of assets (a)	Companies managed by group (percentage owned) (b)	Important investments	Remarks
JCI	Mining financial	0·8	1·0	Free State Development & Investment Corp. ('Freddies') (49)		
	Gold	14·3	20·9	Western Areas (7·4) Randfontein (25·3)		
	Platinum	9·2	10·2	Rustenburg Platinum (28)		World's largest producer
	Diamonds	22·7	12·6		Diamond Purchasing & Trading Co. (16) Diamond Trading Co. (16) De Beers (1)	Part of the Central Selling Organization (see Chapter 16)
	Antimony	3·2	1·9	Consolidated Murchison (25·0)		World's largest producer
	Copper	2·2	6·1	Otjihase (52·5)	Palabora (4·5)	
	Nickel and coal	6·7	9·5	Shangani Mining (49)		Major Rhodesian nickel producer

General Mining						
	Industrial	26·1	20·6	Steel brite (64·0)	Argus Group (18) SA Breweries (19), Johnson Matthey (24)	Newspaper publishers / Leading precious metals refiner
	Mining financial	6·5	23·2	Sentrust Beperk (33·3)	Union Corporation (46·0)	Sentrust has 5·2 per cent interest in Union Corp.
	Gold	31·7	14·5	Buffelsfontein (8·3), S. Roodepoort (13·6), Stilfontein (17·8), W. Rand Consolidated (12·9)		8 per cent of South African gold
	Coal	15·2	3·9	Eleven mines incl. Trans Natal Coal Corp. (43·5)		40 per cent of South African coal
	Other mining	13·9	21·1	Asbestos: Msauli Asbestos (48), Gefco (49); Chrome: Chrome Mines of South Africa (64), Montrose; Fluorspar: Transvaal Mining & Finance (100); Uranium: produced as by-product by gold mines; Copper: Klein Aub	Rössing Uranium (6·8)	Group is largest South African chrome producer; 36 per cent of South African uranium production; New RTZ mine in Namibia; Namibian producer

Table 29 – cont.

Mining group	Category of investment	Percentage of assets (a)	Percentage of profits (a)	Companies managed by group (percentage owned) (b)	Important investments	Remarks
General Mining	Platinum	9·4	3·6	Platinum: Lydenburg platinum (22)		Holding co. with 8·4 per cent in Rustenburg Plat.
	Industrial	23·3	23·7	Tubatse ferrochrome (51) Alpha-Dunswart (84), Hall & Longmore (58)	Mainstraat Belegging (50), Trek Petroleum (23)	With US Steel (49) Steel interests
Anglovaal	Mining financial Investment vehicle			Africa Triangle (54)		With US Steel (30)
	Gold	22	21	Middle Witwatersrand (56) Hartbeestfontein (6·5), Lorraine (7·9)		

Manganese	60	Associated Manganese (27·9)	2nd South African producer
Platinum	25	Atok Platinum (46·7)	Sold to Rustenburg (1977)
Copper	17	Prieska (50·2)	With US Steel (46·2)
Antimony	1	Ferralloys (1)	Consolidated Murchison (7·9)
Industrial Finance and investment	42	AT Industries (59)	
	2	Anglo Transvaal Finance (100)	

(a) Totals may not always equal 100 per cent because of rounding.

(b) Among the mining houses of South Africa, the term 'group' usually has a wider meaning than the statutory definition of a parent company and its subsidiaries, and includes associated companies as well.

Johannesburg Consolidated Investment (JCI)

JCI was formed in 1889 by Barney Barnato and was administered from London until 1963. It still has an important investment in De Beers and other Anglo diamond companies but its most important investments are Rustenburg Platinum, the largest platinum producer in the world, and Consolidated Murchison, the world's largest antimony producer. It has some gold and coal interests and is developing a new copper mine in South Africa and a nickel mine in Rhodesia.[14] The Anglo group has a 50 per cent share in JCI.

Barlow Rand Limited (Barrand)

Rand Mines was formed by Alfred Beit in 1892, but in 1971 it was taken over, with the help of Anglo (then the largest shareholder in Rand Mines), by Barlows, a fast-growing industrial conglomerate. Rand Mines became a wholly-owned subsidiary, and its industrial interests were absorbed into other divisions of Barlows. Rand Mines has extensive gold interests, including Harmony Gold, which is one of the largest gold mines in the world.[15] The group is one of the largest producers of chrome ore in the Republic, and also operates seven collieries. Barlow's wide-ranging industrial interests made it the largest industrial company in South Africa in 1975.*

Gold Fields of South Africa

Gold Fields of South Africa is 49 per cent owned by the British Consolidated Gold Fields group founded by Cecil Rhodes.[16] It produced 21 per cent of South Africa's gold in 1977: controlling seven major gold mines concentrated in the West Wits line† and including West Driefontein, the largest and most profitable gold mine in the world. The group is generally considered the most conservative of the South African mining houses and has resisted

---

*Ranked by turnover, profits and market capitalization, although it ranked second to South African Breweries if measured by total assets.

† See Figure 4.

initiatives to improve the pay of black mineworkers. Of all the mining houses GFSA is the most heavily committed to gold, but it has several other metal-mining interests; the most important of which are the South West Africa Co., which mines zinc and vanadium, and the Zinc Corporation of South Africa, which has the only electrolytic zinc refinery in South Africa. Anglo American holds 11 per cent of GFSA.

General Mining

The present structure of General Mining was created in 1963 by Anglo American (14 per cent) and Federale Mynbou (44 per cent) and is the only Afrikaner-controlled mining house.[17] The group's five gold mines produce 8 per cent of South Africa's gold and 25 per cent of the uranium output. It has extensive coal, metal and mineral interests, including the world's largest blue asbestos mine, the Chrome Mines of South Africa and Montrose chrome mines. The group's steel interests are held through Alpha-Dunswart Beleggings and Mainstraat Beleggings (with Anglo). Since 1975 it has had a controlling stake in Union Corporation, and as a result it is now the second biggest mining house in South Africa.

Union Corporation

Union Corporation was established in 1897, and played a leading role in the development of the East Rand and Orange Free State gold fields, as well as discovering the Evander field. Today Union Corporation administers seven gold mines, producing about 10 per cent of the Western world's output of gold. It has the reputation of being one of the most efficient of the gold-mining groups. Its other major investments include Impala Platinum, which is the second largest producer in the world, and extensive pulp, packaging and paper-making interests. It also owns a beach-sand mining company in Australia and a Mexican mining company.

In 1974 Barlows made a bid for Union Corporation but withdrew the offer when Gold Fields entered with a counter-bid.

Then General Mining made an offer for Union Corporation. After an epic takeover battle, Gold Fields' bid lapsed, to leave General Mining and several other Afrikaner financial institutions with 30 per cent of Union Corporation. Charter Consolidated, Anglo's London-based international mining house, holds 10 per cent of Union Corporation. In 1976 General Mining increased its shareholding to 50 per cent.

Anglovaal

Anglovaal was founded in 1933. It is the smallest of the South African mining houses and has extensive industrial interests. It controls four gold mines, and is South Africa's largest manganese producer. It also has a substantial stake in the Consolidated Murchison antimony mine, and at Prieska in Northern Cape it has developed a major new copper mine with US Steel. It sold the small Atok platinum mine to Rustenburg in 1977.

Anglo American Corporation

The largest of the South African mining houses and the only one with substantial interests outside southern Africa is the Anglo American Corporation. Ernest Oppenheimer built the Corporation on a foundation of diamonds and gold; and since 1958 the Anglo group's assets have comfortably exceeded the combined resources of all the other South African mining houses. In the last fifteen years Harry Oppenheimer has built Anglo into a major international company. It is the biggest mining company in Africa; and although its complex structure makes it difficult to establish the exact size of the group, it is generally reckoned to be one of the twenty-five largest corporations in the world.[18]

The Anglo group controls more than 300 mining, banking, insurance, brewing, building, engineering, investment, and trading companies. One of the group companies, De Beers Consolidated, is the world's largest gem diamond producer and controls the world diamond trade. Either directly, or through its core companies and their subsidiaries, the group has interests in Angola, Botswana, Tanzania, Kenya, Mauritania, Mozambique,

Namibia, Nigeria, Rhodesia, Sierra Leone, Swaziland, Zaire and Zambia. At the centre of the group are three 'core' companies, Anglo American, De Beers Consolidated and Charter Consolidated, and the finance house, Minorco. These companies control a series of investment holding companies like Amgold, Amcoal, Amaprop, Rhoanglo, Amcan, Amic and Anamint.*

De Beers Consolidated

The diamond monopoly established by Sir Ernest Oppenheimer through De Beers and the Diamond Corporation remains as profitable and powerful as ever.† It is less often realized that De Beers has a large portfolio of industrial interests in South Africa, which has been built up to counterbalance its heavy dependence on diamonds. In the 1950s De Beers invested heavily in Anglo's Orange Free State gold mines and today has substantial investments in Anglo American 33 per cent, in the Anglo American Industrial Corporation (Amic) 12 per cent, Anglo American Property Investments (Amaprop) 19 per cent, Barlow Rand, JCI, South African Breweries, Highveld Steel and Mondi Paper. De Beers also has a 42·5 per cent interest in the South African chemical and explosives monopoly, African Explosives and Chemical Industries, whose other main shareholder is the British company Imperial Chemical Industries (42·5 per cent). Investments outside the diamond industry now account for about 30 per cent of De Beers' annual profits.

Charter Consolidated

The main vehicle for the Anglo group's international operations in the sixties was the London-registered Charter Consolidated, created in 1965 by Harry Oppenheimer out of a rag-bag of assorted companies, including the British South Africa Company, the Central Mining and Investment Corporation (whose chairman was Charles Engelhard), and Consolidated Mines

* See Chapter 19 for a fuller description of the controlling mechanisms of the Anglo empire.
† See Chapter 17.

Selection (with which Anglo had been associated since 1917). The aim of Anglo was that

Charter Consolidated would ease the penetration of areas where Anglo American's direct South African connections could be embarrassing and would improve the possibility of support from bodies such as the World Bank.[19]

After the merger, Oppenheimer moved swiftly to broaden the base of the new company and to spearhead Anglo's move into mining outside southern Africa. Charter invested in mining projects in Britain, Canada, Malaysia and Mauritania; in British and French industry; and in Australian merchant banking. Charter has major investments in several Anglo group companies: it holds 33·5 per cent of Rhodesian Anglo American (Rhoanglo); 24·8 per cent of Amcan (Anglo's Canadian Investment company); 20 per cent of Minorco; 15 per cent of Austranglo; 10 per cent of Anamint and 10 per cent of Anglo American itself. Charter is also the largest shareholder in Selection Trust (25·8 per cent) and has investments in Union Corporation (10 per cent), Rio Tinto Zinc, and Société le Nickel. In England, together with I C I, Charter is mining potash in North Yorkshire. Other mining interests are in Malaysian tin mining and a tin and wolfram mine in Portugal; and it controls the Cape Asbestos group of companies in South Africa and Britain.

In the seventies Charter's African mining ventures have run into difficulties and its usefulness as the focal point of Anglo's overseas empire was restricted by the weakness of sterling, Britain's continuing balance of payments problems and restraints on the free movement of capital. In Mauritania, Charter had a 53·5 per cent share of Somima mining copper on the edge of the Sahara. After several years of disastrous losses, the Mauritanian government bought out Charter's stake in May 1975. In Zaire Charter led an international consortium developing a massive high-grade (6 per cent) copper deposit in Shaba province. But in 1976 the project was shelved because of rising costs, political uncertainty in neighbouring Angola and the low price of copper, and it looked as if Charter's place in the Anglo Group might be superseded by Minorco.

Minorco and Rand Selection

In the early seventies, the two major finance investment houses of the Anglo group were the Mineral Resources Corporation (Minorco) and Rand Selection Corporation. They were primarily investment vehicles that did not have any in-house management or technical staffs. Minorco was created in the aftermath of the Zambian takeover of Anglo's copper interests in 1970. The group's Zambian holding company, Zamanglo, was transferred to Bermuda, and Anglo used the compensation paid by the Zambian government to create a major new international mining finance house. The various Engelhard metal refining and processing interests, previously held through a private Luxembourg company, were then injected into Minorco, which is planned as a major vehicle of Anglo's global expansion in the next few years.

Rand Selection was reorganized by Anglo in 1961 to attract and channel foreign investment funds into the Anglo group. It has the right to participate up to 30 per cent in any new Anglo venture. The value of its investments has grown from R46 million in 1961 to R693·5 million in 1974. In March 1974 it made a spectacular and successful bid for the giant South African property and insurance group, Schlesingers. Then, in 1977, Anglo merged with Rand Selection. According to the offer documents this put Anglo 'in an even more advantageous position to compete both locally and internationally for new business'. Taken with De Beers' record profits of R623 million, this restructuring of the group's assets emphasized once more that the Anglo group is the most formidable concentration of economic power in Africa.

13 The Structure of International Mining Companies

The internationalization of the mining companies in the wake of the second industrial revolution has changed the structure and decision-making organization of the companies. In their early days, operating largely in only one country, most mining companies were controlled by one man – usually the domineering entrepreneurs who founded the companies. Cecil Rhodes who controlled Consolidated Gold Fields and De Beers; Barney Barnato at Johannesburg Consolidated Investment, Ernest Oppenheimer at Anglo American, Chester Beatty at Selection Trust, and William Boyce Thompson at Newmont Mining made most decisions single-handed. Subsequent chairmen were often equally powerful commanders who used the same methods: Solly Joel at JCI, or Fred Searls at Newmont. With such personal control the company structure was somewhat sketchy, with information flows and decisions centred on the chairman. The result was often that key men were excluded and complained, as did the local secretary of Consolidated Gold Fields, that they 'never knew what the hell was going on'.[1] While the companies were small, these problems were not too serious; but as the company grew, the organization had to change.

There are still some smaller international mining companies which remain firmly under the control of a flamboyant managing director. Lonrho is a vivid example of this. It reflects the personality and character of Tiny Rowland, who in ten years built up a company with assets of £2·5 million and profits of £158,000 into a mining, brewing, sugar and motor dealing conglomerate with assets of £117 million and profits of £16 million, and interests in over 300 companies in 20 countries. Yet despite the size of the Lonrho empire, there was no organizational structure to compare with those of rival mining houses.

The management of the company has been astonishingly loose and informal. The headquarters, an unimposing set of offices in London's Cheapside, contains no more than 80 people, including clerks and typists. There is no formal corporate planning set-up to control an amorphous collection of more than 300 companies, the finance department has a senior staff of eight and until about 1967 Rowland himself was rarely to be found in London. 'I found it extremely difficult to discover what was going on. Tiny is the only man who knew the whole picture,' said one senior director. To a very large extent the Lonrho board have been content to let the profits roll in and to let Tiny get on with the job.[2]

It was largely Rowland's unwillingness to set up an adequate and professional management structure that led to the liquidity crisis of 1972 and the spectacular boardroom row of 1973.*

Generally, however, the widening spread of company operations and increasing technological complexity has led to the development of a more formal structure, in which the power of the mining company chairmen is more circumscribed. D. A. B. Watson, chairman of JCI through the 1960s, described the company's earlier structure as authoritarian; but 'We have made efforts to decentralize and at this point we have a team that is capable of running the company without constant reference to the top brass.'[3] In the late fifties and early sixties three men, Roy Wright, Val Duncan and Sir Mark Turner, ran Rio Tinto. As Wright, now deputy chairman, tells it: 'We had to do everything ourselves from planning the mine to marketing the product – now with all these planning departments the place is unrecognizable.'[4]

The decision-making process within the corporations has been rationalized and become more formal. Possible investments are examined from all angles by the geological, engineering, marketing and financial departments. The key coordinating and policy-making body is the Executive Committee or its equivalent. This Committee of key executives, managers and strategists meets frequently to discuss current problems, assess major new investments, and decide future growth areas for the company.

*See Suzanne Cronje, Margaret Ling, and Gillian Cronje, *Lonrho: Portrait of a Multinational*, Penguin Books, 1976.

JCI has five executive directors, who meet twice a week. 'Any question which involves the disposal of resources is dealt with by the committee.'[5] The central authority within Anglo is the Executive Committee, chaired by Harry Oppenheimer, which analyses problems of financing and forward planning for the whole group. Each of the specialists on this committee has a back-up team of experts drawn from a centralized secretariat within the chairman's office. The Committee meets three times a week to discuss important company business. Each meeting usually lasts between three and four hours. Oppenheimer explains that the Committee is made up of a number of senior directors:

Mind you, not all, because you get a certain type of senior director who likes an independent command and doesn't want to be concerned with the co-ordination of the various businesses of the group as a whole. Then you get the other sort, who are good at the hammering out of an overall policy but who, if put in charge of a particular division, would be out of their element.[6]

The more formal decision-making process means that there are few gambles like that of Ernest Oppenheimer's investment in the Orange Free State gold field. Adriaan Louw, chairman of the rival company, Consolidated Gold Fields, which also took a risk in the area and failed, says that 'No one would start a mine on the basis of the information that was available on Free State in 1946.'[7] The new style is exemplified by Anglo's Executive Committee, or by Newmont's chairman Plato Malozemoff depending 'much more heavily than his predecessors on a critical study and analysis of a given situation rather than on intuition or a highly personalized approach'.[8] Companies do still misjudge investments, as General Mining did with Msauli Asbestos; or gamble on a new process before it is fully proved, as Anglo and Charter did with the TORCO process in Mauritania.*

One should not exaggerate the decline in the chairman's position. He may still control companies by virtue of his personal dominance, such as Ian MacGregor of Amax and Plato

---

*Although political factors were also important. Oppenheimer was anxious to develop a mine in independent Africa at the time.

Malozemoff of Newmont; or because he is the son of the founder, like Harry Oppenheimer at Anglo, or A. Chester Beatty at Selection Trust. At JCI, according to Watson, the aim was to reach a consensus: 'in the end obviously you cannot avoid the fact that somebody has to say "boo" if necessary, but we are not a one-man band.'[9] In the case of ALCAN, the company magazine explains that the President, Nathaniel Davies, takes the final decisions about the 'combination of investments in raw material, smelting and fabricating capacity that will earn the greatest return on the group's capital and managerial resources'.[10] When asked if he exercised a personal power of veto over the Executive Committee, Oppenheimer replied 'This is a situation that has never arisen and I don't think it will. We always reach a consensus.' But *African Development* claims that 'no major policy decisions are taken without Chairman Oppenheimer's approval'.[11] In fact, Anglo has a complicated machinery to enable Oppenheimer to exercise his control, and no man is given command of a major Anglo group division unless he has worked with Oppenheimer in Johannesburg. The chairman's voice will be particularly important when an assessment of political factors is being made. The different attitudes of Anglo and Amax to the Zambian takeover owe much to the differing personalities and political outlook of Oppenheimer and MacGregor.

The operational control of the mines is left in the hands of experienced managers, but company headquarters decides all major policy, investment and expenditure questions. The key body in the allocation of RTZ's reserves

is the Capital Estimates Committee chaired by Sir Mark Turner in London. All operating companies have a limit beneath which they can spend as they choose, but projects costing more than a certain amount, which varies from company to company, must go to the CEC. So too must acquisitions or expansions which would have a chain effect that would take the group into new fields of activity.[12]

At Anglo the division of responsibilities is similar: managers 'have wide powers, but if they want to go into a new business which involves spending substantial sums of money, the Executive Committee has to authorize it'.[13]

Financial criteria have become more important, both in assessing and in controlling the activities of subsidiaries. Oppenheimer says that in future

top management must be more and more limited, generally speaking, to financial control. . . The central decisions in a company like Anglo must, in the nature of things, be financial decisions. Of course you've got to have the best technical advice, and certainly you want certain people on your board who are technically trained. But basically we are a finance house.[14]

At JCI, the investment division keeps an eye on all the group's holdings to make sure that the performance of each is adequate. When the platinum, mining, industrial and property divisions of JCI are competing for funds, the investment division applies a common discounted cash flow (DCF) yardstick to each project. JCI looks for different rates of return on different projects: it will usually be the profit level which is important, but the 'education' that JCI will derive from the venture can also be taken into account.[15] General Mining ran into trouble in its early years when projects were not under proper financial control, and the company now has a central financial control plotting performance month by month. The company divides its investments into the more important strategic companies and the portfolio. The demands of organic growth in the strategic companies have priority if they offer an adequate DCF return.[16]

THE CHANGING STRUCTURE

The internationalization of the mining companies has led to further changes in the companies' organizational structure. The experience of Newmont Mining Corporation is probably typical of this process. Company historian Robert Ramsey says that while William Thompson, the founder, was the chairman, he 'reserved all critical decisions for himself', although of course he depended on his staff for guidance. Beginning with the advent of his successor, Fred Searls, 'one can detect a spreading of the decision-making process to other members of the Newmont hierarchy', and Newmont acquired a management group of about

ten talented specialists, who divided up the company's operations between them. 'There developed a kind of horizontal
organization wherein responsibility split up along geographical
lines', with different individuals taking responsibility for Canada,
for Africa, for prospecting and new ventures, and so on. But
when Plato Malozemoff became President of Newmont, in 1954,
the management structure began once again to change. 'The old
horizontal division, or geographic split began to disappear . . .'
and further changes created an organizational structure based on
functional divisions, so that today Newmont is divided into
financing, exploration, mining, metallurgy, and engineering
sectors.[17]

This organizational pattern is now fairly common at least
among American mining companies. Amax is divided into major
divisions by product group: aluminium; base metals; molybdenum and speciality metals; fuels; while a fifth division contains
Amax's international and chemical interests. The New York
headquarters provides the overall direction. Each division is
headed by an Executive Vice-President, but overall financial
direction and planning is controlled by an Executive Committee
and a Finance Committee, each with ten or eleven members
selected from the company's board of directors. For administrative convenience, Amax has several other divisions, including
forest products, exploration, and the engineering and technology
division, the environmental services.[18]

ALCAN, which makes and sells nearly half the aluminium
moving across frontiers in the non-Communist world, is
divided into four major divisions: finance, raw materials,
smelting, fabricating and sales, reflecting the process flow from
bauxite deposit to finished article. Significantly this 'mine to
market chain' pays little attention to national boundaries. The
company's interests are conceived as a global whole. The company's divisions take more account of the manufacturing process
and ALCAN's internal lines of communication and transportation, than of such politico-economic divisions as the nation
state.[19]

One of the few multinationally-owned mining companies,
Pechiney-Ugine-Kuhlmann, is the product of a merger between

two major French and German companies. After intensive studies, a holding company was established to control seven major industrial branches: steel and titanium; aluminium; chemicals; mining and electrometallurgy; nuclear and research; special products; and copper fabrication. The general management of the holding company is responsible for directing and controlling the group, and is backed up by centralized finance, general administration, scientific research, market development and technical services. As with Amax, certain foreign operations report directly to the general management of the holding company.[20]

At Rio Tinto Zinc the company's control structure is less formal and is based on frequent contact by members of the main board with RTZ's subsidiaries. All board members 'serve on the boards of a number of subsidiary companies and play an active role in the management of the companies concerned'.[21]

The South African mining finance houses have developed along slightly different lines. They began by acting as holding companies for one or two gold mines and grew into powerful centres of technical, administrative and financial expertise.* As they expanded their activities, and sought new outlets for their central resources, they developed and expanded the original mining finance house concept to cover their other mineral interests and later their industrial and property investments.

Nowhere has this organizational structure been more fully developed than at Anglo American. The vast Anglo American empire is made up of hundreds of separate companies, whose operation is firmly controlled from the head office of Anglo American Corporation through a complex system of holding companies and interlocking shareholdings,† reinforced by the provision of administrative, managerial, technical and financial services. The pool of administrative, financial and technical specialists at Anglo's head office can be deployed whenever and wherever they are needed. When Alan Milne, the Managing Director of African Explosives and Chemical Industries (50 per cent owned by the Anglo group), went to discuss a proposed merger with Triomf Fertilizers, he took with him Grey Fletcher,

*See Chapter 1.   †See Chapters 12 and 19.

the Financial Director of Anglo American.[22] All members of the group draw on Anglo American's administrative and technical services. The wide range of these central services can be seen from Table 30.

Table 30: The administrative and technical services provided by the Anglo American Corporation to the rest of the Anglo group

New Business	Anglo's vast information network keeps it abreast of new investment opportunities; and Anglo's size means that it can create not just new companies but new industries
Prospecting	Aerial, geophysical and geological
Company Finance	Flotation, underwriting, new issues, loans
Company Management	Group companies can hire management services from Anglo on short- or long-term basis
Company Administration	Secretarial, accounting, transfer secretarial
Technical Services	Consulting engineers: mining – mechanical, electrical, civil; consulting geologists; consulting metallurgists; consulting chemists; architects; town planning
General Services	Buying-stores, personnel, public relations, medical services, labour recruiting, metal sales, farming, land and estate, administration
Investment Management	Stock exchange dealing, financial planning, investment advice
Research	Metallurgical, geological, diamond, general
Patenting	New mineral or industrial processes
Manpower Resources	Personnel, labour recruiting

Conclusion

At the beginning of the twentieth century, the mining companies in Africa had mines in only one country: e.g. Rhodesian Selection Trust in Northern Rhodesia; Newmont Mining in the USA; Anglo American in South Africa. As the companies grew, they sought new outlets for the fund of skills, expertise and capital they had amassed. Thus they came to manage a string of mines in a number of countries around the world. Organizational structures grew more complex, and investment decisions became more and more the product of thorough research, metallurgical evaluation and financial planning. At first companies divided their operations along national or geographical lines, but the emphasis has shifted from the profitability of one mine in one country to the overall performance of the group around the world. Reflecting this, companies are subdividing their activities along product lines. The international mining company makes decisions about a mine in any given country, not on the basis of that country's needs, but on the basis of the company's world-wide interests. Powerful executive and financial committees at head office decide when and where to expand existing capacity or establish new mines; which production techniques are to be used; at what rates the deposits are to be exploited. These global evaluations determine the operating characteristics of a mine, and set the course for any discussions with host governments. The capacity of an African government to alter a company's decisions and impose national development objectives is severely limited by the international orientation and organization of the companies themselves.

14 Relations Between the Mining Groups

In the nineteenth century the mining companies competed vigorously for mineral deposits and for available funds in the stock markets of the industrialized nations. Today the power of the international mining groups is increased by the cooperation and connections between them. Their attitudes towards mineral development in Africa are very similar and their cohesiveness as an economic and political force blocks the attempts by African governments to assert their own economic priorities. But although the companies share commercial objectives and operating characteristics they may well pursue different tactics to safeguard or expand their investment. They are also competing against each other within the world capitalist economy. This competition is usually restricted to certain well-defined areas, such as the discovery and management of new deposits. Even so the dominance of the larger international groups is growing and will continue to grow because of the high capital cost of modern mines and the pressure from the international banks. This concentration and centralization of power in the major mining groups reinforces Africa's underdevelopment and ensures that the developmental priorities of Africa are once again overridden.

LINKS BETWEEN THE COMPANIES

The close formal and informal links between the mining companies are created by interlocking shareholdings and cemented by interlocking directorships. One study in the early sixties focused on the major mining companies operating in central and southern Africa and attempted to map the interlocking directorships which constituted 'a financial and industrial network of enormous proportions encompassing all aspects of the mineral industry of Africa, not only in Katanga but southwards to the Cape'.[1] Today the major mining groups control their global empires through a bewildering network of directorships which link parent companies to their subsidiaries; mines to suppliers and customers; and the major groups to each other and to government policy-making bodies.* The significance of these interlocking directorships between the companies has been the subject of vigorous debate.[2]

The importance and centrality of these relationships to the policies and activities of the mining companies varies according to the nature of the relationship between the linked companies and the functions of the interlock. The fact that the parent company and a subsidiary share the same directors does not add a new element to the relationship between the companies, rather it expresses that pattern of ownership. The interlocks between groups and companies occur at different levels. Interlocking directorships between the boards of major mining companies are often very important to an understanding of the companies' actions, as in the Congo.† But it is not enough to identify the interlock. Its significance depends on the size and meaning of the investment. Selection Trust for over thirty years was the largest single shareholder in Amax and was represented on the board, but with only an 11 per cent stake it had in no sense a controlling interest (although one should perhaps not underestimate the importance of the constant two-way flow of information between companies).[3] On the other hand Anglo's 30 per cent stake in De Beers Consolidated very definitely represents a controlling interest, and interlocking directorships guarantee that the diamond company acts in line with the interests of the Anglo group as a whole; as for example when De Beers provided large amounts of capital for the development of the Orange Free State Gold Fields. Interlocking directorships between the Executive Committees of different companies, as in the case of Anglo and De Beers, for example, indicate a close working relationship and are very significant because executive committees

* For more on these links with governments see Chapter 18 below. See also Chapter 10 on the Congo, and Chapter 8 on Rhodesia.

† See Table 20.

are at the centre of the international mining groups, controlling the movement of capital and labour materials, and the siting of new mines, refineries and manufacturing plant through the world.

When two groups both share directors in a jointly owned mine this may reflect a close link between the groups or merely the joint investment in the mine. In some joint ventures, such as the Mauritanian and Liberian iron-ore mines, the interlocking shareholdings and directorships are related not so much to the control and management of the mine but to the percentage of the mine's output to be taken by each of the major mining groups.[4] Sometimes the patterns of ownership and control are more complex, and the mere fact of interlocking directorships does not mean that the companies or groups will act in unison although the interlocks will undoubtedly aid the flow of information and help coordinate their actions. At the height of the struggle for independence in the Congo and Northern Rhodesia each major company, despite the many connections between them, was controlled by a separate and distinct group of shareholders and managers. So the Belgian-controlled Union Minière group, the British-controlled British South Africa Company and Tanganyika Concessions, the South-African-controlled Anglo American group, and the American-controlled group were not always in agreement over tactics, although they of course all shared the same strategic aim of preserving their investments. Similarly the many connections at mine level between the two major copper-mining groups in Zambia did not prevent them taking different positions in their 1969 negotiations with the Zambian government.

The connections between the companies at all different levels feed information and experience to the international mining groups from all over Africa and reinforce their powerful position when confronted by nationalist governments seeking to increase their share of the surplus. The cohesiveness of the mining groups enables them to benefit from each other's experience and to block attempts by African governments to take over existing mines. Both Zaire and Zambia have attempted to encourage new consortia to take over the management of their copper mines, without success, partly because of the reluctance of the mining companies to interfere in the sphere of influence of another company but also because of the information, pressures and threats that can be conveyed along the network of interlocking directorships. These interlocks are the visible signs of the inter-relationships between the companies and they are very important both in reflecting and in reinforcing the cohesiveness of the international mining companies as an economic force in Africa. But these links do not mean that competition between the companies is completely eliminated.

COMPETITION BETWEEN THE COMPANIES

Within the world capitalist economy the companies are constantly competing against each other, and the continuing centralization and integration of the world economy through a welter of acquisitions, mergers, stock manipulations, and a series of technical advances based on new technology such as the computer, has welded the mining companies into ever larger and more powerful aggregations of capital. The mining companies in Africa have had either to expand the scope and scale of their operations or to be absorbed by other companies. In South Africa, Anglo American, the most aggressive and internationalist of the South African mining houses in the early 1960s, began to build up its worldwide operations by taking over an assortment of mining companies, including Cecil Rhodes's old company, the British South Africa Company, which had once ruled Rhodesia, and used them to create a new international mining house, Charter Consolidated. American companies like Amax and Newmont expanded rapidly, absorbing smaller companies and developing new mines.

The skill with which a mining company selects and manages its mines will affect its credit rating with the major banks and international lending agencies and thus affect the ability of the group to go on expanding. Once again the larger groups are in a stronger position than the small mining companies. A large group such as Anglo American, which had a string of technical difficulties with new mines in Mauritania, Botswana and Zaire, was able to ride out the storm, and survive, albeit with a tarnished reputation. But what is an embarrassment to a major group may prove disastrous to smaller companies which are vulnerable to absorption if they over-stretch themselves. Rand Mines, for example, made a disastrous foray into oil exploration, in the wake of which it was taken over by the Barlow's conglomerate.

Although there was a rash of takeovers in the sixties, there were few spectacular takeover battles. The three-way takeover battle, such as that between Barlow's, Gold Fields, and General Mining for control of Union Corporation, is a relatively rare occurrence in the mining world. More often, the takeovers were agreed in advance. The takeover both of Rand Mines by Barlow's and of General Mining by Federale Mynbou were both agreed in advance with Anglo American. Without that approval a similar bid for control of Johannesburg Consolidated Investment failed.

The mining groups compete to identify changing patterns of supply and demand for various minerals and then to bring new mine capacity on stream and take advantage of rising prices. In South Africa, American companies stole a march on local mining houses, by spearheading, with the British company RTZ, a 300 per cent explosion in base-metal mining while the mining houses concentrated on their gold mines. As the long-term projections for nickel began to look very favourable the companies developed new nickel mines; when it was predicted that there would be a shortage of uranium supplies by the end of the nineteen-seventies the companies scoured the world for new uranium deposits, and RTZ found and developed a massive deposit at Rössing in Namibia.

MANAGING THE MINE

The international mining company wants control of its major investments so that production, marketing and cash flow can be adjusted to meet the needs of the company's worldwide operation. The discovery of a new mineral deposit gives the mining company the chance to develop the mine and manage it during its active life, even if other companies help provide some of the finance. But competition over mining rights can be intense.

The Palabora open-cast copper mine in South Africa was a case where the claims of two powerful mining groups were in conflict. In 1953 both Rio Tinto and Newmont were examining the Phalaborwa copper deposit in northern Transvaal. The Phalaborwa deposit is a mineral complex covering an area roughly five miles long and two miles wide. Uranium, vermiculite and phosphate are also found in the area, the centre of the ore-body is marked by an outcrop known locally as Loolekop. Rio Tinto received South African government permission to explore the area in 1953. At the same time Newmont sent an exploration team to investigate. Both companies applied for a mining lease. Val Duncan, chairman of Rio Tinto, and Newmont's chairman, Plato Malozemoff, discussed the possibility of cooperation between the companies. Talks broke down, however, on the question of which company would wield the management responsibility in the proposed joint company. After a break of a few months, Malozemoff contacted Duncan with the suggestion that a management independent of both Rio Tinto and Newmont be established. 'However Val Duncan voiced the opinion that this would be a "kind of Soviet" and once more discussions broke down.'[5] The South African government brought pressure on the two companies to get together, because it was unwilling to divide the property in any way. Agreement was reached in June 1956. Newmont was forced to let Rio Tinto manage the new company, because Rio Tinto held the mineral rights to the Loolekop outcrop in the centre of the area.[6] In the development of the mine, Newmont engineers and a team from Bechtel Corporation worked out the location and design of the mine and the plant, while Roy Wright and Val Duncan of Rio Tinto secured the financing from various banks. The largest loan, for $26·9 million, came from Kreditanstalt für Wiederaufbau, the West German export bank, on the basis of a twenty-year contract to sell between 30,000 and 36,000 tons of blister copper annually to Norddeutsche Affinerie of Hamburg, in Germany. Amax, Selection Trust, Union Corporation, all took substantial stakes in the equity capital, along with Newmont and Rio Tinto. The mine came on stream in 1965 at a capital cost of $103 million and soon proved itself a very profitable undertaking. The ownership of Palabora in 1968, before Amax sold out its 7·7 per cent stake, is shown in Figure 14. Management responsibility remains with Rio Tinto Zinc.*

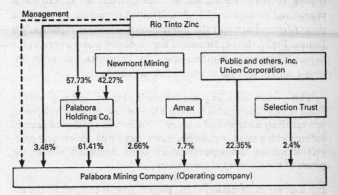

Fig. 14. The ownership of the Palabora Mining Company in 1968
NOTE: Amax subsequently sold its 7·7% stake.

The company which discovers a deposit may not necessarily develop the mine. In Mauritania the Akjoujt copper deposit was developed by Charter Consolidated although it did not discover the deposit. This was because Anglo American's TORCO process was claimed to extract lower grade ore than rival processes.† More recently in Botswana the relations between the various companies constantly changed as the balance of power shifted as a new project at Selebi-Pikwe was developed. The various companies competed for the benefits of controlling the mine, but the benefits to Botswana of the involvement of the companies are not at all clear.

*Rio Tinto became Rio Tinto Zinc after its merger with Consolidated Zinc in 1962.

† In the event the project was bedevilled by technical problems caused by design faults and the extreme heat and dustiness of the location on the edge of the Sahara. Eventually Charter sold its share to the Mauritanian government, although the company still manages the mine.

MINING AND BOTSWANA: THE SELEBI-PIKWE MINE

At the time of Botswana's independence, the country was one of the poorest in Africa.[7] Today, Botswana's economy is being transformed by the discovery and exploitation of a copper-nickel deposit at Selebi-Pikwe, and in some quarters her experience is considered to be a model of the fruitful cooperation between a poor African state and the international mining companies. Sir Ronald Prain, then chairman of the company which operates the Selebi-Pikwe copper-nickel mine in Botswana, certainly believed so. He told his shareholders in July 1971:

> 'This project has a long and interesting history, and may well be found to be a classic example of the effects of new mining development on a relatively undeveloped country . . . What was a backward pastoral country with a small population, is now faced with the exciting prospect of mineral development which could completely change the nature of the economy of the country . . .'[8]

But a closer examination of the project reveals that, while the involvement of the mining companies ensures the development of the mine, it presents an obstacle to the fulfilment of national development objectives, and reduces the benefits of the mine to the host country.

The Early Stages

The story of the Selebi-Pikwe mine begins in 1956 when the Anglo American Corporation of South Africa expressed interest in the area belonging to the Bamangwato tribe. The colonial government was in favour of granting a concession to the company, but Tshekedi Khama, leader of the tribe, was suspicious of the South African company and instead arranged to meet Sir Ronald Prain, the chairman of Rhodesian Selection Trust (RST). The negotiations began, and two years later, on 2 June 1959, Tshekedi and Seretse Khama signed a concession agreement with RST on behalf of the Bamangwato tribe. In November 1959 RST established Bamangwato Concessions Ltd (BCL) to explore the concession. BCL was owned 61 per cent by RST itself, 23 per cent by Minerals Separation Ltd (Minsep), and 16 per cent largely by Zamanglo and Inco subsidiaries.

The Selebi-Pikwe copper-nickel deposit was discovered in 1963, and further prospecting and feasibility studies were encouraging.[9] But Bamangwato Concessions Ltd, though backed by Roan Selection Trust,* lacked the resources to develop the mine on its own. RST's operations on the Copperbelt† were certainly profitable, but the group could not bring the Selebi-Pikwe mine on stream without assistance. A larger group could have developed the mine and then released a proportion of the equity to the public and other interested investors without losing control of the project. But the relatively meagre resources at the disposal of BCL and RST allowed the control of the project to pass out of their hands.

The Chicken and the Egg

By 1967 the development of the Selebi-Pikwe mine had reached an impasse. The difficulty was that although the copper-nickel deposit had been found no one seemed willing to put up the money for it to be proved. Thus began what the business magazine *African Development* described as 'Botswana's Epic Struggle between the Chicken and the Egg'. Without a full evaluation and proving of the deposit, no finance would be forthcoming for the mine; but without additional finance, the deposit could not be proved.

When Bamangwato Concessions Ltd first found the deposit, RST took the position that it would do no more proving unless more infrastructure was provided. The British government was not prepared to pay for the necessary development. When Botswana became independent in September 1966, the new government could not provide the estimated £12 million required. The World Bank was not interested, and the US was revising its aid programmes in Africa. RST's solution was to ask the public. Early in 1968 RST created a subsidiary called

* The company changed its name from Rhodesian Selection Trust to Roan Selection Trust in 1965.
† See Chapter 9.

Botswana RST (BOTREST), to which it transferred all its interests in Botswana, and offered shares to the public. This move was criticized in mining circles as premature; but, strapped for cash and capital, RST felt it had little option.[10] At this stage, RST's Botswana interest consisted of 61 per cent of Bamangwato Concessions Ltd and 64 per cent of a soda mine at Makgadikgadi. Figure 15 shows the various interests in the Selebi-Pikwe mine in 1968 after the flotation. The 61 per cent of BCL originally owned by RST were now held largely in America. The largest single shareholder in Botrest was the American Metal Climax Co. (Amax), which was also the largest shareholder in RST. The public held 56·71 per cent of the shares in Botrest. Most of these shares were represented by publicly owned American Depositary Receipts*, of which the Morgan Guaranty Trust Company of New York acts as depositary. At this stage the Anglo American group held no shares in Botrest.

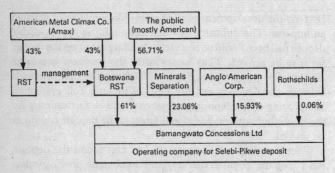

Fig. 15. Interests in the Selebi-Pikwe copper-nickel deposit in 1968

With the capital raised by the Botrest issue, BCL was able to prove the existence of 22·1 million tonnes of ore at Pikwe, grading 1·45 per cent nickel, and 1·14 per cent copper; and a further 10·0 million tonnes at Selebi, grading 0·70 per cent nickel and 1·56 per cent copper. The price and marketability of nickel

*American Depositary Receipts: American investors in foreign companies do not hold the shares directly. Specified banks hold the shares and American investors are issued American Depositary Receipts.

seemed at that time better than those of copper and so the company decided to go ahead with the Pikwe mine first and to bring Selebi into production at a later date (around 1980). The Pikwe mine's annual production was estimated at 14,800 tonnes of nickel and 16,600 tonnes of copper, from an annual ore production of around 2 million tonnes. The cost of bringing the mine to production was estimated at $121 million. The infrastructure to be provided by the government consisted of a dam at Shashi to provide water; a coal-fired power station; a rail spur to transport the metal; and a new township to service the mine and its workers. The estimated cost of the infrastructure was $67 million (£25 million). The company and the Botswana government began a worldwide search for funds.

Financing the Infrastructure

Botswana's negotiators approached the World Bank, the Canadian government, the United States government, and the British government for finance for the infrastructure, initial surveys, training and administration. The Botswana government itself set up the Shashi Project Management Unit to bring into operation and to administer the power and water corporations and the new township.

The infrastructure financing was secured in July 1971 when the government signed an agreement with the World Bank for a loan for the dam, the township and the railway spur. The Bank loaned $32 million at a 7¾ per cent interest rate, with a four-year grace period and repayments spread over 25 years. The Canadian International Development Agency (CIDA) lent $19·5 million interest free, with repayments over 50 years, for the power station and power transmission lines. The United States Agency for International Development (USAID) loaned $6·5 million at 3½ per cent over 40 years; and a further $1·5 million was raised from the British government and other sources. The Botswana government undertook to raise the remaining capital needed. Although the government had succeeded in raising the infrastructure capital, the whole financial structure of the project was like a delicately balanced house of cards. All the loans were dependent on the successful completion of the other financial arrangements. The Canadian loan, for example, was conditional on the Botswana government being able to raise its share of the money, and the World Bank required the mining companies to guarantee the loan. This condition was causing Botrest much difficulty.

Financing the Mine

In view of its meagre paid-up capital of $4 million, Botrest was not, itself, acceptable to the lenders as the sole guarantor of loans totalling $150 million for the infrastructure and the mine, and it was clearly not feasible to raise the required guarantees from the public. Botrest needed to secure long-term metal sales contracts.

The German company Metallgesellschaft AG agreed to purchase a guaranteed amount of the mine's copper and nickel production for fifteen years, provided that it was given a discount of 2–3 per cent on the ruling international metal prices. On the strength of this contract, Botrest approached the German export bank Kreditanstalt für Wiederaufbau for a loan. The bank agreed to organize a consortium of German banks to provide 50 per cent of the finance for the mine ($60·2 million), but only on condition that certain guarantees were forthcoming from the major mining corporations with an interest in the project: Amax, Mineral Separation, and Anglo American. It was also a condition of the World Bank's infrastructural loan that these corporations guarantee the Bank's $32 million.

Minerals Separation (with 23 per cent of BCL) dropped out of the project at this stage. It was unwilling to participate in the long-term guarantees in view of their magnitude. Amax was not prepared to make further substantial investments in Africa because of its experience in Zambia, where the company was suffering from the government's increasing restrictions on dividend remittance. It was prepared to guarantee 50 per cent of the total amount required, but no more. Botrest turned to Anglo for help.

Anglo Muscles In

Anglo looked at the Selebi-Pikwe copper-nickel deposits with covetous eyes. Within the Corporation, the whole of central and southern Africa is regarded as an Anglo fiefdom. Anglo expects to be involved in most major projects in the area, and as a consequence of its technical skills and immense financial power it can reasonably expect to control the projects in which it takes a stake. By 1970 the Anglo group was actively involved in three mining projects in Botswana. It owned a small manganese mine at Kanye in southern Botswana, and it was investigating the largest coal deposits in Africa at Moropule.* In 1967 after a twelve-year search, De Beers found the second largest diamond pipe in the world at Orapa. Four years later the mine went into production. De Beers 'gave' the government a 15 per cent stake.† Now, for a number of reasons, the Anglo group was anxious to increase its stake in Selebi-Pikwe, which at this stage amounted to 16 per cent of BCL. Traditionally the group's main investment was in gold, copper, coal and diamonds; but demand

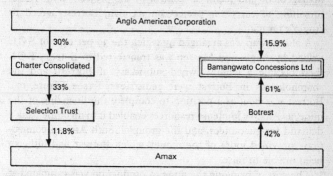

Fig. 16. Interlocking shareholdings of the major mining groups involved in the Selebi-Pikwe project in 1968

*Large though they are, the Moropule deposits cannot compete with the high-grade, low-cost South African and Rhodesian deposits; so development has been limited to a small mine to provide fuel for the Selebi power station.

† In 1975 the government began negotiations which successfully increased this stake to 50 per cent.

projections for nickel were very favourable, and Anglo was keen to develop its nickel-mining experience.

The big mining companies with a stake in Selebi-Pikwe were connected by a series of interlocking shareholdings (see figure 16). We have already noted Amax's 42 per cent stake in Botrest. The largest holder of Amax common stock is Selection Trust. The largest shareholder in Selection Trust is Charter Consolidated, which is controlled by Anglo American. This closed circular relationship accounts for the arm-in-arm approach of the companies.[11] These links do not in themselves, however, explain why Anglo took control of Selebi-Pikwe. The decisive factor was Anglo's financial strength.

The Final Stages

Anglo was willing to take up a large share of the guarantees, but it drove a hard bargain. It insisted that its modest 16 per cent stake in BCL be increased substantially until it was an equal participant with Amax; and that the Anglo group share in the management and technical control of the project. With Amax unwilling to carry the project on its own, Botrest agreed to Anglo's terms.

A share swap was arranged by which the 39 per cent of BCL owned by Anglo and Minsep was transferred to Botrest. BCL then became a wholly owned subsidiary of Botrest, and the shareholdings in Botrest were redistributed (see Figure 17). Botrest was now in a position to complete the financing of the mine, as Anglo's immense resources enabled it to meet the bank's demand for guarantees, and the group's South African connections provided more of the money which Botrest had hitherto been unable to raise.

The cost of bringing the mine to production was estimated at $121 million; $60·2 million, or 50 per cent, of this money came from the consortium of West German banks led by the Kreditanstalt für Wiederaufbau, and including the Deutsche Bank and the Dresdner Bank. Another $18·9 million was loaned by the South African Industrial Development Corporation. An advance on this loan was made by a consortium of South African banks led

by Anglo American's merchant bank, Union Acceptance Ltd.
Anglo's bank also guaranteed the Industrial Development Corporation loan. Rothschilds and Hill Samuel provided revolving credit lines of around $7 million to meet working capital requirements. This left another $42 million to be raised by BCL,

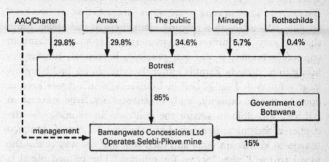

Fig 17. Interests in the Selebi-Pikwe mine in 1971

which it proposed to do by issuing more shares in the company.
BRST, Amax and the AAC/Charter group had to give guarantees that the project would be completed in respect of the UAL guarantee, and the World Bank, KFW consortium and IDC loans. In addition, BRST, Amax and Anglo had to guarantee 10 per cent of the $60 million Deutsche Mark loan from KFW, and 60 per cent of the infrastructure loan made by the World Bank. The other 40 per cent was guaranteed by the West German company Metallgesellshaft AG, the purchaser of the metal.

The Botswana government itself raised $67 million in loans.
This sum was larger than it needed to be, because the low-interest or interest-free loans from the Canadian and US governments were tied to the purchase of US and Canadian goods.
Thus the pipelines and valves had to be imported from the United States when they could undoubtedly have been bought more cheaply elsewhere.

Construction of the concentrator and smelter plants, using processes developed and licensed by the Finnish company Outokompu Oy, began in 1971 and was finished by the end of

343

1973.* Smelting the ore produces a copper-nickel matte of approximately 80 per cent metal content. At this stage the metal has largely been separated from the waste, but the nickel and copper remain intermixed. Because this copper-nickel matte is worth less than the fully refined metal, the government negotiators tried to get the mining company to refine the matte in Botswana. The mining companies argued that it was not economic to establish a refining plant there at this stage. Since the orebody has different characteristics from the Zambian copper orebodies, it was not possible, it seemed, for the refining to be done in Zambia either. Besides, Amax had bought a large refinery at Port Nickel in Louisiana, which it was keen to operate at full capacity, and, because of its large interest in BRST, was able to secure the contract for refining. So the copper nickel matte is shipped out through Maputo (Lourenço Marques) in Mozambique and then sent half the way round the world to the United States for refining. The refined metal is then shipped to Metallgesellschaft in Germany.

Despite the much-vaunted technical proficiency of the mining companies, the Selebi-Pikwe mine ran into serious technical problems. There were difficulties with the Finnish-designed smelter, several miners were killed in an underground explosion, and the ore was unexpectedly complex. It was decided to begin production not from the underground workings but by extracting part of the orebody in the centre of the deposit by open pit methods. This was to ensure more consistent supplies of ore to the concentrator. The company also said that this late change was due to difficulties in training the Tswana labour force.[12] However, the technical problems continued and despite expensive modifications to the mine plant, there was a serious shortfall in production, and therefore of sales. Now the high gearing of the project coupled with the slump in metal prices compounded the technical problems and created a liquidity crisis and Botrest reported an operating loss of R40·3 million in 1974 and a further R20 million in 1975. Botrest's liquidity crisis was resolved by

* But it was still suffering from teething troubles in 1975; and as the production level fell further and further behind schedule, Botrest had to borrow still more money to finance design modifications and the heavy loan charges.

loans of R48·5 million from Amax and the Anglo group to keep the company going.[13] Further design modifications were reported to have overcome the technical problems, and Botrest expected to repay the additional loans within a few years as production rose along with world mineral prices.[14] The cost of commissioning the mine rose from R90 million to R180 million. Low copper and nickel prices produced more losses in 1976 and 1977 and led to a major restructuring of BCL's marketing and financial arrangements. The expensive sales agreement with Metallgesellschaft was severed, while certain loans were prepaid by Amax and AAC to reduce BCL's interest burden, and R75 million of the company's debt was capitalized. The royalty system, which was profit-based, was re-set at 3 per cent of gross sales to be deferred if BCL made any losses during the following three years. However although the technical and financial difficulties may have embarrassed the companies, providing production and sales can reach and maintain the targeted levels, the gross sales revenue of the mine was estimated in 1972 to be some $1·5 billion over twenty-three years after all capital had been repaid.[15]

And so it was that 'Botswana's' new copper-nickel mine came to be financed by British, American and South African capital, managed by a South African mining group, using a Finnish smelting process and an American refinery in Louisiana. The mine output was sold to guaranteed buyers in West Germany. Perhaps it is pertinent to ask just what contribution this operation will make to Botswana's economic development?

Development or Underdevelopment?

There will be few direct benefits from the mine. The additional employment and multiplier effect of the mine will both be small. In a population of 600,000 the new mine employs 2,600 men. The creation of the new township at Selebi-Pikwe will provide additional work, and its population is expected to grow to more than 20,000. (This will make it at least as big as the country's capital, Gaberones, and it should provide a sufficiently large market to encourage local food production.) The mine will not be a major purchaser of local goods and services, and all the capital equipment has to be imported. Spare parts and services will be provided by companies in Finland and South Africa, and so it cannot be said that the mine is contributing much direct impetus for Botswana's development.

The main effect of the mine is to provide additional government revenue from profit sharing and taxation of the mining company; through taxation of the employment income generated by the project; and finally through customs, excise, and sales duty. The customs revenue on imported machinery and supplies was high for the construction phase of the project, at around R7 million a year, but dropped sharply once the mine was completed in 1975, to approximately R1·5 million a year.[16] Personal income tax collection was expected to rise to R500,000 a year during the construction phase and fall to approximately R250,000 thereafter; rising again to R300,000 in the early 1980s. The provisions for profit sharing and company taxation are more complex. Under the terms of the original 1959 agreement, the government gave BCL a mining lease for twenty-five years, and the company issued 15 per cent of BCL's share capital to the government without payment. If the capital of the company is subsequently increased, the government is entitled to that number of shares required to keep its stake at 15 per cent. The government can also increase its stake in BCL, because it will generally have the first right to acquire any other shares in BCL at 'a market value' if Botrest decides to dispose of them.

The tax arrangements between the mining company (BCL) and the government are designed to give the government 50 per cent of total Selebi-Pikwe revenue after allowances for capital repayment. This is not as high as Zambia's effective rate of 73 per cent of mine profits, but Zambia's mines are already built and in operation. A royalty levied under the mining lease is fixed at $7\frac{1}{2}$ per cent of the operating profits (defined as the excess of sales revenue over production costs). The *Rand Daily Mail* calculated this revenue at R1·7 million ($2·5 million) a year. Under the agreement, the government can levy tax on the company profits only *after* the royalty has been deducted. The normal rate of company tax in Botswana is 30 per cent, but for the mining company this has been fixed at 40 per cent. This is subject to an 'escalator' clause, under which corporation tax goes up one per cent for every one per cent by which BCL's operating profit margin exceeds $48\frac{1}{2}$ per cent. However, there is an absolute ceiling, whereby corporation tax cannot exceed 65 per cent of BCL's operating profit margin. Government revenue from this source was estimated at R8·7 million ($13·0 million). But the level of tax revenue will depend on the level of profits that the company wishes to declare.

The taxation agreement is, in fact, well designed to meet the needs of the mining companies. The corporation tax was raised from 30 per cent to 40 per cent at the express demand of BCL, which wanted to get the maximum kickback under the double taxation agreements between Botswana, the UK and the US.[17] Under double taxation agreements, taxes paid in Botswana are offset against taxes in the UK and the US. This reduces the tax liability of the parent company in its home country; and since Botswana's tax authorities are less experienced than those in the US, it is likely to be easier to manipulate the accounts so as to minimize *total* tax payments. But the most important feature of the tax arrangements is that all capital expenditure is repaid before income tax becomes fully payable. So the full tax return to the Botswana government will not begin for ten years.[18] In addition interest charges on the outstanding loans are deductible and represent more of the mine's surplus which escapes Botswana tax.* The government has further agreed that Botrest dividends shall be freely remittable to Botrest shareholders outside Botswana in their respective currencies.[19] This must be a drain on Botswana's foreign exchange. The level at which these payments shall be made is to be determined by the directors of Botrest, who represent Amax, Anglo American, and Charter Consolidated, etc. The government has no say in Botrest's dividend policy, because although it has two directors on the board of BCL, which operates the mine, it has no stake, and therefore no directors, on the board of Botrest.

Total government revenue from company taxation and the

---

* It is estimated that 75 per cent of Botrest's gross profit is deductible before tax (*Financial Mail*, Johannesburg, 17 May 1974, p. 675).

provision of essential services was estimated at R10·4 million
($15·5 million). But the government has first to service the infra-
structure loans from CIDA, USAID, and the World Bank.
These repayments began just after the mine came on stream in
1973.* After servicing these loans, the government's net income
was expected to be around $6·25 million. But this increased
government revenue led the British government substantially to
reduce its aid to Botswana. The last grant in aid made to Botswana for recurrent expenditure was in 1971–2. A World Bank
study concluded that, while mine revenue will give the government a measure of financial independence for the first time, the
mining developments in net terms will not add very much to the
resources available to Botswana for capital formation, since
recurrent expenditure will absorb most of the revenue from the
mine.

Botswana's gross domestic product grew spectacularly as a
result of Selebi-Pikwe and the new Orapa diamond mine, and by
1976 the GDP was expected to be 70–80 per cent above the 1968
figure. But this is misleading, because the high level of payments
abroad means that the effect on the gross national product will be
less than half of this. The previous trade deficit will be turned
into a surplus, but at the cost of creating an unbalanced economy.
Structurally Botswana's economy has all the characteristics of
other underdeveloped mining economies, with a heavy export
orientation, dependent on fluctuating world metal markets for a
large portion of government revenue, and large payments abroad
to the mining companies and international agencies.

The new mine has already caused social and political disruption in Botswana and, as elsewhere in Africa, the government has
supported the company management in its clashes with the
workers. At the establishment of the mine the Botswana government felt it could not insist that no South Africans were em-

---

*Repayments are so arranged that Botswana will not even touch much of
this money. The revenue from water and power supplies has been earmarked
to pay off the World Bank loan. BCL pays for the services with income from
the sale of the copper and nickel to Metallgesellschaft. This money is paid
direct into a Barclays Bank Trustee Account in London, which then services
the World Bank loan. The World Bank clearly does not take any chances!

ployed. The South African managers and miners brought their racist attitudes with them and this led to tension, just as it had done in Zambia. In 1972 during construction of the mine, 400 Botswana housing and construction workers went on strike for nine days because, they alleged, South Africans were being given preference for jobs.[20] Workers at the Botswana Power Corporation went on strike when segregated toilets were introduced by the South African managers.[21] In the second half of 1974 miners at De Beers' Orapa mine went on strike for higher wages and the government was forced to make concessions; but it reacted differently when the 2,000 miners at Selebi-Pikwe went on strike over wages in July 1975.

The vice-president flew to the mine, but the strikers refused to give him a hearing and police broke up the crowd of miners and made numerous arrests. Property was damaged and feelings ran high. President Seretse Khama castigated the strikers for 'flouting the country's laws'. Their action amounted to sabotage, he said. The country expected the few Batswana fortunate to find relatively well-paid employment* 'to share their good fortune with their fellow Batswana and to ensure that we maintain law and order, without which there will be no development ... It is essential for Botswana's development that we continue to retain foreign investment ... (and) this can only be done if the companies who invest here obtain a reasonable return on their investment.'[22]

With the government's backing the company dismissed all the strikers. The strike collapsed and there was a rush of applications for the jobs. About 200 people were not re-employed, including most union members (even though it is not at all clear what role, if any, the union played in the strike).[23]

There is another problem. Because the new mining complex is likely to become the political and economic centre of the country it will divert the government's attention and resources away from the rest of the country, where the majority of the population

---

*The average minimum wage at Selebi-Pikwe was R40 a month, compared with the average of R47 a month for all Batswana in wage employment (*Financial Mail*, Johannesburg, 8 August 1975, p. 318). But this was still higher than most Batswana outside the wage sector.

lives. In fact development in the rest of the country will be affected by the loss of manpower, as young men are attracted to Selebi-Pikwe in search of work that will not be available. Already the shanty town on the outskirts of Pikwe is growing rapidly.

MINING AND DEVELOPMENT IN BOTSWANA

To raise $67 million, the Botswana government was forced to pledge government revenues for twenty-five years to pay for the infrastructure needed by the mines. But the direct fiscal benefits to the government merely offset recurrent expenditure on health, education and administration. The indirect benefits are low in relation to those which would be obtained by a labour-intensive manufacturing investment of comparable size. But of course it is even harder to obtain capital for industrial development than for a mine. There is room for mineral production to be expanded and for the government to ensure a higher revenue in the years to come if it can exert enough pressure on the mining companies. But events so far do not encourage optimism. Botswana wanted to avoid South African control of its mineral resources and decrease dependence on external economic forces. However, the result of the complex sequence of events we have described is that the largest mining company in South Africa, the Anglo American group, controls the three main mines in the country: Orapa, Selebi-Pikwe and Moropule* and the government has exchanged its financial dependence on British aid for dependence on Anglo's mines, which will provide the bulk of the government's tax revenue for the foreseeable future. The level of tax payments will be determined by the company's mining and accounting policies, over which the government has little or no control.

More serious for the people of Botswana, the country's plans for balanced growth have been put aside, and the economy has acquired the structural imbalance of underdeveloped mineral-exporting countries. The mining companies' quest for profits

* In addition, De Beers is also developing two new diamond mines at Letlhakane and Jwaneng.

means that much of the surplus that could provide the basis of a more balanced growth is exported along with the copper and nickel. The profits of Anglo American, Amax, R S T, depend on this continuing transfer of capital: in other words, on Botswana's underdevelopment. Henceforth control of Botswana's economy lies not in the country's capital of Gaberones but in the board-rooms of Anglo American in Johannesburg and of Amax in New York.

15 Mining in Africa Today

Establishing a modern mine is a lengthy, complicated process, requiring a high degree of financial, technical and managerial expertise. At each stage of the mine's development, it is the company's priorities which determine events, for it is the company which has the geological information, the mining skills, the marketing information and above all the capital needed to develop new mines. Moreover the increasing scale of modern mines, the use of loan finance and joint ventures, all reinforce the dependency of Africa on the international mining companies. The behaviour of the companies can be understood only in the context of their overall structure, resources and global strategy, a task made more difficult because many of the functions previously carried out by the market are now decided within the corporation, which makes them both less visible and less accessible to national governments.[1] To counter this, many African governments have taken a majority stake in the major mines, but the companies have also changed their tactics and they have been able to maintain their powerful position.

EXPLORATION

Exploration is expensive, and there is no guarantee of success; but since new mines are the lifeblood of the international corporations, they retain large staffs of geologists to work on worldwide exploration programmes. In 1974, for example, Anglo American was busy prospecting in Africa, Australia, North and South America, Europe and Asia in a total of thirty countries.[2] De Beers was prospecting for diamonds in South Africa, Botswana, Angola and Venezuela.[3] Amax was investigating prospects in New Guinea, Fiji, Indonesia, Iran, Ireland,

Portugal, North America and Australia.[4] In recent years there has been a noticeable shift in exploration expenditure away from the Third World towards the more developed countries: mainly Australia, Canada, South Africa and the United States.[5] Sir Ronald Prain, ex-Chairman of RST, estimated that in 1973 and 1974 about 80 per cent of currently available exploration funds were being spent in the developed countries – in fact 70 per cent was going to Australia, Canada, South Africa and the United States.[6]

Nevertheless an African country with a promising geological structure and relatively safe investment climate can still attract mining companies like bees to a honey pot. In 1971 the companies exploring for various minerals in Botswana read like an international Who's Who of the mining industry: they included Roan Selection Trust, Anglo American, Amax, De Beers, Anglovaal, International Nickel, Société le Nickel, Union Carbide and Johannesburg Consolidated Investment.*[7]

The tendency of the mining groups to reduce the proportion of their exploration expenditure in Africa has been offset to some extent by the United Nations Development Programme (UNDP). In 1961 UNDP launched a programme of geological and mineral surveys in the belief that 'the world is living in a period of fast-growing demand for minerals and there is normally an ample supply of investment capital, national or international, for the development of orebodies of economic importance'.[8] Worldwide, this programme has revealed deposits worth at least $13,000 million. Follow-up investment by governments and private sources in these mineral funds was estimated at over $558 million in 1971.[9] In Africa, UNDP mineral surveys were undertaken in thirty-one countries including Zambia, Liberia, Mauritania, Niger, Guinea and Swaziland; and several important deposits were discovered. Despite the UNDP geological surveys, however, most of the major mineral discoveries are still being made by the mining companies.

*Of course Botswana's proximity to South Africa, and the consequent inhibitions on its freedom of action, make it an exceptionally attractive country, but the general point remains.

The art of prospecting has come a long way from the days of the lone prospectors like Raymond Brooks, looking for copper in Northern Rhodesia, or Hans Merenskey searching for diamonds in South Africa. The companies use a wide range of advanced geological, analytical, and photographic methods to pinpoint valuable mineral deposits. In most mining houses, the senior geologists identify those areas worth exploring in the light of general geological knowledge (sometimes provided, of course, by the UNDP national geological surveys). Then the companies apply for prospecting rights which may be limited to specific minerals: for example, De Beers' prospecting rights in Angola were for diamonds, and Anglo's for copper and petroleum. The next stage is to secure aerial photographs of the area, and locate the main structural features. After examination of the photographs the field geologists move in to sample the most promising areas. Since all soil contains traces of minerals the field geologists are interested only in those soil samples which contain a much higher than average incidence of a mineral. The natural occurrence of copper in the earth's crust must be concentrated more than fifty times, and nickel must be concentrated more than eighty times, before a company will be interested. When the geologists succeed in identifying a promising orebody, the next stage is either 'trenching' or drilling. If the deposit is accessible, the company digs trenches into the orebody at strategic points to discover more about its characteristics. The next, and most expensive, stage is diamond drilling. The aim of the drilling is to delineate the extent, depth and uniformity of the mineralization. Core samples are then assessed by the company's own geological staff and by consultant geologists. When the geologists can confidently state the minimum size and grade of the deposit, the whole mining project is costed by the company's mining, engineering and investment departments. Knowledge is power, and the government concerned has little or no knowledge about the prospect. It does not have its own prospectors, and all the information about the deposit is closely controlled by the company. The mineral reserves announced by the company are those it needs to prove to the shareholders and banks that the mine is a viable prospect.

EVALUATING A MINERAL PROSPECT

The viability of a mineral deposit depends on a combination of interacting factors, including the mineralogical characteristics of the deposit – its probable extent, grade, complexity, uniformity and accessibility; the marketing prospects of that particular mineral over the next ten or twenty years; the position of the ore-body in relation to existing transport facilities; and the availability of skilled labour. Making these calculations, and reworking them according to different cost assumptions and marketing projections, requires a heavy investment in the time of skilled personnel. Because of the high salaries paid, and the large number of projects in which they have been involved, the skills of the mining company are generally far superior to those at the disposal of the host government. In practice, African governments must take the companies' evaluations on trust, lacking as they do the information and ability to check the companies' calculations.

THE INVESTMENT DECISION

The company's evaluation of the deposit is determined by the internal criteria of the company and not the government's development strategy. The aim of the company is to secure the return of its capital outlay and a minimum profit within a foreseeable period. An investment in what is considered a risk-free area (i.e. safe from the fear of expropriation) may be judged satisfactory if the rate of return is 12 per cent; but the rate may have to be twenty per cent or more where the risk is adjudged to be higher. Newmont Mining, for example, requires a minimum after-tax return of 20 per cent on all its investments,[10] and this seems to be about the norm for mining company investments in Africa.[11] Obviously the tax policies of the government will influence the period taken to achieve this rate of return. The company will be interested in the allowances for capital depreciation, and the rate of tax on the company's income.

An example will illustrate how these factors interact. If we suppose that the mine will take three years to construct; that capital expenditure (raised entirely by equity finance) will be

355

spread evenly over the three years; and that, when the mine comes on stream, annual gross profits are equal to 35 per cent of the total capital expenditure, then the capital will be entirely recouped in 2·86 years of operation.[12] But the company will require not just the return of its capital outlay, but also a level of return which at the very least covers the interest which could have been earned on the unrecouped balance, and will also take account of the tax levied by the host government. If we suppose that the rate of interest is 12 per cent and that the government taxes the company's profits at the rate of 73·05 per cent (as in Zambia, for example), then the company's capital will be recovered in ten years.* If the company demands a 15 per cent return on its investment with the same rate of tax, then it will be twenty years before this return is achieved.

But our example is a simplification of the real process, because the rate of return required by the companies is not just a simple calculation of the money invested and the income expected. The value of money varies over time, and usually decreases. £100 today is likely to be worth a great deal more than £100 to be received in ten years' time. The mining companies will take this into account when calculating the rate of return on a given investment. If a company invests £100 million today in a mine, it will expect to earn back in five or ten years not just £100 million, but also *at least* as much as that £100 million could have earned at prevailing rates of interest on the world's money markets, together with enough to cover the fall in value due to inflation. In order to ensure that the project in question will meet these minimum requirements, the mining companies employ the Discounted Cash Flow (DCF) technique.† The purpose of DCF calculations is to consider the present value of future revenue. In effect, the companies calculate what rate of return is required over five or ten years to give an income equivalent to a

*We will assume for the moment that the company can only transfer income on the basis of declared profits. In practice inflated transfer payments to head office for goods and services provide another way of exporting profit.

† We are grateful to Martyn Marriott for drawing our attention to the importance of DCF in mining-company investment decisions.

certain return earned on an investment today. To return to the example given above: what annual gross profit does the company require to give a 20 per cent return on the investment in terms of today's money values? If the company demands a DCF yield of 20 per cent, and if we assume the tax rate in the country to be 73·05 per cent, then the annual gross profit will have to be 50 per cent of the original investment over a period of 20 years to meet the company's criteria. Thus, if the investment is $100 million, and the project starts with three years' expenditure of $33·3 million a year, the company will expect for two years cash flows of $50 million (untaxed because of the country's capital investment allowance) and 18 years of cash flows of $13·475 million (i.e. $50 million minus 73·05 per cent tax). If the company demands a 15 per cent DCF yield requirement under the same conditions, the mine would have to produce an annual gross profit of around $45 million. For a DCF yield of 25 per cent, under the same tax and capital allowance conditions, the mine will have to produce profits of $70 million a year. In general most mining companies require a DCF rate of return around 20 per cent, depending on their view of the risk attached to the investment.

DCF calculations highlight the importance to international corporations of maximizing cash flows. Indeed it is argued that the earnings and financial state of a company are shown more realistically by the cash flow than by the partial and limited figure of net profit, which is an accounting creation largely for the consumption of outsiders and investors.[13] The objective of company management is to maximize the return on invested capital.

Corporations today seek to optimize their profitability not their profits ... The objective of profit accumulation is not important. Instead their interest and the aim of their professional management become maximizing the profitability of the enterprise in terms of how efficiently capital is used and increases itself.[14]

If this is true, then the ratios of cash flow to turnover, net worth or wage costs are better criteria for measuring the annual and long-term results of the company than the traditional measurements of net profits, return on sales, and employee productivity.

Financial calculations are the most important determinant of the company's decision to open a mine, but the political climate, viewed from company headquarters, may dictate a much higher rate of return than the company's norm. For investments in Africa, the companies expect a higher return. An Amax executive has stated that the Botswana Selebi-Pikwe copper-nickel project is only a marginal project as the DCF return is claimed to be only 12 per cent.[15] Some companies have developed elaborate guidelines for assessing the investment climate (see Table 31) although not all companies use such a tightly structured assessment, preferring to rely instead on more informal methods.

Other factors may also enter the mining companies' decision, for an international company takes a long-term view. In Johannesburg Consolidated Investment, for example, there is an investment division which applies

a common yardstick to every project usually by means of discounted cash flow techniques. Clearly the group is looking for different rates of return from its various developments. The DCF test can also take account of considerations other than straight profit, assessing for instance, the comparative value of the 'education' JCI is going to derive from a venture.[16]

The overhead costs of maintaining expensive staffs require a continuous flow of new projects. Charter Consolidated, for example, has a staff of some 600 highly qualified and correspondingly paid technical staff in its exploration, engineering and administrative divisions.[17] Selection Trust, which is one of the smaller groups, has over 200 draughtsmen and engineers in its engineering division alone.[18] But apart from the need to meet these overhead costs, mining companies prefer to invest their capital in mines because of their accumulated expertise in mine development and mine management, even though other investments may offer a higher return.*

* Even if mining companies invest in non-mining projects, it tends to be in areas which have a close affinity to mining in terms of the scale, engineering and cash flow involved. Thus when Anglo diversified into non-mining activities in South Africa in the 1960s, it chose large-scale capital investment projects such as a steel plant and a paper mill.

Table 31: Assessing the investment climate
An example of a company's rating scale for determining a country's investment climate

| | Number of points | |
Item	Individual sub-category	Range for category
Capital repatriation:		
No restrictions	12	0–12
Restrictions based only on time	8	
Restrictions on capital	6	
Restrictions on capital and income	4	
Heavy restrictions	2	
No repatriation possible	0	
Foreign ownership allowed:		
100% allowed and welcomed	12	0–12
100% allowed, not welcomed	10	
Majority allowed	8	
50% maximum	6	
Minority only	4	
Less than 30%	2	
No foreign ownership allowed	0	
Discrimination and controls, foreign versus domestic business:		
Foreign treated same as local	12	0–12
Minor restrictions on foreigners, no controls	10	
No restrictions on foreigners, some controls	8	
Restrictions and controls on foreigners	6	
Some restrictions and heavy controls on foreigners	4	
Severe restrictions and controls on foreigners	2	
Foreigners not allowed to invest	0	
Currency stability:		
Freely convertible	20	4–20
Less than 10% open/black market differential	18	
10% to 40% open/black market differential	14	
40% to 100% open/black market differential	8	
Over 100% open/black market differential	4	
Political stability:		
Stable long term	12	0–12
Stable, but dependent on key person	10	
Internal factions, but government in control	8	

Table 31 – *cont.*

Item	Number of points	
	Individual sub-category	*Range for category*
Strong external and/or internal pressures that affect policies	4	
Possibility of coup (external and internal) or other radical change	2	
Instability, real possibility of coup or change	0	
Willingness to grant tariff protection		
Extensive protection granted	8	2–8
Considerable protection granted, especially to new major industries	6	
Some protection granted, mainly to new industries	4	
Little or no protection granted	2	
Availability of local capital:		
Developed capital market; open stock exchange	10	0–10
Some local capital available; speculative stock market	8	
Limited capital market: some outside funds (IBRD, AID) available	6	
Capital scarce, short term	4	
Rigid controls over capital	2	
Active capital flight unchecked	0	
Annual inflation for last 5 years:		
Less than 1%	14	2–14
1%–3%	12	
3%–7%	10	
7%–10%	8	
10%–15%	6	
15%–35%	4	
Over 35%	2	
Total		8–100

Source: Harvard Business Reviews, September–October 1969, quoted in Christopher Tugendhat, *The Multinationals*, Penguin Books, 1973, pp. 206–7.

TAXATION

The taxation policies of the host governments will be a factor in the investment decisions of the mining companies, but, because of the scale and scope of their operations, international companies are in a much stronger position than locally based companies.

To these giant capital accumulating companies, national governments – even quite powerful governments of developed countries which once had imperial power – are but client states, granted concessions of capital investment only on condition of good behaviour, e.g. tax allowances, state aid, credit guarantees, trade union laws and so on.[19]

Because of their size and financial power the mining companies can frequently negotiate special tax agreements designed to suit the company. In the colonial era the companies typically paid very low taxes. In the post-independence era, they have, after an initial struggle, accepted a higher nominal rate of tax. But, in fact, as a result of the various tax concessions granted, the host economies benefit very little from the economic surplus generated by the mining industry. In Zambia, the 1969 agreement promised the government 73 per cent of company profits, but the exemptions and allowances in the small print of the agreement produced a dramatic fall in government revenue. In Liberia for years the iron-ore companies have profited from the low level of taxation, and in Botswana the new Selebi-Pikwe mine operates under a special tax agreement specifically designed to suit the companies.*

The taxation provisions are crucial to Africa because the high capital intensity and relative unimportance of returns to labour in modern mines means that taxes are the main linkage between the mines and the host economy.† Any attempt to increase the national share of the surplus generated must therefore centre on the relationship between net profits and taxes. But this brings the government into conflict with the companies because

*For more details see Chapters 9 (Zambia), 11 (Liberia), and 14 (Botswana) respectively.
†See Chapter 20.

the attempt to raise revenues immediately brings into the open two business practices where the corporation exerts total discretion, to the detriment of the host economy; the company alone sets prices and it alone determines the optimal values of depreciation, amortization and depletion allowances.[20]

In this conflict the government lacks expertise and is in a weak bargaining position, because the ultimate weapon in the mining companies' hands is that heavier taxation will lead it to withhold investment for a new or an existing mine. The companies may curtail any expansion of productive capacity as they did in Zambia in the 1960s,* or they may even cease production altogether, as Aluminium Ltd did in Guinea in 1962.

The problem of taxing international mining companies is not unique to Africa[21] or underdeveloped countries,[22] but it is particularly serious in Africa. A recent study of mining laws and exploration agreements in Africa concluded that

because of the lack of well-defined laws, the expatriate mining concerns retain all the proceeds of export sales, except those which they must spend to meet their operating outlays in the country concerned ... The flow of outward payments to service mounting external loans and the repatriation of profits, and charges for other 'services' rendered by the private companies do not match the inward flow of fresh capital. The practice of multinational firms today is for the complete and immediate recovery of invested capital, and in the case of subsidiary companies maximum remittance of liquid assets to enable the parent company to register record profits.[23]

In other words Africa exports capital, along with its natural resources. The surplus generated by the mines still leaves Africa under a variety of tax allowances written into tax agreements, by inflated head office charges, transfer prices, and other forms of creative accounting. The net result is that the international company will pay tax wherever it best suits the company. The accounting departments of the major mining companies have a wealth of accounting techniques developed over years with which to evade the underdeveloped and over-stretched tax departments of African governments.

The key taxation provisions which enable the companies to

*See Chapter 11.

export the surplus generated by the mines are the tax deductions allowed against gross profits.[24] The companies want generous allowances for the time allowed and percentage deductible for amortization and capital depreciation. The more generous these allowances, the quicker a company's capital is released for further expansion and investment. More surplus is exported under any allowances granted for transport expenses and handling export sales.

Another significant proportion of gross profits goes into reserve funds for contingencies, equipment replacement, depletion. The companies hold these funds outside the host country and seek favourable tax treatment for the income derived from these funds. In Uganda the funds accumulated by Falconbridge 'for possible future expansion' were used to make special dividend payments of over $6 million in 1970, which was more than twice its share of the profits from the Kilembe mine that year.[25] Head office, management, design and consultancy charges are particularly hard for the government to cost accurately, and once again it is at the mercy of the company's discretion. Then there is the 'loan trick', where the parent company lends the subsidiary money but only on paper and the money is never in fact brought into the country. The subsidiary, however, includes the loan in its capital. This has the dual effect of making the profits seem not so disproportionate in relation to the investment, and providing another route for the export of surplus generated by the mine in the form of loan repayments to the parent company. Finally the pricing of the mine's output is at the company's discretion, and small differences in the price per unit may represent large differences in the declared total gross sales, and thus in net profits subject to government tax.

DESIGNING AND EQUIPPING THE MINE

In designing the new mine, and deciding the relative mix of capital and labour to be employed, the international mining companies use the capital-intensive mine technology developed for the industrial economies of Europe and North America, where labour is relatively expensive and the companies are under constant pressure to increase manpower productivity and reduce unit labour costs.[26] The tendency towards capital intensive mines is accentuated by the availability and relative cheapness of loan capital for the international mining companies, which generally have good credit ratings and a ready access to the major capital markets. The result is that, irrespective of the needs of the host economy, the mining companies design their mines according to the most advanced technology available in the metropolitan centres, even if this means that the company has to import large numbers of highly trained and highly paid expatriates to run the mines.

In recent years the companies have been switching from the mining of relatively small and high-grade underground deposits to open-cast surface mining of low-grade mineral deposits on a massive scale. This trend is partly reflected in the increasing number of open pit mines, but more in the tremendous increase in the size of the new mines.[27] By 1974 some 75 per cent of world metal-mining requirements and an ever-increasing proportion of mineral fuels were produced by surface mining methods.[28] This trend has been reflected in Africa by a new generation of mines such as Palabora in South Africa and Lamco in Liberia, which are essentially large-scale transport operations. Blasting, hauling and shipping of the ore is controlled by computers to reduce unit costs and gain maximum efficiency of operation. At Consolidated Diamond Mines' Namibian operation, where once large numbers of black labourers scratched and scrabbled on their knees for diamonds in the sand, today a R30 million fleet of heavy scrapers and earth-moving equipment operates round the clock shifting millions of tons of overburden and diamondiferous soil a year.

The trend towards larger and larger mines, both underground and open-cast, is closely linked to the development of new mine equipment and computerized analysis and control of the mines. As the companies have sought greater efficiency and low labour costs, so larger and larger machines have been developed; in particular there has been a dramatic expansion in the use of mechanized trackless equipment. In underground mines, whereas one-cubic-yard load-haul-dump (LHD) machines were common fifteen years ago, today five-cubic-yard machines are being rapidly introduced and new mines are being developed around machines of eight-cubic-yard capacity. In 1975, around 60 per cent of the world's largest underground mines were using mechanized trackless equipment to win all or part of their output.[29] Again, in open pit mines, whereas not long ago a 45 ton truck was considered to be fairly large, by the mid-seventies 75–100 ton trucks appeared to be the norm in major open pit mines, while 150 and 200 ton trucks were in use in several parts of the world.[30]

As the scale of the mines, and the complexity of new equipment have increased, the business of designing and constructing the new mines has become more and more specialized and is now the province of a small number of international firms. Mine design and construction is sometimes carried out by the mining groups themselves but increasingly is contracted out to specialist firms like the American giant, Bechtel,[31] or the smaller British company, Costains.

The mining processes are developed and licensed by the mining companies, as for example Anglo's TORCO process used in Zambia and Mauritania, or the Outokompu Oy smelting process being used in Botswana. The equipment comes from the international equipment manufacturers like International Harvester, Caterpillar, Eimco, Joy, Euclid, Wagner, Wabco, and Parnfischer. The tyres, including those specially developed and designed for open pit mining and for modern trackless equipment, come from Firestone, Goodyear and Bridgestone. The provision of drilling rigs and bits is in the hands of a few giants like Atlas Copco, Hughes Corporation, and Boart International.

The global standardization of operations by the international mining companies makes it increasingly difficult to decompose rival processes and make up a combined process geared in cost, scale, and type to the needs of an African economy. In fact there is a tendency for the international mining equipment companies to reproduce their existing technological monopoly as they compete against each other at the frontiers of technology to win a larger share of the world markets. Mine design and management techniques come in ready-assembled packages put together by, and leased from, the international mining companies, who then restrict the spread of these advanced techniques by erecting protective legal barriers in the form of patents and restrictive agreements.

The technological monopoly of the mining companies is reinforced by their policy of centralizing and concentrating their research and development facilities in the metropolitan centres, to reduce costs, and eliminate duplication of research effort. So Amax base metal research and development centre is in New Jersey, Newmont's research centre is in Danbury, Connecticut, Pechiney's research centre is at Ugine in France, while De Beers' research laboratories are in Johannesburg. The location of these research facilities is crucial to the mining groups, because it is their monopoly of the skill, experience, and knowledge required to design and operate modern mines that reinforces their continuing control of mineral development around the world. So far African countries have not attempted to follow the example of the Andean Pact countries in Latin America who have imposed strict control over imported technology with the aim of reducing their dependence on international companies.[32] But without such controls or local research facilities African countries will find it very difficult – if not impossible – to gain the research experience needed to develop the mining technology of tomorrow. Throughout the sixties the Takwa Mining School in Ghana was the only mining school in independent Africa.[33] Only in 1973 was black Africa's second mining school established in Zambia, more than forty years after the establishment of a local copper-mining industry.

FINANCING THE MINE

The vast scale of modern mines means that the 'investment of a half-billion dollars or more in a single mining venture is becoming quite commonplace'.[34] Rarely is a mine brought to development by the unaided activities of one company alone. The diamond mining activities of De Beers are perhaps an exception; but this is because the enormous cash flow generated by its control of the marketing end of the operation makes De Beers less dependent on external sources of finance. Few companies have the resources to go it alone. Smaller mining companies raise the money by inviting other companies to join them in consortia, and by raising a high proportion of the capital in the form of bank loans. Raising such large sums of money for a mine which it may take five years or more to bring to production is a specialized operation, relying on the international banks and the Eurodollar market.[35] Both joint ventures and bank finance reduce the influence of the host government. In a large-scale mineral development, joint ventures are attractive, according to Amax chairman Ian MacGregor,

because of their cost and risk-sharing features and their flexibility. They also make it easier to provide for participation by companies or government of the host country when such participation is required or encouraged.

In addition to accomplishing the objectives of risk-sharing and foreign equity or management participation, the joint venture is often selected because each participant can finance its own needs. If the venture is performed through a subsidiary, the financing can be accomplished without recourse to the parent company. Incorporation of the subsidiary can take place in whatever country a participant chooses. Tax considerations may be critical.[36]

The scale of investment means that bank loans are needed in addition to the capital generated by issuing shares in the mine. This is partly because

private investors will not take an owner's risk over the life of a project for all the capital needed. To put it another way, a rate of return that will induce private investors to undertake the risks of large-scale and long-term mining projects is achieved by obtaining some of the capital from lenders who will be satisfied to earn a fixed return for a fixed period in the early years *plus* having drastic power to foreclose and take over the property if anything upsets the fixed terms of the loans.[37]

The banks have responded to this new demand by setting up special departments which concentrate on mining projects, and successfully tapping the Eurodollar market for the large capital requirements.[38] The companies also feel that states will be less likely to default on a bank loan or expropriate the company's investment when the banks are involved. The dependence of African countries on the international mining companies is increased by the reliance on loan financing. Banks lending vast sums of money required for a modern mine look for an assured cash flow to guarantee repayments. As the mine has not come into production,

the cash flow is only in prospect and must therefore be defined. This is normally done by a firm sales contract with fixed or minimum prices (or take-or-pay arrangements) plus fully detailed arrangements to assure the satisfactory commencement of production to meet the sales contracts. This assurance that the project will be satisfactorily commissioned is the least publicized part of the financing agreements but is obviously critical. The borrower must demonstrate that there is not only the management and technical capability to bring the project to production but also adequate funds to meet any cost and/or time overruns if necessary.[39]

Because of the companies' greater financial resources, technical expertise, and superior marketing knowledge compared to anything the African governments can muster, the banks will in general lend only to the companies. By the same token, they prefer lending to the large mining groups rather than the smaller companies.

FINANCING THE INFRASTRUCTURE

If a mine is to be developed in some remote area of Africa, then the cost of providing the necessary roads, railways, and water and power supplies forms a large component of the total cost. Very often the companies ask the government to provide the infrastructure, and in such cases the World Bank and bilateral aid agencies are usually prepared to help with the financing. The cost to an African state of providing such infrastructure may be high. Servicing the necessary loan may well absorb the income from the mine for twenty years or more, leaving very little surplus to promote economic development. In addition the country's freedom of action will be severely reduced by the conditions attached to the loans. The World Bank and the international funding agencies demand guarantees that the loans can be serviced, i.e. that the revenue from the mines will cover the loan charges. To guarantee that the mines will produce sufficient income, the World Bank and its associates demand that the major mining corporations manage the mine. The companies believe that World Bank participation makes the project far less vulnerable to expropriation. This is especially true where the borrowing government agrees, as in both Botswana and Zambia, that any major disputes with outside investors be submitted to arbitration by the World Bank-sponsored International Centre for the Settlement of Investment Disputes (ICSID).

PROCESSING THE MINERAL OUTPUT

The ore has to go through several stages before it is ready for sale as metal to manufacturers.* After mining, the ore is milled, which usually involves crushing the different-sized lumps of ore to a smaller and more uniform size. The ore is then ground to a powder and the mineral-bearing particles in the powdered ore are concentrated by various chemical processes. This concentrate is then smelted to produce a matte, the metal content of which is steadily improved by further smelting to remove impurities and by-products. Then the final refining processes produce the metal in different grades for sale to the manufacturers.

Each stage in the smelting and refining process increases the value of the product and thus also the profit accruing to the mining companies. The underdeveloped countries of Africa therefore want the smelting and refining processes to be carried out locally for it is these stages which produce the highest additional value to the raw mineral and hence also the highest profit to the mining companies. So Zaire has now insisted that all Zairean copper must be locally refined by 1980.[40] And even South Africa, which is the most developed economy on the continent, feels that it exports too high a proportion of its base mineral output in an unprocessed state and is attempting to increase the proportion which is beneficiated and processed

* Minerals and gemstones go through a similar process of separation from the ore, sorting and final preparation for sale to consumers, and the problem of valuing the stones is a contentious issue. (See Chapter 17.)

locally.[41] Apart from anything else, a high-value mineral export will produce correspondingly higher revenue from export duties. Once again the interests of the mining companies are completely different from those of the host government.

The international mining companies locate the smelting and refining plant according to the needs of their global operations, not where Africa needs them. Low-value mineral export has the advantage for the company that it will attract relatively low taxes in Africa and will also escape tariff penalties levied by the developed countries.

The companies want the smelting and refining processes where they can achieve the highest economies of scale, and have most control of the marketing of the final product. They prefer, therefore, to refine and sometimes smelt the ore as far as possible in the metropolitan centres. Iron ore which typically grades between 40 and 65 per cent metal content is often shipped direct, but copper ores which typically grade anywhere between 1 and 6 per cent metal content are concentrated and smelted close to the mine before being shipped. But even then the company may not refine the copper locally. Union Minière preferred to produce only blister copper in Zaire because it involved a smaller foreign investment per final ton produced (and lower local tax liabilities), and because it had a centralized refinery at Hoboken in Belgium serving several mines.[42] Union Minière also benefited from the valuable by-products recovered in the refining of Zairean ore. A mining company may wish to keep an existing refinery which it owns elsewhere in the world running at full capacity and may therefore be unwilling to build a refining plant in Africa. In Botswana, Amax insisted that the copper-nickel matte produced at Selebi-Pikwe be refined at its Port Nickel refinery in Louisiana which it had just bought and which needed a guaranteed source of minerals to maintain full operating efficiency.

Locating the mining, refining and manufacturing processes in different parts of the world reduces the companies' vulnerability to local pressure. Kaiser Aluminium decided for economic and political reasons to process Jamaican bauxite in its US plants to smelt alumina with cheap Ghanaian power from the Volta

Dam and export the aluminium. Since the alumina was imported, the smelter in Ghana was located at the port and the local bauxite reserves remained untouched. Similarly Pechiney-Ugine-Kuhlmann ships Guinean alumina to its smelter in Cameroun.[43]

As the industrialized nations develop their technology so the international mining groups alter their beneficiation and refining policy, but always it is the changing needs of the metropolitan centres and the companies which determine plant location in Africa, and not the needs of Africa. So, for example, the development of the massive open-cast iron-ore mines of West Africa was closely linked to the development of bulk ore ocean carriers which made long hauls of over 10,000 miles economic.[44] Several orebodies have become exploitable because of the lower cost of ocean transport.[45] At first the ore was shipped direct, but as the percentage of pelletized and sintered ore used in the metropolitan blast furnaces increased from 16 per cent to 65 per cent between 1950 and 1964[46] so the mining companies have responded by building pelletizing and sintering plants in Africa, as in Liberia, for example.

This trend is by no means universal: for example MIFERMA in Mauritania was firmly opposed to local processing or upgrading of mine product, and still exports run-of-the-mine ore. However, the rise in fuel costs may well lead to a restructuring of the world trade in bulk materials,[47] and the trend in steel technology towards direct reduction processes may mean a further change in the materials demanded by metropolitan steel companies.[48] The next decade may well see giant-sized complexes sited near cheap energy sources to produce semi-finished steel which is then transshipped to the metropolitan centres for further conversion.[49]

TARIFF BARRIERS

The locational preferences of the mining companies for centrally sited refineries are reinforced by the level of tariffs set by the industrialized nations, which are designed to protect their

*See below, page 433.

domestic refining and manufacturing industries. These industries are often either owned by or closely linked to the major international mining companies. In 1932, during the economic depression, the United States used a tariff of 4 cents a pound on copper to seal off the market from European competitors.

Today the tariffs are generally either very low or non-existent for unrefined ores and rise sharply if the product is smelted or refined. For example, the United States imposes no duty on copper-bearing ores, but copper wire is taxed at US 1·85 cents per pound plus a 15 per cent ad valorem tax.* Copper seamless pipes and tubes are subject to a duty of 4·5 cents per pound; and as an example thumbtacks made of copper were subject to a 14 per cent ad valorem tax.[50] Similarly whereas unprocessed bauxite is free of import duty, unwrought aluminium is taxed at 1 cent per pound and wrought aluminium in the form of plates, sheets, bars, rods, circles and discs is subject to a 2 cents a pound tariff.[51] The Common External Tariff of the EEC countries is very similar. All metallic ores and concentrates are imported free of duties, but smelted and refined metal products are subject to a rising ad valorem percentage tax.[52]

MINERAL TRANSPORT

As with all other aspects of mining in Africa, the transport of the minerals is firmly under the control of the mining companies. In fact the network of mineral transport in Africa is a separate system, almost completely divorced from the local economies. Minerals were the magnet which drew many of the existing railway lines across the continent.[53] The result is that today there are two distinct types of African transport, one based largely on the railways and catering for the export of minerals and other primary products, and the other based on roads, that handle imports, local traffic and generally serve the domestic markets.[54] Although African governments, for example Liberia and Swaziland, have tried to influence the routing and design of the mineral railways, they are primarily designed to facilitate the company's movement of minerals around the world and do not generally

*ad valorem = charged in proportion to the value.

make a significant contribution to the growth of domestic markets. This is because railways geared to the export of minerals, such as those in Liberia* and Mauritania, only permit development at selected points along the line of rail and at the ports, which have often been specially constructed to handle the mineral exports.[55]

The minerals are usually shipped in the mining companies' own ore carriers, supplemented by ore carriers on charter. LAMCO uses the Providence Shipping Company, which it owns, to ship its iron ore; similarly in Ghana, Kaiser Aluminium imports alumina for the Tema smelter in its own ships.† Even if the ore carriers are not owned or contracted to the mining companies the African countries are in a poor position to ship their own minerals. Most of the world's shipping is owned and controlled by companies based in the industrialized nations. In 1970 the Third World owned only 7·8 per cent of total tonnage and an even smaller proportion of world bulk carriers.[56]

BIG COMPANIES, SMALL NATIONS

The dominance of the international mining companies in the African economy is revealed at each stage of the development of a new mine. This dominance is reinforced, as in the Selebi-Pikwe project in Botswana, by the demands of the banks and the international financial agencies for completion agreements and guarantees which only the international giants have the financial and technical resources to meet. Neither small countries nor small companies can expect to finance and develop an important mine within the world capitalist economy without the participation of the international mining companies, and as the price of their participation the companies demand total control of the project. This does not put African nations in a very strong position to control the marketing of their minerals in world markets.

*See Figure 10.   † See below, page 429ff.

16 The Marketing of Africa's Minerals

The level of world metal prices significantly affects foreign exchange earnings, government revenue, and consequently economic development in Africa. The booming commodity prices of 1972-3 and their subsequent collapse in 1974 focused attention on the wild fluctuations of market prices for minerals, and promoted much speculation about collective action by mineral-exporting countries. But at the moment African mineral-exporting countries exercise very little influence over the price, because their mineral trade is still firmly controlled by a small number of international mining companies which also manipulate world markets.

IRON ORE

Most of the world's iron ore is not in fact traded on any market, because a large proportion of world exports come from mines owned or controlled by steel works. Out of the 176 million tons of ore exported in 1964 about one third came from mines in which steel concerns owned more than 50 per cent of the capital.[1] Most of Africa's major iron-ore mines are owned by steel concerns.*

Traditionally iron ore was sold by agreement over the quantity and price of ore for the coming year. In the last twenty-five years, the high capital cost of new mines has encouraged contracts covering much longer periods, because the companies and the banks need a guaranteed market until the mine's debts have been paid. The LAMCO contracts run for fifteen years, and some contracts run for forty. It is possible that when a new mine

*See Chapter 12 and Appendix 1.

has established its ore on the market, and the long-term contracts expire, it will revert to annual contracts.[2] But if it is owned partly or wholly by a steel company, they may insist on long-term contracts, which was one of their reasons for investing in the mine in the first place.

The price for any given iron ore is a function of both its grade and its physical characteristics, and the attractiveness of these particular qualities to the steel works. A fully integrated steel works with adequate sintering* capacity can accept a far greater proportion of fines† than can a works without this capacity. A relatively small steel plant equipped with electric or other small capacity reduction furnaces will require a higher grade of ore as it cannot handle large amounts of slag. In short, the metallurgical value of an ore cannot be universally defined, but will vary from one consumer to another, which is why there is no quoted market price for iron ore as there is for metals like copper, and bilateral agreements are the most convenient method of setting prices. As an example of the possible range of prices, the Japanese iron and steel industry signed contracts with Liberia in 1965 for 130,000 tons of 65 per cent Fe grade ore at an F.O.B. price of US $7·6 per ton; and in the same year contracted for 5·1 million tons over six years from Angola, grading 62–64 per cent Fe at an F.O.B. price of US $6·04 per ton.[3]

ALUMINIUM

Aluminium is a relatively new metal that was smelted commercially for the first time in 1910. And it

has from the beginning had a strenuous fight to wrest business from age-old competitors such as iron and steel, copper, brass, lead, etc. This fight could obviously not have been successful if the price of aluminium had not been sufficiently low to have encouraged substitution on an economic basis.[4]

---

* Sintering is fusing a mass of metal particles by pressure and heating below melting point.

† Fines are fine fragments or tiny particles of crushed rock, separated by screening.

World aluminium production is controlled by six major companies: Alcan, Alcoa, Kaiser, Amax, Alusuisse, and Pechiney-Ugine-Kuhlmann. Tight control of world bauxite mining, alumina smelting, and aluminium production has enabled the companies to keep aluminium prices both low and stable. To reduce unit costs, production facilities are installed on a high-volume basis, and production capacity has frequently run ahead of demand, so intensifying the companies' search for new sales outlets and discouraging any price increases. Indeed:

The high capital cost and the excess capacity have resulted in the acceptance of sales at low price simply for the purpose of covering the high fixed costs.[5]

The companies have consciously decided to encourage future demand at the expense of present profits, and the low prices reflect

the determination, and discipline of the producers to offer aluminium on terms which would virtually compel users to switch from other metals to aluminium.[6]

The aluminium companies' control of production and marketing has enabled them to eliminate the violent price fluctuations that afflict so many minerals. Aluminium contracts are made on the basis of prices ruling at the time of delivery. The fabricators accept this arrangement because prices have been stable over the years. The aluminium producers thus prevent the possibility of buying forward or hedging, so that no group of speculators and agents can play havoc with the market price, as happens in the case of copper.

The only potential threat to the aluminium pricing structure comes from the marketing policy of the USSR. In 1958 there was a brief period of panic among the big companies, when aluminium from the USSR was sold on the British market at prices below the ruling producer price. But after negotiations, the USSR agreed to restrict exports of ingots, scrap and semi-manufactures to Western Europe. The big six, for their part, agreed to purchase all ingot aluminium offered for export by the USSR and East European countries at an agreed price, which was below the world price but above that at which the socialist states would generally be able to sell on the Western market.*

PLATINUM

The world platinum market is controlled by the world's largest producer, Rustenburg Platinum, which sets its price without worrying about being undercut by other producers. The primary consideration is what the market will bear.[7]

It is perhaps a little misleading to talk of a world market for platinum at all. Rustenburg sells the bulk of its production on contract. Until 1966, sales were simply between Rustenburg (then the only South African producer) and the two major refiners, Johnson Matthey and Engelhard Metals. The small London market consisted of the bullion ring, a few platinum specialists like Sam Ayrton, and the large metal merchants who made occasional forays into the market. The New York market was, and remains, equally small and club-like. These markets handle the supplies from the USSR, for which Ayrton Metals† is the agent; production from a few small mines in America and Canada; and scrap. In 1966 the first of the new South African producers came on stream. Today Union Corporation's Impala Platinum, Lonrho's Western Platinum, and Anglovaal's Atok Platinum, all sell the bulk of their production on contract; following Rustenburg's producer price. The market price thus indicates whether the consumers need additional supplies or not, and Rustenburg buys or sells on the market to bring the price more into line with the producer price.

Rustenburg has consistently tried to persuade consumers to use platinum more extensively, by guaranteeing adequate supplies and maintaining a constant price even in the face of rising demand. In 1963 a shortage of platinum developed almost overnight, because the petrol companies needed more platinum catalysts to make high octane petrol. Rustenburg kept the pro-

---

*Western fabricators demand a heavy discount on aluminium coming from USSR and Eastern Europe, since supplies are uncertain.

†Now a Union Corporation subsidiary.

ducer price steady despite the temptation to go for short-term profits.

They did this although they probably suspected that some of their customers, who were paying about £50 per ounce for their monthly quota, were immediately selling it on the free market for more than £100 per ounce ...

The rationale for a steady producer price is that by this means customers will not be encouraged to use cheaper substitutes as, for example, happens periodically in the copper market. A stable producer price moreover does not discourage consumers from maintaining their own stockpile of platinum products.[8]

Rustenburg's response was to institute a massive expansion programme, increasing its output for eight consecutive years up to 1971.

Throughout the 1960s Rustenburg made an enormous investment in research, promotion and productive capacity to win new industrial markets for platinum. The main aim was to get platinum used in the automobile emission control units, needed to meet anti-pollution legislation in the USA. As research was intensified, Rustenburg emphasized the unique properties of platinum and the stability of both supplies and prices. To convince the motor manufacturers that the industry could meet the demand if a platinum catalyst was chosen, both Rustenburg and the new Impala mine expanded production and stockpiled large quantities of platinum. In 1971, however, declining sales, due to a recession in the USA, Russian sales on the free market, and the expanded capacity in South Africa, led to falling prices and a serious crisis. The producers' stockpile reached 1·5 million ounces; or more than one year's output in South Africa. Rustenburg was forced to cut back production. Large numbers of African mineworkers, and a smaller number of white miners, were dismissed at short notice. The workforce was cut from 35,000 to 14,000. Ford had announced in June 1971 that they would use a platinum-base emission control unit developed by Engelhard Minerals and Chemicals. But the breakthrough came in 1973: General Motors, Chrysler and Toyota all announced contracts with South African producers for large quantities of platinum. A vast new market worth $250 million a year had been won by Rustenburg's marketing strategy.

NICKEL

The world nickel market is dominated by three large mining companies; two Canadian and one French. The world's largest nickel producer, accounting for almost half of world production, is the International Nickel Co. (INCO). Most of INCO's nickel comes from its mines in Sudbury, Ontario. With its long-established mines in New Caledonia, IMETAL (formerly Société le Nickel and controlled by Rothschilds) is the world's second largest producer. The price set by INCO is taken as the producer price and followed by the other Canadian producer, Falconbridge Nickel; the new Australian producers such as Western Mining; and the smaller mines, such as the Anglo/Amax Selebi-Pikwe mine in Botswana. In fact, the Selebi-Pikwe mine's fifteen-year contract with its German customers stipulates that the price will be 'the INCO price', less a small discount.[9] Although INCO's position is gradually weakening as new mines come on stream, it is still true that if any producer tries to set an independent price, as Falconbridge did briefly in December 1974, INCO's marketing muscle will ensure that prices are brought back into line.[10] Rustenburg Platinum produces substantial quantities of nickel as a by-product, which it sells under contract direct to INCO at well below market price. In return INCO, which produces platinum as a by-product, ensures that its sales do not disrupt Rustenburg's marketing of platinum.

ANTIMONY

The South African company, Consolidated Murchison, controlled by JCI and Anglovaal, is the only significant antimony producer outside China and Bolivia. A relatively unimportant proportion of its output is sold on the open market. Most goes direct to the British company Associated Lead, which is the biggest refiner of antimony in the world. Nearly all the rest goes

379

to three US refineries. Deals on the open market are invariably for small quantities, apart from the Chinese supplies. If Consolidated Murchison feels that the market price is getting too far out of line with the producer price, it adjusts its supply of antimony on to the market. This deters marginal suppliers and new small-scale antimony producers from springing up.[11]

CHROME AND ASBESTOS

Two other important South African mineral exports are asbestos and chrome. The large Canadian asbestos producers set the prices for chrysolite asbestos, but General Mining's Gefco produces almost the entire world output of blue asbestos and so can minimize price fluctuations to a certain extent. Prices for low-grade South African chrome remained constant for most of the sixties and early seventies, not because the producers exercised control but because they undercut each other unmercifully, allowing merchants and consumers to manipulate the market.[12] Rhodesia is a major producer of high-grade metallurgical chrome, which commands a better price than chemical-grade chrome.

GOLD

Gold is unique among African metal exports because of the crucial role it plays in the world monetary system. In consequence its price has been held stable for long periods at a time, first by Britain and then by the USA, as the world's major financial powers. Such was, in effect, the first international commodity agreement. But in the early seventies, largely as a result of world monetary instability, the majority of the world's gold began, like other mineral commodities, to be sold at a fluctuating price on the free market. There were two prices at which gold could supposedly be sold. The 'official' rate was the price (in 1972: of $42·22 an ounce) which governed sales between the world's central banks. But with the free market price so much higher, the 'official' one was in practice a price at which central banks would gladly buy but never sell. The devaluation of the dollar in 1972 simply meant that there was then 'a new price at which Washington refuses to sell gold, namely $42·22 per ounce'.[13] The other price was the 'free market' price, which is the price at which gold is bought and sold on the London and Zurich markets. This price has rocketed from around $38 an ounce, when the two-tier system was first introduced in 1967, to over $100 an ounce at the height of intense currency speculation in early 1973, and about $190 an ounce in 1974 before falling back to $160–170 for most of 1975. In 1976 the two-tier system was abandoned and the official price of gold abolished. The price fell to $103 an ounce in August that year, depressed by the proposed IMF gold auctions, but it resumed its upward movement as the dollar weakened and reached more than $200 an ounce in mid-1978.

Most of the world's gold is produced from mines controlled by the seven South African mining finance houses (see Figure 18). The gold is first refined at each mine and then sent to the Chamber of Mines Rand Refinery at Germiston, just outside Johannesburg, where it is refined to a standard of 99·5 per cent gold. The South African Reserve Bank acts as the selling agent for the mining companies, and the gold bars are sent to the London and Zurich markets. The traditional route was by Union Castle passenger ships to Southampton, but Zurich is now the more important of the two markets and the gold is flown there in specially chartered jets.[14] The role of the South African Reserve Bank, interposed between the mining companies and their markets, is a unique one. Under South African exchange control regulations, the mines must offer all their gold to the Reserve Bank for sale. As a central bank, the South African Reserve Bank will then decide how much of the gold should go into South Africa's gold and foreign currency reserves, so affecting the amount of gold available on the free market and thus the price. Reserve Bank retentions from April to October 1972 had a direct impact on the free market price, as Figure 19 shows. The retention was due partly to balance of payments considerations, but in part also to the desire of the South African government and

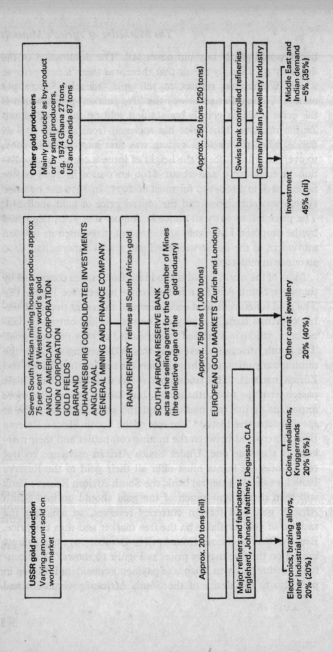

USSR gold production
Varying amount sold on world market

Approx. 200 tons (nil)

Other gold producers
Mainly produced as by-product or by small producers, e.g. 1974 Ghana 27 tons, US and Canada 87 tons

Approx. 250 tons (250 tons)

Seven South African mining houses produce approx 75 per cent of Western world's gold

ANGLO AMERICAN CORPORATION
UNION CORPORATION
GOLD FIELDS
BARRAND
JOHANNESBURG CONSOLIDATED INVESTMENTS
ANGLOVAAL
GENERAL MINING AND FINANCE COMPANY

RAND REFINERY refines all South African gold

SOUTH AFRICAN RESERVE BANK acts as the selling agent for the Chamber of Mines (the collective organ of the gold industry)

Approx. 750 tons (1,000 tons)

EUROPEAN GOLD MARKETS (Zurich and London)

Swiss bank controlled refineries

German/Italian jewellery industry

Major refiners and fabricators:
Englehard, Johnson Matthey, Degussa, CLA

Electronics, brazing alloys, other industrial uses
20% (20%)

Coins, medallions, Krugerrands
20% (5%)

Other carat jewellery
20% (40%)

Investment
45% (nil)

Middle East and Indian demand
–5% (35%)

mining companies to establish the free price of gold in the $60 to $70 range.

The whole gold market has changed radically since South Africa switched sales from London to Zürich. Most gold is not sold on the market as in London, but direct to the major Swiss banks buying on their own account, who then offer gold to buyers. The result is that the market has now gone 'underground'. The secretiveness of Swiss bank operations enables speculators and even central banks to buy gold without embarrassing disclosures. With accelerating worldwide inflation, there has also been a rapid increase in the proportion of gold bought for hoarding. To meet this demand the South African Central Bank began minting Kruger rands, or one-ounce gold coins, which offered the public at large the opportunity to buy gold direct.

1974 was an exceptional year, with a massive increase in private bullion purchases and a collapse of industrial demand (see Figure 18). The pattern of sales subsequently returned to a pattern broadly similar to that of 1970. In 1977 an estimated 1,300 tonnes went into industrial uses, including jewellery (979 tonnes) and dentistry (81 tonnes), with coins and medallions taking 180 tonnes. About 220 tonnes were hoarded or used for speculation. The gold came from mine production of around 965 tonnes, while the communist bloc provided some 400 tonnes, and net official sales by the central banking system, including the IMF, contributed a further 241 tonnes to the net total of 1,607 tonnes available in that year.

Fig. 18. The world gold trade, 1974

NOTES: All production figures and market shares are approximate as the price of gold changes. Figures in brackets give the position in 1970.

1970: Gold price US $35 an ounce. World production 1,273 metric tons.

1974: Gold price US $170 an ounce. World production 1,016 metric tons.

SOURCE: *Financial Mail* supplement, 'Gold' Johannesburg 17 November 1972, p. 60. *Mining Annual Review 1975*, Mining Journal, p. 35.

URANIUM

Uranium is of great strategic importance to the industrialized nations, and so governments are involved in the world trade of uranium. Government agencies are the major consumers, and most contracts for military or atomic energy supplies cover several years at fixed prices. Companies mine the uranium but contracts are often settled at government level. In June 1975 uranium companies responsible for 60 per cent of world production established the Uranium Institute to coordinate their activities. Prices have risen from about US $6·00 a pound in 1973 to US $43 a pound at the end of 1977.

COPPER

In contrast to the stable prices of the vertically integrated and government or producer controlled industries, copper is notorious for its violent price movements.

Shortages and threats of shortages send prices rocketing – often out of all proportion to the realities of the situation – and every boom is followed by recession as production inevitably catches up with, and frequently overtakes, the world demand.

A stable copper market has long been the dream of producers and consumers and some of the best brains in the industry have been applied to solving the problem as to how this can be brought about. Alas, despite recent new attempts, the solution appears to be as elusive as ever and the only remaining certainty about the copper market seems to be its traditional uncertainty.[15]

The instability of the copper market stems from the fragmented structure of the industry and a competition between American and European companies which undermines all attempts to control copper prices. In the 1890s a European syndicate temporarily doubled the price of copper by buying up all mine supplies; but the high price brought a flood of new and scrap metal on to the market, and the prices collapsed.* From 1918 to 1923, the US copper companies ran the Copper Export Association, which successfully curtailed US domestic produc-

*This was the famous Secretan corner.

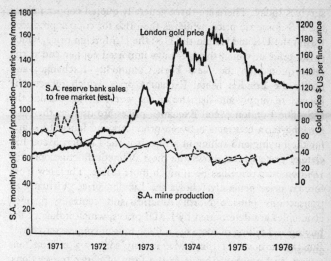

Fig. 19. The relationship between South African gold sales and the free market price of gold 1971–October 1976.

SOURCE: *Mining Journal*, 29 October 1977, 'Analysis of Rand and OFS Quarterlies', p. 9.

tion while the post-war surplus was absorbed. The Association collapsed under the rival claims of the domestic producers and those with extensive foreign interests.[16] In 1926 Copper Exporters Inc. was established. This cartel included not only the major US companies but also Union Minière and Rio Tinto, and controlled some 95 per cent of world production. 'The aim of the cartel was price stability and its target was the London Metal Exchange merchants and brokers.'[17] In the boom leading up to 1929 supplies were insufficient, prices rose, and new production from Canada and Northern Rhodesia threatened the cartel. As the world depression took effect, the US producers persuaded the US government to impose a four cents a pound tariff on imported copper in 1932. The foreign members of the cartel resigned in protest, and concentrated on ensuring their own self-sufficiency.

The division between the American and European companies

survives today. There are three generally quoted copper prices: the US domestic price, which is the price for copper produced within the US and sold in the US; the US foreign price, which is the price at which the US buys imported copper and is the price quoted on the New York Commodity Exchange; and finally the London Metal Exchange price, which reflects the balance of supply and demand on the world market outside the US. The London Metal Exchange prices are used as the basis for long-term contracts between producers and fabricators, and for the buying and selling of scrap. It is the London Metal Exchange price which shows the most dramatic fluctuations; the US domestic price has been much more stable. The New York foreign price generally follows the London price. Virtually all transactions outside North America and centrally planned economies are determined by LME prices, which influence the buying and selling of some 6·5 million tons of copper per year.[18] But the turnover of the LME is only some 2·3 million tons a year, and much of this is in the form of paper transactions. The actual metal handled by the market is a mere 500,000 tons a year. It was estimated in 1968, for example, that only 14 per cent of copper imported in the UK was handled by the London Metal Exchange. Most producers sell direct to customers, and LME warehouse stocks come largely from custom smelters.

Apart from establishing a guide price for long-term contracts, the London Metal Exchange price measures the balance of supply and demand. It is the marginal imbalance of supply and demand in the copper trade which underlies the extreme sensitivity of the LME prices. Marginal influences on marginal balances lead to enormous price movements.[19] Figure 20 shows the fluctuations in copper prices from 1965 to 1978. In 1965 Sir Ronald Prain, Chairman of Roan Selection Trust and a widely respected authority on the copper industry, put the position succinctly:

The London Metal Exchange, the foremost of the metal commodity exchanges, is a fine institution, almost perfectly designed, if it is desired to have a sensitive barometer which will reflect the marginal

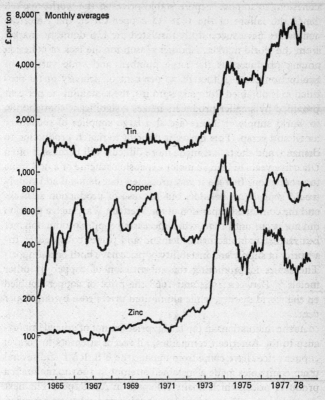

Fig. 20. Copper, tin and zinc prices on the London Metal Exchange, 1965–75
SOURCE: LME figures.

supply and demand. However, several developments have led to a growing questioning of whether an industry such as the copper industry can afford to allow its price to be based on such a sensitive barometer.[20]

The price fluctuations continue because no group of companies or countries has sufficient copper production, or the necessary cohesion, to impose a more stable price on the world market. Since the failure of the 1928–32 copper cartel, the American companies have successfully insulated the US domestic market from the world market. Another reason for the lack of cohesion among producers is the large number, and wide variety, of production costs. Although 70 per cent of primary metal production is obtained from large groups, the remaining 30 per cent provided by smaller producers makes a significant contribution to world supply.[21] There are also large supplies of secondary metal and scrap. This makes it difficult to match production to demand, and the task is made more difficult still because it often takes five years to bring a major expansion scheme or a new mine to production. In 1964 it was predicted that demand and supply would soon be in balance, but because of production setbacks and the continued expansion of the Vietnam War, such a position did not occur until 1970, when increasing copper production met contracting manufacturing demand and prices collapsed.[22] Insecurity of supply and instability of price have both been important factors in promoting the substitution of copper by other metals.[23] Between 1964 and 1968 the price of copper doubled on the world market, while aluminium prices rose by only 7 per cent.

As the fluctuations in the LME price are not of crucial importance to the American companies, all recent attempts to control copper prices have come from outside the US. RST and several other companies made a sustained attempt in 1961 to maintain a producer price, which finally collapsed in April 1966. The next attempt to coordinate copper production and marketing came in 1967, when a group of producing countries – Zambia, Zaire, Chile and Peru – got together to form the Copper Exporters Council (CIPEC – Le Conseil Intergouvernemental des Pays Exportateurs de Cuivre) in imitation of the successful oil producers' group (OPEC). But the copper-producing countries have not shown the same degree of cohesion as the oil producers. They have sometimes been able to agree on production cutbacks; but when the market begins to pick up again, political differences and the different production costs lead the producers in different directions. The aim of CIPEC is to exert enough influence on the market to minimize violent fluctuations (such as occurred, for example, in 1973 and 1974) while maintaining CIPEC members' share of the total market. But

> The real options open to CIPEC to exert any substantial influence are limited. It would be a matter of great practical difficulty to support a floor price during hard times and local political expediency would almost certainly inhibit agreement or a cutback programme except during periods of exceptionally low prices ... While world economies shake under the impact of successive currency crises and economic activity cycles reach peaks and troughs of greater amplitude at an increasing frequency rate, it is to be expected that the cycle in commodities such as copper will surely follow. CIPEC's problem is to look after the long-term interests of its member nations, whilst accommodating their immediate political necessities and it must attempt to do this in an economic climate which exerts a very great deal of influence on the world market, in which the organization's members operate but which currently seems to be running out of control.[24]

Although CIPEC members produce approximately 70 per cent of the world's copper exports, they are simply not powerful enough as a group to dictate price levels on the world market.

> CIPEC members have been able to do no more than wait on the sidelines and watch the economic game develop, while internal political and production problems of some of the members have limited the organization's ability to act positively.[25]

One recent attempt to exert some control over world copper markets came in April 1975. The export of surplus copper by Japanese smelters was the major influence behind the collapse of world copper prices from £1,400 to £500 a ton in 1974. Finally, in November 1974, Japan banned copper exports, but the surplus stocks building up threatened to bankrupt the smelters in 1975. So RTZ, which is a major supplier of both copper and iron ore to Japan, tried to organize a copper stabilization scheme, in which a financial consortium would remove the huge surplus of copper in Japan, estimated at 250,000 tons.[26] The attempt failed, and the huge stocks continued to hang over the copper market, depressing prices below the costs of production in some CIPEC countries. By 1978 the price of copper had fallen to its lowest level, in real terms, for twenty-five years.

The creation of a buffer stock has frequently been canvassed as a solution to the price fluctuations of the copper market. A UNIDO monograph on the non-ferrous metals industry argues for the establishment of a considerable stockpile, financed by both governments and mining companies:

With the correct approach and with a suitable surplus capacity backed by stocks, it would be possible to preserve a measure of stability in the economic situation resulting from the competition of alternative materials.[27]

But the difficulties of a buffer stock arrangement for copper, similar to that operated under the International Tin Agreement, are formidable. Agreement on the price range would be extremely hard to secure in view of varying producer costs and the widely fluctuating price levels of recent years. Even if an agreement could be reached, the kind of investment involved would be enormous. It is estimated that the size of the stockpile would have to be about one million tons, but since buffer stocks also have to buy in excess supplies, the maximum holding could, in certain circumstances, rise to double this amount. The cost of financing a stockpile of one million tons of copper, and reserves to buy an additional one million at a cost of perhaps £700 per metric ton, would be massive. The copper producers outside the US would find it a long-term and difficult task to build up such a buffer stock and financial reserve without additional funds. Only the US government, the EEC, or the OPEC countries could finance a stockpile of this magnitude.

TIN AGREEMENT

The advocates of a buffer stock for copper often point to the success of the International Tin Council's buffer stock operation in evening out the fluctuations on the world tin market. The price of tin had moved almost as erratically as that of copper and tinplate users were reducing their dependence by developing more economical methods of tinplating and by using alternative materials, when the first International Tin Agreement was signed in 1956. It was to run for five years. The current agreement is the fifth and came into effect in July 1976.

The Agreement, concluded under the auspices of the United Nations, aims to 'prevent excessive fluctuations in the price of tin and in export earnings from tin'.[28] It also aims to increase the export earnings of the producing countries. It uses export quotas in the producer countries to control supply; and a buffer stock of approximately 20,000 tons (or the equivalent in cash) on the free market to even out price fluctuations. The export quotas of the main producing countries are established from time to time by the International Tin Council, and it is the responsibility of each producing country to keep production and exports in line with the agreed quota. The aim is to adjust supply to demand as far as possible and prevent fluctuations. The buffer stock manager, who was given increased power and flexibility under the Fourth Agreement, buys excess supplies of tin coming on to the market if they threaten to push prices below the agreed floor level. If prices go above the agreed ceiling, the manager is a net seller of tin from the stockpile. The floor level in 1966 was £1,100. In 1970 this was raised to £1,350 and the ceiling level was fixed at £1,650 and by 1975 the floor level had reached £2,300, and the ceiling £3,230.[29] The combination of the two controls is necessary, because while export control is 'undoubtedly a more effective weapon than is the buffer stock in adjusting supply to demand . . . it is a weapon which may have harsh effects on immediate employment and it may be subject to long-term ill effects'.[30] Should there be a radical increase in demand, producer countries might be unable to take advantage of it, if they had had to cut back mining activities too severely in the previous slack period. Dual controls give the agreement added flexibility. In 1971, for example, no export controls were imposed, but the buffer stock manager bought in the market on a small scale. An important feature of the Fourth and Fifth International Tin Agreements was the arrangement for financing the buffer stock operation. The International Monetary Fund has made it clear that it regards the Tin Agreement as one of the appropriate type for inter-governmental commodity control, and it will permit countries contributing to the buffer stock to finance such contributions through their IMF drawing rights. This is the first time that the IMF has offered such facilities in support of a commodity agreement.

The International Tin Agreement is signed by two groups of countries, all members of the International Tin Council. Signatories to the agreement have gradually increased until almost all the major producing and consuming countries are now included. Each group is apportioned a number of votes corresponding to the relative size of either its production or consumption.*

The ITC has succeeded in minimizing price fluctuations, but this is only partly due to the activities of the producer countries. The key factor differentiating the world tin market from the world copper market is that the USA and the other developed countries do not themselves produce significant quantities of tin. They are almost totally dependent on the Malaysian, Indonesian and Bolivian tin producers, and so it is in the consumers' interests to minimize price fluctuations. Another factor is the distribution of refineries. The US has not developed a refining industry based on foreign ores, largely because of Britain's traditional importance as a smelter and refiner of tin. To protect its weak position in the market the US leant its general support to the International Tin Council, while building up a large stockpile which is now an ever-present threat to the Tin Agreement. The existence of these large stocks and the dominance of the consumer countries in the ITC held prices low and discouraged investment, so that although for the first time the USA was a signatory to a new Agreement, the ITC was unable to maintain control over the market. The shortfall in production was so great (over 15,000 tons in 1977) that the buffer stock was exhausted in January 1977 and the manager could do nothing to

*The producers on the ITC are: Malaysia, Bolivia, Thailand, Indonesia, Nigeria, Zaire, and Australia. The major consumers are Japan, UK, Federal Germany, France, Italy, Netherlands, Canada and India.

prevent the price soaring to £7,335 per tonne in December that year. (See Figure 20.)

LIMITATIONS OF THE MARKET

The market is a very imperfect mechanism. The market price brings into relationship only immediate demand and immediate supply, although speculation about future demand and supply is also an influence. Prices are affected by the level of world production, of available supplies and of industrial demand, but they are also manipulated by the international mining companies for profit. Forward buying allows mineral users to hedge their bets on future market trends. But it also allows speculators to distort the market. Finally the market does not take into account the long-term diminution of world mineral reserves, or the true cost to Africa and the other underdeveloped nations of their lost resources. So mineral-exporting countries have in recent years been exploring alternative marketing arrangements.

COOPERATION AMONG PRODUCER COUNTRIES

Most African minerals are not marketed or traded in any meaningful sense, because of the manipulation and control of world markets by the international mining companies. The degree of control exercised by the companies depends on the importance of the producing company, the number of smaller producers, and the relationship of the mining company to the major refineries. But in all cases the profit that market control brings accrues to the companies. Some idea of the level of surplus that was being extracted by the companies came when OPEC pushed the price of oil up from US \$2·00 to US \$10·00 a barrel and the Jamaican government pushed the price of bauxite up from US \$3·00 to US \$10·00 a ton.

The success of the OPEC countries in raising oil prices showed the benefits that cohesion and joint action can produce. In quick succession the major bauxite-exporting countries set up the International Bauxite Association, and the iron-ore exporters set up the Iron Ore Exporters Council. But as the experience of

CIPEC has shown, the creation of an exporters' collective does not by itself remove price fluctuations. It is difficult for producing countries to agree on a common policy, but even if this is achieved there are still formidable obstacles to be overcome.

THE USE OF THE STOCKPILE

The vulnerability of the underdeveloped nations is increased by the measures adopted by the industrialized nations to protect domestic mineral producers and manufacturing industry from foreign competition. The USA, which is the world's largest producer and consumer of metals and minerals, has frequently imposed tariffs and quotas to insulate the domestic economy from world price movements. It also maintains a large stockpile of minerals which it can use to influence world prices (see Table 33). The US strategy in the face of its unusually weak position in the world tin market has been to reduce its dependence on tin and to support an international commodity agreement, while building up its own stockpile. In effect, the ITC has helped the US keep tin prices low and stable, while Americans developed alternative materials and technologies to minimize their dependence on foreign supplies. The same technique of forcing outsiders to bear the brunt of adjusting supply to demand by insulating the US market was used in the lead and zinc industry. The US is a major lead and zinc producer, but at the end of the 1950s production and employment were falling. The US government imposed protective quotas; restricting imports and encouraging domestic production to increase rapidly. The US in effect exported the depression in lead and zinc production, while creating the boom at home. By the summer of 1960, US zinc prices were more than one sixth higher, and lead one quarter higher than the ruling LME prices.[31]

The US was not a signatory to the Fourth Tin Agreement, although it had an understanding with the International Tin Council not to release stockpiled tin at a rate which would disturb market stability. There is, however, no guarantee that this undertaking will continue to be observed. The US stockpile is an ever-present threat to the world's major tin exporting nations. In March 1973, as part of a series of measures to control domestic inflation, President Nixon announced that large quantities of tin would be released from the US strategic stockpile. As the tin stockpile of 270,000 tons was equal to more than one year's total world production, the effect of the announcement was dramatic. The price of tin fell immediately by more than £50 a ton on the London Metal Exchange.[32] Producing countries expressed considerable alarm. The Bolivian Minister of Mines said that his country would 'consider it economic aggression if the United States sell their reserves'.[33] In April the US stockpile objective was slashed to 40,500 tons, thus releasing 191,500 tons for sale.[34] Intensive lobbying by the tin-producing countries, and the State Department's realization that rapid sales would have serious political repercussions, persuaded the US government to release stocks more slowly than had been intended.

COMPANY CONTROL

Even the brief survey in this chapter, summarized in Table 33, shows that most of Africa's mineral exports are sold in tightly controlled markets, where prices are very largely determined by the companies. The companies are interested in the steadily rising profits and predictable cash flow that comes from orderly marketing. Company control of world mineral markets enables them to determine where they take their profits: at the mining, processing, refining, marketing, or manufacturing stage. The greater the degree of vertical integration, the harder it is for African countries to win back some of the monopoly profit that accrues to the companies; for then, as in the iron and aluminium industries, export is merely an internal transfer from one branch of an international mining company to another. In the case of diamonds, where De Beers controls production and marketing, the company also has a monopoly of pricing and sorting expertise, which buttresses its power, making it very difficult for an African country to know the value of its own diamonds.* Other markets are not so tightly monopolized, but where one company

* See Chapter 17 below for an analysis of the De Beers diamond monopoly.

Table 32: The US stockpile of selected minerals, 31 December 1974

Material	Unit	Objective	Total on hand	Excess available for disposal	Sold during 1974	US import dependence 1974, as a percentage	Major foreign suppliers
Antimony	short tons	0	40,700	0	4	46	South Africa, Mexico
Asbestos (Amosite)	short tons	0	46,593	28,193	11,404	87	Canada, South Africa
Aluminium	short tons	0	13,183	13,183	453,545	88	Jamaica, Australia
Bauxite, Jamaica	l. tons (dry)	4,638,000	8,858,881	1,370,077			Jamaica, Australia, Surinam
Chromite, chemical	s. tons (dry)	8,400	250,000	0	322,886		
Chromite, metallurgical	s. tons (dry)	444,710	2,504,560	0	899,949	91*	USSR, South Africa, Turkey
Chromite, refractory	s. tons (dry)	54,000	399,960	0	571,163		
Chromium, ferrochrome	s. tons	11,476	783,706	0	3,182		
Cobalt	lb.	11,945,000	59,797,947	12,597,947	9,325,667	98	Zaire, Belgium†
Columbium	lb	800,000	997,134	1,372	251,106	100	Malaysia, Zaire
Copper	s. tons	0	489	489		18	Canada, Peru, Chile, South Africa
Diamond Industrial bort	carats	0	35,905,479	12,205,479	2,921,500	n.a.	
Diamond Industrial stones	carats	0	21,069,182	1,069,182	1,502,451	n.a.	
Lead	s. tons	65,100	599,743	69,745	229,294	21	Canada, Peru

Manganese ore, metallurgical	s. tons	750,500	4,201,562	1,595,962	498,185	98	Brazil, Gabon, South Africa, Zaire
Nickel	lb.	0	0		0	73	Canada, Norway
Platinum	oz. troy	187,500	452,645		0	86	UK,† USSR, South Africa
Tin	l. tons	40,500	207,458	6,832	23,554	86	Malaysia, Thailand, Bolivia
Tungsten ores and concentrates	lb.	4,234,000	114,643,672	89,475,710	6,071,137	60	Canada, Bolivia, Peru, Thailand
Zinc	s. tons	202,700	372,473	169,773	266,758	61	Canada, Mexico, Peru

* Ores and metals.
† Mainly refined from foreign ores from Africa.
Source: *Mining Annual Review 1975*, Mining Journal, pp. 305 and 307, quoting US government and US Bureau of Mines statistics.

Table 33: The marketing of African minerals

Metal	Market Characteristic	Remarks
Iron	Vertical integration	Backward linkage by steel companies
Aluminium	Vertical integration/ producer monopoly	Market controlled by North American producers. Bauxite producers are trying to combat this through the IBA
Nickel	Vertical integration/ producer monopoly	Dominated by INCO, whose monopoly is, however, slowly being eroded
Diamonds	Vertical integration/ producer monopoly	De Beers regulates world production and marketing
Gold	Closed market/ producer monopoly	South African government restricts sales according to its needs
Uranium	Vertical integration	North American and British companies dominate
Platinum	Producer control	Rustenburg Mines and South African companies largely successful in stabilizing price
Tin	Producer/consumer control	Fifth International Tin Agreement backed by IMF
Lead and zinc		American market protected
Copper	Unstable marketing	Producers' cooperative so far without effect. Speculators active on market. US market protected
Chrome	Unstable marketing	Due to company competition

produces a large proportion of world output and there are not too many small producers, it can, and does, manipulate world prices. This is especially true of the mining company which owns or has close links with the major refineries, as does Rustenburg Platinum. Other markets are not so rigidly controlled but they are still more influenced by the companies than by the producing countries because of the companies' financial strength reinforced by their superior information network. They are based in the industrialized nations and have close contacts with those who use the metal. Thus, within the limits set by the overall levels of demand in the industrialized world, the companies are much better placed to maximize their income on a rising market or to protect themselves in a world recession such as began in 1974.

17 Africa and the World Diamond Monopoly

The luxury status and investment value of diamonds largely depend on their rarity. Diamonds have been in potential over-supply ever since the discovery of the great Kimberley diamond fields in 1867; and so long tradition in the diamond industry has sanctified the principle of controlled world production marketed centrally through a single channel. Forty years ago Ernest Oppenheimer established the principle that the producers should also control the selling organization. Since that date, De Beers Consolidated has controlled the world diamond trade in one of the most enduring and profitable monopolies of the twentieth century.

WORLD DIAMOND PRODUCTION

Africa is the world's largest source of both industrial and gem diamonds and accounted for more than 60 per cent of world production worth £360 million in 1974.[1] Gems account for 20 per cent of world trade by volume but about 80 per cent by value. The two major groups of diamond producers are the South African companies and the rest of the world's producers in Africa, South America and the USSR. There are six major producing mines in South Africa (Premier, Wesselton, Finsch, Koffiefontein, De Beers and Dutoitspan) as well as the State and De Beers diggings in Namaqualand. In Namibia, De Beers controls the fabulously rich Consolidated Diamond Mines, which produce 80 per cent gem-quality diamonds. De Beers accounts for about 80 per cent of South Africa's production, but it also has extensive interests in other parts of Africa.

The other major African diamond-producing countries are Botswana, Zaire, Angola, Sierra Leone and Ghana. De Beers has a 50 per cent stake in the world's largest diamond mine at Orapa in Botswana, which has an annual output of 2·2 million carats, about 75 per cent industrial-quality stones. In 1975 a new agreement was reached between the government and De Beers to increase production to 4·4 million carats to increase the government's stake from 15 to 50 per cent and to increase the level of taxes to 70 per cent of profits. New mines at Letlhakane (40 per cent gem) and Jwaneng will make Botswana the third largest diamond-producing country in the world.

The largest producer of industrial diamonds in the world is Zaire. The main mining company there is the Société Minière de Bakwanga (MIBA) which was owned by the Belgian company SIBECKA but is now controlled by the Zaire government.* Local diggers account for up to a third of Zaire's production, but most of their production is smuggled through the Congo People's Republic.

In Angola the De Beers-controlled DIAMANG company is responsible for the bulk of the country's production, 70 per cent of which are gems. Production ceased in 1976 as a result of the civil war, but in September 1977 the government increased its stake in DIAMANG to 61 per cent and production was expected to pick up again.

In Sierra Leone diamonds are produced by DIMINCO (51 per cent government; 49 per cent Sierra Leone Selection Trust) and by independent diggers who sell some of their production to four licensed diamond buyers and smuggle the rest through Liberia and Guinea.

In Ghana, the government now has a 55 per cent stake in the Consolidated African Selection Mine at Akwatia; although the diamonds are mainly industrial quality they have a safe market. There are also local diggers, most of whom smuggle their stones to Togo and Dahomey.

The less important African producers are Tanzania, Lesotho, Ivory Coast, Guinea, Liberia and the Central African Empire. In Tanzania the Mwadui mine is 50 per cent owned by De Beers

---

*The Zaire government announced it was taking 100 per cent control in November 1973, but legal complications delayed implementation of the decree for more than eighteen months.

and 50 per cent by the government, as the result of a pre-independence arrangement.* Although it mines the world's largest diamond pipe, covering between 5 and 6 square miles, Mwadui's production has fallen in recent years, and the mine has an estimated life of only ten years. In Lesotho, after many years of prospecting by large mining companies, De Beers developed a R23 million mine at Letseng la Terai which started production in 1977. Until now most of Lesotho's production has been mined by independent diggers in the Kai district. In the Ivory Coast there are two small diamond mines, and in Guinea the diggings are closed for most of the year, as priority is given to agricultural production. Some diamonds are illegally exported to Liberia and Sierra Leone. Local diggers working alluvial deposits produce the majority of the Central African Empire's production and account for half the country's exports.

Outside the African continent the main diamond-producing countries are the USSR, Venezuela, Brazil and Guyana. Soviet production is about 70 per cent industrial and comes from generally high-cost mines in or close to the Arctic circle. The South American diamonds come from alluvial deposits and are mainly mined by independent diggers.

CONTROL OF PRODUCTION

To preserve orderly marketing and to prevent the wild fluctuations in supply and demand which most primary commodities suffer, De Beers keeps supplies in step with demand. Production in South Africa and South-West Africa is coordinated by the Diamond Producers Association, managed by a board of five, three members of which are appointed by the mining companies and the Diamond Corporation, and one each by the governments of South and South-West Africa (Namibia). The chairman is appointed by the government of South Africa. The Association is dominated by De Beers, and the South African government would intervene only in exceptional cases, such as those which led to the inclusion of the government in the first place.† Production is controlled by a quota system. The level of the quotas

*See below, page 413.   † See Chapter 2.

is adapted to the sales of the Central Selling Organization (CSO).

Production outside South Africa is controlled by the contracts that independent producers have signed with the Diamond Corporation. The basis of these contracts, which usually run for five years, is that the Diamond Corporation agrees to buy a minimum quantity of rough diamonds annually. Whether the Corporation will buy more is dependent on the level of world sales. If a company or mine produces more diamonds than the Diamond Corporation is prepared to buy, the contract stipulates that the producer must stockpile the excess. It is not allowed to sell to any buyers other than the Diamond Corporation.[2]

South African production is controlled by De Beers itself, which alters mine production and grade recovery to fit prevailing market conditions. When world sales increase after a slack period, it is De Beers' production which increases to meet rising demand. This means that, as Sir Ernest Oppenheimer put it:

> The sales of the big South African producers are dependent on the volume of world trade, while practically all other sources of production are limited on the basis of a maximum yearly figure.[3]

The level of De Beers' profits therefore depends partly on the proportion of total sales that come from its own mines.

CONTROL OF SALES

De Beers and its subsidiaries buy up almost all of the world's diamond supplies for the market. Diamonds exported by the USSR are sold through the CSO. In Zaire MIBA's production is sold through De Beers, while BRITMOND, a CSO subsidiary based in Bermuda, buys the diggers' production. In Angola the production was sold to the CSO and to a Portuguese diamond factory in which De Beers also has an interest. The Diamond Corporation buys the diggers' production in Sierra Leone through DICORWAF and the Mwadui mine's production in Tanzania through DICORTAN. In countries where the CSO does not have a contract with the major producers, De Beers buys in the open market to protect its marketing policy. The only production which is not sold through the CSO is that of Ghana, and the smuggled stones from Liberia and other West African countries, which are sold in the diamond markets of Antwerp. The CSO handles around 85 per cent of world gem sales. The USA is the world's major importer of diamonds, taking about half the world's gemstones and around 60 per cent of industrial diamonds.

THE CENTRAL SELLING ORGANIZATION

Diamonds from the South African Producers and the Diamond Corporation pass to the Central Selling Organization, which is the collective name for a group of De Beers controlled companies (see Figure 21). The stones are first sorted. The larger and more valuable stones are called gems; while the smaller but more numerous are classified as industrials.* Gem diamonds remain essentially a luxury item; but since the Second World War many new applications have been developed for the smaller industrial stones, which are now used for drilling, cutting and grinding tools in industry. Industrials are sold on demand to CSO-approved buyers, but the system for gems is more complex.

The diamond-cutting industry is very volatile, and highly sensitive to fluctuations in world economic conditions. There are a large number of small manufacturing units, many of them specializing in different types of diamonds. Specialist banks lend against stocks and work in hand. The high value of the stones encourages a host of intermediaries, operating with small margins on a large turnover. They can shift rapidly from one category of stone to another, accentuating the forces of supply and demand in the market. The many small firms are under-capitalized, and this reduces the industry's capacity to absorb

---

*In fact, of course, the classification of stones is much more complex than that. Gemstones are divided into basic series based on the processing required. Each of the series has its sub-classifications. The series are: Stones (round sawable stone); cleavage (stones that require cleaving or splitting); Maccles (these are found or broken pieces); Chips (small cleavage); Melee (small stones); Flats; Near gem (those stones between industrial and gem); and Industrial (these are further sub-divided into die stones, dressers, drilling and bort). In all, the CSO uses some 2,000 separate categories. Stones above 14 carats are sold singly.

periods of slack demand; but De Beers' unique selling system forces the cutting industry to absorb some of the cost of stabilizing the diamond industry.

Once a month the Diamond Trading Company arranges the 'sights' at which 200 selected buyers view the gems. Only those buyers whom the Diamond Trading Company considers of sufficiently high reputation and financial backing to help preserve the stability of the diamond trade are admitted to these 'sights'. On arrival at the CSO's buildings in London, each buyer is shown into a room where there is a box of diamonds. Inside each box is a selection of stones arranged according to the CSO's detailed classification. After inspection, the buyers indicate whether or not they will buy at the going price. If they do not buy, they are not offered another box. If buyers buy very little or irregularly, they may be struck off the list. When the market is weak, registered buyers continue to buy from the CSO, even if they cannot sell the stones: because the CSO is a monopoly, and if they do not buy from the CSO when the market is weak, they will not be allowed to buy when the market improves. The consignments are then resold by classification to cutters in the main diamond-finishing centres of the world – Antwerp, Amsterdam, Tel Aviv, New York, Bombay, Puerto Rico and London. After they have been cut, the diamonds pass to the jewellers, who then sell them to the public.

PRICING POLICY

Prices are constantly adjusted upwards to the level that the CSO thinks the market will bear.* With correct timing in a tightly controlled market, there is no reason for a price increase to excite a fall in demand. But if prices are increased too sharply, it would encourage those producers outside De Beers' control to

---

*For example, increasing demand and currency realignments led to the following changes in 1971–3: gem prices were raised by 5 per cent in November 1971; 5·4 per cent in January 1972; 9·6 per cent in September 1972; 11 per cent in February 1973 (to take account of the dollar devaluation); 7 per cent in March, 10 per cent on larger gems in May and another 10·2 per cent on all diamonds in August 1973.

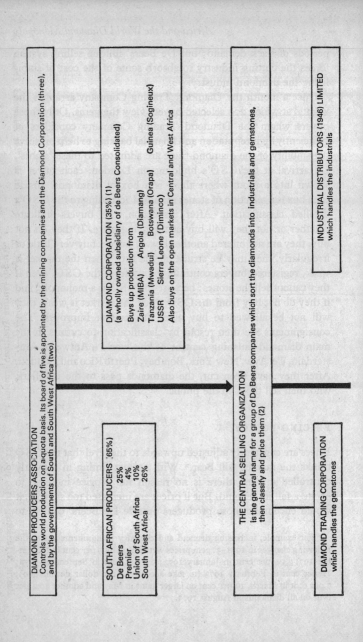

DIAMOND PRODUCERS ASSOCIATION
Controls world production on a quota basis. Its board of five is appointed by the mining companies and the Diamond Corporation (three), and by the governments of South and South West Africa (two)

SOUTH AFRICAN PRODUCERS (65%)
De Beers   25%
Premier   4%
Union of South Africa 10%
South West Africa   26%

DIAMOND CORPORATION (35%) (1)
(a wholly owned subsidiary of de Beers Consolidated)

Buys up production from
Zaire (MIBA)   Angola (Diamang)
Tanzania (Mwadui) Botswana (Orapa)   Guinea (Sogineux)
USSR   Sierra Leone (Diminco)
Also buys on the open markets in Central and West Africa

THE CENTRAL SELLING ORGANIZATION
is the general name for a group of De Beers companies which sort the diamonds into industrials and gemstones, then classify and price them (2)

DIAMOND TRADING CORPORATION
which handles the gemstones

INDUSTRIAL DISTRIBUTORS (1946) LIMITED
which handles the industrials

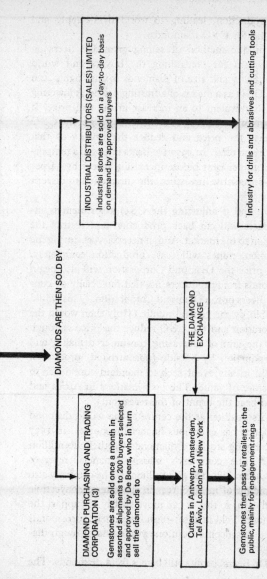

DIAMONDS ARE THEN SOLD BY

INDUSTRIAL DISTRIBUTORS (SALES) LIMITED

Industrial stones are sold on a day-to-day basis on demand by approved buyers

Industry for drills and abrasives and cutting tools

DIAMOND PURCHASING AND TRADING CORPORATION (3)

Gemstones are sold once a month in assorted shipments to 200 buyers selected and approved by De Beers, who in turn sell the diamonds to

THE DIAMOND EXCHANGE

Cutters in Antwerp, Amsterdam, Tel Aviv, London and New York

Gemstones then pass via retailers to the public, mainly for engagement rings

Fig. 21. The world diamond trade

NOTES: (1) Percentage figures represent the relative size of the diamond sales quotas. (2) The actual position is more complex, as there are many 'desk drawer' companies in the West Indies and other tax havens. (3) Shareholdings, all firmly within the Anglo group, include De Beers 45%, Anamint 16%, JCI 16%, Consolidated Diamond Mines 7%.

SOURCE: Based on information in G. Lenzen, *The History of Diamond Production and the Diamond Trade*, Barrie & Jenkins, 1970, pp. 184–7, and various company annual reports.

increase their production, leading to world over-supply and weakening demand for CSO diamonds.

The CSO's unique method of selling gives De Beers an additional mechanism for controlling the buyers and world trade. Both the quality and size of diamonds in the 'sights' can be varied by the CSO as a means of adjusting prices. A lowering in the quality is equivalent to an increase in the real price. If demand for a particular category of stone is very high, the CSO may both increase the price and reduce the quality of that particular category on offer. In 1977 De Beers imposed a temporary surcharge of 40 per cent before increasing prices by 34 per cent to head off speculative investors who threatened to disrupt the market.

In a recession, and if adjusting the CSO assortment is insufficient, De Beers will cut back production and restrict the supplies coming on to the market. And, if necessary, as during the 1929–32 depression, mines will cease production completely. To support the price the Diamond Corporation will also begin to buy up diamonds from producers not tied financially or contractually to De Beers or the Diamond Corporation. (This would include stones sold by the general public.) Only then would the Diamond Corporation and the CSO reduce the price of rough diamonds with the aim of increasing consumer demand, and discouraging production by outside (uncontrolled) producers. The CSO would in any event seek to maintain confidence in diamonds as a store of value. The open markets in Africa and elsewhere would bear the brunt of the recession.

To maintain its position at the centre of the world diamond monopoly, De Beers has enormous financial resources. In 1977 the CSO was carrying stocks of diamonds worth R220 million ($253 million).[4] The company's massive financial reserves amounted to R1,401 million ($1,611 million).[5] The company also holds a large amount of its resources in short-term convertible investments and cash, so that it can move swiftly to support the market. The amount held in short-term investment corresponds approximately to the income from one year's sale of rough diamonds.[6]

The bulk of De Beers' profits still comes from diamonds. The group made a pre-tax profit on its consolidated diamond account of R751·2 million and income from investments was R169 million in 1977.[7] Table 34 shows De Beers' profits for the last ten years. It is not easy to discover which is the most profitable part of the De Beers operation, especially since the Diamond Corporation became a wholly-owned subsidiary of De Beers in 1972. But in 1969 the CSO showed a 6 per cent profit on turnover. A more realistic idea of the profitability would be the level of return on investment made by the CSO companies (the Diamond Trading Company, the Diamond Corporation, Industrial Distributors Ltd) in their diamond trading. *After tax* this appeared to be 21 per cent for the Diamond Trading Company (selling gems) and 17 per cent for the Diamond Corporation.* De Beers has firmly resisted all attempts to break its profitable monopoly or to market diamonds independently.

Table 34: De Beers diamond sales and profits, 1965–77

Year	Reserves Rm.	Investments† quoted and unquoted Rm.	CSO sales Rm.	Profits after tax Rm.
1965	312·5	412·8	350	70·6
1966	349·1	415·1	360	81·8
1967	382·7	483·0	350	87·7
1968	430·5	576·5	420	105·8
1969	474·1	543·1	500	112·1
1970	522·7	481·6	380	77·1
1971	551·7	468·8	450	100·7
1972	629·2	605·4	660	161·5
1973	751·8	660·5†	920	235·9
1974	822·2	560·9	850	199·7
1975	920·8	575·6	849·1	218·4
1976	1,067·9	573·4	793·5	306·7
1977	1,401·9	814·9	1,803·0	621·5

*Industrial Distributors made a small loss in 1967, 1968 and 1969, reflecting the over-supply of industrial bort and small stones on the world market and the competition from synthetic stones.

†Listed at market value, plus unlisted at book value 1965–72 and at directors' valuation 1973 onwards.

MAINTAINING THE MONOPOLY

After Rhodes' reorganization of De Beers and the Kimberley mines, the group controlled world production because it owned all the important mines. Then De Beers' position as a producer began to be eroded as new diamond deposits were found and exploited. Ernest Oppenheimer's reorganization and vertical integration of producers and buyers has protected De Beers' position down to the present day. Although De Beers' own mines account for only about 30 per cent of world production, they produce over 60 per cent of the world's gemstones, largely from Consolidated Diamond Mines in Namibia. De Beers has been careful to buttress its position by skilfully adjusting the production from its own mines and by buying all significant mine production either on contract or in the open market. But despite these protective measures, the monopoly is still vulnerable. A large independent producer, or association of producers, might market diamonds separately from the CSO. At the very least this could upset the orderly marketing by which De Beers sets so much store, and at most it might fatally weaken the monopoly. The manufacturers of synthetic diamonds, the diggers in the West African and South American diamond rushes, and the important gemstone mines in Tanzania and Sierra Leone have all tried to market diamonds independently in the last twenty-five years; but on each occasion De Beers moved swiftly to counter the threat.

The first synthetic diamonds were produced by a Swedish company in 1953, but they were tiny and discoloured and there were no plans for commercial production. Then, in 1955, the diamond world was rocked by the announcement from General Electric that the company had devised a payable method of producing synthetic diamonds. De Beers initiated a crash programme of research and by 1958 had discovered its own method of making such stones. De Beers set up factories in South Africa and Eire to produce the synthetic diamonds, which are for industrial use in drilling and abrasive equipment.

A long legal battle between De Beers and General Electric over the patents for their rival processes ended with an agreement to split the world market between them. General Electric produced 90 per cent of the 19–20 million carats produced in the US in 1974. But much of this production was exported, and the US imported 19 million carats in 1974, of which between 8 million and 10 million were synthetic, produced by De Beers.*[8]

INDEPENDENT DIGGERS IN WEST AFRICA

Another threat to the De Beers' monopoly has been the diamond rushes in West Africa. The independent diggers panning the swamps and river beds have frequently smuggled their production across borders to escape taxes and take advantage of currency fluctuations. Agents bought this production and sold it direct to Antwerp and the other diamond markets, completely bypassing the CSO. It was in Sierra Leone that De Beers first developed the techniques to meet this threat.

Diamonds were first mined commercially in Sierra Leone by Chester Beatty's Selection Trust group in 1934. Consolidated African Selection Trust (CAST) established a wholly-owned subsidiary, Sierra Leone Selection Trust (SLST), to exploit the diamond concession, which covered virtually the entire country. For nearly twenty years SLST mined and exported diamonds at a steady, if unspectacular, rate. Then in 1952, after years of watching Sierra Leone Selection Trust prospectors, local people began mining on their own account. The diamond rush worried SLST (whose pre-tax profits slumped from £1·43 million in 1953 to only £590,000 in 1957), the Sierra Leone government, and, of course, De Beers. Technically the activities of the diggers were in violation of SLST's exclusive mining rights, but there was little that the government or the company could do about the influx of diggers: although in Kono district

---

*In April 1975 the US Justice Department fined two of De Beers' industrial diamond distributors for price fixing and market allocation. The case was seen partly as a precedent-setting move to show the Administration's ability to act against foreign corporations not based in the US and partly to encourage American firms to enter the production of synthetic diamonds because GE's patents have only a few years to run. (*Financial Mail*, 25 April 1975.)

the company had minimized 'illegal' digging by the use of its own Security Force.* But there was another problem.

The company paid tax on the diamonds it produced and exported, but the independent diggers' diamonds were usually smuggled out of the country to avoid tax. A new system was needed. The government and the CSO had a joint interest in preventing smuggling: the government wanted the tax revenue, and the CSO wanted to prevent independent marketing. The Diamond Corporation recruited diamond buyers and in 1956 set up offices in the diamond fields, to buy diamonds from the diggers according to published prices. In 1959 this was replaced by a Government Diamond Office, managed by the Diamond Corporation, which became the sole legal exporter of the diggers' diamonds. The GDO reviewed its prices more frequently to keep them in line with outside prices, and therefore was much more attractive to the diggers. It was also attractive to SLST, whose profits recovered to reach £2·55 million in 1961. In 1961 a new company, Diamond Corporation of West Africa (DICORWAF), was formed to manage the GDO. This arrangement continued until 1974, when the Sierra Leone government ended DICORWAF's exclusive export licence and allowed other firms to come in as buyers and exporters. The object was to reassure diggers and dealers that they were getting a fair price for their diamonds, and so reduce smuggling.† When prices are high in Europe, it is estimated that up to 50 per cent of production is smuggled out of the country. For De Beers, its experience in Sierra Leone allowed it to experiment with ways of protecting its monopoly from diggers; and later rushes in

---

* See Ian Fleming, *The Diamond Smugglers*, Cape, 1957. The James Bond book *Diamonds are Forever* is a fictional account of the same situation.

† President Siaka Stevens said in an interview: 'I spoke to Mr Oppenheimer and I said "Human nature being what it is, if you have got only one buyer people are never satisfied, even if they get the best price in the world." So I said to him, "Times have changed, so let us bring in a few more buyers", and he said "Steve, I agree." So they brought in four or five more buyers and the people are very well satisfied. We think it better all round, and it discourages to a certain extent the smuggling business.' (*African Development*, April 1975, Sierra Leone supplement, p. S.L.6).

Guinea, Liberia, Ivory Coast, Congo and South America did not disrupt the market.

INDEPENDENT MARKETING

Mines producing a high proportion of gemstones have often chafed at the restrictions of De Beers' marketing policy. Good-quality stones are often resold on the Diamond Exchange at a premium over the CSO price, and there has always been a temptation for gemstone producers to bypass the CSO and sell direct to the market. The two most important examples of this have been in Tanzania and Sierra Leone.

In Tanzania the Canadian prospector John Williamson discovered the Mwadui mine; but he was short of funds to develop it, and after an injection of South African capital he agreed to market his production through the CSO. Then after a few years, he decided that it would be more profitable to market his stones independently, so he stockpiled his production and refused to sell any stones to the CSO. The British Colonial Secretary, Alan Lennox-Boyd, visited Williamson to persuade him to change his mind, but to no avail. Harry Oppenheimer was dispatched by his father to reach an agreement with Williamson and ensure the orderly marketing of Mwadui's production. Williamson finally gave way and agreed to sell through the CSO again.[9] On Williamson's death in 1957, De Beers bought the mine from Williamson's brother and offered 50 per cent to the Tanganyika government, which waived estate duty on the mine. Since Tanzania's independence, Mwadui's production has steadily fallen, but all production has been marketed through CSO channels.

Sierra Leone and De Beers

The threat to the De Beers' diamond monopoly posed by the independent marketing of Sierra Leone diamonds had been recognized since the beginning of commercial operations in the country. In 1935 a consulting engineer working for De Beers reported to Ernest Oppenheimer that Sierra Leone 'will produce more diamonds in value than Angola and the Congo combined ... these fields are a great menace to De Beers ... particularly in a moderate market'.[10] Sierra Leonean diamonds are of good quality and colour, and a high proportion are large gemstones. For the past thirty years the diamonds have been sold through the De Beers-controlled CSO under five-year renewable contracts. But since the price schedule of the five-year CSO contracts is based on CSO selling prices and not on those of the market, there has always been a tendency for Sierra Leonean producers to seek a higher price for their output.

When the 1956 contract ended in 1960, a major conflict developed between SLST and the Diamond Corporation over the price that SLST was receiving for its stones. The company compared the prices it got for its output with the prices that New York cutters were paying for stones of like quality, and decided that the CSO was not paying enough. But the sharpest comparison was with the price that the Diamond Corporation was paying for stones in the Government Diamond Offices (GDO). In order to prevent the diggers from smuggling the stones to Monrovia and Antwerp, the Diamond Corporation had to offer prices that were close to the ruling world market price. Then in 1961 when President Nkrumah of Ghana ordered all CAST diamonds to be sold on Ghana's diamond exchange, SLST (owned by CAST) was able to see even more clearly the margin between the price that CSO was offering the company and the ruling market price.

CAST's break with the CSO came at an opportune moment. Harry Winston Inc., the largest diamond-cutting firm in the world, was looking for new supplies. Winston had pioneered the selling of diamonds in non-traditional outlets (such as supermarkets) and had cutting workshops in the United States, Puerto Rico, Holland, Belgium, France, Germany and Israel. He was anxious to develop sources of supplies independent of the CSO, which had not permitted expansion at the rate he wished.[11] Winston offered CAST a higher price for the SLST diamonds than the CSO was prepared to give. Since SLST's concession area had been much reduced in the fifties, and since there were continual incursions by diggers on the concession areas that it had retained, the company was out to extract as much profit as possible in the shortest possible time. Winston offered a £10 million two-year contract, promising SLST profits of around £250,000 a year. Although the contract was only to run for two years, compared with the five-year CSO contract, SLST judged the Winston contract worth the risk of conflict with the CSO.

But in the government's eyes the prospect of increased tax revenue did not warrant breaking with the CSO. In its discussions with the government, the CSO argued that the sale of the important SLST production outside of the normal CSO marketing channels would lead to a deterioration in the world price of diamonds, which, in turn, would lead to a reduction in the prices paid to the diggers and which would be politically unpopular for the new government. The diggers would seek to maximize their return on a falling market by smuggling the diamonds to Liberia, and government revenue would fall. The government was convinced, and passed an act to control the marketing of diamonds in Sierra Leone. Henceforth all diamonds, whether produced by the diggers or by SLST, had to be sold to the GDO, which became the only legal exporter of Sierra Leonean diamonds. The GDO, which had been created in 1959 to buy the diggers' production, was still to be run for the government by the Diamond Corporation.

If De Beers had once again proved its strength, SLST had not given up hope of breaking away from the monopoly. There was nothing in the new act that forced SLST to sell diamonds at all. So for sixteen months the company stockpiled stones and, with Harry Winston, lobbied the government. A compromise was reached in July 1962. In future SLST diamonds would be sorted in the offices of the GDO and the government valuer, a Belgian diamond merchant, N. Zollman, would prepare a valuation list. SLST would sell at least half of its production to the Diamond Corporation: while the remainder could be sold to the three American diamond-cutting firms which were to be given buying licences, Harry Winston Inc., Templemens Inc., and Lazare Kaplan Inc. This arrangement lasted until the end of the sixties.

The contract between the SLST and the government was due for renewal in 1972. Negotiations began in June 1970 and almost immediately were reported to be running into trouble.[12] The government had acquired a much firmer grasp on the complexities of the diamond trade in the years since independence, and seemed determined to improve its share of the diamond profits. The Minister of Finance visited the USSR and almost certainly discussed the marketing of diamonds.[13] At the same time the government was talking to Lonrho,* which had ambitions to break De Beers' diamond monopoly.[14] The government announced the formation of the Commercial and Industrial Corporation (COMINCOR) in June 1970. The company was to be a joint venture with Lonrho: the government taking 55 per cent and Lonrho the remaining 45 per cent. The aim of the company was stated to be 'the development of all known viable mineral resources in the country'. In Sierra Leone that essentially referred to diamonds, which accounted for 63 per cent of the country's exports and a substantial proportion of the government's revenue.

What did Lonrho's chairman and guiding force, Tiny Rowland, hope to achieve? There was strong speculation that Lonrho's aim was to set up a rival marketing organization to compete with De Beers. Lonrho had a diamond concession in Lesotho and strong connections in Zaire, and was actively seeking an alluvial concession in Ghana. If Lonrho could market Sierra Leonean diamonds and perhaps even the Soviet production (was this the purpose of the Finance Minister's trip to the USSR?), then it might be able to compete with De Beers. But there was one major gap in the latest of Tiny Rowland's imaginative plans: the new marketing combine would not be a match for the marketing expertise of the CSO.

While the diamond trade buzzed with speculation, the government was negotiating with SLST. In December 1969, prime minister Siaka Stevens had announced his 'New Mining Policy for Sierra Leone', subtitled 'Partnership for the Future'.

---

*See Chapters 8 and 10 for more information about Lonrho. See also Suzanne Cronje, Margaret Ling, and Gillian Cronje, *Lonrho: Portrait of a Multinational*, Penguin Books, 1976.

The government declared its intention to purchase 'for a fair value' a majority interest in each of the four mining companies* operating in Sierra Leone. The Prime Minister said that the government was anxious to know from the inside 'exactly how the mining companies conducted their affairs and invoiced their shipments'.[15] Sierra Leone, clearly influenced by the Zambians' successful takeover, proposed payment for 51 per cent of S L S T assets of £2,550,000 through bonds bearing interest at $5\frac{1}{2}$ per cent. The government would redeem the bonds in 16 half-yearly payments of sterling in London. The similarity of the arrangement to the Zambian takeover was emphasized when, on President Kaunda's recommendation, Andrew Sardanis, Zambia's 'Mr Fifty-one per cent', was appointed to the board of the new National Diamond Mining Company (DIMINCO).†[16] Another appointment was that of the American, Theodore Sorensen, who had advised the Zairean government during its 1966–7 battle with Union Minière, and now advised the Sierra Leone government in its negotiations with S L S T.[17] The new company, Diminco, would be subject to approximately 70 per cent tax, compared to the 55 per cent tax on S L S T. In addition, of course, the government would get 51 per cent of the dividends.

It was against this background that the five-year contract with the Diamond Corporation came up for renewal in 1972. The government hoped to make the Diamond Corporation pay a large sum to compensate for past exploitation and as a fee for continuing to market Sierra Leonean diamonds.[18] The presence of an eager Lonrho, ready to snap up the business, strengthened

---

* Sierra Leone Selection Trust (diamonds); Sierra Leone Development Co. (iron ore); Sierra Leone Ore and Metal Co. (bauxite); Sherbro Minerals (rutile). The government has since withdrawn its proposals to take a stake in the three mining companies apart from S L S T.

† The appointment of Sardanis to Diminco raised an interesting question because he was no longer managing director of Zimco, the Zambian state holding company, but had joined Lonrho to reorganize their interests north of the Zambezi. The situation was thus that S L S T representatives sat on the Diminco board along with Sardanis, who, although there in his private capacity, was closely connected with S L S T's closest competitor anxious not only to do business with the government, but even to take over the S L S T concession. (See *African Development*, April 1971, p. 51.)

the government's hand in the negotiations. The two Diamond Corporation executives, Anthony Oppenheimer and Derek Cliverd, argued that the Diamond Corporation was not making exorbitant profits from Sierra Leone's £20 million diamond production. They pointed out the dire results of uncontrolled marketing and the lack of marketing expertise of both Lonrho and the government. The government back-pedalled and, deciding to look closely at alternative marketing arrangements before breaking away from the Diamond Corporation, renewed the contract for five years. Many Sierra Leoneans felt that the government could have struck a harder bargain.[19]

Since 1961 the Diamond Corporation has managed the GDO through its wholly-owned subsidiary, Diamond Corporation West Africa. The GDO bought half the Diminco output, as well as the independent diggers' production, through its own offices, and licensed diamond dealers. There was believed to be an understanding between the government and the Diamond Corporation that as long as the Corporation managed the GDO, it would get at least half of the Diminco production. The Diamond Corporation paid the government £165,000 a year for the right of being the sole exporter of GDO diamonds and guaranteed to buy all diamonds offered to the GDO unless it had a stockpile of £3 million.[20] But the key issue remained the price that Sierra Leone got for its diamonds. The Diamond Corporation guaranteed to pay a minimum price – which was the ruling CSO price, less export duty (7 per cent), less 10 per cent commission. Given that CSO prices are not the same as the market prices, and that Sierra Leone's good-quality large stones command a premium on the market, to allow the CSO a 10 per cent discount on top of the premium seemed very generous.

The conflicts in 1960-63 and 1970–72 shows that the Sierra Leone government, and before them the SLST, were well aware of the high value of the diamonds that the country produced and of the profits taken by De Beers. The CSO maintained its control of the diamond marketing by convincing the government that it was giving a fair price for the stones and that an alternative channel of marketing would, in the long run, produce less, rather than more, revenue for the government.[21]

But the doubts remained and in 1974 new buyers were introduced to provide the option of an alternative to the pricing and marketing offered by the CSO.

The problem of valuing the stones remained. On the takeover, Diminco absorbed the sorting organization of the SLST, which had been valuing and classifying the diamonds for ten years. But despite this experience, the example of a CSO assortment, and help from the American cutting firms, the CSO still sent valuers once a month to check and amend the Diminco assortment. The CSO jealously guards the expertise and skill which is required to sort diamonds into more than 2,000 categories. It was the lack of this expertise that deterred the government from marketing on its own account, or assisting Lonrho to build up a rival marketing organization.*

Undervaluation of diamonds in Sierra Leone would mean that the government's share of the diamonds' selling price was reduced, with lower profits for Diminco and a loss of export tax revenue. Assuming the Diamond Corporation sorting staff do not operate this form of transfer pricing deliberately, they must always be inclined to play safe in their valuation. There will obviously be more concern by their employers (the Diamond Corporation) if they overvalue than if they undervalue a stone. Even if this only happens on a small scale, a small percentage drop in the price that the Sierra Leoneans receive for their stones could amount to a sizeable sum on an annual production of £20 million.

VALUATION OF STONES

The experience of Sierra Leone shows that one of the principal problems for African diamond-exporting countries is to establish whether or not they are receiving a fair price. Diamonds come in a wide range of sizes and qualities, and valuation is a highly skilled task. It is very difficult for producers to check the assortment and valuation of their diamonds. African governments can either employ independent diamond merchants or train their

*Nothing has so far (1979) resulted from the founding of COMINCOR

own staff from scratch.* In neither case are the government's valuers able to match the expertise of the CSO, which has a formidable store of technical knowledge and experience of diamond sorting and marketing. It uses this knowledge and its position in the diamond trade to gain the maximum profit from Africa's diamonds while paying a low or fixed price to the producer. When the diamonds have been sorted in the country of origin they still have to be checked by the CSO, which naturally will concentrate on correcting mistaken overvaluation, while being less anxious to remedy undervaluation. As African governments increase their knowledge of the diamond industry, it seems certain that they will try to win higher prices for their production: but whether they will risk an alternative marketing organization is more problematical. Until such time, the CSO, and De Beers, will continue to profit at the expense of Sierra Leone and other African producers, both from its monopoly of sorting and valuing expertise and from its control of the world market.

AFRICA AND THE DIAMOND MONOPOLY

Harry Oppenheimer has justified the De Beers' monopoly control of the world diamond trade on the grounds that:

A degree of control is necessary for the well-being of the industry ... Whether this measure of control amounts to a monopoly, I would not know, but if it does it is certainly a monopoly of the most unusual kind. There is no one concerned with diamonds whether as producer, dealer, cutter, jeweller, or customer who does not benefit from it.[22]

But De Beers does not provide a stabilizing function for the world market out of the goodness of its heart. 'It is in the business to make money. The name of the game is market protection but the sub-title is profit.'[23] The question of whether the trade needs a body like the Central Selling Organization to stabilize the diamond trade must be distinguished from the question of whether De Beers should control such a body. The stabilizing role of the

*Tanzania, Angola and Botswana have their own sorting organizations, while Zaire is advised by a Belgian diamond merchant.

CSO is welcomed by producers and buyers alike; but one wonders how long the CSO can remain under the control of a South African company producing less than half of the world's diamonds.

The company is vulnerable to political action. Namibia is De Beers' main source of gemstones (and 22 per cent of its profit in 1977), and independence for this South-African-held international trust territory could at one stroke undermine De Beers' dominance of world diamond production. To protect its political position, De Beers has moved CDM's head office from Kimberley to Windhoek, and in other countries, like Sierra Leone, it employs influential local individuals in its operations, who can provide a counterweight to economic nationalism.[24] But political manoeuvring may not be enough if the producers in the rest of Africa, in South America and the USSR, who together account for more than 50 per cent of world production, should combine to force De Beers to make the CSO a genuine producers' collective on the lines of OPEC and CIPEC. This could then force De Beers to dismantle the elaborate web of companies that make up the CSO; open up its workings to the public gaze; and reduce the monopoly profit that at present accrues to De Beers.

18 Power Politics and the Diplomacy of Private Enterprise

The enormous economic power of the mining companies is accompanied by extensive political influence. In the familiar lexicon of company statements, the major mining groups favour 'stability' and 'a favourable investment climate'. To secure such seemingly peaceful aims, the companies have deployed a formidable range of military, diplomatic and political effort both in Africa and in the developed nations. In the course of the violent and turbulent pursuit of profits over the last hundred years, the companies have changed the face of Africa. When economic muscle and financial manipulation proved insufficient to secure 'stability', and a favourable investment climate the companies detonated coups d'état, bankrolled armies, organized wars, launched invasions, hired mercenaries, de-stabilized governments, started political parties, corrupted politicians and uprooted millions of African peasants.

In the last twenty years the power and influence of the companies in Africa and in the metropolitan countries has been crucial because the whole process of decolonization is an uncertain historical movement. Its direction and meaning are constantly being defined and re-defined, because the relative plasticity of political and social formations in newly independent African countries renders them susceptible to many influences.[1] The mining companies are among the most important of the external influences and their interventions during colonization, the colonial era and since have been crucial in determining the general patterns of economic and political development in Africa and in defining the relationship of the continent to foreign capital in particular. In Africa, the mining companies exert heavy and continuous pressure to ensure that the newly independent countries remain firmly within the world capitalist economy. At a more fundamental level, the companies are in such a powerful economic position that they can divert and undermine the best-laid plans for economic independence. In the advanced capitalist nations the companies exercise powerful influence on the foreign-policy-making institutions and company directors develop close links with prominent politicians and well-connected businessmen.

The mining companies also control African mineral production, through their monopoly of financial resources and marketing power, technical and managerial skills. But it is not just this monopoly of skills that places the companies in such a dominant position. It is the sheer scale of economic resources at their disposal. In 1971, for example, the *profits* alone of Anglo American Corporation were bigger than the entire gross domestic product of Botswana that year.[2] In the same year the combined assets of the Anglo group were over $3,780 million, which was more than the total foreign exchange reserves of South Africa ($1,290 million), South West Africa ($320 million), Nigeria ($348 million), Zaire ($165 million), and Zambia ($52 million) combined. The combined assets of the major South African mining houses in 1976 (R6,000 million) were greater than the gross national product of any African country on the continent excluding South Africa and Nigeria. The combined assets of the twenty-one mining companies listed in Table 22 were greater than the GNP of every country on the continent apart from South Africa in 1974.[3]

THE DIPLOMACY OF PRIVATE ENTERPRISE

This economic power is reinforced by the cultivation of close personal contacts with the ruling families and politicians. In Liberia, for example, the iron-ore companies have appointed members of the leading Whig families to their boards. But the company which has made the most extensive use of these top-level personal contacts is Lonrho. The company's chairman, Tiny Rowland, has cultivated close relations with African heads of State and members of their families are frequently found on the boards of the local Lonrho subsidiaries. In Kenya, President

Kenyatta's son-in-law, Udi Gecaga, is on the board of local Lonrho companies, and in the Ivory Coast Lonrho employs the nephew of President Houphouet-Boigny.[4] Lonrho's West African manager is Gil Olympio, second son of the late president of Togo. Lonrho also maintains close links with key ministers. In Zaire, citizen Mboti Litho, ex-Minister of Finance, Minister of Agriculture and a cousin of President Mobutu's father, is on the board of local Lonrho companies.[5] Citizen Litho is reputed to be the richest man in Zaire, apart, that is, from the President himself. However, not all of Lonrho's personal contacts have stayed in office, and when, as in Sierra Leone and Zaire, they left office, Lonrho's plans for that country fell dormant.

In the white-minority-ruled states of southern Africa, the companies, whilst exploiting the minerals and the black population, have been careful to make contact with local nationalist politicians.

They have been deeply involved in the manoeuvrings which surround the future decolonization of the white-minority-ruled states of southern Africa. In Angola, as the rival movements struggled to assert themselves, Lonrho backed Dr Jonas Savimbi's UNITA movement and *New African* magazine reported in August 1978 that through its subsidiary, Armitage Industrial Holdings, it had provided a discreet air service ferrying arms and mercenaries from Lusaka to UNITA-occupied territory in Angola. In Rhodesia as Ian Smith and the African Nationalists were being pressured into negotiations by President Kaunda and Prime Minister Vorster, Anglo flew the African National Council members from Salisbury to Lusaka and used its contacts in support of detente. In Namibia, RTZ has held negotiations with the liberation movement, SWAPO, on the future of its Rössing mine.

In the advanced capitalist nations the mining companies exercise a powerful influence on the foreign-policy-making institutions. Prominent political figures sit on the boards of the major companies and the companies spend large sums on propaganda, lobbying governments and influencing the mass media. On occasion the influence of a company can be crucial in determining the passage of special legislative provisions to protect its mines. A few examples will give an indication of the range of influential positions held by mining company executives and indicate their importance in the evolution of foreign policy. Charles Engelhard, chairman of several South African mining companies and founder of the American South Africa Investment Corporation, was an important and prominent supporter of the Democratic Party and was leader of the State Department's team which visited Zambia and represented President Johnson at the Independence celebrations. Harold and Walter Hochschild, board members and important stockholders in the American Metal Climax Company (Amax), financed the Africa–America Institute, which, although unknown at the time was later revealed to have been a conduit for CIA funds to African trade union and political leaders like Tom Mboya in Kenya.[6] The chairman and chief executive of Amax, Ian MacGregor, sat on the Council of Foreign Relations Study Group on the evolution of US policy towards Africa in 1968.[7]

In England the political lobbying of the mining companies has had a powerful influence on British foreign policy from the time of Rhodes, through the period of the Central African Federation, to recent times. At the time of its merger into Charter Consolidated in 1964, the board of the British South Africa Company read like a Who's Who of Britain's financial and political establishment and included Lord Salisbury, the 'kingmaker' of the Conservative party. The embattled Lonrho has cultivated leading members of the Conservative party establishment, and, notwithstanding Edward Heath's damning comment that the company represented the 'unacceptable face of capitalism', in 1977 Lord Barber, Lord Duncan-Sandys, and Edward du Cann were all on the board. Sir Val Duncan, chairman and chief executive of RTZ until his death in 1975, was also chairman of the committee set up by the British Foreign Office in August 1968 to assess the effectiveness and direction of Britain's diplomatic service. It was not perhaps surprising that the Duncan Report recommended that the Foreign Office disengage from black Africa and other less economically important areas and concentrate its efforts on the more developed areas of the world, such as Australia, Canada and South Africa.[8] This was exactly the policy which RTZ and other major British mining groups were pursuing at the time.

The most ambitious and highly organized attempt to win political friends and influence is the South Africa Foundation. This powerful lobbying organization was set up by the South African mining and manufacturing industry to improve the country's image abroad.[9] Important mining company chairmen like Harry Oppenheimer (Anglo), E. Pavitt (Union Mining), Slip Mennell (Anglovaal), Adriaan Louw (Gold Fields) and Punch Barlow (Barrand) are all members. Charles Engelhard was a founder member and Vice-President of the Foundation. The aim of the Foundation is to influence prominent opinion-makers in the leading Western industrial nations. It invites prominent politicians and non-specialist journalists to visit South Africa and gives them a guided tour of the country with the chance to meet the leaders of South Africa's business community. Over 200 such visitors were taken to South Africa by the Foundation between 1960 and 1970.[10] British visitors included Anthony Barber, Reginald Maudling, and Sir Alec Douglas-Home, ex-Prime Minister, who were respectively Chancellor of the Exchequer, Home Secretary and Foreign Secretary in the 1970–74 Heath administration. Selwyn Lloyd, Duncan Sandys and Lord Montgomery of Alamein also visited South Africa at the Foundation's invitation.[11] As the official historian of the Foundation proudly noted, 'Every Foundation-sponsored guest from Westminster between 1968 and 1970 became a member of the new Government except one (Selwyn Lloyd) and he became the Speaker of the House of Commons!'[12]

Through the UK South Africa Trade Association (UKSATA) the Foundation kept close links with the British business community supporting trade with South Africa, including influential mining men such as Sir Val Duncan.[13]

In America, the President of the Foundation had a long interview in Washington with President Nixon and Henry Kissinger.[14] The Foundation also invited to South Africa influential Americans like Clarence B. Randall, former President of Inland Steel Company of Chicago, a special adviser to President Eisenhower, consultant on the Marshall Plan, and later Chairman of the US Council on Foreign Economic Policy.[15] Important visitors from the continent of Europe included Herr Franz Josef Strauss, West German Minister of Finance, and Hubert Beuve-Méry, the founder and editor of *Le Monde*, the influential French newspaper.

NEWSPAPERS

In addition to developing a wide range of personal contacts, the mining companies have felt the need to create and secure a friendly press. For example, in 1971 RTZ financed a trip by the industrial editor of the London *Sunday Times*, Keith Richardson, to visit the company's mines in Canada, South Africa and Australia. The three articles which followed were very sympathetic to RTZ and appeared at a time when RTZ was being heavily criticized for conditions at Palabora in South Africa and its involvement in the Rössing uranium mine in Namibia.[16] In America the Africa–America Institute, supported by Amax directors, publishes a monthly magazine called *Africa Report*. In Katanga, Northern and Southern Rhodesia, the companies have established and run local newspapers.*

In South Africa the companies have been supported in their political activities by their ownership of the two largest English-language newspaper groups. The Cape-based Argus group of newspapers was originally controlled by Rhodes, Barney Barnato and Solly Joel, before passing to the Central Mines and Rand Mines. Today the largest shareholder is Johannesburg Consolidated Investment. The other main newspaper group, which included the famous *Rand Daily Mail*, was owned 60 per cent by Sir Abe Bailey, the mining magnate, whose interests passed on his death to the Anglo American group. In 1955 the paper was merged into the South African Amalgamated Newspaper Group (SAAN) and the Bailey interests fell to 50 per cent.[17] Although today the ownership of both newspaper groups is more diffuse than in the days of Rhodes, neither newspaper group is noted for its attacks on the working conditions and low pay in

*See Chapter 8.

the gold mines and they have in the past submitted articles about the mines to the companies before publication.[18]

THE COMPANIES' INFLUENCE ON GOVERNMENTS

The influence of the mining companies can secure the adoption of special legislative or administrative measures. The worldwide diamond monopoly of De Beers relies heavily on the continuing supply of large high-quality diamonds from Namibia. In Namibia under an early ordinance the administration is not allowed to put up taxes on diamonds without the consent of Consolidated Diamond Mines.[19] To protect the monopoly De Beers has persuaded both the South African and British governments to take steps which will make it more difficult for rival producers to assess the company's production policy. In Britain, at De Beers' request, the Department of Trade no longer publishes the source of Britain's diamond imports, the majority of which come from De Beers-controlled mines to be sorted at the De Beers Central Selling Organization.[20] In South Africa, again at the instigation of De Beers, the government passed section 2 of the General Law (1975) Act, which prohibits the company from disclosing any information to foreign governments or parliamentary inquiries.[21]

ECONOMIC INDEPENDENCE

The international mining companies are the principal savings and investment mechanism in much of Africa, determining the structure and growth of the host economies through their investment and export policies. Mining projects all over Africa show that, notwithstanding the heavy commitment of government resources, the linkage with and benefits for the rest of the economy are often minimal.[22] Despite the massive investment in Pechiney's FRIA smelting plant based on cheap hydroelectric power in Guinea, the local benefits are few.[23] The tax revenue from such projects is also frequently meagre, as Botswana has found with the Selebi-Pikwe mine. Almost invariably it is the company's priorities which prevail, as the examples of Ghana, Mauritania and Sierra Leone show.

Kaiser Aluminium and the Volta River Project

A celebrated example of the way the mining company's priorities prevail over national plans for national development is provided by Volta River Project in Ghana. In 1914 an Australian geologist working for the British government found large deposits of bauxite in the Gold Coast (as Ghana was then called); and he prepared detailed plans to process the bauxite, using hydroelectric power from a dam that he proposed at Akosombo on the lower stretches of the great Volta river.[24] Over the next forty years, the juxtaposition of large supplies of bauxite and potential hydroelectric power seemed to make the Gold Coast an ideal site for an integrated aluminium production plan. In 1955 a British government White Paper backed the scheme; as an escape from the post-war monopoly of the American aluminium producers from whom it was buying more than four fifths of her supplies. The Canadian company ALCAN was invited to build an aluminium production plant. ALCAN wanted electricity from the dam to be supplied at an initial cost of only 2·5 mills* per unit, with reductions later. But the Preparatory Commission had decided that the price would have to be 5 mills per unit at the outset, with subsequent reductions to 2·5 mills. No agreement was reached; ALCAN withdrew, and the scheme foundered.[25]

It was revived in 1957 after Ghana's independence, when the USA took an interest in the project after a meeting between the Ghanaian Finance Minister, Dr Gbedemah, and President Eisenhower. Although there was substantial surplus capacity in the American aluminium industry, and the companies had asked the Administration to help the industry by building up a stockpile of aluminium, the USA was anxious to regain the prestige lost in Africa by the withdrawal of US funds from the Egyptian Aswan dam, where the Russians had stepped in to help.[26] After a meeting between Edgar Kaiser and Kwame

*A mill is one thousandth of a dollar.

Nkrumah in New York on 28 July 1958, the Kaiser Corporation was asked to investigate and reappraise the Volta Project.

The Kaiser Reassessment Report was completed within six months, and it contained several surprises. Kaiser slashed some £60 million from the estimated cost, but there was a considerable revision of the scheme. The original Volta plans provided not only for an aluminium factory but for a large-scale irrigation project and the development of a fishing industry on the Volta Lake created by the dam. The Kaiser Report dropped the irrigation and fishing industry plans; but most important of all, there was to be no integrated aluminium complex using Ghanaian bauxite. The smelter would use imported alumina instead. Kaiser estimated that alumina would have to be imported for at least ten years.

The Ghanaians were appalled. As originally conceived, the Volta River Project was to have been a more expensive and more ambitious venture: the dam, hydroelectric and integrated aluminium industry complex were seen as the hub from which would spread out a variety of connected activities – bauxite mining, irrigated agriculture, lake fishing, transport and various industries. It was to be vehicle and symbol for a total transformation of the Ghanaian economy. Ghana's revenue from the Kaiser proposals would amount to only half of those that an integrated industry would have provided. Moreover the proposals would leave undeveloped the large bauxite deposits at Kibi, the true extent of which had been discovered in 1956. Since Kibi was much closer to both Akosombo and Tema than the other deposits, the Ghanaians had hoped that Kibi bauxite would be used. But Kaiser was adamant that the project would have to use imported alumina.

Both Nkrumah and Gbedemah were totally committed to the project, and they continued to explore ways of funding even this truncated scheme. ALCAN offered to take the initiative in forming a consortium, but the company still baulked at the cost of the electricity from the Volta. So President Nkrumah asked Kaiser to head another consortium. Until now, Kaiser had only been concerned with the engineering and technical evaluation of the project; but it had, of course, extensive aluminium interests in the USA. The Volta Aluminium Company (VALCO) was created in November 1959 as a consortium of aluminium interests. The companies involved at the start were Kaiser Aluminium, ALCAN, Aluminium Company of America (ALCOA), Olin Mathieson (an American aluminium group associated with the Rockefeller interests), and Reynold Metals. ALCAN dropped out in 1960. In 1961 ALCOA dropped out, and Olin Mathieson decided to concentrate on its Guinean deposits. This left Kaiser and Reynolds as the sole participants in VALCO, with interests of 90 per cent and 10 per cent respectively.

Table 35: Financing the Volta river project

---

1. Akosombo dam and power station

	£m.	
World Bank (IBRD)	16·8	(at 5¾% over 25 years)
US (AID)	9·6	(at 3½% ,, ,, ,,)
US (EX-IM BANK)	3·6	(at 5¾% ,, ,, ,,)
Britain	5·0	(at 6% ,, ,, ,,)
Total external loan finance	35·0	
Ghana government	35·0	(Equity)
Total cost	70·0	

---

2. Tema aluminium smelter (VALCO)

Kaiser Corporation	44·0	(Equity 90%)
Reynolds Corporation		(Equity 10%)

---

3. Ancillary investment at Tema

Ghana government	7·2
Total investment	121·2

Source: The Volta River Project, Government Printer, Accra, 1961.

The total cost of the dam and smelter was estimated at £114 million. Of the estimated £60 million for the dam and infrastructure, Ghana would find half from her own resources, and the rest would be provided in the form of loans from the World Bank and the US government (see Table 35). These loans were larger than they needed to be, because they were tied to the purchase of American goods. Even the World Bank felt that the loans were too restrictive, and the Ghanaians were able to negotiate a partial relaxation, with some of the contracts put out to international tender. The US Export Import Bank loaned VALCO £34·5 million for the smelter, while AID guaranteed Kaiser and Reynolds' investment to the tune of £9·5 million. In addition the Ghana government had to give a written guarantee not to expropriate the £44 million smelter. These arrangements gave Kaiser relatively little financial exposure, as most of the risk was borne by the US government. Even so, the company demanded substantial concessions in the form of tax relief and minimal charges for electricity.

In its 1961 assessment of the Volta project, the World Bank pointed out that the main benefit to the Ghanaian government would be in the form of taxes, royalty and income from the sale of the electricity. The Bank's advice was that Ghana should negotiate with VALCO to sell electricity at a fixed rate of 4·5 mills per kilowatt, with a flat rate of 15 mills per kilowatt for all other customers. In certain circumstances the Bank advised the Ghanaians to sell power for 3·5 mills per unit. But VALCO was insisting on the same figure as ALCAN had several years earlier, 2·5 mills per unit. Edgar Kaiser wrote to Nkrumah, pointing out that the aluminium industry was in a depressed state and that there was idle smelting capacity in the USA. In these circumstances, the project would go ahead only if VALCO's shareholders could be sure of a sufficient return on their commitment of £125 million. Kaiser concluded by referring to the dissipation of what he called a 'healthy climate' for discussions and expressed the hope that this could be restored. At the same time, having obtained a copy of the World Bank Report unofficially, Kaiser argued with the Bank that its calculations had been too cautious and that the electricity could be sold at a lower price. The Ghanaians agreed to a lower price, largely because Kaiser seemed to be the only company prepared to carry out the long-cherished Volta project. VALCO would pay a special rate of 2·625 mills per kilowatt, and agreed to purchase 300,000 kilowatt of Volta power per day for 30 years. The cost of the electricity to VALCO would be a mere £2·5 million a year, only a fraction over the cost price. Over thirty years, this income would meet the capital cost of the Volta project, estimated at £70 million.[27]

The importance of cheap electricity to aluminium production can be seen when one breaks down the cost into its various stages (see Table 36). The major cost in producing aluminium is the

Table 36: The distribution of aluminium production costs

Percentage of the total cost	Process	Additional Input	Product	Location of VALCO Operations
10%	Extraction of ore		Bauxite	Jamaica
10%	Beneficiating		(Bauxite exported)	Jamaica
20%	Conversion to alumina	Caustic soda	Alumina	USA
60%	Reduction to aluminium	Electricity, Cryolite	Aluminium	Ghana

Note: Percentages are approximate; exact figures depend on variable factors that fluctuate over time.

Source: M. S. Brown and J. Butler, *The Production, Marketing and Consumption of Copper and Aluminium*, Praeger, 1968, derived from data on p. 5 and chart 3, p. 142.

reduction stage, when aluminium is reduced by the electrolytic process from alumina to aluminium. It is the cost of electricity rather than the quality of the bauxite and alumina that differentiates between the high- and low-cost aluminium producers. One can see why both ALCAN and later Kaiser were eager to secure the lowest possible unit cost for electricity. A difference of one mill in power costs will add some $16–$18 per ton of ingot aluminium. The aluminium companies will usually invest in smelters overseas only if they can get power more cheaply than in the US.[28]

The low cost of the electricity meant that it was more profitable for Kaiser to import Jamaican bauxite, process it into alumina in the US, and then trans-ship the alumina to Ghana for smelting into aluminium, than to develop Ghana's Kibi bauxite deposits. But another advantage of the scheme for Kaiser was that without an alumina plant Ghana did not have the facilities for an integrated aluminium industry, which would have been much more vulnerable to expropriation. With the essential alumina plant in the USA, Kaiser felt more secure. If Ghana had any intention of expropriating VALCO, it would be dissuaded by the fact that without imported alumina the smelter could not operate; and without the income from the smelter, the loans on the dam could not be met. The Kaiser scheme went ahead, and the dam was inauguarated on 22 January 1966, just a few months after Nkrumah had published his book *Neo-Colonialism*, which argued that Africa's development was restricted by the power of foreign capital. The US government was so incensed by the book that it lodged a formal diplomatic protest.[29]

The World Bank estimated that the net contribution of Kaiser's reduced project, including the smelter when fully operational, would be only £7–8 million a year, or about 1½ per cent of Ghana's GDP in 1961. Apart from the temporary employment opportunities created during the construction phase, the contribution of the project to employment was only about 200 at Akosombo and 1,500 in the smelter and at the port of Tema. Net foreign exchange earnings from the smelter were expected to amount to between £16 million and £19 million.[30] To build the project Ghana committed £77 million, which was more than half of the total capital budget for all other public sector projects planned for 1959–64.[31]

In 1963, at a time of anti-American demonstrations in Accra, Nkrumah again pressed Kaiser to produce alumina from Ghanaian bauxite, but Kaiser firmly rejected the idea:

Under conditions that exist in Ghana today, I would not finance 10 cents and I simply do not know when conditions will allow the financing of an alumina plant.[32]

Whatever these conditions are, they have yet to materialize.

The VALCO smelter continues to process alumina imported from the US, using cheap power from the Akosombo dam. In 1979 Ghana had no alumina plant; and the bauxite reserves at

Kibi, which could supply the VALCO smelter at its planned rate of production for more than 250 years, remained undeveloped.

MAURITANIA

The evolution of the relationship between the mining companies in Mauritania typifies the experience of many African countries. The country was a poverty-stricken colony in French West Africa when, in 1952, a consortium of French, German, British, and Italian steel companies decided to exploit Mauritania's massive iron-ore deposits and to replace less profitable operations in France itself, which had been closed, creating severe unemployment and social dislocation.[33]

The consortium established the Société de Mines de Fer de Maurétanie (MIFERMA) in 1959, and the Mauritanian government mortaged virtually all of its investable surplus to build the infrastructure needed by the mine. The loans from the World Bank were jointly guaranteed by the French and Mauritanian governments.[34] The Mauritanian government was involved in the guarantees largely to safeguard against the threat of expropriation after Independence. Presumably the same reasoning prompted the granting to the government of a derisory 5 per cent stake in MIFERMA in 1964.

The new mine was a state within a state and in the early days even had its own army.[35] A 650-kilometre railway was built to link the mine in the Kedia of Idjil with the specially constructed port at Nouadhibou. The mine came into production in 1962 and exports rose quickly from 1·3 million to 4 million tons in 1964. The operations of MIFERMA were entirely responsible for the high level of capital investment in Mauritania. Over sixty per cent of all capital investment in the years after independence was connected with the iron-ore mines.[36] The mine was also responsible for the rapid growth of the gross domestic product, which increased 2·4 times in seven years.[37]

This impressive economic growth was, however, incapable of providing the basis for economic development. Any expansion or contraction in the mining sector was immediately reflected in the gross domestic product. Mauritania was in fact the classic example of a dualist economy driven from outside because of its mineral exports and whose various sectors were completely unrelated. The mining sector remained an isolated enclave. Fifteen years of economic growth and an apparently impressive increase in the *per capita* product from $60 in 1959 to $130 in 1970 meant little, because the growth was restricted to the mining sector and its direct subsidiaries. The direct linkages with the rest of the economy were few, and the share of the mining product which accrued to Mauritania was very small.[38] Although MIFERMA contributed a third of Mauritania's tax revenue, this was only a small proportion of the surplus generated and exported by the mine.[39] In the nineteen-sixties, payments to the local staff made up less than 20 per cent of the value added in the mineral sector and government revenue was fixed at a mere 9 per cent of export sales.[40]

The highly paid expatriate engineering and management personnel earned far in excess of the Mauritanian workers, who then found promotion to higher posts within MIFERMA blocked. What appeared to be growth was largely an increase in the surplus extracted and exported by the mine. The net result was that Mauritania, 'once an undeveloped colonial reserve, is now a true underdeveloped country'.[41]

The government accepted this state of affairs in the vain pursuit of 'export-led development'. It even lightened the tax levied on MIFERMA and granted it extensive prospecting rights along the line of rail.[42] In 1968 the government intervened on the side of the company to break a strike of local mineworkers.[43] The government was anxious to maintain the flow of revenue and supported the increase in iron-ore exports to almost 10·5 million tons in 1973. But despite this support and encouragement, MIFERMA was not responsive to the government's plans for national economic development.

The government wanted MIFERMA to explore and develop the lower-grade reserves in the Kedia area and prolong the life of Mauritania's mining industry. The company resisted these pressures and refused to undertake any processing of the ore locally. Finally in 1973 the Mauritanian government, caught in the worldwide inflationary spiral, limited MIFERMA's freedom of action by restricting the movement of capital and levying heavier taxes on the company.[44] Two years later in a further attempt to increase its revenue the government took a 51 per cent share in MIFERMA, which was paid compensation of $90 million. The new company operating the mines was called COMINOR and is a wholly owned subsidiary of the state-owned Société Nationale Industrielle et Minière (SNIM). Production fell, however, when the French technicians left and again when Polisario, the liberation movement fighting for the independence of Western Sahara, attacked the mine in retaliation for Mauritania's annexation of Western Sahara.

STATE PARTICIPATION

Throughout the continent, governments have struggled with the problems created by the fact that the mines developed to service the profitability of the international mining companies are the sole major source of foreign exchange and capital investment. The governments had no control over the prices their mineral exports might fetch either because of violent market fluctuations or because of monopoly control.* Often the companies determined export price earnings by their pricing decisions within the firm. For example, the long-term contracts that the steel companies signed with their iron-ore mining subsidiaries and associates encourage the mines to sell extra quantities on the free market relatively cheaply, because their major objective is not to make a profit on these sales but to lower the unit cost of raw materials delivered to their parent companies.[45] And again the companies decide at what rate the deposits will be exploited through their day-to-day control of management. For example, in Liberia in 1972, when the cost of shipping iron ore dipped sharply, LAMCO, without reference to the government, quickly increased the rate of mining, milling and the export of ore to take advantage of the lower shipping rates.[46]

All over Africa, the rulers of the newly independent nations

* See above, Chapters 16 and 17.

went through a process similar to that in Mauritania. They recognized the prime importance to their power, and to the government revenues, of the continuing export of minerals. They have therefore identified closely with the policies of the mine management, while at the same time seeking to increase their share of the surplus. The governments first encouraged foreign investment with tax concessions and then increased the level of taxation and finally took a direct stake in the mines (see Table 37). In fact the trend to government participation was so pronounced that a small group of economists and mining experts has grown up to advise governments in their negotiations with the mining companies.[47]

The Response of the Companies

The mining companies, for their part, have evolved a strategy designed to minimize the shock to the corporate system caused by state participation and even to improve their position. The changing political climate requires a change in the companies' tactics, but their strategic aim remains as always to develop the resources of Africa for profit, so at first

> they will hang on to their position of strength for as long as they can . . . then they will try to support moderate (some would say stooge) African politicians likely to be favourably disposed towards them; finally . . . they will . . . come to terms with the government of the day.[48]

In the takeover negotiations the power of the company to disrupt the government's revenue and wreck the country's balance of payments puts it in a very strong position. The strength of the company is reinforced by Africa's dependence on imported technology and technicians for the mines.[49] The company can underline its strength, as Union Minière did, by threatening to destroy the mineral maps of the Katangan subsoil built up over fifty years, but usually there is no need for the companies to make any such direct threat. African governments are fully conscious of the power wielded by the companies. Should they be in any doubt the companies use their powerful diplomatic and political muscle in Africa and the industrialized nations in sup-

Table 37: Majority government participation in the mines of Africa

Country	Mine	Product	Foreign mining interests and percentage owned before government participation	Year of state participation	Company's present interest percentage	State interest percentage
Angola	Diamang	diamonds	De Beers (100)	1977	39	61
Botswana	Orapa	diamonds	De Beers (85)	1976	50	50
Ghana	Ashanti	gold	Lonrho (80)	1972	45	55
	Akwatia	diamonds	CAST (100)	1972	45	55
	Nsuta	manganese	Union Carbide (100)	1972	45	55
Guinea	Fria	bauxite	FRIGUIA (51)	1969	51	49
	Boke	bauxite	Halco (51)	1960	51	49
Mauritania	Miferma	iron ore	Miferma (95)	1975	49	51
	Akjouit	copper	Charter Consolidated (33)	1975	nil	53
Sierra Leone	Tongo, etc.	diamonds	SLST (100)	1972	49	51
Tanzania	Mwadui	diamonds	De Beers (100)	1967	50	50
Togo	Kpogame	phosphate	Various US and French cos. (80)	1972	nil	100
Uganda	Kilembe	copper	Falconbridge (72·8)	1975	nil	100
Zaire	Union Minière	copper	Belgian and British cos. (approx. 66)	1969	nil	100
Zambia	RCM	copper	Amax (40)	1970	20	51
	NCCM	copper	Anglo American group (56)	1970	49	51

port of their investments. Occasionally, however, a company faced with government participation may decide to liquidate its investment leaving a hole both in the ground and in the government's pocket, as happened in Sierra Leone.

Sierra Leone and DELCO

The Sierra Leone Development Co. (DELCO), a subsidiary of William Baird Inc. registered in Scotland, began mining iron ore at Marampa in Sierra Leone in 1933. The ore was hauled fifty-five miles over the company's private railway from the mine to a specially constructed deep-water port at Pepel. For forty years DELCO shipped the ore at a rate of up to three million tons a year, most of it to the British iron and steel industry. Then in 1972 President Siaka Stevens announced that his government would take a 51 per cent stake in all the country's major mines.

At this point, according to the Government Report by a deputy Governor of the Central Bank, DELCO decided to go into liquidation rather than be nationalized.[50] In 1973 the company wrote down its assets from Le20 million (£10 million) to Le2 million (£1 million) and registered a trading loss which it reported to the government. On the basis of this 'loss', the government decided not to proceed with the takeover, and as the accounts were not presented to the Sierra Leone Auditor General for two years, the government remained ignorant of the true reasons for this loss. Meanwhile in November 1974 DELCO asked the government for a loan of Le2 million to keep the mine going while discussions about its future continued. Bethlehem Steel was approached to see if it would take over management of the mine. The government made another loan of Le2 million to DELCO in July 1975. In September the company asked for monthly loans of Le 0·5 million through to the end of the year. The government, in the middle of a financial crisis, scraped together the money to keep the mine going, even though DELCO had now paid no taxes for four years, while it continued to bank the foreign exchange earned by the iron ore. The government was trying to preserve the employment and government revenue provided by the mine. Negotiations with Bethlehem Steel for a 'rescue operation' continued, but the American company was more interested in the concession to mine the Tonkolili iron-ore deposit than in taking over DELCO. Finally in December 1975 DELCO went into liquidation, putting the mine out of operation, making thousands of workers redundant, dissipating an experienced workforce built up over the years, and creating a sharp drop in Sierra Leone's export earnings. The company had managed to liquidate its assets and repatriate its capital leaving Sierra Leone with an abandoned mine, railway and port. Moreover the iron deposit was almost exhausted and the government was left with a substantial and unsecured debt.[51]

COMPENSATION

If a mining company accepts a demand for government participation, its main objective is then to ensure what the companies are wont to call 'full and fair' compensation for their assets. There is of course no such thing as a 'fair price' for a company's assets, merely the price that both parties can agree to and obtain what they want from the deal.[52] No African governments have yet attempted to apply the Chilean formula of ignoring possible future profits, and assessing any historical return on capital above 12 per cent as excess profits and reducing compensation accordingly. This is perhaps surprising as the compensation payments involve yet another massive export of locally generated surplus, and the original capital investment has usually been repatriated with interest long ago. This indicates once again the weak bargaining position of African governments. The power of the companies enables them to demand and receive compensation in foreign currency freely remittable to wherever the company designates. The companies use this capital to build up their mining interests in other parts of the world. In the case of Anglo American's Zambian subsidiary Zamanglo it was allowed to move to Bermuda without even the formality of winding up.[53] The bonds with which African governments have usually paid compensation have sometimes themselves become high yielding investments when heavily discounted by metropolitan investors.[54] Typically the final element in an agreed government takeover in Africa has been the awarding of a generous management contract to the original mining company.[55]

Government participation in African mines has encouraged the trend towards loan financing and joint ventures by the mining companies, for, although they are partly demanded by the sheer size of modern mining projects, they are also seen as a protection against expropriation.

> The experience of companies and the particular unpopularity of nationals of one country may be submerged by the organization of multi-national consortia . . . from several industrial states . . . Multinational participation may produce a more sober [sic] approach by governments of less developed countries who may also have enough concern for future capital supplies not to injure relations with all capital-producing nations at one time.[56]

Loan financing reduces the international mining companies' risk exposure. Moreover, the heavy interest charges built into the cost structure of the mine allows most of the surplus wealth generated by the mine to be exported without being subject to local taxes.

In a parallel development, although the mining companies previously provided much of the capital for the supporting infrastructure for new mines either directly or through portfolio investment, in recent years they have departed from this practice, and the necessary loan capital is now often provided by the international and bilateral aid agencies. This trend has been accentuated by the aggressive lending policies of the World Bank under Robert MacNamara. So the companies have invested less and less of their own money in African mining ventures, reasoning, no doubt correctly, that African governments were much less likely to default on loans to international agencies or expropriate multinational consortia than to expropriate a single, easily identifiable foreign mining company.

Most companies have accepted government partnership in new mines, and as Anglo's chairman Harry Oppenheimer put it in his company's 1973 *Annual Report*,

A group like ours must be prepared to accept, provided it is wisely exercised, a greater measure of direct government participation and control in the enterprises we undertake in developing countries. On the other hand governments that wish to attract capital and administrative and technical know-how must be prepared to allow profits to be made and to be paid out on a scale which is commensurate with the real value of this know-how and with the high risks inseparable from mining.

The point was reinforced by the authoritative *Mining Annual Review* in 1974:

At bottom, free enterprise is not dedicated to any particular form of ownership. It is dedicated to making profits, and, providing the terms are right, it should be no more difficult (and quite a lot less risky) to make profits from the sale of mining skills and management skills than from the discovery and exploitation of mineral deposits.[57]

But not all companies share this view: Union Minière and Selection Trust have moved all their interests out of Africa; and in early 1976 thirteen of the biggest Western mining groups submitted to the European Economic Community a document which said that, unless countries in Africa (and elsewhere) treat mining investors more favourably, investment from European sources is likely to dry up completely. The companies threatened an investment strike and said that unless the EEC protected the companies there was bound to be a very sharp fall in mining investment, which in turn would lead to a shortage of raw materials by the mid-eighties. Some commentators have linked the document and its demands to suspension of the Tenke-Fungurume Project in Zaire and note that the World Bank has told Zaire that it would not loan any of the $250 million required to meet cost increases.

It cannot be denied that state participation does restrict the mining companies' freedom of action to some extent. But the relative imbalance of the partners remains, for the international mining groups retain their superior technical, information, financial and managerial expertise. Moreover, as day-to-day management is invariably left in the hands of the mining company it can make apparently technical alterations in mining policy by altering shipping rates or stripping ratios, which do not benefit the host but do improve the cash flow and profitability of the parent group. These decisions may well hasten the depletion of local mineral resources, but this is not usually an important factor for the international mining company.

State participation can give the host government a greater knowledge of the internal operations of the mining company, but this does not necessarily lead to greater control. In Zambia and Sierra Leone, 51 per cent takeover has proved insufficient for effective control. In Sierra Leone, DIMINCO (although 51 per cent government-owned) appeared to be holding back production simply to force the government to take action against illicit diggers, and in 1975, as the government was seeking a much larger say in management, production fell for the first time in fifteen years.[58]

State participation also has advantages for the mining group in that the host government will now have a vested interest in defending the companies against political attacks, in preserving a 'stable environment', and in making the local subsidiary as profitable as possible to maintain a high level of government earnings from its 51 per cent share. In Zambia the government put pressure on the companies to maintain production and dividends at high levels so that the government could meet the compensation repayments and absorb at least a proportion of the country's rising unemployment.

If it is politically unwise to declare a high level of profits the international mining groups have a wide range of techniques to siphon off the surplus generated by the mine. Creative accounting, head office charges, transfer pricing, and paper loans are all proven methods of maintaining the companies' income. If the government takes a stock participation in the mine, its income is then dependent on the level of profits declared and taxes paid by the companies. As profit figures can so easily be manipulated, it is difficult for the government to be sure that it is getting the income to which it is nominally entitled.

African governments, realizing that the vital decision-making processes which affect their national economic development are based on the allocation of resources within the firm, have sought to incorporate the firm into the state decision-making process, but the effect of state participation so far has been to incorporate the government into the international mining company's decision-making structure.

19 The Oppenheimer Complex*

The Anglo American group of companies is the unchallenged colossus of the African mining industry. Both in the white-ruled states of the south and in black Africa, the group mines a wide range of base and precious metals. The overall value of the interests of the group was valued by Anglo's 1975 *Annual Report* at R5,300 million. By comparison the gross domestic product in that year of a medium-sized African state such as Tanzania was only R1,800 million, or about a third the size of Anglo.[1]

Anglo's head office stands massively squat on Main Street, close to the heart of Johannesburg's business section. The building is immense and imposing, and from it Anglo's chairman, Harry Oppenheimer, controls one of the largest business empires in the world. Urbane, intellectual, and articulate, Oppenheimer can give visitors the impression that he almost considers the complex affairs of the Anglo group a mammoth intellectual puzzle to be explored with almost philosophical detachment. Nevertheless, he is one of the world's most powerful men.

The base of the Anglo empire is twofold: De Beers' control of the world diamond trade and the group's gold mines, producing 37 per cent of South African output in 1977 (27 per cent of non-Communist world production). Within South Africa the Anglo group dwarfs all competition. De Beers is only one part of the Anglo group, and yet De Beers alone is five times the size of the top two South African banks combined.† In 1970, which was not a good year for De Beers, it made more profit than the twenty

* This chapter is a somewhat shortened, but revised and updated, version of G. Lanning and M. Mueller, 'The Oppenheimer Complex', Johannesburg, mimeo, 1971.

† Ranked by market capitalization.

most profitable South African companies combined.[2] Seven years later its position, after a wave of takeovers and mergers among leading South African industrial companies, was less dominant but its pre-tax profits still equalled the combined total of the eight most profitable industrial companies in South Africa.[3]

Anglo American dominates the South African gold-mining industry. In 1977 the group had substantial interests in nine of the top ten gold mines (ranked by production) in South Africa and through its mine management and technical services administered three of the top five and six of the top eleven.*

Also falling within the orbit of the Anglo American Corporation group in 1976 were three of the major mining houses, and the five top mining finance houses, the largest life assurers and the largest retail motor organization in South Africa. After the government, the group is the largest taxpayer and the largest employer of labour in South Africa.[4] It should come as no surprise to learn that the largest private steel company, one of the largest coal-mining groups, and two of the top ten property companies are all in the Anglo family. And, to make sure it's all safe, Anglo has an interest in a prominent South African manufacturer of burglar alarms.

The total profits of this enormous group are difficult to estimate because of a complex system of interlocking companies, but the profits of the most important companies for the years 1966–77 are given in Table 38. Anglo American's profits after tax have risen without a break for twenty years, from R7·5 million in 1956 to R39·2 million in 1970, and R195·3 million in 1978.† De Beers Consolidated has declared even higher profits. In its peak year of 1977, profits were R621·5 million (compared with R42·6 million in 1961). The Anglo group's investments in South Africa and South West Africa accounted for 79 per cent of Anglo investment and 76 per cent of group income in 1977. Anglo's investments in the rest of Africa accounted for 6 per cent of the

* In 1963, on a visit to Anglo's deepest mine, Harry Oppenheimer was quoted as saying, 'It's quite amusing but I wouldn't like to work there' (*Sunday Times* (Johannesburg), 25 June 1963).

† Because of the merger with Rand Selection this figure is for fifteen months.

Table 38: The profits of the main Anglo group companies, 1966–77 (all figures R million, after tax)

	1966	1967	1968	1969	1970	1971	1972	1973	1974	1975	1976	1977	Total 1966–77
Anglo American Corp.	30·5	30·5	32·7	36·2	38·7	40·9	45·4	57·9	75·5	84·4	86·0	195·0	753·7
De Beers Cons.	81·8	87·7	105·8	112·7	77·0	100·7	161·5	235·9	199·7	218·4	306·7	621·5	2309·4
Charter Cons.	15·6	13·4	16·7	17·4	24·1	33·1	26·8	21·0	27·5	30·2	31·5	32·2	289·5
TOTAL	127·9	131·6	155·2	166·3	139·8	174·7	233·7	314·8	302·7	333·0	424·2	848·7	3352·6

Note: All figures are approximate. Because of rounding, individual years and totals may not correspond.

Figures represent only *declared* profits after tax, and preference dividends as given in annual reports.

Charter's profits are converted at prevailing rates of exchange.

Anglo's profits for 1977 cover fifteen months and include Rand Selection which became 100 per cent subsidiary that year, and therefore are not comparable with those for previous years.

investment and 6 per cent of the income in 1972, and generally reflect a much higher return on investment than the South African operations, as for example in 1972, when 8 per cent of investments produced 16 per cent of the income. The group's copper interests, which are mainly in Zambia, have given a particularly high proportionate return on investment. As the main administrator and technical adviser to the group, Anglo gets a large slice of its profits from loans and fees, which in 1977 contributed R85·8 million, about a third of total profits.

The great strengths of the Anglo group, apart from its size and profits, are its capital resources, financial skills, vast information network and large-scale engineering know-how. Where other companies run into difficulties financing major projects, Anglo's high reputation in international financial circles means that it can attract fresh capital almost at will. The group has links with banks in all the important financial centres of the world. Its banking friends include Banque de Paris et des Pays Bas, Deutsche Bank, the Union Bank of Switzerland, First National City Bank of New York, Morgan Guaranty, Rothschilds, Morgan Grenfell, and Banca Commerciale Italiana. Oppenheimer himself is a director of Barclays Bank. The group's ability to raise overseas finance is strengthened by an agreement with the South African government. Under the terms of this agreement, De Beers supports long-term state loans and, in return, has permission to raise funds abroad to finance developments in other countries.[5] The ability to raise capital, together with its information network, means that Anglo is very good at exploiting a potential first revealed by others. This was shown, for example, in Botswana, where Anglo took no part in the early work of proving the Selebi-Pikwe deposit, and yet now controls the mine. Above all, it is Anglo's sheer size that is so important and enables the group to out-manoeuvre competitors. According to the Johannesburg *Star*, in June 1970, when the state government of Western Australia lifted the ban on claim pegging, local Australian prospectors in jeeps looked on with some amazement as Anglo pegged its claims with three helicopters and a light aircraft!

THE FINANCIAL STRUCTURE

The complex pattern of interlocking ownership* established by the group's founder, Ernest Oppenheimer, is designed to maintain control of the ever-growing Anglo empire without on the one hand tying up too many resources and endangering expansion or on the other hand losing control of existing investments. A simplified version of this structure is given in Figure 22. Despite the size and the complexity of the group, control rests firmly with Anglo.

The pre-eminence of Anglo both in the control structure and in the management system makes it clear that although Anglo's executives prefer to speak as if their group were a narrowly circumscribed agglomeration of subsidiary and directly associated companies, De Beers and the other major entities are in practice part of one enormous Anglo family.[6]

The key to the control of this 'family' is the concept of 'effective control' and Anglo's highly developed use of the holding company mechanism. 'Effective control' means that a minimum outlay by Anglo secures maximum control. It is not necessary to hold 51 per cent of the shares to control a company. If the Anglo group holds more than 30 per cent of a company's shares, with the remaining shares widely distributed and firmly held, then Anglo's control is secure. The group does not tie up more capital than is necessary to secure control, because this would hinder further expansion. A holding company is a company that controls one or more subsidiary companies by owning all or part of their share capital. Holding companies are often established with purely nominal capital, but they can control direct and indirect subsidiaries and affiliates which control much larger financial resources. Taking full advantage of both the holding company and the concept of effective control it is possible for Anglo to control a mining company through a 30 per cent stake in a holding company which in turn has only a 30 per cent stake in the mining company. In theory Anglo is in a weak position to control the mine owning only 30 per cent of 30 per cent, but in

* For a broad outline of the major group companies see Chapters 12 and 13.

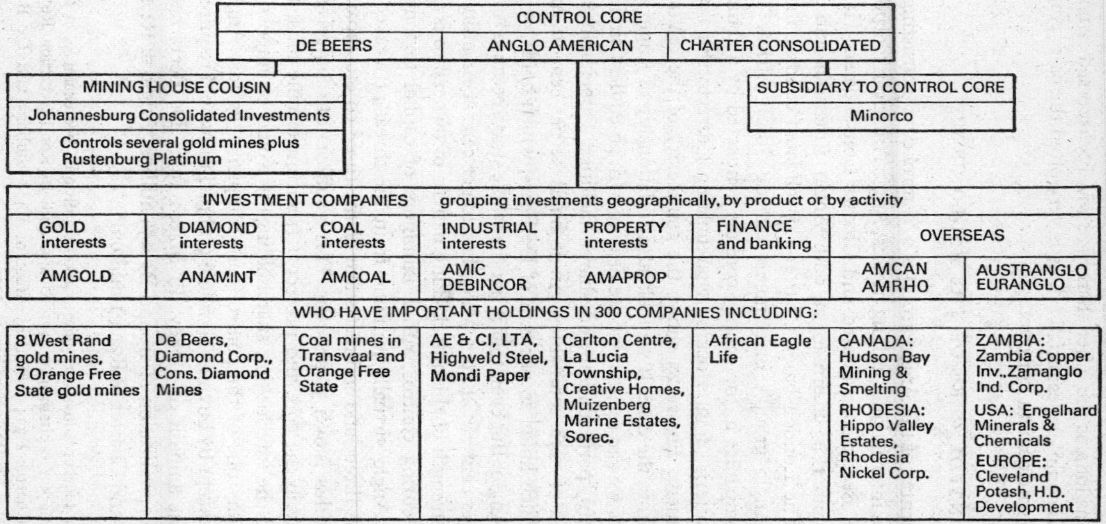

CONTROL CORE

DE BEERS	ANGLO AMERICAN	CHARTER CONSOLIDATED

SUBSIDIARY TO CONTROL CORE

Minorco

MINING HOUSE COUSIN

Johannesburg Consolidated Investments

Controls several gold mines plus Rustenburg Platinum

INVESTMENT COMPANIES grouping investments geographically, by product or by activity

GOLD interests	DIAMOND interests	COAL interests	INDUSTRIAL interests	PROPERTY interests	FINANCE and banking	OVERSEAS	
AMGOLD	ANAMINT	AMCOAL	AMIC DEBINCOR	AMAPROP		AMCAN AMRHO	AUSTRANGLO EURANGLO

WHO HAVE IMPORTANT HOLDINGS IN 300 COMPANIES INCLUDING:

8 West Rand gold mines, 7 Orange Free State gold mines	De Beers, Diamond Corp., Cons. Diamond Mines	Coal mines in Transvaal and Orange Free State	AE & CI, LTA, Highveld Steel, Mondi Paper	Carlton Centre, La Lucia Township, Creative Homes, Muizenberg Marine Estates, Sorec.	African Eagle Life	CANADA: Hudson Bay Mining & Smelting RHODESIA: Hippo Valley Estates, Rhodesia Nickel Corp.	ZAMBIA: Zambia Copper Inv., Zamanglo Ind. Corp. USA: Engelhard Minerals & Chemicals EUROPE: Cleveland Potash, H.D. Development

Fig. 22. The structure of the Anglo American Corporation group (1978)

practice as long as the other shares are widely dispersed Anglo's control is complete, especially if, as is very often the case, Anglo has the management contract.

THE CONTROL CORE OF THE ANGLO GROUP

At the centre of the Anglo group is a 'control core' consisting of the three international mining houses, Anglo American Corporation, De Beers Consolidated and Charter Consolidated. Harry Oppenheimer is chairman of both Anglo American and De Beers. The London-based Charter Consolidated controls many of the Anglo group's investments outside South Africa. The three companies in the control core are connected by a complicated pattern of interlocking shareholdings, directorships and management. Figure 23 shows the complexity of the relationships within the core. If we look at the relationship of Anglo and De Beers we can see that we are dealing with an endless circle of ownership, participation and shared facilities. Oppenheimer is chairman of both companies. Anglo holds 52 per cent of Anamint, which holds 26 per cent of De Beers, which holds 33 per cent of Anglo. But even that is not the whole story, because Anglo has 36 per cent of Charter, which has 10 per cent of Anamint.

The strength of this interlocking pattern of ownership is that while assuring control with a minimum of capital tied up it renders Anglo virtually immune from the threat of a takeover bid. The direct and indirect stake of the three core companies in each other is over 30 per cent. This is sufficient to control each company in the core and protect it from unwelcome bids. Because of the interlocking shareholdings it would be impossible to buy any one of the control core companies against Anglo's wishes except by buying the whole group. This would require an enormous amount of money. In March 1978, De Beers had a market capitalization of around R1,953 million, Anglo of R1,130 million, and Charter of R224·1 million.*

* These market values vary with market conditions. For example, in 1973 Anglo's market capitalization was R934·9 million, Rand Selection R630·6 million, Charter R934·9 million, Anamint R461 million; and De Beers market value hit R3,600 million in 1969.

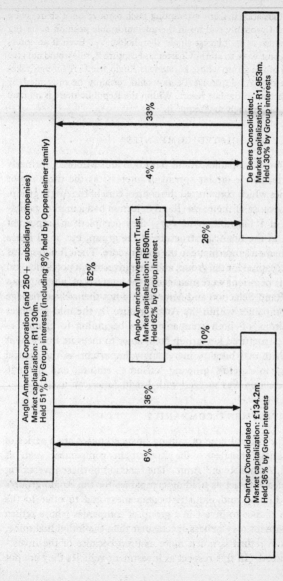

Fig. 23. The control core of the Anglo American group
SOURCE: Anglo-American *Annual Report 1978*. (Market capitalization as at 31 March 1978.)

Anglo American Corporation (and 250+ subsidiary companies)
Market capitalization: R1,130m.
Held 51% by Group interests (including 8% held by Oppenheimer family)

De Beers Consolidated.
Market capitalization: R1,953m.
Held 30% by Group interests

Anglo American Investment Trust.
Market capitalization: R590m.
Held 62% by Group interest

Charter Consolidated.
Market capitalization: £134.2m.
Held 36% by Group interests

33%

4%

26%

52%

10%

36%

6%

Any international giant attempting such a move on a share swop basis would probably end up in the uncomfortable position of having Oppenheimer as its biggest single shareholder ... Even if an international giant were to storm Charter and capture it, this would not give it control of the group whose keystone is Anglo itself. A foreign takeover of either Anglo or De Beers would certainly be prevented by political action in the last resort. Within the Republic there is no rival remotely big enough to attempt it.[7]

CLOSELY ASSOCIATED COMPANIES

Two finance companies, Rand Selection and Minorco, formerly Zamanglo, had a similar spread of interests as the three major companies which constituted the control core of the Anglo group. If only because of their size (Rand Selection had a market capitalization of R389 million in 1975) they occupied an important position in the financial structure of the group, but at all times they remained subordinate to the control core. Their function was to attract capital for the group, and their investment portfolios and financial operations were managed in the interests of the group as a whole. Rand Selection and Minorco did not themselves manage other companies within the Anglo group. By the mid-seventies the position of both companies was beginning to change as Anglo restructured key group companies to meet its investment needs. Minorco became increasingly important as the central company in Anglo's growing 'offshore' empire, and in 1976 Rand Selection was merged with Anglo American itself.

THE INVESTMENT COMPANIES

Below the control core of mining finance houses are a series of participation vehicles – the investment companies, such as Amgold, Amaprop and Amic. The function of these investment companies is to act as holding companies for the Anglo group's various mining and industrial companies; and to offer to the public a chance to invest in a group of companies whose return on investment may be less spectacular than the individual mine, but whose return is much more assured because of the investment spread. (In this respect as investment vehicles they are not unlike unit trusts, although, of course, they are commercial companies and not managed trusts.) The major investment companies and their most important activities are shown in Figure 22. It is these investment companies which in turn control the many mining, industrial and financial companies.

THE OPERATING COMPANY

To show how the system of control works in practice, let us look at Anglo's control of one of its gold mines. One of the main gold-producing areas in South Africa is the Orange Free State. In 1976 there were ten operating gold mines there. In none of its seven Orange Free State gold mines did Anglo have an interest of more than 25 per cent, but its control of them was totally assured.

One of the richest mines was Free State Geduld. In 1977 the total profits of the company amounted to R92·3 million, making it the fourth most profitable gold mine in the country. (The most profitable gold mine in South Africa that year was GFSA's West Driefontein, in which Anglo also has an interest.)

The control structure for Free State Geduld is shown in Figure 24. Anglo exerts its control over Free State Geduld in three ways: first through Amgold (Anglo's gold-mining investment company) the group had a 21 per cent stake in the mine; secondly Anglo administered the mine on behalf of Amgold; and thirdly Harry Oppenheimer was one of several Anglo directors of the mine. In addition other Anglo group companies had a small direct stake in the mine. Anglo's control of Free State Geduld is secure for an additional reason. The public shareholders in the mine (40 per cent of whom are American) will support Anglo's continued control in the face of any challenge, because they have confidence in the quality of Anglo's mine management. They are unlikely to be persuaded that another group can manage the mine more profitably. In return, Anglo demonstrates its confidence in the future of the mine by buying shares in Free State Geduld when the market price is falling. This maintains the share price and the value of the shareholders' investment.

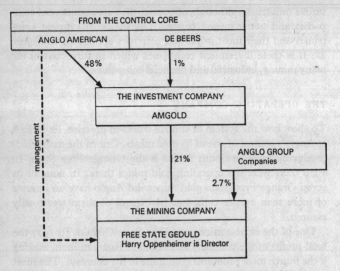

Fig. 24. The ownership and control of an Anglo gold mine
SOURCE: Anglo American *Annual Report 1977*, and 'Inside the
Anglo Power House', *Financial Mail*, 4 July 1969.

The same pattern of control is evident in Anglo's investments
outside South Africa. For example, the investment company
which groups all Anglo's Canadian interests (over $152 million)
is AMCAN (Anglo American Corporation of Canada). In 1977
AMCAN was 83 per cent owned by the control core companies.
Anglo itself and De Beers each held 29 per cent of AMCAN,
and Charter Consolidated 25 per cent. AMCAN had a 38·1
per cent interest in Hudson Bay Mining and Smelting Company
operating mines in Canada.

In Africa the pattern is more varied, presumably because it is
not always politically wise to use the South-African-based companies. So in Mauritania, Charter Consolidated, which is based
in London, had a direct 33 per cent stake in the Société Minière
de Maurétanie (SOMIMA), which is mining copper at
Akjoujt.* In Zaire, Charter has a 14 per cent share in the

* Until Charter sold its stake to the Mauritanian government in 1976.

Société Minière Tenke-Fungurume (SMTF). In Southern Rhodesia and Botswana the 'classic' Anglo pattern is used. The Rhodesian Nickel Corporation, which owns four nickel mines in Rhodesia, is 85 per cent owned by the Anglo group, largely through the Rhodesian holding company AMRHO, which is in turn owned by Minorco (47 per cent), Charter Consolidated (34 per cent), Anglo American (17 per cent), and De Beers (2 per cent). In Botswana the Anglo group's interest in the Selebi-Pikwe mine is held through Anglo American Botswana (AMBOT) which is 100 per cent owned by Anglo group members.

THE HOEK REPORT

The size and influence of the Anglo group have made it the subject of political debate within the Nationalist Party.* When Hendrik Verwoerd was still Prime Minister, a special study was initiated within the National Party to assess the Anglo American Corporation and its power in South Africa. The report, undertaken by P. W. Hoek at the University of Pretoria, was completed after Verwoerd's assassination and was sent to his successor, John Vorster. Instead of publishing the report, Vorster suppressed it. But the Hoek Report reached right-wing dissidents, and in August 1969 Ras Beyers, a former General Secretary of the Mineworkers Union, planned to disclose its contents. When asked about the report, Hoek denied both its existence and his authorship but nevertheless sought an injunction to prevent the document from being published.

The report, which we have seen, suggested that Anglo's power was of sufficient magnitude to obstruct the aims of the government. It reported that Anglo American was the single largest force in the South African economy and that it exercised control over 918 companies through direct ownership, the command of other shares, management services, interlocking directorships, and by-product control (i.e. controlling a key step in the manufacturing, marketing or distribution of a commodity). The report also showed that under the existing tax laws, Anglo paid a dis-

* See Chapters 6 and 7 above for earlier instances of this.

proportionately small amount of tax in relation to its profits, and alleged that in some Anglo-operated firms the gross rate of tax was only 6 per cent, compared with the average rate of 40 per cent for other South African companies. Hoek pointed out that this represented a loss of annual revenue to the government of millions of rands. In his general recommendations, he suggested that government measures be used to curtail Anglo's oligarchical powers by limiting its operational boundaries in South Africa and by placing special restrictions on Anglo's foreign-based companies like Charter Consolidated and Zamanglo. Hoek also suggested that a more equitable tax base be applied so that Anglo companies came to share a larger part of the tax burden. Hoek argued that government control over companies crucial to South Africa's national security was essential and pointed out that the Anglo group was a key supplier of strategic materials needed for South Africa's military defence.

During the controversy over the Hoek Report, Vorster's position was being challenged by right-wing Nationalists. The Herstigte Nasionale Partei (HNP), a right-wing breakaway from the National Party, led by Albert Hertzog, argued that Vorster should have used the report

to warn the nation about the economic grip that Oppenheimer has on South Africa. If he were to do so, the real threat to South Africa's independence and the Afrikaaners' economic freedom would have become an important factor in South African politics.

The HNP paper *Die Afrikaner* said: 'The question arises amongst informed people whether or not Vorster is prepared to do political battle against this economic might.'[8] Vorster's handling of the case indicated that he was not prepared to challenge Oppenheimer. He allowed the political storm to blow over.

Another incident which illustrates the government's reluctance to challenge the Anglo group occurred during the 1970 General Election campaign, when the former Minister of Planning and Mines, Dr Carel de Wet, publicly challenged Oppenheimer over Anglo's attitude to the government's border industries programme, in the Bantustans. Oppenheimer was in

Australia at the time; when he returned he bluntly denied de Wet's charges:

I have said innumerable times that a country cannot develop its full economic potential if it does not make the best use of its labour force. But this is quite a different thing from trying to sabotage your government's policy by the way you run your company.

He said that his companies would continue to

carry out any agreements governing the employment of labour they had entered into and have respect for the conventions which governed these matters in South Africa.[9]

A prominent Johannesburg businessman was quoted by the Johannesburg *Sunday Times* as saying, 'If de Wet takes on Oppenheimer you know who is going to win, don't you . . .' The paper commented that 'Any threat singling out Mr Oppenheimer's companies can only be regarded as a threat to the total industrial development of South Africa.'[10] Vorster reprimanded de Wet, and in the next Cabinet reshuffle removed one of his portfolios.

ANGLO AND WHITE MINORITY RULE

A distinguishing feature of the Anglo group is the fact that, to a degree unusual among mining company chairmen, Harry Oppenheimer is a frequent and articulate exponent of his companies' operating philosophy.

There is, I believe, a special need at the present time for a large mining and industrial group such as ours, operating in many different countries and concentrating attention not on the political differences which divide them but on their common need to raise the standard of living of the people. Some years ago my father defined the aim of the Anglo American Corporation as being to make profits for our shareholders, but to do it in such a way as to make a real contribution to the welfare of the countries where we operate.[11]

And indeed one of the problems for a group like Anglo, which has extensive interests in white-minority-ruled South Africa and also in independent black Africa, is to satisfy political groups on both sides of the black–white divide. Clearly a group so dependent on cheap black migrant labour, and operating extensively in Namibia and Rhodesia, is vulnerable to political attack in independent Africa.* Anglo's size and local connections obviously protect it to a certain extent from such attacks, but it cannot adopt the strategy of a company like Lonrho which draws a discreet veil over its South African and Rhodesian interests.[12] However, if Anglo could be seen to be a highly visible and vocal critic of the worst aspects of apartheid and the low wages paid to black workers in South Africa, then any criticism would be more easily defused, and make the company more acceptable in black Africa and indeed throughout the world.

OPPENHEIMER AND POLITICS

Oppenheimer's public statements over the last twenty years show a preoccupation with the need for stability within South Africa and with the need to prevent the isolation of South Africa from foreign capital, both of which are clearly vitally important to an international mining group like Anglo. In 1957 while still a member of the United Party he attacked the Nationalist Government for 'declaring that we do not need capital from abroad, I do want to say that we need it very badly'.[13] As the African nationalists' public campaign for basic political rights reached its height in South Africa, Oppenheimer outlined his position. He believed that

there were very good grounds for discrimination in South Africa. There were different backgrounds and the legitimate right of the white worker to have his standard of living protected.[14]

Indeed,

because of the different standards of education and civilization white leadership will continue as far as one looks ahead. As the native people become capable of more responsibility, however, they should be given

---

* In view also of the group's position and activities in the South African gold-mining industry, individually and through the Chamber of Mines, in Rhodesia, in Zambia, in Botswana and in the world diamond trade. See Chapters 6–9 and 17.

an effective share in the government under which they live, particularly in local government, but also in central government without running the risk of destroying white leadership. If a situation develops in which the natives can take the final decision in a matter, it will only bring complete chaos.[15]

Above all, said Oppenheimer,

what we should not do is to put uneducated people, still in a semi-barbarous state, in charge of a developing country like South Africa . . . We do not need to go in for some kind of head-counting democracy – which in the long run will turn over the government of the country to blacks who will be just as nationalistically inclined as we whites . . . We must build up a self-respecting Native middle class as the greatest guarantee against lawlessness and Communist agitation.[16]

For Oppenheimer, the

civilized standards which were brought to Africa by Europeans can by no means be reduced to the doctrine of manhood suffrage and in South Africa manhood suffrage or anything approaching it, instead of being a guarantee of individual liberty, would lead directly to inefficiency, corruption and tyranny.[17]

The African National Congress continued to press its campaign, and by 1959 Oppenheimer was clearly concerned at the continuing agitation. He felt that

the political demands of the small number of politically conscious Africans are pitched high – indeed unreasonably high. Justice and expedience, however, both require the political advance of the Africans.[18]

There was no sign, however, that either the Nationalist government or the opposition United Party was prepared to introduce even minimal reforms. Fearing that the stability of South Africa was in jeopardy, and remembering that as he himself had said earlier, 'reform is the true conservatism',[19] Oppenheimer and his colleagues broke away from the United Party to launch the Progressive Party. He felt that

South Africans are unduly worried about a supposed threat to White leadership and standards in the Union. Personally, I am sure the civilized population is big and strong and wise enough to cope with any such threat.[20]

The aim of the Progressive Party was to cope with that threat.

THE PROGRESSIVE PARTY

The Progressive Party was a descendant of that strand of nineteenth-century liberalism which advocated the abandonment of the more 'primitive' aspects of colonialism in order to preserve a stable economic base for capitalism and to avoid the more dangerous possibilities of revolution. This attitude traditionally found support among Cape liberals, among politicians like the late Finance Minister J. H. Hofmeyer, and among liberal capitalist groups. It was vigorously opposed by the extreme right-wing Afrikaner nationalists, whose platform was anti-Semitic, anti-capitalist, and attacked British imperialism. The Progressive Party urged that some traditional white supremacist policies be abandoned in favour of more pragmatic policies, provided they were compatible with modern capitalism.

The Progressive Party is often portrayed as a firm and courageous opponent of apartheid. Yet, if the Progressives appeared to represent the most liberal end of the spectrum of white politics, it was only because more radical parties have been outlawed or forced to disband. A closer look would indicate that the policies of all the white political parties in South Africa share the common aim of maintaining the economic privilege of the white population against the threat of revolution. In this sense, the Progressive policy differs little from that of *verligte* Nationalists.*

There remains, to be sure, a crucial difference of strategy. The Progressives and their allies are prepared to extend the franchise to blacks if this can be done in a controlled manner which can ensure economic stability. Nationalists still feel that this is too high a price. For most traditional Afrikaners, white political rule, with a monopoly of the franchise, must be maintained, even

* *Verligte* is the Afrikaans word meaning 'enlightened', used to describe the less conservative wing of the Nationalist Party and their policies. Similarly, *verkrampte* describes the old guard and more fundamentalist section of the Nationalist Party.

at the cost of restricting economic advancement. For the Progressives and their supporters, the vote is not the dominant issue; they urge the creation of a black bourgeoisie with economic interests similar to their own. To ensure this the possession of property or sufficient standards of income, with perhaps the alternative of certain educational levels, would be a prerequisite for the franchise. In this way they seek to limit the potential political effect of giving the vote to South African blacks. The other reforms advocated by the Progressives are very limited and are the minimum consistent with maintaining their economic interests.

The founders of the Progressive Party and most of its supporters can afford to be liberal. They are well off, and not threatened by the prospect of upward mobility for black South Africans; a gradual extension of material and even political benefits to a black bourgeoisie cannot threaten their position. In any case, the qualified franchise which the party officially proposes would provide only token representation for blacks. According to one study, a franchise based on education and property qualifications would allow fewer blacks to vote than participated in the 1886 Cape Colony elections.[21] Such a restricted franchise would not reduce the economic disparities between blacks and whites, nor would it change basic living conditions for Africans.

Support for the Progressive Party among the white electorate has slowly grown, and in 1976 it merged with a breakaway section of the United Party to form the Progressive Reform Party. The general position of the new enlarged party differs little from that of the old Progressive Party, but its aim of supplanting the United Party as the main opposition party in the South African Parliament is likely to lead the party to move to the right in search of greater electoral support among white South Africans.

LABOUR POLICIES

In addition to Oppenheimer's support of the Progressive Party, the Anglo group has been in the forefront of those within South Africa who have urged a change in the country's rigid industrial colour bar, believing it has become a barrier to further economic growth. In 1964, Oppenheimer said:

> If South Africa is to advance economically, a change must be made in the way in which labour is used. It has to be used in such a way as to justify additional capital investment.[22]

Throughout the sixties, Oppenheimer pursued this theme, and in 1970, when the growth rate of the South African economy slumped sharply, he blamed this on the country's acute labour shortage.[23]

> I have said innumerable times and I say again – a country cannot develop its economic potential if it does not make the best use of its labour force.[24]

The truth is, there is no shortage of labour in South Africa. There is a shortage of skilled *white* labour, and Oppenheimer and other industrialists realize that if the black labour force on the mines and in industry could be more fully utilized then the South African economy would grow much faster. They are not, however, proposing the complete abolition of apartheid and the industrial colour bar, but something rather less.

> One thing should be clear through a close scrutiny of the statements of even the most liberal industrialists. Their desires are precise. They do not ask for an abolition of apartheid, nor even the abrogation of the industrial colour bar, but merely for the relaxation of some restrictions which would enable them to fit non-whites into jobs where whites are no longer available. The under-class would be allowed to move a small number of 'representatives' up the pyramid, but the essential pyramidal power relationship (whites on top, blacks on the bottom) ... would not have altered one inch.[25]

Indeed, Oppenheimer has said something similar:

> I am not arguing about the system of division of labour between races (whether it is good or bad). We are in the position that we can maintain this system and can allow the whole structure to float upwards, so that everybody benefits.[26]

Later, in a Progressive Party publication, Oppenheimer returned to this theme:

We don't live in the thirties where the White worker is out in the streets, where white and non-white are competing to do pick and shovel work for pitiful wages. We live in times when jobs which are done by skilled white workers can be taken over and done effectively by non-white workers, freeing the white worker to do better work for himself, better work for the country – work which really can carry forward the country economically as it should be carried forward.[27]

ANGLO AND THE NATIONALISTS

An analysis of Oppenheimer's public pronouncements and the policy of the Progressive Party reveals clearly that the argument between the Nationalist government and Oppenheimer is an argument between different elements of the white power establishment in South Africa. The dispute is not a debate about *who* should wield economic and political power, the present alliance of government and white capitalists or the dispossessed black majority who are exploited by that alliance. The argument is about *which* economic and political priorities shall take precedence, economic growth or separate development. Oppenheimer and Anglo do not challenge the basic structure of the political system which is responsive only to a privileged white minority, nor does Oppenheimer oppose the class system in which the economic power of the whites is firmly rooted. His 'liberal' policies are not designed to lead to an essential change in the political and economic relationship between blacks and whites in South Africa. What he is, in effect, proposing is not the abolition of black powerlessness in South Africa, but rather the cultivation of slightly better-fed black workers who could ensure the growth of the Anglo group and its profits in the future.

COMMON INTERESTS

Whatever arguments Oppenheimer and the Nationalists may have, they are but minor irritants which do not alter the underlying communality of interests between Anglo and the white minority in South Africa. Oppenheimer himself said in 1958,

I think that South Africans themselves often fail to grasp the extent to which they are united about the things that matter most, or how artificial in many ways are the barriers between the parties.[28]

For Oppenheimer, as for mining companies down the years, the most important requirement is a 'stable' environment, but the potential for racial conflict in South Africa could still upset that stability. So although in the rather different political climate of the 1970s one does not find Oppenheimer speaking about 'natives' and the need to avoid giving 'semi-barbarous people' the vote, his preoccupations remain unaltered. South Africa must avoid any severance of its links with the capital markets of the Western world, for in his experience, 'isolation is a continual trouble and can cause severe difficulties in financing companies and selling goods'.[29]

In addition, the patterns of labour use in South Africa must be changed to allow further expansion.

In the years ahead such acute shortages of skilled manpower are anticipated that it seems evident that the main impediment to the continued growth of the South African economy will be our human and financial resources, not lack of viable projects.[30]

Meanwhile, the Anglo group continues to invest heavily in South Africa, building the economy and buttressing the power of the white minority. It supports the Nationalists' policy of separate development by investing in the Bantustans, and helps the Afrikaner business community to expand. In addition, the Anglo group uses its influence and finance to support the government's outward policy in southern Africa. Oppenheimer is a powerful member of the South Africa Foundation, and his group is an important conduit for foreign capital into the country. In turn, the government protects Oppenheimer and his empire from serious attack, by the surviving disciples of an Afrikaner national socialism on the right and by the forces of revolution on the left. The Vorster regime may not be all that Oppenheimer would like it to be; it may not be moving as far or as fast towards reform as Oppenheimer or the Progressive Reform Party might want; but meanwhile it is guarding the stability of the country and as long as it does that Oppenheimer is unlikely to make any serious attempt to displace it. Indeed, it may be said that the interests of the Vorster regime, and of Anglo, coincide so closely that Anglo can scarcely advance its own interests without advancing those of the white minority at the same time.

20 Namibia – The Last Colony

In the early 1970s Namibia was the largest refined lead, the second largest cadmium, the third largest zinc and the fourth largest diamond producer in Africa.* It also was an important producer of copper. But, as elsewhere in the continent, the practice of crediting these exports to the nation hides a disturbing reality. For what is happening is that the last colony in Africa is being ruthlessly exploited by South Africa, which controls the territory, and by the mining companies, which are digging out the country's wealth as rapidly as modern techniques can devise, without any consideration for the future development of the territory.

Denied any effective control over the disposal and exploitation of the country's natural resources, Namibians have seen the country's mining industry grow to massive proportions. Encouraged by low taxation and generous concession areas, mining companies – based in South Africa, Britain, America, Germany and Canada† – have made the mining industry the largest employer of labour and the largest single contributor to Namibia's exports, gross domestic product and government revenue. Little of the wealth generated by the mines remains within the country. The companies enjoy a high rate of return on the capital invested, and with the low level of taxation they are free to repatriate capital and profits. The result is that from 1946 to 1962 some 31·7 per cent of the gross domestic product accrued to foreign capital.[1] And it is estimated that over one third of the new wealth currently generated is being expatriated.[2]

* Measured by value.
† For a full list of the companies and their mines, see Appendix 2.

THE MANDATE

The German colony of South West Africa was occupied by South African forces during the First World War. At the Versailles Peace Conference in 1919, South Africa was granted a mandate over the territory. The mandate did not grant South Africa full sovereign power over the territory, but only, in accordance with the principles of the mandate, the power of administration in trust for the inhabitants.[3] Moreover it was a principle of the League of Nations that, since they were trustees, the countries granted a mandate should derive no benefit from such trusteeship.[4]

Nevertheless, from the time the mandate was granted, South Africa has not only gained considerable economic benefit from Namibia, but has consistently sought to incorporate the territory within South Africa.[5] In 1919 the Union government extended the application of South African laws to Namibia. The aim was to institutionalize and reinforce the segregation of the black from the white population, and to establish the migrant labour system to provide cheap labour for the mines and farms. The Land Settlement Act and succeeding legislation divided the territory in two, so that the 16 per cent of the population which was white occupied 60 per cent of the land, which contained the best farm land, the major diamond- and mineral-rich areas, and all the ports.

Namibians swiftly lost their freedom of movement and contract as the mining companies took control of the territory's mineral resources. In 1919 the country's main mineral exports were diamonds, copper and tin. Ernest Oppenheimer bought up eleven diamond mining concessions for £3·5 million and established the Consolidated Diamond Mines alongside the British- and German-owned South West Africa Co. as one of the two most important mining companies in Namibia. Together they set up the Northern Labour Organization in 1926 to procure migrant labour largely from Ovamboland in the north to work in the mines to the south. The land available to Africans was of poor quality and kept in short supply, so as to force African subsistence farmers into the money and wage-earning economy.

Movement in and out of the impoverished reserves was controlled by the pass laws. Thus, as in neighbouring South Africa and Rhodesia, the subsistence economy became the hub of the cheap labour system. Again as in neighbouring territories, such as Zambia, it became a criminal offence for any person other than a duly registered mineowner to prospect and dig for minerals.

In the twenties, the mining industry grew, but it suffered a temporary setback during the world economic depression of the thirties, before expanding once again during the Second World War. To meet the need for more efficient regulation of migrant labour for the mines, and to accommodate the growing demand from farms and government service, in 1943 the NLO was expanded and renamed the South West Africa Native Labour Association (SWANLA).

The South African government persisted with its plans to incorporate the mandated territory into the Union. In 1964 the Odendaal Commission recommended the creation of ten 'homelands' for each of the official ethnic groups in the territory, as well as both a coloured and a white area. The full implementation of the report's recommendations will require that two thirds of the black population outside Ovamboland will have to be resettled.* It also recommended closer integration of the territory with the Republic. The South African government accepted many of the recommendations and proceeded to transfer powers from the territorial administration to the capital of the Republic in Pretoria.

ILLEGAL RULE

The General Assembly of the United Nations reacted to the implementation of the Odendaal plan by revoking South Africa's mandate and placing Namibia under its direct administration. Then in May 1966, the General Assembly established the United Nations Council for South West Africa to administer the territory as the successor to South Africa until independence. Subse-

* Total population of Namibia (1971) was 746,328: whites 90,658; blacks 655,670 (including Ovambo 342,455, of whom approximately 290,000 were in the 'homeland').

quently the International Court of Justice spelled out the kind of dealings with the South African government which, under the UN Charter, and under general international law, were inconsistent with the Security Council's declaration of illegality and invalidity, because they might imply recognition of a legal South African presence in Namibia. These actions included 'entering into treaties with the South African government purporting to act on behalf of the people and territory of Namibia ... (and) entering into economic or other relations or dealing with South Africa on behalf of or concerning Namibia, which may entrench its authority over the territory'.

The UN was unable immediately to enforce its policy in Namibia, and the South African government continued its legislative programme to systematically destroy the unity and territorial integrity of Namibia, by delineating and establishing the first of the homelands recommended by the Odendaal Commission. The Republic also consolidated its hold over the territory. The 1969 South West African Affairs Act adjusted many administrative, legislative and financial matters relating to the territory and transferred direct control of several spheres to Pretoria, including the control of mining and matters relating to minerals, to companies and to fishing, thus confirming and reinforcing its continuing control of Namibia's great material wealth and natural resources.

The tax revenue generated in Namibia goes not to the territory, but to the South African government in Pretoria, which collects the taxes levied on the mines, companies, prospecting claims and undistributed profits, as well as the diamond export duty. This is then paid into the South African Consolidated Revenue Fund.[6]

THE SCRAMBLE FOR MINERALS

Overseas mining companies have continued their profiteering in Namibia, undeterred by the World Court ruling that South Africa's administration of Namibia is illegal and that therefore all prospecting and mining rights issued by the administration are invalid. Despite UN requests that foreign governments and companies avoid involvement in Namibia, foreign investment, especially in mining, has multiplied considerably in the last ten years. The incentive of high rates of return on capital investment, and the freedom to repatriate a substantial portion of the profits, have so far proved far stronger than the right of the Namibian people to independence.

Foreign investment has increased rapidly since 1966. Four new copper mines were opened between 1966 and 1971, and in the early seventies some forty companies were prospecting for a wide variety of minerals. The value of mineral exports increased from R53·1 million in 1961 to more than R130 million in 1969. In 1977 they were estimated to be about R250 million.[7] One study stated that, despite the absence of accurate figures, it was clear that in the early seventies the capital assets of the three major companies, Consolidated Diamond Mines, the Tsumeb Corporation, and the South West Africa Co., exceeded the GDP of Namibia.[8] Consolidated Diamond Mines is a subsidiary of De Beers, and together with the American-controlled Tsumeb Corporation in the early seventies accounted for about 90 per cent of the territory's mineral output and 60 per cent of Namibia's total exports. Both companies have been highly profitable. In the five-year period to 1967, the annual profits of CDM and Tsumeb averaged £7·5 million and £6 million respectively after tax.[9] This is equivalent to an average rate of return of 500 per cent and 350 per cent respectively on their original investments. And their profits continue to rise. In 1972 these two companies generated gross profits of $92 million, over half of which went to foreign shareholders.[10]

Consolidated Diamond Mines

CDM mines the large diamond fields in the south of the territory. Huge earthmoving machines scrape and transport the overburden on the foreshore to be sorted by migrant black labour for the rich gemstones which make this concession so important to De Beers. The high value of the diamonds and the low wages paid to the black miners have produced pre-tax profits for CDM of R500 million over the period 1963-73.[11] The pre-tax profits of CDM increased from R100·7 million in 1972 to R153·4 million in 1973[12] and to R250 million in 1977. The value of the large production is enhanced by the high proportion of large gemstones recovered by CDM, and these gemstones are crucial to the maintenance of the De Beers diamond monopoly because they ensure the company's dominance of the world gem diamond market.*

Tsumeb Corporation

Tsumeb was a small and inactive mining company owning a unique orebody in the north of the territory when it was bought in 1945 by a consortium of American and British companies led by American Metal Climax, and Newmont Mining, for a mere £1 million. Subsequently the consistent profitability of the Tsumeb mine, which produces copper, zinc, lead, cadmium and silver, has lifted Newmont to the front rank of American mining companies and enabled it to expand dramatically in North America.[13] Tsumeb is the largest single employer in Namibia. Most of its employees are migrant labourers from Ovamboland. The company now operates four mines: the original Tsumeb mine; Kombat, which produces lead and zinc, the Matchless copper mine, some 300 miles to the south of Tsumeb; and its latest mine at Asis Ost. The company operates its own copper smelter and lead refinery. Profits more than doubled from R5 million in 1972 to R13·2 million in 1973. The company then planned to open a large new refinery to process all the territory's blister copper to be operated jointly with O'Okiep Copper company, which is also managed by Newmont. Because of foreign pressure not to invest in Namibia, this refinery was to be built in Cape Province in South Africa;[14] however the drastic fall in the world price of copper in 1974 led to the postponement of the scheme.

The South West Africa Co. (SWACO)

SWACO is the oldest of the major mining companies still operating in the territory. It secured its Damaraland concession

* See Chapter 18.

from the German authorities in 1892. It still owns the mining and prospecting rights to large areas of Namibia. It operates two mines at Berg Aukas and Brandbert West. The main output is zinc, but the mines also produce useful quantities of lead, vanadium, tin and wolfram. In addition to its own mines the company has a 2·4 per cent interest in Tsumeb. It is managed by the Gold Fields of South Africa Group, of which it is now a wholly owned subsidiary.

Rössing Uranium

Encouraged by the low level of taxation and the generous concession areas offered by the South African government, many companies have been investing in Namibia. The most important of these new ventures has been Rio Tinto Zinc's enormous open-cast uranium mine at Rössing,* which began production in 1976. Rössing is the largest uranium mine in the world, processing 100,000 tons of ore to produce 5,000 tons of uranium oxide per year. The mine has a key place in South Africa's nuclear strategy† and is a major exporter of uranium to the industrialized world. Originally Japan was to have been a major customer, but it withdrew in 1976 because of the political implications of importing uranium from Namibia. The uranium produced will go in the first place to the British Nuclear Fuels Corporation, which has signed a long-term contract to purchase 7,500 tons of uranium oxide worth £25 million between 1976 and 1982.

Other Companies

New mines have also been developed by General Mining group (copper: Klein Aub); Nord Mining (tin and wolfram: Kranzberg); Falconbridge (copper: Oamites); Navarro Exploration

---

*The mine is managed by Rio Tinto Zinc and owned 45·5 per cent by RTZ; the South African Industrial Development Corporation, 13·2 per cent; 11 Minatome SA, 10 per cent; General Mining, 6·8 per cent.

†See Barbara Rogers and Zdenek Cervenka, *The Nuclear Axis*, Times, 1978.

Co. (copper: Onganje); and JCI (copper: Otjihase). Other mining companies prospecting in South West Africa in the early seventies included a large number of North American companies. Etosha Petroleum, owned by Briland Mines of Canada, is reported to have discovered a large zinc deposit at Grootfontein. Bethlehem Steel, another US firm, which prospected extensively for iron ore, has joined Tsumeb in exploring at Grootfontein for fluorspar, an important mineral in steel smelting. Other North American companies prospecting include Consolidated Mining and Smelting of Canada, Phelps Dodge, and Hanna Mining, while an important new South African venture is the development of a mine producing lead and zinc concentrates at Rosh Pinah by Iscor, the South African Iron and Steel Corporation. This mine, together with the SWACO mine at Berg Aukas, will enable South Africa to fulfil all its domestic requirements for zinc, a metal which at present it imports.[15] In addition, US firms were prospecting widely for oil along the Namibian coast.

DISAPPEARING RESOURCES

The Odendaal Report urged the rapid economic development of known and determinable resources.[16] The beneficiaries of this rapid exploitation of known mineral deposits would be South Africa and the mining companies. Namibia's mineral resources, while large, are not infinite, and various estimates put the life of both the gem diamond deposits and the Tsumeb deposits at no more than twenty years.[17] One UN estimate even suggests that the Oranjemund gem diamond deposits will be almost exhausted by the 1980s.[18] Although the report of the Commission of Inquiry into the Diamond Industry in 1973 was less pessimistic, it still forecast a fall in total diamond production to 22 per cent of present levels by 1990, because of depleted reserves. At Tsumeb, in 1971, the General Manager gave the mine an estimated life of only some 12–15 years. By the time depletion occurs, foreign companies will have taken out a billion dollars' worth of minerals from Namibia. This rapid rate of mining and the impending exhaustion of established mineral resources will cripple the prospects of development for the economy of an independent Namibia in the future unless the Namibian people can succeed in winning their independence and the right to control their own economy.

MINERAL PRODUCTION AND TAXATION

It is the policy of the South African government not to release information on current production rates, concessions, and prospecting within Namibia. Detailed figures for 1966 – the last date for which official figures are available – showed that minerals produced were worth a total of R127·1 million. Diamonds accounted for R84·7 million (66 per cent); blister copper R19·2 million (15 per cent); refined lead R12·3 million (10 per cent); zinc, vanadium, lithium ores R10·9 million (8 per cent).[19] Since 1966, Namibia's annual production statistics have only been published by the South African Department of Mines consolidated with figures for mines in the Republic, but output by main producing mines can be estimated from company reports and journals. The underlying trend indicates a relative decrease in the importance of diamonds and a corresponding increase in base minerals due to the new copper and uranium mines being developed. Tsumeb remains the major producer of base metals: in 1970–71 it produced R26 million worth of mineral products, or 20 per cent of total production.[20] In 1973 diamond production reached nearly 1,600,000 carats, worth an estimated R127 million.[21]

MINERAL EXPORTS

Namibia's principal export markets are South Africa (50 per cent), Britain, North America and the EEC. Again, although there are no recent official data on mineral exports, the 1966 official figures indicate that the largest buyer of gem diamonds was Britain, while the four largest buyers of base minerals were the US (R15·7 million), Belgium (R9·4 million), West Germany (R3·9 million) (copper and vanadium), and South Africa (R3·3 million) (zinc and lead). The principal base mineral was blister copper, which accounted for 76 per cent of US mineral purchases.[22] Sixty-three per cent of South Africa's purchases in Namibia were in refined lead. In return, eighty per cent of Namibia's general imports were from South Africa. West Germany is a key source of imports, providing electrical machinery and transport equipment, largely for mining company use.[23]

THE CONTRACT LABOUR SYSTEM

The burgeoning mining industry of Namibia is built on the system of cheap migrant black labour established in the 1920s. It remained virtually unchanged for over fifty years. The International Commission of Jurists described the contract labour system as 'unique in its organized and efficient application of conditions that are akin to slavery'.[24] And a more recent study concluded that

> In practice, the provisions of the laws on mining rights coupled with the discriminatory labour policies operated by the mining companies under the aegis first of the NLO, then of SWANLA, effectively deny the indigenous inhabitants ownership or participation on a level other than that of indentured labourer, in the development of the natural resources of the country in which he lives.[25]

The contract labour system prevents African workers from acquiring real skills, and keeps wages at subsistence level. In 1971 wages received by Africans in the mining industry ranged between R17 and R45 a month. The minimum income required to maintain a family for a month was estimated at R78[26] (white miners earned R300 a month or more). As in the Republic, Africans are barred from forming their own unions and from striking for higher wages.

Discontent with the labour system boiled over in December 1971. A government official claimed that the workers at Walvis Bay, the centre of the fishing industry, freely accepted the contract system because they allowed themselves to be recruited voluntarily. The men, through an elected committee, rejected the contract system and demanded an end to it. Drawing attention to the officials' remark that they 'freely' accepted the contract, they 'freely' handed in their contracts, and demanded to be repatriated. As news spread of the strike at Walvis Bay, 5,500 contract workers in the capital, Windhoek, went on strike. Within a week some 12,000 workers at a dozen centres, including the Consolidated Diamond Mines in the south, were on strike, and a month later the number had risen to 13,500. Almost all the strikers were repatriated. The mines and much of industry was brought to a complete standstill.

The main demand of the strikers was an end to the contract system. Ovambo workers claimed they were handcuffed by the contracts, which were on terms established unilaterally by the employers through SWANLA. Workers entered the system because they had no other way of earning money, and despite the pitiful level of wages. They objected to being recruited by SWANLA, instead of being allowed to find their own employment; they also objected to the pass laws and to the compulsory repatriation to Ovamboland at the end of their contracts. Workers described the system as slavery, since they were 'bought' by SWANLA and then housed in jail-like compounds.*[27]

The South African government responded to mining management complaints by sending in police and army reinforcements from the Republic. Workers' compounds were sealed off and Africans were imprisoned or shuttled back to the reserves. Finally, negotiations between strikers' delegates, employers and government officials were held at Grootfontein on 19 and 20 January 1972. The settlement provided for token wage rises and some changes in the recruitment for contract labour; but these reforms were not fundamental. The main change was the abolition of the compulsory minimum wage scale and of the labour recruitment organization, SWANLA, which formerly had graded African labour and negotiated mining contracts for

* The authors visited Namibia and Katatura, the large compound outside the capital, Windhoek, in early 1971, some months before the strike. The worst conditions were in the compounds which housed the male workers. They were surrounded by high walls and barbed wire, and accessible by the large entrance gates only. However, one visit was curtailed by the arrival of the police, who confiscated the film in our cameras and escorted us from Katatura.

black workers. Under the new system, the mines contract directly with the workers. But the operation of vagrancy and pass laws still prevents unemployed workers from having the necessary mobility to choose their own jobs. The essentials of apartheid and the contract labour system remained, for the restrictions on the workers' freedom of movement and of association rendered most of the changes in the contract ineffective.[28] African workers returning to the compounds found that although wages were increased by fractional amounts, employers in all sectors of the economy were collaborating to enforce uniform wage rates and thus to prevent the emergence of a fluctuating labour market based on a competitive wage scale.

To maintain the system the authorities launched a vigorous campaign to enforce the vagrancy and pass laws, declared a state of emergency and attempted to intimidate the Ovambo population by a sweeping series of arrests and public floggings. But all the indications were that the contract system was no longer working smoothly.[29] There were further disturbances including a riot at Katatura in March 1973 when workers damaged the compound and were reported to have destroyed records kept on contract workers.[30]

RESPONSES TO ILLEGALITY

More than ten years after the UN General Assembly resolution, the control of South Africa over the territory of Namibia remains as strong as ever, and the mining companies continue to exploit the country's natural resources at a furious rate. In violation of the terms of the mandate South Africa has incorporated the territory ever more closely into the political, legal and administrative framework of the Republic; despite Namibian resistance South Africa has also pursued its plans to undermine the territorial integrity of Namibia by creating a string of homelands on the pattern of the South African Bantustans; and the Republic has benefited directly from its presence in Namibia. Uranium from the new Rössing mine is crucial to South Africa's strategy to become a fully fledged member of the nuclear club, while the revenue from the diamond and base-metal mines provides valuable foreign exchange. Namibia's incorporation into the South African economy has meant that the South African government has been able to finance much of its own expenditure (on the Kunene hydroelectric scheme and the homelands policy, for example) from Namibia's resources.

The most important Namibian sources of revenue for the South African government are CDM and Tsumeb, of which CDM's contribution is the largest. In the financial year 1973–4, taxes on the mining industry provided R53·2 million of a total estimated revenue of R93·5 million. Taxes on diamond mines contributed R24·633 million; taxes on base minerals were R12·143 million. Diamond export duties added R7·165 million, and diamond profits' tax an additional R9·161 million. The total tax on diamonds levied by the local administration in 1973–4 was R40·959 million.[31] In 1973, the De Beers Group *Annual Report* showed that the taxation provision made by CDM of SWA was R59·93 million.

Foreign governments have so far done little to support the UN resolution and have in fact defied it. The British government signed a long-term contract for uranium supplies with RTZ and the South African government from the Rössing mine in direct contravention of the World Court ruling. Moreover, although the British government abrogated its double-taxation agreement with the white administration, thus apparently complying with the 1966 UN resolution, in 1967 the same government specifically extended the double-taxation agreement between Britain and South Africa to include Namibia![32] As for the United States, in 1970 the government issued a statement officially discouraging American investment in Namibia, calling South African rule there an 'illegal occupation' and stating that Export Import Bank loans would not be made available for trade with Namibia. However, since the US Internal Revenue Service has continued to grant tax credits to Newmont and Amax for taxes paid to the South African government, it is not surprising that US corporations have not reduced their activities in Namibia. In 1971 in response to a request for clarification of American policy, the State Department said, 'In the last analysis the decision whether or not to invest in South West Africa remains with the individual ... Under United States law, it is not illegal *per se* to invest or do business in the territory.' J. P. Ratledge, General Manager for Tsumeb, America's largest mining operation in Namibia, was quoted in 1970 as saying that official US discouragement of investments did not affect the situation 'one bit'.[33]

The flurry of diplomatic activity which followed the independence of Angola and Mozambique produced many statements, much speculation, but little significant change for the people of Namibia, while South Africa and the mining companies continued to profit handsomely from their investments in Africa's last colony. In July 1978 it was announced that an agreement had been reached for elections and independence under UN supervision. Namibians could only hope that their independence would enable them to halt the plundering of the mineral wealth before the country's main deposits are exhausted.

... with the authority ... Superintendent Chief ... likely an open lever ... of corruption in the resource ... of Rebelato, General Manager for Portugal ... Angola ... putting pressure on Mandume ... question ... that these companies' officials ... discount ... or investigators did but after the ... summons was ...

The history of apartheid, partisan which followed the bitter ... ideologies of Angola and Mozambique, produced many ... gains, many speculations, but little identity was change for the people of Namibia. South Africa ran not the mining companies continued to profit ... share holders for this foreign running. Namibia ... last colony. In July 1978 it was announced that an agreement had been reached for elections and independence, under a UN supervision. Namibians could only hope that their independence would enable them to halt the plundering of the natural world, before the country's riches deposits are gone, ...

Part Four

Africa Undermined

Part Four

Africa Undetermined

21 Mining Companies and the Underdevelopment of Africa

Orthodox economic theory urges the developing nations to concentrate on the export of primary goods. It is argued that by participating in international trade and selling their agricultural products and minerals in an expanding world market the poor nations can generate sufficient capital to build up their own economic structures and invest in a growing range of industries, producing manufactured goods for the home and international market. African countries with rich mineral deposits should encourage foreign capital to develop mines and export minerals to the industrialized world. There is assumed, therefore, to be a sufficient identity of interest between African nations and the mining companies to establish a 'partnership for development'.[1] In this view, the mining company brings its financial, technical and marketing expertise to Africa, provided that it is given an adequate return on its investment. Africa gains, it is argued, because mineral resources are turned into income-producing assets, because foreign exchange earnings and local employment opportunities increase, and because the multiplier effect of the mining companies' expenditure on local labour and stores expands the domestic economy.[2]

But the situation on the African continent today is in general very different from that predicted by orthodox theory. Africa is confined to the export of primary goods, and Africa's mineral resources are being depleted without generating economic development. Government revenue, employment, and foreign exchange earnings in many African countries are totally dependent on minerals mined, refined and exported by the companies. Planning for economic development is difficult, if not impossible, because of fluctuating prices and because control of the mineral exports is firmly in the hands of the mining companies, who exploit the mineral resources at a rate and in a manner consistent with their interests and not with those of the host nation. Most of the surplus generated by the mineral exports accrues not to the host countries but to the companies who control the mining, shipping, marketing and fabricating of the minerals.

DIRECT BENEFITS: CLAIMS AND REALITY

The major direct benefits of a mine are said to be the expansion of local markets for both labour and goods and the additional foreign exchange income. Local labour will be used in both the construction and operating phases of a mine's development. The incomes of these workers will, it is argued, create a larger market for local manufacturers, and the market will expand further if the company buys supplies locally. The minerals produced will largely be sold abroad, and the foreign exchange receipts can be used to import capital and consumer goods not produced locally.

The experience of African mineral-producing countries has been very different. The promised direct benefits of mining to employment are reduced by the trend to massive open-cast mines, with their smaller unit production costs and increased capital intensity.[3] The investment of two or three hundred million dollars will establish a mine employing only a few hundred workers. Furthermore, because of the technical problems involved, most of the managerial, engineering and technical posts are filled by expatriates. Local labour is generally used only for the construction stage; and then only for unskilled and semi-skilled work. The number of wage-earners on a modern mine will be small both proportionately and absolutely. The copper mines of Zambia and the gold mines of South Africa are obvious exceptions to this; but they employ large numbers of men because these mines were initially based on cheap unskilled labour. Indeed, the pattern is changing even there, and production has constantly expanded for the last twenty-five years without any corresponding increase in the labour force.

The mines have few linkages with the local economy. Typically the mining operations are specially established, in self-contained communities whose whole activity is oriented to the export market. Examples of these mining enclaves are the MIFERMA iron-ore mine and the Akjoujt copper mines in Mauritania; most of the Liberian iron-ore mines; and the British Aluminium Company's bauxite mine at Awaso in Ghana. This isolationism is, of course, most marked in diamond-mining operations, and mines like the Orapa mine in Botswana, Consolidated Diamond Mines in Namibia, and Diamang in Angola are completely sealed off for security reasons. Modern mines and their communities often have better communications with the advanced industrialized nations that they serve than with the capitals of the countries in which they are situated. Mine stores and consumer goods tend to be imported from abroad, along the same route as the ore is exported. This tendency is reinforced by the demands of the expatriate managerial and supervisory staff. It was to meet such demands that LAMCO built a Swedish town at the Mt Nimba mine in Liberia.

An agricultural or industrial enterprise often uses local road and river transport, or creates new facilities which can be used by local farmers and traders; but a mine often exports its production along specially built high-volume railway lines running directly to the port. The FOSBUCRAA phosphate mine in Western Sahara transports the ore from mine to port along a 62-mile conveyor belt, and the COMILOG manganese mine in Gabon uses an overhead bucket system to carry the ore 48 miles to the railhead, 303 miles from the sea.

For several reasons, few of the mine's supplies come from the host country. In the present state of African industry, it is not possible for the mining companies to purchase their complex and expensive mine machinery and capital equipment in Africa. Only South Africa can meet a large proportion of its mine equipment needs from local manufacturers. South African companies also export some mine equipment to the neighbouring countries of Zambia and Botswana. Because the mines employ only a small labour force, the demand for local products is also likely to be relatively small. The only local supplies consumed by the mine are likely to be energy and water. The Botswana Selebi-Pikwe mine uses local coal and the Akjoujt mine local water supplies; but sometimes even supplies such as these are imported, because it is more convenient for the company. At one time all of the coal for Zambia's copper mines came from the Anglo American controlled Wankie coal mine in Southern Rhodesia. Only after UDI was the Zambian government able to force the companies to develop local coal deposits at Maamba.

SUBSIDIARY BENEFITS: CLAIMS AND REALITY

It is argued that as the workers gain experience of working in an advanced industrial unit (i.e. the mine) a pool of skilled labour will be created to facilitate the introduction of other modern industries. It is also argued that the demonstration effect of advanced technology and advanced managerial techniques will promote faster economic progress in the country as a whole. To the extent that the workers on the mine save their incomes, new investment funds will be created within the country. Finally, local manufacturing and fabricating industries will have access to cheaper supplies of minerals; to the extent, of course, that they can use the product of the mine.

While it is true that many industrial skills are badly needed in Africa, it seems unlikely that the mining companies will provide them. The local labourers that the mine employs are almost exclusively unskilled or semi-skilled. The more skilled workers often come from outside the country and return there at the end of their contracts (e.g. Zambia and Liberia). This is very important, because, while even a small group of skilled workers might have a beneficial effect on the rest of the economy, a large group of unskilled labourers cannot. In fact, the influence of the unskilled miners may be very damaging to the economy, because they are likely, as in Zambia, to copy the consumption patterns of the highly-paid expatriate staff. This 'imitation effect' is partly responsible for the high-import, high-wage and high-cost structure of the Zambian economy. Zambia has acquired the consumption pattern of an advanced industrial society without the skills or structure to support it.

Nor are the incomes generated by the labour force likely to provide a source of new investment funds, for two reasons. A high proportion of the managerial staff will be foreign, and their salaries and savings will be remitted overseas. Moreover, local miners are more likely to spend their wages in an attempt to raise the low living standards of themselves, their families and their relatives in the cities and rural areas, before saving a high proportion of their income. In any case, savings in a capitalist economy more often come from company profits than from the incomes of manual workers. But as the mines are invariably established with foreign capital, the bulk of the profits are also paid overseas, except of course for the taxes levied by the government. Skilful use of transfer accounting can further reduce the amount of tax paid by the companies. Even if more savings and profits were channelled through the commercial banking sector, there is not, in most African states, an indigenous entrepreneurial class waiting to utilize the capital. If funds are available locally, the mining company with its superior credit rating will take advantage of them to finance mine renewal or expansion. Then, as in Zambia, the companies will use bank funds, while exporting their own incomes to their metropolitan base.

The low level of economic development in Africa means that very few countries are able to establish industrial plants which can use the metal produced by the mines. This is not surprising since the mines were established and their scale determined by the needs of the industrialized nations of Europe and America.* Even in South Africa, where industry is well developed, a very high proportion of minerals produced are exported. Only the production of iron ore and coal is geared to local consumption; and even here, companies are beginning to export both iron and coal in increasing quantities to Japan. In the rest of Africa the only notable example of industrial development on the country's mineral base is in Zambia, where the ZAMEFA copper-wire factory has been established. However, its annual requirement of 20,000 tons of copper is tiny beside the Copperbelt's production of 700,000 tons a year. Even if African governments set up manufacturing plants based on local mineral production, the small domestic markets mean that the bulk of production would

* Nowhere in Africa, except in Rhodesia and the diamond-producing countries of West Africa, is there even the proliferation of small mines alongside the large-scale export sector, such as exists, for example, in Chile.

have to be sold abroad. And in the world market, unprotected by high tariff barriers, these industrial products would be exposed to the fierce competition of the large producers in the developed world. So unless the mine's level of production is designed to meet the needs of the domestic economy, which is rarely the case in Africa, the importance of the mine in the provisions of local low-cost supplies to local manufacturers is likely to be small.

THE FISCAL BENEFITS

It is argued that even if the mine remains an enclave, cut off from the rest of the economy, the country still benefits financially from the mine. In return for a licence to develop the mineral deposit, the company will undoubtedly have to pay taxes. The government can use this income to develop the country's educational, technical and industrial infrastructure. Alternatively the income can be channelled through the central and commercial banks to provide risk capital and encourage new enterprises and local entrepreneurs.

The revenue accruing to the government from taxes will depend on the value of the mineral, the profitability of the mine, and the division of profits between the mining company and the government. In the colonial era, the funds diverted to Africa were negligible in relation to the developmental needs of the continent. Since independence, nationalist governments have sought to increase their share of mine profits. But although they have made some progress, they have not succeeded in diverting enough of the surplus created by the mining industry to generate economic development. Liberia, for example, is as far from industrialization as ever; and despite more than twenty years of iron-ore production, the country still imports all its steel.

The government's income from mining in Africa is often very small, and despite the heavy capital expenditure it is not enough to lay the basis for further economic development. The income is used to meet the government's rising recurrent administrative costs, and may well be offset by a consequent reduction in aid, as in Botswana. There is a small gain in economic independence, but little or no help for balanced economic development. Even where the government has taken a large stake in a mining company, this does not necessarily mean that the government's income will increase. The compensation agreements involve the payment of large sums of capital, which have to be paid out of the country's foreign exchange earnings for many years. However, in the long run African governments should receive a higher income from mines in which they have a majority equity stake, and in theory this can be used to foster the development of other sectors of the economy.

Whether the funds diverted from the mining operation will be used to promote economic development will naturally depend on the economic and social perspective of each particular government. Is such productive reinvestment likely to occur? In part it will depend on the size of the mine being established, or in the case of an existing mine the speed with which the expansion takes place. Where the receipts from the mine are large, both absolutely and in proportion to the government's existing income, or where the income increases in a sudden spurt, there is a strong likelihood that this income will be allocated to developmental expenditure.

If, on the other hand, the mine produces only a small income, or the payments increase gradually, the funds are much more likely to be absorbed into the general revenue and not be treated in a special way. In other words, it is only if the funds increase sharply or are large enough to be noticeable that the mining revenue will be credited to a development fund; otherwise, they will tend to finance everyday government functions. Since many mines produce only a gradually increasing income, especially while capital debts are being repaid, the most likely effect of a new mine in Africa today is that the revenue will be absorbed into the general account and be used to finance a concomitant expansion of government services and bureaucracy.*

The low level of industrial and economic development in Africa means that a large mine tends to dominate the host

---

* This tendency is reinforced by the class interests of the rulers; see below, page 499. Of course services do need to be expanded, but the key to development is productive investment, and job creation in the government service – however necessary – does not generate more employment.

economy to an extent unknown in the developed world. The more important the new project is within the monetary sector of the economy, the greater will be the attention it receives, because it is from the monetary sector that the state derives its revenues and with which its activities are mainly concerned. The tendency will be, as in Zambia and Zaire, to maintain at all costs the operation and profitability of the mines. Furthermore, the establishment of a mineral export industry focuses the country's attention and energies to an unwarranted degree on the export sector of the economy, with a consequent neglect and even abandonment of the internal economy. Zambia is a particularly clear illustration of this, as is Liberia.

The benefits of mineral production for export are less than sometimes imagined. It seems that in Africa today, leaving aside the ideological and economic priorities of individual governments, the mere establishment of a mining industry brings with it no guarantee of increased economic development. But it is not merely that the benefits are less than expected: they are completely outweighed by the cost of obtaining them through the agency of international mining companies in a world capitalist economy.

INTERNATIONAL COMPANIES IN THE WORLD ECONOMY

In a capitalist system, such as embraces Europe, North America, Japan, Africa and most of the Third World, there is constant pressure from the market to speed up the reproduction of the available capital. Savings in the time taken to turn over capital are reflected in lower costs and increased profits. Time is the key to this process. The companies and the market will save time through economies of scale, specialization, the improvement of communications and the tightening of overall control. The ideal industrial structure will be as vertically integrated and concentrated as is possible. We can see this more clearly by looking at the production process. Any production process involves a number of stages, from the extraction of the raw material through to the finished product. In order to lower costs and increase profits, time must be saved. Coordinating the activities of labour and materials at each stage of the process will save time. If the product is made by a number of independent firms, then the function of coordination and control is fulfilled by the market. But there is a time cost involved in the flows of information, in the quotations, the bargaining and the delivery agreements required by market exchange. If, however, the whole process is under the control of one firm, many of these processes can be eliminated, and others significantly speeded up. Effective coordination and control rely on swift two-way information flows. If these exchanges of information take place within the single firm, then the cost is reduced and the reliability of the information transmitted is improved. The process of concentration and integration encouraged by the market has, in its latest stage, produced the multinational corporation and the new production techniques of the second industrial revolution.[4]

The advantages of concentration in the already existing industrialized areas are reinforced by the tendency for the scale of modern industrial plant to increase dramatically with technical advances.[5] These two tendencies have the effect of keeping the world in its existing division of labour, with the underdeveloped countries as the suppliers of raw materials and the industrialized nations as producers of manufactured goods. The world division of labour created in the nineteenth century continues to reproduce itself, through the advantages of investing in the existing areas of concentration. International corporations will accentuate this process in their search for internal economies. Again the very integration of the international company will weaken the growth pole effects of a mine in the underdeveloped periphery. An international mining company is in a much better position to transfer the surplus generated in the periphery to the metropolitan centre, because this transfer is within the company and therefore much less open to government scrutiny than a similar transfer by an indigenous company could be. In addition, the massive technical, financial and managerial power of the international mining company restricts the ability of the periphery to compete. Rival local companies are no match for their international competitors at any level.

The international mining companies are all, with the exception of the South African mining houses, owned and controlled from the metropolitan centres of the industrialized world. The structure of these companies, increasingly organized on product lines, groups together production units from all parts of the world. Decisions are usually made by a small executive committee at the head office, in the light of the company's worldwide operations. It is the global profitability of the company that is the criterion of investment decisions and not the developmental needs of a small African economy. Insofar as the company feels vulnerable to political pressures, it will take account of national aspirations; but whatever concessions are made, the company's first aim will be to generate a high return on its investment, and use the surplus generated by the mine, not for the growth of the country, but for the further expansion of the company's activities. This in turn will ensure that the company transfers a large part of the surplus created out of Africa and reinvests it in other parts of the world. Ever since African countries became independent, the mining companies in Africa have consistently exported their profits, in order to create new mines in Canada, Australia, and other parts of the industrialized world. When capital is made available to African countries, it is on terms that involve restricting the whole fiscal and employment policies of the states, and indeed the whole growth path of their economies.[6]

International companies, to increase internal efficiency and economy, standardize production techniques around the globe, so that their investment in the periphery tends to be highly capital intensive. Modern techniques of large-scale production require specialized machines which have to be imported from the industrialized nations. The reliance on imported capital goods reduces the investment in the capital goods sector of the African economy, postponing the development of an indigenous capital goods industry and the growth of the local labour market. The imported capital goods were designed for the developed nations, where labour is both scarcer and more skilled. Capital-intensive methods of production when used in the periphery ensure that the expansion of employment opportunities for unskilled labour will be slow. This in turn restrains the growth of demand for peasant agricultural produce. The tendency to increase capital intensity, which is a feature of both multinational manufacturing and mining companies, is producing a relative impoverishment of the population in the rural areas:

The spiral process of rising wages and mechanization tends to produce a situation of rising productivity and living standards in a limited and shrinking modern sector, while the wage employment opportunities in that sector for the unskilled, semi-proletarianized peasantry . . . are reduced.[7]

As in the colonial period, the rural areas are left to decay, while the expansion of the mining sector does not promote additional industrial activity. Even the techniques and machinery required for the transformation of traditional patterns of agriculture are dependent on external forces. A local capital goods industry could develop machines and techniques embodying a modern labour-intensive technology, suitable for a continent with large reserves of unskilled labour. Increased participation of the peasant labour force in the monetary economy would increase the size of the internal market and make self-sustained economic development possible. But as long as the investment decisions are made and controlled by the international metropolitan-based corporations, the developmental needs of a continent with large supplies of unskilled labour will remain unsatisfied.

Foreign mining companies created Africa's dependent economic structure and incorporated the continent into the world economy. And today Africa's subordinate position in a world economy dominated by the advanced industrial nations is maintained by the giant international companies. The obstacles blocking the way are too great, and the forces too powerful, for a poverty-stricken African state, however richly endowed with resources, to develop its potential as part of the world capitalist system.

SOUTH AFRICAN EXPERIENCE

But if the benefits of mineral production for export are so few, and if international companies create underdevelopment, how, then, has South Africa been able to develop a modern industrial economy within the world capitalist economy, on the basis of a mining industry with a large amount of foreign investment? Does not the South African experience suggest that capitalist economic development in Africa is possible? The answer is no. To the extent that it has managed the structural shift into heavy industry and manufacturing, South Africa is a very special case. Its limited success is due partly to the timing of its development; partly to the nature of gold as a commodity; partly to the interplay of a vicious racism and a vigorous Afrikaner nationalism; but above all to the massive exploitation of a non-unionized, unskilled, disenfranchised black labour force.

In South Africa significant participation by locally-based capitalists, and the smaller size of foreign mining companies at the end of the nineteenth and the beginning of the twentieth century, left open the possibility of effective nationalist intervention. The development of the diamond industry did not require large sums of capital. The surplus generated in the diamond industry was then invested in the gold mines of the Transvaal. Although some concentration was taking place, most of the mining industry was in the hands of relatively small companies based in either London or South Africa. A political alliance between white mineworkers, other white workers, and a vigorously nationalist, culturally unified, white rural bourgeoisie won control of the state machine. It then encouraged the existing trend for the mining companies to become locally owned and controlled, while using the state apparatus to finance the heavy industry sector of the economy, and to protect the nascent manufacturing industry from foreign competition. This ruling nationalist bourgeoisie, unlike its classic European counterpart, was not rooted in the entrepreneurial manufacturing sector of the economy. Its political base was in the rural areas; and so the state gave massive loans, educational facilities, subsidies and grants to transform the agricultural sector. The white government, companies, and labour force built their growing economy on the basis of a massive exploitation of cheap black unskilled labour in the mines, in industry, and on the farms. And the mining companies were willing participants in this economic and political exploitation, for it was the cornerstone of their wealth and influence. Throughout the forties, fifties and sixties, the continuing strength of the world gold market, the influence of foreign investment, and the exploitation of the cheap unskilled black labour force enabled the South African economy to sustain a formidably high level of domestic capital formation behind high protective tariff barriers. The result was an impressive record of economic growth directed by the state, and South Africa is now a relatively independent centre of production within the world capitalist economy. Indeed, while remaining subordinate in many ways to the advanced nations, it is beginning to expand its sphere of influence in Africa.

THE UNDERDEVELOPMENT OF AFRICA

The movement of African minerals in world trade for the last hundred years through the agency of the companies has had a profound effect on Africa. The mining companies have determined the pattern of mineral exploitation in Africa, transformed trading patterns and incorporated African mineral resources into the world capitalist system. Assisted and supported by the colonial authorities, they created dependent economic, political, and social structures in Africa. Formerly self-sufficient subsistence economies became increasingly dependent on mineral exports to the industrialized world. The mines and their associated services sucked the young and able-bodied men from the rural areas and deposited them in the companies' camps and towns. Traditional society, already weakened by the effects of the slave trade, and then frozen at a time of political and social change by the colonial conquest, could not survive this haemorrhage of young men. In their absence the remaining villagers, the older men, the women and the children, could not maintain the agricultural productivity of the rural areas, let alone promote the transformation in scale and methods of production needed to meet the needs of the growing rural population and the mushrooming urban communities. Neither the mining companies nor the colonial authorities were prepared to inject the capital and manpower needed to transform agricultural production in the rural areas. Both required a pre-capitalist agricultural sector to provide the continuing supply of cheap unskilled labour which the mines, white farmers, plantations and colonial administration needed. While the rural areas were left to decay, the mining companies created an overdeveloped mining industry out of all proportion to Africa's needs, so as to satisfy the companies' need for profit and to supply the industrialized nations with minerals.

Since Independence many governments have taken majority stakes in the local mining operations. But state participation in the African mining industry has not yet significantly curbed the outflow of minerals and capital from Africa. Though we may reasonably expect African governments to make greater efforts to control mining companies, the fundamental question remains whether state participation can or will bring economic development to Africa.

The companies remain in a powerful position because of their superior management skills, superior access to information, superior financial and technical resources; all of which are underpinned by the political, economic and sometimes military support of the industrialized nations in which the companies have their base. In return for their technical expertise and financial investment, the companies demand a large share of the surplus generated by the mines. Because the companies are owned and based overseas, the surplus must be removed from the domestic income stream and remitted to foreign shareholders. The claims of the international mining companies on the investable surplus make it impossible for locally originated industrial development to occur, or agricultural productivity to increase, at a rate sufficient to generate self-sustaining economic development.

Even if African governments succeeded in winning a larger share of the investable surplus generated by the mining companies, can they achieve economic development without interrupting the free flow of minerals to the developed states? The investable surplus that the country's rulers do capture is first being used to reinforce and extend the power and patronage of the government machine, to provide the tools and pay the salaries for an expanded civil service and army. The proportion of investable surplus that is available for economic development in Africa is very small. Moreover, the industrialized countries have in general given strong protection to their infant industries and state support for their development. They have in effect suspended free trade in order to build up their economies. But in Africa, governments are unable to suspend free trade and to halt the outflow of economic surplus and minerals without losing the technical, financial, and managerial skill of the mining companies and risking the loss of revenue which accrues to the state from the mines. This, the ruling elites of Africa have not so far been prepared to risk. To understand why, one must consider the nature of the post-colonial state and the class interests of these elites.

THE POST-COLONIAL STATE

In Africa, the political and administrative structure which was established in the colonial period was based on the needs of the metropolis. It did not emerge as a result of internal political and economic evolution, but was imposed from the outside to ensure continuing metropolitan control, and to subordinate pre-capitalist social formations to the imperatives of colonial capitalism.[8] In the post-colonial states of Africa, the state dominates society. At independence the new rulers in Africa lacked an economic base in society, and used the patronage and power of government to consolidate their own position. Partly because of this and partly because of the nature of an underdeveloped economy,

the state in Africa is the main source of capital and its accumulation. The state plays a major role in economic activity and development. The state is the principal employer of labour, the chief dispenser of jobs, benefits, patronage, contracts, foreign exchange and licence to trade ...[9]

Underpinning the power of the state in many African countries is the revenue that accrues to the Treasury from the mining companies. The new rulers could not afford to lose this revenue for any significant length of time without destroying the base of their power.

The importance of the state in post-colonial Africa means that those who staff and run the state apparatus form the basis of the emergent ruling class in Africa. This new ruling class is based on the petty bourgeois salariat of clerks, store-keepers, teachers, which emerged in the colonial era. This is not a fully formed class. Its relative social autonomy and susceptibility to multiple determinations and influences leave open the question of which direction development should take. But its freedom of manoeuvre is limited by the economic and social distortions of the colonial era. One path to development is that explored with varying degrees of consistency by Nkrumah, Sekou Touré, and Nyerere, and which is based on an assertion of economic and political independence from the metropolitan powers. The other path is one of accommodation with external capital and is represented by most leaderships in the continent. But both strategies are based on control of the ex-colonial state apparatus; it is only in Guinea-Bissau, Mozambique and Angola that new political structures have been evolved in conflict with the colonial state.

In South Africa, where the political and economic base of the ruling party lay in the rural areas and among the urban white communities, the government developed the agricultural, manufacturing and heavy industrial sectors of the economy as well as expanding the state bureaucracy. In the rest of Africa the political bases of the governing elites lie in the urban, clerical and administrative employees of the state and the large international companies. These elites, accustomed to, and buttressed by, their intermediate role between international capital and national resources, have not been under such political pressure to increase the productivity of the agricultural sector, nor have they chosen to solve the unemployment problem by building up manufacturing industry. Rather they have expanded the government bureaucracy and armed forces at the expense of productive investment in other sectors of the economy.

In the seventies, when many of the ruling political and military elites in Africa took 51 per cent participation in the mines, it was not primarily to further a broad economic strategy, aimed at reducing Africa's dependence on mineral exports, suspending free trade, and encouraging industrial development. On the contrary, the first demand to be made after state intervention was usually for an increase in mineral production: involving an increase in the country's dependence on mineral exports and of its integration with the world capitalist economy. State participation in the mining industry was designed to buttress the political power of the new rulers by bolstering the power of the new state bourgeoisie. Recognizing and encouraging a powerful wave of economic nationalism, the emergent ruling class in Zambia, Zaire, Liberia and other parts of Africa inserted itself as the intermediary between the foreign mining companies and Africa's abundant mineral resources. But the process was not a smooth or an easy one; for the companies were still immensely powerful, and the price of their continued technical, financial and managerial presence was the maintenance of free trade in minerals. In this their interests coincided with those of the state bourgeoisie, and a new alliance was formed. As the partners in this alliance are wedded by political and economic self-interest to the maintenance of free trade, the economic outlook for Africa is generally one of continuing dependence and underdevelopment, with its chances of meaningful development undermined by the activities of the international mining companies.

More minerals have been mined in the last fifty years than in the whole period since people first appeared on the earth, but the world is clearly entering an era when its finite resources will have to be carefully rationed. The danger for Africa and the other underdeveloped countries is that the industrialized nations will use their undoubted political, economic and military power to ensure that their share of world mineral consumption does not diminish. Should this happen, Africa will be condemned to a permanent state of poverty and underdevelopment.

Appendix 1 Major Mines of Africa

Major mines in Africa producing more than 150,000 tons of ore per year,* in 1977 – summary.

	Open Pit						Underground					
	TOTAL	150,000 to 300,000 ton/year	300,000 to 500,000 ton/year	500,000 to 1 million ton/year	1 to 3 million ton/year	More than 3 million ton/year	TOTAL	150,000 to 300,000 ton/year	300,000 to 500,000 ton/year	500,000 to 1 million ton/year	1 to 3 million ton/year	More than 3 million ton/year
†Algeria	6	3	1	1		1	3	1		2		
Angola	1					1						
Botswana	2				1	1	1				1	
Congo							1	1				
Egypt	1			1			4	3		1		
Gabon	2			1	1							
Ghana	2	1	1				3	1	1	1		
Guinea	3				2	1						
Lesotho	1			1								
Liberia	5				1	4						
Malagasy	1	1										
Mauritania	4				2	2						
†Morocco	1			1		2	6	2			2	2
Niger	1				1							
†Rhodesia	10	3	3	1	3		15	2	5	5	3	
Senegal	2		1		1							
Sierra Leone	1			1								
†South Africa	16	2	2	1	7	4	63	3	11	9	26	14
South West Africa	3			2		1	7	2	3	1	1	
Sudan	1	1					1	1				
Swaziland	1			1			1				1	
Tanzania	2		1		1							
Togo	1			1								
Tunisia	1		1				8		1	4	3	
Uganda	1	1					1	1				
Western Sahara	1				1							
Zaire	6		1		2	3	5		1	1	2	1
Zambia	2		1	1			9		1	2	2	4
TOTAL	77	12	10	10	24	21	128	17	23	26	41	21
World Total	462	56	56	61	137	152	590	141	131	121	141	56

There are estimated to be more than 6,000 mines producing less than 150,000 tons/year worldwide. Countries marked with a dagger are

*Data abstracted from *Mining Magazine*, March 1978, 'Annual International Survey of Mining Activity'.

those where small mines represent an important sector in that country.
Alluvial mines are listed separately below.

MAJOR MINES IN AFRICA

Key: U = underground A = more than 3 million tonne/year
P = open pit B = 1 million to 3 million tonne/year
A = alluvial C = 500,000 to 1 million tonne/year
D = 300,000 to 500,000 tonne/year
E = 150,000 to 300,000 tonne/year

Mine	Location	Mining Method	Size of Operation	Product
Algeria				
El Abed	El Abed	U	C	Zn, Pb
Beni Saf	Tlemcen	P	E	Fe
Bou Khadra	Annaba	U	C	Fe
Khanguet	Tebessa	P	E	Fe
Ouenza	Annaba	P	A	Fe
Timezrit	Timezrit	P	E	Fe
Zaccar	Zaccar	U	E	Fe
Djebel Kouif	Djebel Kouif	P	D	Phosphate
Djebel Onk	Djebel Onk	P	C	Phosphate
Angola				
Cassinga	Cassinga	P	A	Fe
Botswana				
Pikwe	Pikwe	U/P	B	Cu, Ni
Orapa	Orapa	P	A	Diamonds
Letlhakane	Orapa	P	B	Diamonds
Congo				
Holle	Holle	U	B	Potash
Egypt				
Bahariya	Bahariya	U/P	B	Fe
Sebairya	Isna	U/P	E	Phosphate
Hamrawein	Hamrawein	U/P	B	Phosphate
Quseir	Quseir	U/P	E	Phosphate
Safaga	Safaga	U/P	E	Phosphate
Gabon				
Ogooué	Moanda	P	B	Mn
Comuf	Franceville	P	C	U

Mine	Location	Mining Method	Size of Operation	Product
Ghana				
Ashanti Mines	Obuasi	U	B	Au
State Gold Mining	Prestea	U	D	Au
State Gold Mining	Tarkwa	U	E	Au
Nsuta	Wassaw	P	E	Mn
Awaso	Awaso	P	D	Al
Guinea				
Boke	Boke	P	A	Al
Friguia	Kimbo	P	B	Al
Kindia	Kindia	P	B	Al
Lesotho				
Letseng la Terai	Letseng	P	B	Diamonds
Liberia				
Bomi Hills	Bomi Hills	P	B	Fe
Bong	Bong Range	P	A	Fe
Lamco JV	Tokadeh	P	A	Fe
Mano River	Mano	P	A	Fe
Nimba	Mt Nimba	P	A	Fe
Malagasy				
Comina	Andriamena	P	E	Cr
Mauritania				
Somima	Akjoujt	P	B	Cu
Rouessa	Kedia d'Idjil	P	A	Fe
F'Derik	Kedia d'Idjil	P	B	Fe
Tazadit	Kedia d'Idjil	P	A	Fe
Morocco				
Touissit	Beddiane	U	E	Pb, Zn
Zeida	Midelt	P	B	Pb
Mines de Fer du Rif	Nador	U/P	E	Fe
Imini	Trans Atlas	U	E	Mn
Khouribga	Khouribga	U/P	A	Phosphate
Youssoufia	Youssoufia	U/P	A	Phosphate
Kettara	Kettara	U/P	C	Pyrrhotine
Niger				
Mines de l'Air	Arlit	P	B	U

Mine	Location	Mining Method	Size of Operation	Product
Rhodesia				
Dalny	Chakari	U	E	Au
Pickstone	Eiffel Flats	U	E	Au
Inyati	Headlands	U	D	Cu
Mangula	Mangula	U	D	Cu
Alaska	Lomagundi	P	E	Cu
Shackleton	Lomagundi	U	C	Cu
Norah	Mangula	U	D	Cu
Perseverance	Chakari	U	D	Ni
Shangani	Inyati	P	C	Ni
Trojan	Bindura	U	C	Ni, Cu
Madziwa	Shamva	U	C	Ni, Cu
Empress	Gatooma	U	D	Ni, Cu
Buchwa Mining	Belingwe	P	E	Fe
Norie	Belingwe	P	E	Fe
Que Que Iron Ore	Que Que	P	D	Fe, Mn
Dorowa	Dorowa	P	B	Phosphate
Kamativi	Kamativi	U/P	C	Sn
Boss Asbestos	Mashaba	P	E	Asbestos
Kudu	Essexvale	P	B	Asbestos
Pangini	Filabusi	P	B	Asbestos
Rex	Belingwe	P	D	Asbestos
Vanguard	Belingwe	P	D	Asbestos
Gaths	Mashaba	U	B	Asbestos
King	Shabani	U	C	Asbestos
Shabani	Shabani	U	B	Asbestos
Rhodesia Chrome	Selukwe	U	D	Cr
Senegal				
Taiba	Taiba	P	A	Phosphate
Thies	Thies	P	D	Phosphate
Sierra Leone				
Sierra Leone Ore and Metals	Moyamba	P	C	Al
S Africa				
Blyvooruitzicht	Transvaal	U	B	Au, U
Bracken	Transvaal	U	C	Au
Buffelsfontein	Transvaal	U	A	Au, U
Crown	Transvaal	U	D	Au
Doornfontein	Transvaal	U	B	Au

Mine	Location	Mining Method	Size of Operation	Product
Durban Roodepoort Deep	Transvaal	U	B	Au
East Driefontein	Transvaal	U	B	Au
East Rand Pty.	Transvaal	U	B	Au
Eastern Transvaal Cons.	Transvaal	U	E	Au
Free State Geduld	O.F.S.	U	B	Au
Free State Saaiplaas	O.F.S.	U	B	Au
Grootvlei	Transvaal	U	B	Au
Harmony	O.F.S.	U	A	Au, U
Hartebeestfontein	Transvaal	U	A	Au, U
Kinross	Transvaal	U	B	Au
Kloof	Transvaal	U	B	Au
Leslie	Transvaal	U	B	Au
Libanon	Transvaal	U	B	Au
Loraine	O.F.S.	U	B	Au
Marievale	Transvaal	U	B	Au
President Brand	O.F.S.	U	A	Au, U
President Steyn	O.F.S.	U	A	Au, U
Randfontein	Transvaal	U	B	Au, U
St Helena	O.F.S.	U	B	Au
South Roodepoort	Transvaal	U	D	Au
Stilfontein	Transvaal	U	B	Au
Vaal Reefs	Transvaal	U	A	Au, U
Venterspost	Transvaal	U	B	Au
Welkom	O.F.S.	U	B	Au, U
West Driefontein	Transvaal	U	B	Au, U
West Rand Cons.	Transvaal	U	B	Au, U
Western Areas	Transvaal	U	A	Au
Western Deep Levels	Transvaal	U	A	Au, U
Western Holdings	O.F.S.	U	A	Au, U
Winkelhaak	Transvaal	U	B	Au
Witwatersrand Nigel	Transvaal	U	E	Au
Messina	Transvaal	U	C	Cu
Carolusberg	Cape Province	U/P	B	Cu
Nababeep	Cape Province	U	C	Cu
Palabora	Transvaal	P	A	Cu, Fe, U, Zr
Prieska	Cape Province	U	B	Zn, Cu
Beeshoek and Bruce	Cape Province	P	B	Fe
Cons. African	Cape Province	P	E	Fe
Griqualand Iron Ore	Cape Province	P	E	Fe
Lilyfeld	Cape Province	P	B	Fe
Manganore	Cape Province	P	D	Fe
Sishen	Cape Province	P	A	Fe

Mine	Location	Mining Method	Size of Operation	Product
Thabazimbi	Transvaal	P/U	B	Fe
Mapochs	Transvaal	P	B	Fe, V
Hotazel	Cape Province	P	C	Mn
Lohathla	Cape Province	P	D	Mn
Mamatwan	Cape Province	P	B	Mn
Mancorp Mines	Cape Province	P/U	B	Mn
Wessels	Cape Province	U	C	Mn
Foskor	Transvaal	P	A	Phosphate
Langebaan	Cape Province	P	B	Phosphate
Rooiberg	Transvaal	U	D	Sn
Groothoek	Transvaal	U	E	Cr
Henry Gould	Transvaal	U	D	Cr
Millsell	Transvaal	U	D	Cr
Winterveld	Transvaal	U	D	Cr
Zwartkop	Transvaal	U	D	Cr
Kuruman Asbestos	Cape Province	U	C	Asbestos
Pomfret	Cape Province	U	C	Asbestos
Koegas	Cape Province	U	D	Asbestos
Penge	Transvaal	U	C	Asbestos
Griqualand Asbestos	Cape Province	U	D	Asbestos
Danielskwi Asbestos	Cape Province	U	D	Asbestos
Msauli	Transvaal	P	D	Asbestos
De Beers Kimberley	Cape Province	U	A	Diamonds
Finsch	Cape Province	P	A	Diamonds
Koffiefontein	O.F.S.	U/P	B	Diamonds
Premier	Transvaal	U/P	A	Diamonds
Atok	Transvaal	U	B	Pt, Ni
Impala	Transvaal	U	A	Pt, Ni
Rustenburg	Transvaal	U	A	Pt, Ni
Union Platinum	Transvaal	U	A	Pt, Ni
Western Platinum	Transvaal	U	D	Pt, Ni
Cons. Murchison	Transvaal	U	C	Sb

SW Africa (Namibia)

Mine	Location	Mining Method	Size of Operation	Product
Klein Aub	Rehoboth Gebiet	U	E	Cu, Ag
Kombat	Tsumeb	U	D	Cu, Pb
Oamites	Windhoek	U	C	Cu, Ag
Otjihase	Windhoek	P	B	Cu, Pyrites
Tsumeb	Tsumeb	U	D	Cu, Pb, Zn, Ag
Berg Aukas	Grootfontein	U	E	Zn, Pb, V
Rosh Pinah	Rosh Pinah	U	D	Zn, Pb

Mine	Location	Mining Method	Size of Operation	Product
Brandberg West	Brandberg	P	C	Sn, W
Uis	Brandberg	P	C	Sn
Rössing	Swakopmund	P	A	U
Sudan				
Sudan Mining	Ingessana	U	E	Cr
Nile Mining	Ingessana	P	E	Cr
Swaziland				
Ngwenya	Bomvu Ridge	P	B	Fe
Havelock	Havelock	U	B	Asbestos
Tanzania				
Alamasi	Alamasi	P	C	Diamonds
Mwadui	Mwadui	P	A	Diamonds
Togo				
Mines du Benin	Hahotoe	P	B	Phosphate
Tunisia				
Tamera-Douaria-Djerrissa	Djerrissa	U/P	C	Fe
Kalaa Djerda	Kasserine	U	D	Phosphate
Kef es Schfair	Gafsa	P	C	Phosphate
M'Dilla	Gafsa	U/P	C	Phosphate
Metlaoui	Gafsa	U	C	Phosphate
Moulares	Gafsa	U	C	Phosphate
M'rata	Gafsa	U	B	Phosphate
Redeyf	Gafsa	U	B	Phosphate
Sehib	Gafsa	U	B	Phosphate
Uganda				
Kilembe	Kilembe	U	C	Cu, Co
Western Sahara				
Bu-Craa	Bu-Craa	P	A	Phosphate
Zaire				
Dikuluwe	Shaba	P	B	Cu, Co
Kakanda	Shaba	P	A	Cu, Co
Kambove	Shaba	U	C	Cu, Co
Kamoto	Shaba	U/P	A	Cu, Co
Kipushi	Shaba	U	B	Cu, Zn
Mupine	Shaba	P	B	Cu, Co

Mines	Location	Mining Method	Size of Operation	Product
Musonoi	Shaba	P	A	Cu, Co
Musoshi	Shaba	U	B	Cu, Co
Mutoshi	Shaba	P	A	Cu, Co
Tshinsenda	Shaba	U	D	Cu, Co
Kisenge	Kisenge	P	D	Mn
Zambia				
Baluba	Luanshya	U	B	Cu, Co
Bwana Mkubwa	Ndola	P	C	Cu
Chambishi	Kalulushi	U	C	Cu, Co
Chibuluma	Kalulushi	U	C	Cu, Co
Kanshaushi	Kansaushi	P	D	Cu
Kalengwa	Kalengwa	P	D	Cu
Konkola	Chililabombwe	U	B	Cu
Luanshya	Luanshya	U	A	Cu
Mufulira	Mufulira	U	A	Cu
Nchanga	Chingola	U/P	A	Cu
Rokana	Kitwe	U/P	A	Cu, Co
Broken Hill	Kabwe	U	D	Zn, Pb, Ag, pyrites

MAJOR ALLUVIAL MINES IN AFRICA (1977)*

A = alluvial/beachsand mines

Mine	Location	Size of Operation	Product
Angola			
Diamang	Dondo	A	Diamonds
Ghana			
Ghana Cons. Diamonds	Akwatia	A	Diamonds
Ghana Cons. Diamonds	Edubia	A	Diamonds
Ivory Coast			
Saremci	Seguela	A	Diamonds
Watson	Torkiya	A	Diamonds
Nigeria			
Amalg. Tin Mines of Nigeria	Jos	A	Sn
Bisichi Tin	Bukuru	A	Sn
Ex Lands	Barakin Ladi	A	Sn
Golds and Base Metal Mines	Jos	A	Sn
Kadiena Syndicate	Jos	A	Sn

Mine	Location	Size of Operation	Product
Rwanda			
Georwanda	Rwinkavu	A	Sn
Minetain	Kigali	A	Sn
Somuki	Rutongo	A	Sn
Sierra Leone			
Diminco	Yengema	A	Diamonds
South Africa			
Annex Kleinzee	Cape Province	A	Diamonds
Dreyers Pan	Cape Province	A	Diamonds
Richards Bay	Natal	A	Ti, Zr
South West Africa (Namibia)			
Cons. Diamond	Oranjemund	A	Diamonds
Zaire			
Cie, Grand Lacs Africains	Kivu	A	Au, Sn
Kilo-Moto	Kivu	A	Au
Symetain	Kalima	A	Sn, Cb, Ta
Kivumines	Kivu	A	Sn
Miluba	Kivu	A	Sn
Minerga	Kivu	A	Sn
Zaire-Etain	Maurno	A	Sn
Miba	Kasai	A	Diamonds

*These are not included in main list because of difficulty in making direct comparisons.

MAJOR NEW PROJECTS AND EXPANSION PROGRAMMES FOR 1976/7

Company	Location	Design production (ore, unless otherwise stated)	Completion date	Capital	Type of operation*	Remarks
Algeria						
Soc. Nationale de Sidérurgie	Gar Djebilet	10–12 million tonne/year Fe			P	Bids for feasibility study contract called; ultimately 30m.–40m. tonne/year
Soc. Nationale de Sidérurgie	Ouenza	Fe		Fr48m.		Fives Cail Babcock contract for mine expansion/modernization
Govt	M'Sila	Al	1980			Contracts signed with USSR to establish smelter; with Jamaica for alumina feed
Govt	Kherzet Youcef	10,000 tonne/year Zn metal plus 4,000 tonne/year Pb metal	1977–8			Mine/smelter development underway
Sonarem	Djebel Onk	900,000 tonne/year Phosphate rock				2nd treatment plant to handle expanded mine output
Sonarem	Hoggar Mts	U			P	Feasibility studies in progress by Pechiney/Sofremines

Botswana

Company	Project	Capacity/Product	Date	Cost		Notes
Bamangwato Concessions	Selebi	2 million tonne/year Cu, Ni	1978	R120m.	U, Sm	Mine development after depletion of Pikwe (P) now operational; flash smelter working towards design capacity of 3,500 tonne/month matte from 1,000 tonnes
Debswana (De Beers)	Letlhakane	396,000 ct/year diamonds	1980		P	Stage II programme
Debswana	Orapa	4·5 million ct/year diamonds	1978	R20m.		Expanding Orapa operation from 2·4 million ct/year
Debswana	Jwaneng	Diamonds	1978		P	Basic agreement reached with government

Central African

Company	Project	Capacity/Product	Date	Cost		Notes
Soc. de l'Uranium Centrafrican	Bakouma	500–700 tonne/year U_3O_8 concs.	1981	$8m.	P	Mine development considered by Govt/CEA/Cie Francaise de Minerais de Uranium

Egypt

Company	Project	Capacity/Product	Date	Cost		Notes
Govt	Nag Hammadi	100,000 tonne/year Al	1978–9	£E16m.	Sm	Soviet-assisted expansion from 36,000 tonnes; later 160,000
Govt	Shaglia	1·2–1·4 million tonne/year Phosphate; 600,000 tonne/year concs., 33·6% P_2O_5		$400m.	U	Rumanian-assisted mine development; costs include procession/harbour facilities

MAJOR NEW PROJECTS AND EXPANSION PROGRAMMES FOR 1976/7 — cont.

Company	Location	Design production (ore, unless otherwise stated)	Completion date	Capital	Type of operation*	Remarks
Govt	Abu Tartour	10 million tonne/year Phosphate 7 million tonne/year concs. (33% P₂O₅)	1985	$800m.	U	Engineering design contract to Sofremines/Alusuisse
Gabon						
Comifer	Belinga (Mekambo)	15 million tonne/year Fe	1981		P	Government/consortium mine development (Guilder 900m. for rail link to coast)
Comilog	Moanda	5 million tonne/year Mn	1981		P	Expanding company output from 2·3 million tonnes following completion of Trans Gabon railway and Santa Clara port development
Comuf/Govt	Mouana	1,500 tonne/year U₃O₅	1982		U/P/Rf	Refinery to be established
Ghana						
Bascol	Kibi	600,000 tonne/year Alumina	1980	$240m.	P/Rf	Revised feasibility study for mine/refinery by Kaiser following Japanese withdrawal but no development in short term

Consortium	Tema	300,000–400,000 tonne/year Al	1980	$450m.	Sm	Mitsubishi-led consortium feasibility studies for 2nd smelter complete this year
Volta Aluminium	Tema	200,000 s ton/year Al	1977	$65m.		Kaiser contract for fifth potline to provide additional 50,000 s tons complete by year end
Govt	Nyinahin	Bauxite	1980	C0·5m.		For feasibility study (government funded) on possible mine development; Chemokomplex to undertake
Govt	Wuowiso	200,000 tonne/year Fe	1980	C600m.	P	Costs for mine/iron-steel complex at Sekondi; work under way
Guinea						
Mifergui-Nimba (Govt/consortium)	Mt Nimba	8 million tonne/year Fe	1979	$200m.	P	Feasibility studies near completion (ultimately 15 million tonne/year). Also considering development of Simandou Fe reserves and rail/port facilities for $500m. Kaiser now withdrawn
Bauxites de Boke Guinée (Govt/Halco)	Boke	9 million tonne/year Bauxite	1980	$385m.	P	Mine expansion from 6 million tonnes; costs include mine ($180m.) rail/port development. Alusuisse

MAJOR NEW PROJECTS AND EXPANSION PROGRAMMES FOR 1976/7 – cont.

Company	Location	Design production (ore, unless otherwise stated)	Capital	Completion date	Type of operation*	Remarks
Alugui	Ayekoé, Boke	9 million tonne/year Bauxite; 2 million tonne/year Al			P/Rf	Arab-financed mine/smelter development to go ahead. Alusuisse contract for feasibility studies and prelim. design
Govt/Yugoslavia	Dabola	2 million tonne/year Bauxite			P/Rf	Mine development under way; refinery considered possibly in cooperation with Somiga
Somiga (Govt/Alusuisse)	Tougue	8 million tonne/year Bauxite		1979–80	P/Rf	Eventually 13 million tonnes output planned; 1 million tonne/year alumina refinery considered
Friguia	Fria-Kimbo	1·3 million tonne/year Alumina			Rf	Considering doubling refinery output
Ivory Coast Consortium	Mt Klahoyo	10–12 million tonne/year Fe pellets	$500m.	1980	P/Cn	Multinational consortium considering mine/pellet venture (rail or pipeline transportation undecided). Decision expected this year

Liberia						
Liberia Iron/consortium	Wologisi Range	10 million tonne/year Fe pellets	1979	$350m.	P/Cn	Further feasibility study; mine/pellet venture; 1 million tonne/year fines at Tokadeh ($7·2m.)
Lamco JV	Tokadeh	7 million tonne/year Fe; 4·5 million tonne/year concs.		$159m.	P/Cn	Considering mine expansion and new plant (eventually 20 million)
Bong Mining (Govt/consortium)	Bong	7·5 million tonne/year Fe	1978	$120m.	P/Cn	Mine expansion from 6 million tonnes capacity planned; 2nd pellet plant also considered to double output to 4·8 million
Libya						
Govt	Wadi Shat	5 million tonne/year Fe	1980			Considering mine development to feed 1 million tonne/year planned steelworks at Minsurata
Mauritania						
SNIM (Govt)	Tiris	6 million tonne/year Fe	1980		P	Awaiting World Bank loan to develop Rhein reserves and later (1986) Oum Arwagen reserves for total 12 million tonnes to replace Kedia mine

MAJOR NEW PROJECTS AND EXPANSION PROGRAMMES FOR 1976/7 – cont.

Company	Location	Design production (ore, unless otherwise stated)	Completion date	Capital	Type of operation	Remarks
Morocco						
Cie Minière de Toussit	Toussit	900 tonne/day Pb			U	Expansion at 2 mines from 600 tonne/day
OCP	Ben Guerir	2 million tonne/year Phosphate rock	1978	£100m.	P	Mine/plant; later 9·75 million
OCP	Sidi Hajjaj	3–5 million tonne/year Phosphate rock	1983		P	Expanding to 8 million by 1990
OCP	Youssou fia	7 million tonne/year Phosphate rock	1980		U	Expanding from current 5 million tonne/year
Niger						
Akouta	Akouta	2,000 tonne/year U metal; 600,000 tonne/year ore	1978	$70m.	U	Govt/French/Japanese mine development planned
Conoco/Cogema/ Govt	Imouraren	4 million lb/year U_3O_8	1983		U	Mine development studied
Nigeria						
Gold and Base Metal Mines/ Nigerian Mining Corp.	Liruie, Kano	900 tonne/day Sn/Zn		$45m.	U	New mine development

Operator	Location	Capacity	Commodity	Date	Cost	Status	Notes
Nigerian Steel Dev. Authority	Ikakpe, Kwara	4 million tonne/year Fe concs.		1980s		P	Sofremines contracted for mine engineering
Rhodesia							
Messina MTD (Mangula)	Avondale		Cu				Mine development
	Norah		Cu	1977	$R14m.	U	Doubling concentrator capacity. Expanding Miriam shaft output
Shangani Mining (JCI)	Shangani		Ni			U	Work under way at existing P mine for later switch to underground
De Beers	Beit Bridge	Diamonds				P	Pilot plant testing of diamond deposit underway
Senegal							
Govt/Brazil/Iran	Tobene	2 million tonne/year Phosphate		1980	$200m.	P	Mines (2) development plan plus $100m. for port expansion at Dakar: Iranian finance in exchange for ore
Cie Sénégalaise de Phosphates de Taiba	Taiba	Phosphates				P	Finance for expansion from 1·5 million tonne/year
Sierra Leone							
SL Ore and Metal (Alusuisse)	Port Loko	1·2 million tonne/year Bauxite			$500m.	P	Mine/500,000 tonne/year refinery planned
Govt/Sierra Rutile	Bangbama	100,000–125,000 tonne/year Ti, Zr concs.		1978	$41m.	A	Restart old Sherbro Minerals property; pilot plant for processing ore

MAJOR NEW PROJECTS AND EXPANSION PROGRAMMES FOR 1976/7—cont.

Company	Location	Design production (ore, unless otherwise stated)	Capital	Type of operation*	Completion date	Remarks
Bethlehem	Tonkolili	Fe	$700m.	P		Considering mine development
Bayer-Preussag	Rotifunk	Beachsands		A		Evaluating reserves; pilot programme under way
South Africa						
East Driefontein	Carletonville, Transvaal	210,000 tonne/month Au		U	1977	Expansion complete by year end
Deelkraal	Carletonville, Transvaal	120,000 tonne/month Au	R125m.	U/Cn	1982	Development under way. Initially 75,000 tonne/month in 1980
Elandsrand	Carletonville, Transvaal	180,000 tonne/month Au	R138m.	U	1980	New mine shaft sinking in progress
East Rand Gold and Uranium	Springs, Transvaal	1·5 million tonne/month Au/U	R100m.	Cn	1978	Complex to treat dumps to produce 6,500 kg Au+200 tonne/year U_3O_8
Free State Saaiplaas	Welkom, O.F.S.	200,000 tonne/month Au	R80m.	U	1979	Doubling capacity by No. 3 shaft development by 1979. R12·5m. mill expansion to 145,000 tonne/month capacity
Harmony	Virginia, O.F.S.	590,000 tonne/month Au/U		U	1977	New shaft/milling expansion
Kloof	Westonaria, Transvaal	2 million tonne/year Au		U	1978	Expansion behind schedule. Will further build up to 2·5 million tonne/year by 1981

Company	Location	Capacity	Year	Cost	Type	Notes
Loraine	Loraine, O.F.S.	200,000 tonne/month Au	1979	R34m.	U	Expansion from 135,000 tonne/month
Randfontein	Randfontein, Transvaal	105,000 tonne/month Au, 800–900 tonne/year U_3O_8	1978–9	R130m.	U	Expanding from present capacity of 80,000 tonne/month. Will increase to 250,000 tonne/month with new Au/U plant at Cooke No. 2 shaft
Unisel	Welkom, O.F.S.	100,000 tonne/month Au	1979	R61m.	U	Developing Jurgenshof lease area
Black Mt Mineral Development (Phelps Dodge/GFSA)	Aggeneys, C.P.	1,125,000 tonne/year Cu/Pb/Zn/Ag	1980	R150m.	U/Cn	Pilot plant testing by Phelps Dodge, mine development planned on series of major sulphide orebodies
O'Okiep Copper	Springbok, C.P.	Cu	1981	R17m.	U	Sinking shaft to the Carolusberg Deep orebody which has reserves of at least 11.2 million tonnes grading 1.8% Cu
Zincor	Springs, Transvaal	75,000 tonne/year Zn	1978	R14m.	U	Expanding from 68,000 tonne/year
AAC O'Okiep/Newmont	Gamsberg, C.P.	350,000 tonne/year Zn; Pb/Cu	1980	R170m.	U/Cn	Mine development on major orebody. Start-up on limited scale and build up over several years with Zn/Pb refinery at Saldanha; pilot plant testing under way
Rooiberg	Vellefontein, Transvaal	600,000 tonne/year Sn	1978	R1.5m.	U	Mine expansion

MAJOR NEW PROJECTS AND EXPANSION PROGRAMMES FOR 1976/7 – cont.

Company	Location	Design production (ore, unless otherwise stated)	Completion date	Capital	Type of operation*	Remarks
Iscor	Sishen	15 million tonne/year Fe	1980	R600m.	P	Mine expansion
AAC	Middelplaats, C.P.	1 million tonne/year Mn	1979	R40m.	U	Developing new mine
Rustenburg	Rustenburg, Transvaal	1·63 million oz/year Pt	1978	R97m.	U	Production expansion (deferred from 1976) including 225,000 oz/year from new mine at Amandelbult/Middellaagte
Samancor	Bophuthatswana	164,000 tonne/year Cr	1978	R2·5m.	U/P	Ruighoek mine capacity expansion due complete 1978
Samancor	Rustenburg, Transvaal	20,000 tonne/month Cr	1980	R13m.		Developing new mine on reserves on Elandskraal farm
Transvaal Cons. Land	Transvaal	2,000,000 tonnes/year Cr	1980s			Expanding output from Winterveld/Millsell/Henry Gould mines
De Beers	Finsch, C.P.	3 million ct/year Diamonds	1979	R40m.		Mine expansion from 2 million
De Beers	Koingnass, Namaqualand	470,000 ct/year Diamonds	1978	R20m.	P	Restarting development on work suspended in 1971
De Beers	Langhoogte, C.P.	60,000 ct/year Diamonds	1978	R3·6m.		

Company	Location	Capacity	Date	Cost	A	Mine/smelter development
QIT/Union Corp./ IDC/S.A. Mutual Life	Richards Bay	96,000 tonne/day Ti, Zr	1977–8	R250m.	U	Beachsand mine/smelter development
AAC	Klerksdorp, Transvaal	U	1981			Major study programme on Dominion Reefs/Afrikander Lease uranium properties
AAC	O.F.S.	16 million tonne/year U	1977	R60m.		Gold ore slimes treatment complex to serve 6 O.F.S. gold mines and produce uranium, gold and pyrites
Vaal Reefs	Orkney Transvaal	720,000 tonne/month U	1980	R106m.		Expanding existing recovery plants and constructing new plant for byproduct recovery from gold ore and tailings
AAC	Welkom, O.F.S.	360,000 tonne/year U	1980			Sales contracts arranged, will require extension of slimes treatment at President Brand from 180,000 tons
Harmony	Virginia, O.F.S.	U		R30m.		Seeking finance/markets; construction start advanced for Merriespruit property plant
Stilfontein	Klerksdorp, Transvaal	U				Considering resuming production from treatment of existing slimes

MAJOR NEW PROJECTS AND EXPANSION PROGRAMMES FOR 1976/7 – cont.

Company	Location	Design production (ore, unless otherwise stated)	Completion date	Capital	Type of operation*	Remarks
South West Africa (Namibia)						
Rössing Uranium	Swakopmund	5,000 tonne/year U_3O_8 concs.	1978		P	Mine on stream – building up to rated capacity
GFSA	Trekkopje	U_3O_8			P	Examining large reserves said to be similar to those at Rössing
General Mining	Langer Heinrich	U_3O_8			P	Feasibility studies on calcrete orebody now show development to be viable
Sudan						
Govt/Japanese	Ingessana Hills	50,000–100,000 Cr concs.	1980	$50–60m.	P	Feasibility study on mine expansion
Johns/Manville/ Gulf International	Ingessana	100,000 ston/ year Asbestos products		$115m.		Feasibility studies under way
Tunisia						
Govt	Mrata/Ste Barbe	5·5 million tonne/ year Phosphate	1978–80	$40m.	P/U	To replace declining output from present ops

Upper Volta

Govt/Consortium						
	Tambao	625,000 tonne/year Mn	1980	$24m.	P	Finance needed for mine development; 50% output to Japan

Zaire

Gecamines	Shaba	600,000 tonne/year Cu metal; 20,000 tonne/year Co	1980	$435m.	U/P	Development programme of expansions and new mines and metallurgical plant raising output from 470,000 tonnes Cu and 16,000 tonnes Co
SMTF	Shaba	130,000 tonne/year refined Cu		$800m.	P/Sm	Development halted after spending $200m. Re-assessing feasibility on smaller scale Replacing Musoshi
Sodimiza	Tshinsenda	60,000 tonne/year refined Cu	1977–8		U	
Société Minière de Kisenge	Kisenge, Shaba	Mn concs.			Cn	Mitsubishi considering concentrator but finance and transportation problems

Zambia

NCCM	Kansanshi	16,000 tonne/year Cu metal		£30m.	P	Programme suspended, but detailed engineering still in progress
RCM	Chambishi	Cu	1978		U	Mine expansion to replace pit
Mines Devel. Corp. Lumwana Ltd	Lumwana	Cu			P	New company established to develop low-grade reserves

*U, Underground mine; P, open pit; A, alluvial; S, solution mining; Cn, concentrator; Sm, Smelter; Rf, refinery

Appendix 2 Mining in Namibia*

(1) MAP SHOWING MINES

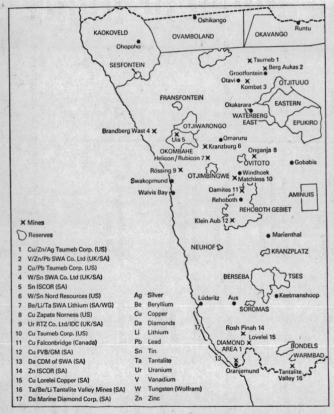

X Mines

Reserves

1 Cu/Zn/Ag Tsumeb Corp. (US)
2 V/Zn/Pb SWA Co. Ltd (UK/SA)
3 Cu/Pb Tsumeb Corp. (US)
4 W/Sn SWA Co. Ltd (UK/SA)
5 Sn ISCOR (SA)
6 W/Sn Nord Resources (US)
7 Be/Li/Ta SWA Lithium (SA/WG)
8 Cu Zapata Norness (US)
9 Ur RTZ Co. Ltd/IDC (UK/SA)
10 Cu Tsumeb Corp. (US)
11 Cu Falconbridge (Canada)
12 Cu FVB/GM (SA)
13 Da CDM of SWA (SA)
14 Zn ISCOR (SA)
15 Cu Lorelei Copper (SA)
16 Ta/Be/Li Tantalite Valley Mines (SA)
17 Da Marine Diamond Corp. (SA)

Ag Silver
Be Beryllium
Cu Copper
Da Diamonds
Li Lithium
Pb Lead
Sn Tin
Ta Tantalite
Ur Uranium
V Vanadium
W Tungsten (Wolfram)
Zn Zinc

*An earlier version of this survey appeared in L. Lazar, *Namibia*, Africa Publications Trust, 1972. It has been revised and updated by Roger Murray for this book.

(II) MINING COMPANIES AND MINES IN NAMIBIA (1976)

compiled by Roger Murray

Namibian Company	Mines and Minerals	Ownership
Diamonds		
Consolidated Diamond Mines of South West Africa Ltd; (Marine Diamond Corporation (Pty) Ltd) 1919	Oranjemund: Diamond Area No 1 alluvial deposits. Gem diamonds.	Wholly owned by De Beers Consolidated Mines Ltd.
Base Metals		
Tsumeb Corporation Ltd 1947 (T C L)	Tsumeb, Kombat, Matchless, Asis Ost. Arseni; mine and refined cadmium; mine and blister copper; mine and refined lead: mine and smelter silver; mine zinc.	29·6% Amax Inc (US); 29·6% Newmont Mining Corporation U S); 14·2% Selection Trust (U K); 9·5% O'Okiep Copper Company (Newmont); 9·4% Union Corporation (S I A); 2·4% Swaco (S A).
South West Africa Company Ltd (Swaco) 1898	Berg Aukas, Brandberg West, Asis Ost. Lead-vanadate concentrates; lead and zinc sulphides; zinc sillicate concentrates; tin/tungsten concentrates.	Until 1976, 44% Anglo-American, 43% Consolidated Gold Fields Ltd (UK); 2% Charter Consolidated (UK); 11% other. Now 100% owned by Kiln Products, unlisted Gold Fields subsidiary.
Kiln Products Ltd 1969	Berg Aukas. Waelz kiln production of zinc oxides.	55% owned by Consolidated Gold Fields and its associates.
Klein Aub Koper Maatskapy Beperk 1966	Klein Aub. (Rehoboth) Copper, silver concentrates.	Administered within the General Mining/Federale Mynbou group (S A).
Oamites Mining Company (Pty) Ltd 1971	Oamites. (Rehoboth) Copper concentrates.	Falconbridge Nickel Mines (Can.) 74·9%, Industrial Development Corporation of South Africa, 25·1%.

Namibian Company	*Mines and Minerals*	*Ownership*
Otjihase Mining Company (Pty) Ltd 1975	Otjihase. (Windhoek) Copper concentrates, sulphur, pyrite.	67% Johannesburg Consolidated Investment, JCI, (SA); 33% joint Tsumeb/Rössing Uranium
Navarro Exploration Company (Pty) Ltd 1967	Onganja. (Windhoek) Copper concentrates.	Navarro Exploration Corporation, wholly owned by Zapata Norness Inc. (US).
Imcor Zinc (Pty) Ltd 1971	Rosh Pinah. Lead and zinc concentrate.	51% ISCOR, the Iron & Steel Corporation of South Africa, 49% Zinc Corporation of South Africa.
Uis Tin Mining Company (SWA) Ltd	Uis (Namib) Tin concentrate.	ISCOR.
Nordex Joint Venture Ltd 1972	Krantzberg. Tungsten concentrate.	Nord Resources Corporation (US) 40%; Ebco Mining Corporation (US) 60%.
SWA Lithium Mines (Pty) Ltd	Karibib. Lithium ores; ambligonite, lepidolite, petalite.	Wholly owned by Metalgesellschaft AG (Ge).
Lorelei Copper Mines Ltd 1960	Warmbad. Copper concentrates.	33% each Moly Copper Mining, Industrial Diamonds of SA Ltd, Diamond Mining & Utility Co. Ltd (SA).
Tantalite Valley Minerals (Pty) Ltd	Karasburg. Bismuth, beryllium, scheelite, tantalite.	Local.
Dr Berger's Mines (Pty) Ltd	Karibib. Marble, wollostonite	Local.
Bantu Mining Corporation 1970	Oshakati, Khorixas. Sodalite, copper, iron.	South African Govt. para-statal.

Uranium

Rössing Uranium Ltd 1968	Rössing, nr Swakopmund Uranium oxide by solvent extraction, ion-exchange method.	46·5% Rio Tinto Zinc Corporation Ltd. (UK); 13·2% IDC of South Africa; 10% Rio Algom (RTZ); 10% Minatome SA (Fr); 6·8% General Mining (SA); 14·5% other (as of 1976). RTZ controls only 26% of the voting rights.

(III) MINERAL PRODUCTION
(metric tons)

Commodity	1974	1975	1976
Diamonds (carats)	1,569,961	1,747,739	1,693,994
Silver (oz.)	1,556,000	1,500,000	1,500,000
Cadmium	114	109	83
Copper			
blister	46,775	36,400	36,100
ores/concentrates	50,000	55,000	39,300
Lead			
refined	64,200	44,300	39,600
ores/concentrates	51,300	48,300	42,200
Lithium ores	6,060	n.a.	n.a.
Tin concentrate	1,100	1,117	1,110
Vanadium concentrate	8,348	5,771	n.a.
Zinc concentrates	44,900	45,600	480,000

Sources: World Bureau of Metal Statistics, *World Metal Statistics*, September 1972.

    World Mining, Catalogue, Surrey, June 1976.

References*

Introduction

1. Those who have examined the phenomena of mining companies in Africa include J. A. Hobson, *The Causes of the South African War*; Alvin Wolfe, 'The Team Rules Mining in South Africa' in *Towards Freedom*, January 1962; Alvin Wolfe, 'The African Mineral Industry: Evolution of a Supranational Level of Integration' in *Social Problems*, fall 1963; Alvin Wolfe, 'Capital and the Congo' in J. A. Davis and J. K. Baker, eds., *Southern Africa in Transition*, Praeger, New York, 1966. For an important African analysis, see Kwame Nkrumah's *Neo-colonialism*, Nelson, 1965. See also Walter Rodney, *How Europe Underdeveloped Africa*, Bogle L'Ouverture, 1972. The mining companies have justified their involvement through the speeches of F. Taylor Ostrander (AMAX), Sir Ronald Prain (formerly Roan Selection Trust) and Harry Oppenheimer (Anglo American), available from the companies.

2. Richard Jolly, 'The Aid Relationship; Reflections on the Pearson Report' in B. Ward, L. d'Anjou, J. O. Runnals, eds., *The Widening Gap*, Columbia University Press, New York, 1971, p. 284, Table 1.

3. Towards the end of the first United Nations Development Decade (1960–70) the President of the World Bank, George Woods, called for an international commission to examine the whole issue of development and the role of aid in this process. His successor, Robert Mac-Namara, took up the suggestion and invited the Canadian Lester Pearson to head the Commission. Pearson and his seven colleagues (Sir Edward Boyle, Roberto de Oliveria Campos, C. Douglas Dillon, Wilfried Guth, Arthur Lewis, Robert E. Marjolin, Saburo Okita) published their report at the end of 1969 under the title *Partners in Development: Report of the Commission on International Development*, Praeger, New York. It has come to be known more commonly as the Pearson Report.

4. A. G. Frank, *Capitalism and Underdevelopment in Latin America*,

*All books published in Britain unless otherwise stated.

revised edition, Monthly Review Press, New York, 1969; A. G. Frank, *Latin America: Underdevelopment or Revolution*, Monthly Review Press, New York, 1969; Celso Furtado, *Development and Underdevelopment*, University of California Press, 1964; Ernesto Laclau, 'Feudalism and Capitalism in Latin America', *New Left Review*, No. 67, May–June 1971; see also H. Bernstein, *Underdevelopment and Development*, Penguin Books, 1973, and C. Harding and C. Roper, eds., *Latin American Review of Books*, No. 1, London, 1973, for other theorists of underdevelopment.

5. A. G. Frank, *Latin America: Underdevelopment or Revolution*, op. cit., p. 225.

6. The literature on international companies is now vast. See for example Michael Barratt-Brown, *The Economics of Imperialism*, Penguin Books, 1973, and H. Radice, *International Firms and Modern Imperialism*, Penguin Books, 1975, and the bibliographies therein.

7. See the works already cited by Barratt-Brown, Laclau and Radice. See also G. Kay, *Development and Underdevelopment*, Macmillan, 1975; H. Magdoff, *The Age of Imperialism*, Monthly Review Press, New York, 1969; A. Emmanuel, *Unequal Exchange: A Study of the Imperialism of Trade*, New Left Books, 1972, and the theoretical comments by C. Bettelheim in the same volume; the work of C. Palloix in Radice, op. cit.; and the debate among Marxists in *New Left Review* and *Capital and Class*.

Chapter 1 The Incorporation of African Minerals into the World Economy

1. David Livingstone, *Missionary Travels and Researches*, 1957, quoted in Basil Davidson, *The African Past*, Penguin Books, 1966, p. 81.

2. See Basil Davidson, *Black Mother*, Gollancz, 1961; Basil Davidson, *The Africans*, Longmans, 1969; and Walter Rodney, *How Europe Underdeveloped Africa*, Bogle L'Ouverture, 1972.

3. R. Oliver and A. Atmore, *Africa Since 1800*, Cambridge University Press, 1967, p. 108.

4. Adrian Boshier and Peter Beaumont, 'Mining in Southern Africa and the Emergence of Modern Man', *Optima*, Vol. 22, No. 1, Johannesburg, March 1972, pp. 2–12. *Optima* is the house magazine of the Anglo American Corporation of South Africa.

5. Al Bekri (A.D. 1067) quoted in Basil Davidson, *The African Past*, op. cit., p. 81.

6. Alan McPhee, *The Economic Revolution in British West Africa*,

1926, p. 50, quoted in M. J. Herskovits and R. Horwitz, *Economic Transition in Africa*, Northwestern University Press, Evanston, 1964, p. 300.

7. J. D. Fage, *Ghana – A Historical Perspective*, Madison, Wisconsin, 1959, p. 15, quoted in Herskovits and Horwitz, op. cit.

8. Richard Brew, *A Treatise upon the Slave Trade*, 1771, quoted in Basil Davidson, *The African Past*, op. cit., p. 226.

9. Richard Hall, *Zambia*, Pall Mall, 1965, pp. 245, 249.

10. Antonio Gamitto, *The Land of the Kazembe*, 1954, quoted in Basil Davidson, *The African Past*, op. cit., p. 289.

11. Muhammed al Idrisi (1100–1166), in 1154, quoted in Basil Davidson, ibid., p. 118.

12. Manoel Baretto, 1667, quoted in Basil Davidson, ibid., p. 172.

13. João dos Santos, 1609, quoted in Basil Davidson, ibid., p. 166.

14. Raymond Brooks, quoted in Theodore Gregory, *Ernest Oppenheimer and the Economic Development of Southern Africa*, Oxford University Press, 1962, p. 401.

15. C. W. De Kiewet, *The Imperial Factor in South Africa*, Frank Cass, 1965 (original edition, 1935), p. 18.

16. J. G. Lockhart and C. M. Woodhouse, *Rhodes*, Hodder & Stoughton, 1963, pp. 54–5.

17. A. Wilmot, *Life and Times of Sir Richard Southey*, Cape Town, 1904, p. 241, quoted in H. J. and R. E. Simons, *Class and Colour in South Africa 1850–1950*, Penguin Books, 1969, p. 36.

18. H. J. & R. E. Simons, op. cit., p. 37.

19. ibid., p. 36.

20. ibid., p. 37.

21. De Kiewet, op. cit., p. 53.

22. Godehard Lenzen, *The History of Diamond Production and the Diamond Trade*, Barrie & Jenkins, 1970, pp. 140–44 for further analysis of the boom and its collapse.

23. De Kiewet, op. cit., p. 53.

24. ibid., p. 52.

25. ibid., p. 54.

26. H. J. and R. E. Simons, op. cit., p. 42.

27. ibid., p. 39.

28. *Financial News*, 1889, quoted in Paul Emden, *The Randlords*, Hodder & Stoughton, 1935.

29. J. G. Lockhart and C. M. Woodhouse, op. cit., p. 114.

30. A. P. Cartwright, *Gold Paved the Way*, Macmillan, 1967, p. 51.

31. Paul Emden, op. cit., p. 225.

32. A. P. Cartwright, op. cit., p. 63.

33. Ralph Horwitz, *The Political Economy of South Africa*, Weidenfeld & Nicolson, 1967, p. 24.

34. ibid., p. 48.

35. Francis Wilson, *Labour in the South African Gold Mines, 1911–1969*, Cambridge University Press, 1972, p. 45.

36. S. H. Frankel, *Capital Investment in Africa*, Oxford University Press, 1938, p. 76.

37. J. A. Hobson, *The Evolution of Modern Capitalism*, 1894, reprinted Allen & Unwin, 1956, p. 272.

38. Letter of 10 August 1889 from Lobenguela to Queen Victoria, quoted in E. D. Morel, *The Black Man's Burden*, 1920, reprinted Monthly Review Press, New York, 1969, p. 35.

39. Patrick Keatley, *The Politics of Partnership*, Penguin Books 1963, p. 167.

40. R. Robinson and J. Gallagher, *Africa and the Victorians*, Macmillan, 1961, p. 251.

41. ibid., p. 250.

42. Keatley, op. cit., p. 200.

43. S. H. Frankel, op. cit., p. 97. Note that this profit of £7½ million does not include all mining companies, only those which survived until 1932.

44. Richard Hall, *Zambia*, Pall Mall, 1965, p. 64.

45. George Middleton, quoted in Hall, op. cit., p. 74.

46. The horrific exploitation of Leopold's Congo Free State is chronicled in E. D. Morel, op. cit., and Ruth Slade, *King Leopold's Congo*, Oxford University Press, 1962.

47. *Conjoncture Économique No. 11, Année 1970*, Kinshasa, 1971, Ministère de l'Économie Nationale, Table 3, 'Copper production 1911–1974', p. 158.

Chapter 2 The Growth of the Mining Companies

1. S. H. Frankel, *Capital Investment in Africa*, Oxford University Press, 1938, p. 39.

2. ibid., Table 50, p. 211.

3. Francis Wilson, *Labour in the South African Gold Mines, 1911–1969*, Cambridge University Press, 1972, p. 45.

4. S. H. Frankel, op. cit., Table 12.

5. Ralph Horwitz, *The Political Economy of South Africa*, Weidenfeld & Nicolson, 1967, p. 66.

6. ibid., p. 180.

7. Frankel, op. cit., p. 94.

References

8. Figures for ore crushed and gold produced from Chamber of Mines of South Africa *Annual Report 1972*, and dividends from Frankel, op. cit., Table 14, p. 95 and p. 56.

9. Frankel, op. cit., Table 16, p. 108.

10. ibid., Table 49, p. 208.

11. Horwitz, op. cit., p. 225.

12. Theodore Gregory, *Ernest Oppenheimer and the Economic Development of Southern Africa*, Oxford University Press, 1962, p. 86.

13. *The Times*, 29 September 1917.

14. Gregory, op. cit., p. 373.

15. Solly Joel, quoted in Ivor Herbert, *The Diamond Diggers*, Tom Stacey, 1971, p. 100.

16. Frankel, op. cit., Table 11, p. 73.

17. Frankel, op. cit., p. 235.

18. ibid., Table 51, p. 212.

19. 1913 production figures, taken from Gregory, op. cit., p. 389. 1920 production figures, ibid., p. 417.

20. Gregory, op. cit., p. 417.

21. Frankel, op. cit., p. 292.

22. ibid., pp. 219, 220.

23. ibid., Table 97, p. 372.

24. ibid., p. 313.

25. ibid., p. 319, and Table 78, p. 320.

Chapter 3 The Structural Transformation of the African Economy

1. S. H. Frankel, *Capital Investment in Africa*, Oxford University Press, 1938, p. 193.

2. ibid., Table 27, p. 153.

3. ibid., p. 204.

4. ibid., Table 28, p. 158.

5. ibid., p. 213.

6. ibid., p. 214.

7. ibid., p. 165.

8. ibid., p. 374, for all figures on railways quoted in this paragraph.

9. ibid., p. 47.

10. ibid., Table 5, p. 55.

11. ibid., Table 16, p. 108.

12. ibid., Table 75, p. 300.

13. ibid., p. 325 and p. 74.

14. ibid., chapter 2, p. 213.

15. ibid., Chapter 5, p. 212.

16. ibid., p. 67.

17. ibid., p. 53.

18. ibid., p. 53.

19. ibid., p. 294.

20. G. Arrighi, 'The Political Economy of Rhodesia', in G. Arrighi and J. S. Saul, *Essays on the Political Economy of Africa*, Monthly Review Press, New York, 1973, p. 336.

21. Quoted in Theodore Gregory, *Ernest Oppenheimer and the Economic Development of Southern Africa*, Oxford University Press, 1962, pp. 395–6.

22. Ralph Horwitz, *The Political Economy of South Africa*, Weidenfeld & Nicolson, 1967, pp. 72–3.

23. ibid., p. 230.

24. Michel Merlier, *Le Congo de la colonisation belge à l'indépendance*, Maspéro, Paris, 1962, p. 131.

25. ibid., p. 134.

26. ibid., p. 135.

27. Richard Hall, *Zambia*, Pall Mall, 1964, p. 129.

28. G. Arrighi, 'Labour Supplies in Perspective; Rhodesia', in Arrighi and Saul, op. cit., p. 210. See also Charles van Onselen, *Chibaro – African Mine Labour in Southern Rhodesia 1900–1933*, Pluto Press, 1976.

29. See Horwitz, op. cit., Chapter 3, pp. 38–40, and Chapter 9.

30. See Horwitz, op. cit., pp. 34–40, and Arrighi and Saul, op. cit., pp. 180–234.

31. Frankel, op. cit., pp. 120–27.

32. Hall, op. cit., p. 128.

33. Merlier, op. cit., p. 131. This also happened in Rhodesia; see Arrighi, op. cit., p. 200.

34. Merlier, op. cit., p. 143.

35. Hall, op. cit., p. 261.

Chapter 4 International Mining Companies and the Post-Colonial State 1935–70

1. A. G. Frank, *Capitalism and Underdevelopment in Latin America*, revised edition, Monthly Review Press, New York, 1969.

2. Theodore Gregory, *Ernest Oppenheimer and the Economic Development of Southern Africa*, Oxford University Press, 1962, Chapter 7; and A. Hocking, *Oppenheimer and Son*, McGraw-Hill, Johannesburg, 1973, p. 171.

3. Francis Coleman, *The Northern Rhodesian Copperbelt, 1899–1962*, Manchester University Press, 1971, Table 2, p. 75.

4. Richard Hall, *Zambia*, Pall Mall, 1965, p. 262.

5. Ioan Davies, *African Trade Unions*, Penguin Books, 1966, p. 116.

6. Francis Wilson, *Labour in the South African Gold Mines, 1911–1969*, Cambridge University Press, 1972, p. 70; see also map of the recruiting stations in 1946 on p. x.

7. *Survey of Economic Conditions in Africa 1971*, United Nations Economic Commission for Africa, New York, 1972, Table 12.3, p. 159.

8. ibid., p. 159.

9. ibid., Table 8.2, p. 100.

10. Percentage for 1969, *Engineering and Mining Journal*, New York, November 1972, p. 149.

11. Various issues of *African Development*, 1971, and United Nations *Survey of Economic Conditions in Africa 1971*, op. cit.

12. Presidential Address, South Africa Chamber of Mines, 1972.

13. Michael Barratt-Brown, *From Labourism to Socialism*, Spokesman Books, 1972, Chapter 1.

14. ibid., p. 39.

15. *West Africa*, 18 December 1972, p. 1679.

16. R. Green and A. Seidman, *Unity or Poverty?*, Penguin Books, 1968, p. 119. *Mining Journal*, 24 November 1961, p, 553; 9 March 1962, p. 236.

Chapter 5 African Minerals in the World Economy

1. Car figures from an advertisement for Fiat in *Newsweek*, 25 March 1974. For English consumption for cars, *Drive* magazine, summer 1974, p. 72. See also *Mining Annual Review 1975*, p. 304, for the consumption on a typical US car.

2. *African Development*, November 1971, p. 57.

3. *Mining Magazine*, November 1971, p. 15.

4. *Engineering and Mining Journal*, New York, November 1971, Table p. 85.

5. 'Africa Annual Survey 1970', *Africa Magazine*, 1970, pp. 143–9.

6. Figures prepared in September 1971 for 'What Mining means to the United States', American Mining Congress, March 1972, US Bureau of Mines, 1972, quoted in A. Sutulov, *Minerals in World Affairs*, University of Utah Printing Services, Salt Lake City, 1973, pp. 92–3.

7. *Engineering and Mining Journal*, New York, March 1973, p. 9.

8. *Mining Annual Review 1972*, Mining Journal, 1972, p. 9; see also *Mining Journal*, 10 August 1973, p. 105.

9. P. Angeloni, ed., *Jane's World Mining – Who Owns Whom*, Sampson Low, Marston, 1970, Introduction.

10. Sutulov, op. cit., p. 67.

11. ibid., p. 107.

12. ibid., pp. 108–9, Table XXXIII.

13. Michael Barratt-Brown, 'The EEC and Neo-colonialism in Africa', in *Essays on Imperialism*, Spokesman Books, 1972.

14. *African Development*, June 1975, pp. 23–4.

15. Sutulov, op. cit., p. 98.

16. *Fortune*, Chicago, October 1972, p. 174.

17. 'Ocean Mining Sweepstakes', *Engineering and Mining Journal*, New York, April 1975, Sweepstakes, p. 75.

18. ibid., p. 75.

19. ibid., pp. 80–81.

20. R. Bailey, *Problems of the World Economy*, Penguin Books, 1967, p. 45.

21. Timothy Green, *The World of Gold*, Michael Joseph, 1968, p. 16.

22. Bailey, op. cit., p. 48.

23. *World Trade in Steel and Steel Demand in Developing Countries*, United Nations Economic Commission for Europe, 1968, ST/ECE/STEEL/22, p. 149.

24. Calculations by Preston Cloud, University of California, quoted in *Fortune*, Chicago, October 1972, p. 176.

Chapter 6 Gold, Nationalism, and Economic Development in South Africa 1900–1948

1. R. Robinson and J. Gallagher, *Africa and the Victorians*, Macmillan, 1961; and M. Barratt-Brown, *The Economics of Imperialism*, Penguin Books, 1974, especially Chapter 6.

2. R. Robinson and J. Gallagher, op. cit., p. 427.

3. ibid., p. 429.

4. According to J. Van der Poel, *The Jameson Raid*, Cape Town, OUP, 1951, p. 83, quoted in Robinson and Gallagher, op. cit., p. 429.

5. Robinson and Gallagher, op. cit., p. 460.

6. H. J. and R. E. Simons, *Class and Colour in South Africa 1850–1950*, Penguin Books, 1969, p. 316. See also F. A. Johnstone, *Class, Race and Gold*, Routledge & Kegan Paul, 1976.

7. Francis Wilson, *Labour in the South African Gold Mines, 1911–1969*, Cambridge University Press, 1972, p. 9.

8. Ralph Horwitz, *The Political Economy of South Africa*, Weidenfeld & Nicolson, 1967, p. 181.

9. ibid., p. 117.

10. ibid., p. 180.

11. Wilson, op. cit., p. 10.

12. Horwitz, op. cit., p. 99.

13. ibid., p. 98.

14. ibid., p. 183.

15. ibid., p. 216.

16. H. J. and R. E. Simons, op. cit., p. 336. The nature of this alliance and its significance has recently been the subject of a vigorous debate. See Simon Clarke, 'Capital, Fractions of Capital and the State', in *Capital and Class*, 5, pp. 32 ff. and the bibliography, p. 75.

17. Horwitz, op. cit., p. 165.

18. Brian Bunting, *The Rise of the South African Reich*, Penguin Books, 1969, p. 375.

19. Horwitz, op. cit., p. 196.

20. S. H. Frankel, *Capital Investment in Africa*, Oxford University Press, 1938, p. 133.

21. ibid., p. 115.

22. ibid., p. 119.

23. ibid., p. 127.

24. ibid., p. 383.

25. D. Hobart Houghton, *The South African Economy*, third edition, Oxford University Press, 1973, p. 59.

26. Horwitz, op. cit., Chapters 9 and 10.

27. Theodore Gregory, *Ernest Oppenheimer and the Economic Development of Southern Africa*, Oxford University Press, 1962, p. 250.

28. ibid., p. 277.

29. Horwitz, op. cit., note 37, p. 474.

30. ibid., p. 228.

31. ibid., p. 231.

32. Frankel, op. cit., p. 94.

33. Horwitz, op. cit., p. 231.

34. Frankel, op. cit., p. 116, Table 18.

35. Horwitz, op. cit., p. 230.

36. ibid., p. 229.

37. Frankel, op. cit., p. 94 and Table 15, pp. 96–7.

38. ibid., p. 93, footnote 2.

39. Gregory, op. cit., p. 523.

40. Frankel, op. cit., p. 104.

41. President of the Chamber of Mines in 1942, quoted by Gregory, op. cit., p. 542.

42. See Bunting, op. cit., and A. Hepple, *Verwoerd*, Penguin Books, 1967.

43. Quoted in Bunting, op. cit., p. 377.

44. Bunting, op. cit., p. 378.

45. A. P. Cartwright, *Gold Paved the Way*, Macmillan, 1967, Chapters 14 and 15.

46. Horwitz, op. cit., p. 257.

47. Wilson, op. cit., p. 78.

48. ibid., p. 79.

49. Transvaal Chamber of Mines, *Tribal Natives and Trade Unions*, Johannesburg, 1946, quoted in Wilson, op. cit., p. 79.

50. Bunting, op. cit., p. 379.

51. Dr Albert Hertzog (not General Hertzog), quoted in B. Bunting, op. cit., p. 380.

Chapter 7 The Gold Mines, Labour, and Economic Growth in South Africa, 1948–75

1. For a more detailed account of the South African economy see D. Hobart Houghton, *The South African Economy*, third edition, Oxford University Press. 1973, and works by Horwitz, Wilson and Bunting cited below. See also Simon Clarke, 'Capital, Fractions of Capital and the State', *Capital and Class*, 5.

2. Ralph Horwitz, *The Political Economy of South Africa*, Weidenfeld and Nicolson, 1967, p. 276.

3. Francis Wilson, *Labour in the South African Gold Mines, 1911–1969*, Cambridge University Press, 1972, p. 26.

4. Theodore Gregory, *Ernest Oppenheimer and the Economic Development of Southern Africa*, Oxford University Press, 1962, p. 37.

5. Horwitz, op. cit., pp. 291–2.

6. ibid., p. 358.

7. Brian Bunting, *The Rise of the South African Reich*, revised edition, Penguin Books, 1969, p. 369.

8. ibid., p. 379.

9. ibid., pp. 380–81.

10. *Mining Journal*, 16 June 1961, p. 706.

11. Morton Dagut, 'The South African Economy through the Sixties', *Optima*, Johannesburg, September 1968.

12. Horwitz, op. cit., p. 287, footnote 44.

13. *Mining Journal*, 30 June 1961, p. 769.

References

14. ibid.

15. Anglo American Corporation *Annual Report 1961*.

16. Horwitz, op. cit., p. 398.

17. *Financial Mail* supplement, 'Inside the Anglo Power House', Johannesburg, 4 July 1969, p. 31; Anglo American Corporation *Annual Report 1974*, p. 30.

18. *Financial Mail*, Johannesburg, 29 May 1959, quoted in Wilson, op. cit., p. 26.

19. South African Minister of Finance, Dr T. E. Dönges, in his budget speech of 2 March 1960, quoted in Anglo American Corporation *Annual Report 1959*, p. 14.

20. ib d., p. 14.

21. A. Hocking, *Oppenheimer and Son*, McGraw-Hill, Johannesburg, 1973, p. 372.

22. Bunting, op. cit., p. 391.

23. *Sunday Times*, Johannesburg, 30 August 1964, quoted in Bunting, op. cit., p. 391.

24. *Mining Journal*, 24 July 1953, in Wilson, op. cit., p. 77.

25. Horwitz, op. cit., p. 410.

26. For a more detailed examination of the interaction between these costs of production and the paramount importance of cheap black mineworkers, see Wilson, op. cit.

27. Wilson, op. cit., p. 46.

28. ibid., p. 47.

29. *Financial Mail*, Johannesburg, 30 March 1973.

30. *Guardian*, 29 January 1975; see also *Chamber of Mines Accident Statistics*, 1971, which also gives annual accident statistics back to 1903; see also *Annual Reports* of Chamber of Mines.

31. H. J. and R. E. Simons, *Class and Colour in South Africa 1850–1950*, Penguin Books, 1969, p. 615.

32. Wilson, op. cit., p. 113.

33. ibid., p. 137.

34. ibid., p. 43.

35. ibid., p. 107.

36. ibid., p. 107. footnote 1.

37. ibid., p. 81.

38. *Financial Mail*, Johannesburg, 13 December 1974.

39. Wilson, op. cit., p. 85.

40. ibid., p. 83.

41. *Financial Mail* supplement, 'Gold', Johannesburg, 17 November 1972, p. 75; *Financial Mail*, Johannesburg, 25 October 1974, p. 339.

42. 'Gold', op. cit., p. 75.

43. W. D. Wilson, Deputy Chairman, Anglo American, *Financial Mail*, Johannesburg, 9 January 1976, p. 71.

44. General Mining *Annual Report 1974*, p. 7.

45. Quoted in Heribert Adam, *Modernizing Racial Domination*, University of California Press, 1971, p. 172.

46. See for example *Financial Mail*, Johannesburg, 28 February 1975, p. 691.

47. *Financial Mail*, Johannesburg, 13 August 1974, p. 1043.

Chapter 8 From Primitive Accumulation to Boom: the Mining Companies in Southern Rhodesia

1. See for example Harry Oppenheimer, *Financial Mail*, 'Top Companies Survey', Johannesburg, 6 June 1975, p. 34.

2. G. Arrighi, 'Labour Supplies in Historical Perspective: A Study of the Proletarianization of the African Peasantry in Rhodesia', in G. Arrighi and J. S. Saul, *Essays on the Political Economy of Africa*, Monthly Review Press, New York, 1973, p. 195.

3. G. Arrighi, 'The Political Economy of Rhodesia', in Arrighi and Saul, op. cit., p. 337.

4. G. Arrighi, 'Labour Supplies . . .', op. cit., p. 191.

5. ibid., pp. 183 ff.

6. ibid., p. 197.

7. Charles van Onselen, *Chibaro – African Mine Labour in Southern Rhodesia 1900–1933*, Pluto Press, 1976, p. 95.

8. G. Arrighi, 'Labour Supplies . . .', op. cit., p. 202.

9. ibid., p. 208.

10. Van Onselen, op. cit., p. 89.

11. ibid., p. 63.

12. ibid., p. 81.

13. ibid., p. 103.

14. ibid., p. 104.

15. ibid., p. 108.

16. ibid., p. 105.

17. ibid., p. 106.

18. ibid., p. 158.

19. ibid., p. 159.

20. ibid., p. 33.

21. ibid., pp. 125–6.

22. ibid., p. 114, Table D.

23. G. Arrighi, 'Labour Supplies . . .', op. cit., p. 214.

24. ibid., p. 207.

25. G. Arrighi, 'The Political Economy of Rhodesia', op. cit., pp. 339f., on the interests of the various groups, including the clash between the national bourgeoisie and the BSAC which led to the 1923 transfer of power.

26. ibid., p. 345.

27. ibid., p. 346.

28. S. H. Frankel, *Capital Investment in Africa*, Oxford University Press, 1938, p. 238.

29. Arrighi, 'The Political Economy of Rhodesia', op. cit., p. 353.

30. Arrighi, 'Labour Supplies . . .', op. cit., p. 218.

31. ibid., p. 216.

32. L. H. Gann and M. Gelfand, *Huggins of Rhodesia*, 1964, quoted in Arrighi, 'The Political Economy of Rhodesia', op. cit., p. 351.

33. *Central African Post*, 3 March 1949, quoted in Richard Hall, *Zambia*, Pall Mall, 1965, p. 64.

34. ibid., especially Chapter 6.

35. Theodore Gregory, *Ernest Oppenheimer and the Economic Development of Southern Africa*, Oxford University Press, 1962, p. 462.

36. Anglo American *Annual Report 1951*.

37. Hall, op. cit., p. 150.

38. ibid., p. 283, and see also p. 226, note 16.

39. Chairman's Statement, Anglo American *Annual Report 1956*, quoted in Gregory, op. cit., p. 464.

40. Hall, op. cit., p. 162.

41. ibid.

42. Arrighi, 'The Political Economy of Rhodesia', op. cit., p. 356.

43. Gregory, op. cit., p. 465; Hall, op. cit., p. 150.

44. M. L. O. Faber and J. G. Potter, *Towards Economic Independence*, Cambridge University Press, 1971, p. 22.

45. Patrick Keatley, *The Politics of Partnership*, Penguin Books, 1963, p. 465.

46. Anthony Martin, *Minding Their Own Business*, Hutchinson, 1972, p. 124.

47. Keatley, op. cit., p. 448.

48. Ian Waller, 'Pressure Politics', *Encounter*, 3 August 1962, p. 11.

49. ibid., p. 10.

50. Keatley, op. cit., p. 452.

51. Arrighi, 'The Political Economy of Rhodesia', op. cit., p. 355.

52. Keatley, op. cit., p. 453.

53. ibid.

54. Gann and Gelfand, op. cit., p. 224.

55. Arrighi, 'The Political Economy of Rhodesia', op. cit., p. 355.

56. ibid., pp. 369–71.

57. Arrighi, op. cit., p. 367.

58. Arrighi, op. cit., p. 350.

59. *Africa South of the Sahara*, 1972, Europa Publications, p. 599.

60. ibid., p. 607.

61. Statement of Fred C. Kroft Jr, President of Ferro Alloys division of Union Carbide, to the Senate Sub-Committee on African Affairs, 7 August 1971.

62. *Africa South of the Sahara*, op. cit., p. 599.

63. Mr J. Clayton Stephenson to Senate Sub-Committee on African Affairs, August 1971.

64. *Mining Annual Review 1972*, Mining Journal, p. 340. Plans for this mine were announced in 1965.

65. *Financial Times*, 30 October 1969.

66. *Mining Annual Review 1972*, Mining Journal, p. 340.

67. *A Survey of the Mining Industry in Rhodesia*, British Sulphur Corporation, 1972, quoted in Alan Baldwin, *Token Sanctions or Total Economic Warfare*, Justice for Rhodesia Campaign, 1972, p. 14.

68. S. Cronje, M. Ling, G. Cronje, *Lonrho – Portrait of a Multinational*, Penguin Books, 1976, pp. 169–70. See also Department of Trade, *Lonrho Limited – An Investigation under Section 165(b) of Companies Act 1948*, paragraphs 4. 78–4. 135, for a fascinating insight into the internal workings of this international mining group.

69. Stephenson, loc. cit.

70. *Sunday Globe*, Boston, 12 December 1971; quoted in Reed Kramer and Tami Hultman, *Rhodesian Chrome – A Portrait of Union Carbide and Foote Mineral*, Corporate Information Centre of the National Council of Churches, New York, May 1972, p. 11.

71. *Newsweek*, 10 April 1972, p. 45.

72. ibid.

73. ibid.

74. ibid.

75. *Wall Street Journal*, as reported in Colin Legum, 'Nixon in Trouble on Rhodesian Chrome', *Observer*, March 1972.

76. *Washington Post*, 19 March 1972, p. 82.

77. *Sunday Times*, 30 January 1972.

78. Colin Legum, op. cit.

79. *Rand Daily Mail*, 30 June 1970.

80. Chairman's Statement, Anglo American Corporation *Annual Report 1975*, p. 2.

Chapter 9 Copper, Labour, and Underdevelopment in Zambia

1. See *Annual Reports* of Rhoanglo and Rhodesian Selection Trust. For analysis, see Special Paper No. 1, 'The Copper Mining Industry of Northern Rhodesia' (May 1963), and Special Paper No. 6, 'The Financial Position of the Northern Rhodesian Copper Mines 1959–1963' (May 1964), African Research Office of the International Confederation of Free Trade Unions, Kampala, Uganda.

2. Special Paper No. 6, op. cit., p. 67.

3. Richard Hall, *The High Price of Principles*, Penguin Books, 1973, p. 74.

4. Richard Hall gives a brilliant description of the final denouement in Hall, op. cit., Chapter 5. He gives the full history of the mineral rights in Richard Hall, *Zambia*, Pall Mall, 1965. In neither book does he reveal that he played an important part in drawing attention to the weak legal basis of the mineral rights.

5. Hall, *Zambia*, p. 230.

6. Hall, *The High Price of Principles*, pp. 71–2.

7. ibid., p. 63.

8. ibid., p. 63.

9. ibid., p. 94.

10. ibid., p. 93.

11. R. Bates, *Unions, Parties and Political Development*, New Haven, Yale University Press, 1971, Table 25, p. 82.

12. Hall, *The High Price of Principles*, p. 196.

13. Brown Commission, quoted in Pamphlet 16, *The Politics of Copper Mines in Zambia*, Europe/Africa Research Project, 103 Gower Street, London WCI, 1971.

14. Brown Commission, quoted in Anthony Martin, *Minding Their Own Business*, Hutchinson, 1972, pp. 147–8.

15. Hall, *The High Price of Principles*, p. 177.

16. ibid., Chapters 9, 10, 11.

17. M. Bostock and C. Harvey, eds., *Economic Independence and Zambian Copper*, Praeger, 1972, p. 121.

18. ibid., p. 112.

19. ibid., p. 121.

20. Introduction to the Mulungushi Declaration, see note 21.

21. K. Kaunda, 'Zambia Towards Economic Independence', the

speech given at the National Council of the United National Independence Party at Mulungushi on 19 April 1968, known as the Mulungushi Declaration, reprinted in D. de Gaay Fortman, *After Mulungushi*, Nairobi, East African Publishing House, 1969, pp. 34–74.

22. *African Development*, September 1969, p. 12.

23. ibid.

24. Hall, *The High Price of Principles*, p. 199, and W. Tordoff, ed., *Politics in Zambia*, Manchester University Press, 1974, especially Chapter 3, 'Cleavage and Conflict in Zambian Politics; A Study in Sectionalism', by Robert Molteno.

25. Tordoff, op. cit.

26. Martin, op. cit., p. 165.

27. See Martin, op. cit., and Bostock and Harvey, op. cit.

28. Bostock and Harvey, op. cit., p. 235.

29. ibid., particularly Appendixes A and B.

30. Discussion with Mindeco staff members in 1973.

31. *Times of Zambia*, 20 June 1973.

32. M. Burawoy, *The Colour of Class on the Copper Mines*, Lusaka, University of Zambia, Institute for African Studies, Zambian Paper No. 7, 1972, p. 78; and see also Bates, op. cit.

33. See Burawoy, op. cit., Bates, op. cit., and also A. Gupta, 'Trade Unionism and Politics on the Copperbelt', in Tordoff, op. cit., pp. 288ff.

34. Burawoy, op. cit., p. 79.

35. ibid., p. 105.

36. G. Simwinga, 'Decision-making and Control in a Partially Nationalised Industry', University of Zambia, mimeo, 1973; see also Burawoy, op. cit., and Bostock and Harvey, op. cit.

37. Simwinga, op. cit., p. 20.

38. *Times of Zambia*, 13 July 1973, p. 5.

39. Moreover outside contractors were paying skilled artisans double the companies' rates and hiring them back to the mines on contract at still higher rates (*Investors Chronicle*, 24 August 1973, p. 843.)

40. Tad Szulc has claimed that the White House (worried about the possibility of Kaunda's overthrow by radicals who might then seize US investments) sent special assistance to President Kaunda in 1970 in the form of electronic equipment to bug the phones and homes of Zambians he suspected of plotting against him (*New Republic*, New York, 29 December 1973, pp. 19–20).

41. See, for example, Tordoff, op. cit., Chapter 4.

42. Ann Seidman, 'A Note: Haves and Have-Nots in Zambia –

What Happens to the Investable Surpluses in Zambia ?', University of Zambia, mimeo, 1973, p. 16.

43. *African Annual 1974–5*, Africa Magazine, p. 199.

44. *African Development*, October 1973, p. 23.

45. For example, *Times of Zambia*, 16 October 1973.

46. Quoted in *African Development*, October 1973, Zambian supplement, p. 15.

47. For more details, see *African Development*, June 1974, p. 29, and December 1974, p. 45; and *Mining Journal*, 28 February 1975, p. 151.

48. *African Development*, December 1974, p. 75.

49. *Mining Journal*, 22 November 1974, p. 438.

50. NCCM borrowed $140 million from a Citicorp and Bank of America consortium (Zambia *Daily Mail*, 21 March 1975) and RCM $40 million (Zambia *Daily Mail*, 18 March 1975).

51. *Mining Journal*, August 1975, p. 163.

52. Ruth Weiss, *Guardian*, 7 December 1972.

53. ibid.

54. Ann Seidman, op. cit., pp. 6–7.

55. Martin Meredith, 'Kaunda's Economic Philosophy', *African Development*, October 1971, Zambian Survey, p. 219.

56. *African Development*, October 1973, p. 239.

57. Hall, *The High Price of Principles*, op. cit., p. 178.

58. Tordoff, op. cit., p. 371.

59. ibid., p. 378.

60. ibid., see especially Chapters 3 and 10.

61. *Africa Digest*, February 1974, p. 13.

62. An example of these is President Kaunda's marathon six-hour 'Watershed' speech of 30 June 1975, but, like other reforms, it does not tackle fundamental problems and is stronger on rhetoric than action. See *African Development*, August 1975, p. 29, September, p. 41, and November, 'Economic Survey of Zambia', p. 25.

Chapter 10   The Mining Company and the State in Zaire

1. See Michel Merlier, *Le Congo de la colonisation belge à l'indépendance*, Maspéro, Paris, 1962. Pierre Joye and Rosine Lewin, *Les Trusts au Congo*, Société Populaire d'Éditions, Brussels, 1961.

2. J. Gerard-Libois, *Katanga Secession*, University of Wisconsin, 1966, Appendix 1, p. 320.

3. Alvin Wolfe, 'Capital and the Congo', in A. Davis and J. K.

Baker, eds., *Southern Africa in Transition*, Praeger, New York, 1966, p. 373.

4. Union Minière, *Annual Report 1960*.

5. Joye and Lewin, op. cit., p. 218.

6. T. Kanza, *Conflict in the Congo*, Penguin Books, 1972, p. 241.

7. See C. C. O'Brien, 'The Congo, the United Nations and Chatham House', in *New Left Review*, No. 31, May–June 1965, p. 6. Conakat was set up and guided by the Europeans of Elizabethville, notably the local agents of the Union Minière, in order, by exploiting tribal rivalries, to provide a counterpoise to black nationalism.

8. ibid., p. 134.

9. Patrick Keatley, *The Politics of Partnership*, Penguin Books, 1963, p. 454.

10. Jules Chome, *La Crise congolaise*, Brussels, 1960, p. 172, quoted in C. C. O'Brien, *To Katanga and Back*, Hutchinson, 1962.

11. For a full account of the events in the months after independence, see Catherine Hoskyns, *The Congo Since Independence*, Oxford University Press, 1965 (but see the critical review by C. C. O'Brien in *New Left Review*, loc. cit.); Conor Cruise O'Brien, *To Katanga and Back*, op. cit.; Kwame Nkrumah, *The Challenge of the Congo*, Nelson, 1967; Thomas Kanza, *Conflict in the Congo*, Penguin Books, 1972; Andrew Tull, *CIA: The Inside Story*, W. Morrow, New York, 1962; and various publications of the Centre de Recherche et d'Information Socio-Politiques in Brussels (CRISP), including *Congo 1959*, *Congo 1960* (2 vols.), *Congo 1961*.

12. *Daily Telegraph*, 27 July 1960.

13. Nkrumah, op. cit., p. 195.

14. Keatley, op. cit., p. 463.

15. Quoted in Nkrumah, op. cit., p. 196.

16. Tanganyika Concessions *Annual Report*, 1960.

17. C. C. O'Brien, *To Katanga and Back*, op. cit., p. 215.

18. ibid., p. 175.

19. Richard J. Barnett, *Intervention and Revolution*, Paladin, 1972, p. 249. Mineral supplies (cobalt, etc.), were also important.

20. ibid., pp. 248–57.

21. C. C. O'Brien, *To Katanga and Back*, op. cit., p. 59.

22. C. C. O'Brien in *New Left Review*, op. cit., p. 13. The effect of England's and Belgium's reluctant support of the UN was that US policy prevailed in Leopoldville and Anglo-Belgian policy in Katanga.

23. Nkrumah, op. cit., p. 198.

24. Deputy Assistant Secretary of State for Public Affairs, Carl T.

Rowan, quoted in Hempstone Smith, *Rebels, Mercenaries and Dividends*, Praeger, New York, 1962, p. 222.

25. For more details of the personalities in the Rhodesia–Katanga lobby, see Keatley, op. cit., and Chapter 8 above.

26. C. C. O'Brien, *To Katanga and Back*, op. cit., p. 214.

27. C. C. O'Brien, *Transition*, July–August 1966, Uganda.

28. The coup is widely believed to have been arranged, or at least backed, by the CIA. See various recent studies of CIA including the 1975–6 US Senate Report, and *African Development*, December 1975, p. 17.

29. See Richard Gott's excellent pamphlet *Mobutu's Congo*, Fabian Research Series 266, Fabian Society, 1967, from which this account draws.

30. Gott, op. cit., p. 24.

31. Kinshasa Radio on 20 February 1967, as quoted in Gott, op. cit.

32. Richard Hall, 'What's Going on with Union Minière', *African Development*, April 1969, p. 10.

33. *African Development*, March 1974, p. 27.

34. Union Minière *Annual Report 1974*.

35. J. Gerard-Libois, 'New Class and Rebellion in the Congo' in R. Miliband and J. Saville, eds., *The Socialist Register 1966*, Merlin, 1966, pp. 270–71.

36. C. Hoskyns and K. Whiteman, 'Congo (Kinshasa)' in Colin Legum, ed., *Africa Handbook*, revised edition, Penguin Books, 1969, p. 234.

37. Gerard-Libois, op. cit., p. 270.

38. Crawford Young, *Politics in the Congo*, Princeton University Press, 1965, p. 100.

39. *African Development*, September 1972, Zaire Economic Survey, p. 25.

40. *African Development*, July 1975, p. 48.

41. See, for example, *Newsweek*, 22 November 1971 and 14 May 1973.

42. Apparently Nixon sent an emissary to ask Mobutu for an explanation of his China journey and the unfortunate diplomat was put back on the next plane: *African Development*, September 1975, p. 48.

Chapter 11 Liberia and the Mining Companies

1. William A. Hance, *African Economic Development*, revised edition, Praeger, New York, 1967, pp. 56–7.

2. *African Development*, July 1973, Liberia Survey, p.L.9; the latest figure is for 1971.

3. R. U. McLaughlin, *Foreign Investment and Development in Liberia*, Praeger, New York, 1966, p. 190.

4. ibid., p. 191.

5. R. W. Clower, G. Dalton, M. Horwitz and A. Walters, *Growth without Development – An Economic Survey of Liberia*, Northwestern University Press, Evanston, 1966, p. 71.

6. ibid., p. 80.

7. *African Development*, August 1970, p. 25.

8. Clower, Dalton, Horwitz and Walters, op. cit., p. 72.

9. ibid., p. 72.

10. Hance, op. cit., p. 83.

11. Clower, Dalton, Horwitz and Walters, op. cit., p. 207.

12. Richard West, *Back to Africa*, Jonathan Cape, 1965, p. 305.

13. ibid., p. 327.

14. Clower, Dalton, Horwitz and Walters, op. cit., p. 222.

15. *The Times*, 17 April 1973, special supplement on Liberia, p. iv.

16. *African Development*, July 1973, Liberia Economic Survey, p. L.24.

17. *West Africa*, 18 December 1972, p. 1681.

18. ibid.

19. *African Development*, July 1975, Liberian supplement, p. L.21.

20. McLaughlin, op. cit., p. 104.

21. *African Development*, August 1970, p. 23.

22. *African Development*, July 1972, Liberia Economic Survey, p. L.38.

23. Clower, Dalton, Horwitz and Walters, op. cit., p. 67.

24. ibid., pp. 64–5.

25. ibid., p. 66.

26. *West Africa*, 19 February 1973, p. 223.

27. *The Times*, 17 April 1973, Liberia survey, p. iv.

28. *West Africa*, 18 December 1972, p. 1681; see also *Africa*, August 1972, p. 59.

29. *African Development*, July 1975, p. L.11.

30. ibid., p. L.21.

31. *Mining Annual Review 1978*, Mining Journal, 1978, p. 499.

Chapter 12 The Major Mining Groups in Africa

NOTE: The main sources of information for facts and figures in this chapter are company reports and various industry publications. The references cover only additional sources.

1. N. Girvan, *Copper in Chile – A Study in Conflict between Corporate and National Economy*, Institute of Social and Economic Research, University of the West Indies, Jamaica, 1972, p. 64.

2. The official company history is A. P. Cartwright, *Gold Paved the Way*, Macmillan, 1967; a useful corrective is *Consolidated Gold Fields Ltd – Anti-Report*, Counter Information Services, 1973.

3. For a favourable account of RTZ, written after visits at the company's expense to Canada and Australia, see Keith Richardson, 'The Mining Moguls of RTZ', *Sunday Times*, 7, 14 and 21 November 1971. For a critical assessment of RTZ, see *The Rio Tinto-Zinc Corporation Limited – Anti-Report*, Counter Information Services, 1971, and Richard West, *River of Tears*, Earth Island, 1972.

4. See *RTZ Anti-Report*, op. cit., and *Management Responsibility and African Employment in South Africa*, Raban Press, Johannesburg, 1973.

5. *African Development*, June 1975, Japan supplement, p. J.7.

6. See S. Cronje, M. Ling, G. Cronje, *Lonrho: Portrait of a Multinational*, Penguin Books, 1976; and *Africa Report*, March–April 1974, pp. 43–5.

7. See *Observer*, 27 October 1971; *Sunday Times*, 28 November 1971 and 6 March 1972; Cronje *et al.*, op. cit.

8. See Robert Ramsey, *Men and Mines of Newmont – A Fifty Year History*, Octagon Books, New York, 1973.

9. *African Development*, May 1975, p. 47.

10. *Newsweek*, 10 April 1972, p. 45.

11. *African Development*, June 1975, Japanese supplement, p. J.6.

12. Theodore Gregory, *Ernest Oppenheimer and the Economic Development of Southern Africa*, Oxford University Press, 1962, p. 16.

13. *Financial Mail* supplement 'Gold', Johannesburg, 12 November 1972, p. 69.

14. See *Financial Mail* supplement, 'Gauging JCI's Mettle', Johannesburg, 25 September 1970; and on Barney Barnato, see Paul Emden *The Randlords*, Hodder & Stoughton, 1935.

15. See A. P. Cartwright, *Golden Age*, Purnell, Johannesburg, 1968, for the history of Rand Mines and Central Mining.

16. See A. P. Cartwright, *Gold Paved the Way*, and the C.I.S. *Anti-Report*, both cited in Reference 2, above.

17. See *Financial Mail*, supplement 'A Sense of Direction', Johannesburg, 5 October 1973, and Brian Bunting, *The Rise of the South African Reich*, revised edition, Penguin Books, 1969, Chapter 14, especially pp. 390–92.

18. See Gregory, op. cit., A. Hocking, *Oppenheimer and Son*, McGraw-Hill, Johannesburg, 1973; and *Financial Mail* supplement, 'Inside the Anglo Power House', Johannesburg, 4 July 1969.

19. Richard Hall, *The High Price of Principles*, Penguin Books, 1973, p. 89.

Chapter 13 The Structure of International Mining Companies

1. A. P. Cartwright, *Gold Paved the Way*, Macmillan, 1967, pp. 55–6.

2. 'Lonrho's Great African Tightrope', *Sunday Times*, 28 November 1971.

3. D. A. B. Watson, interviewed in *Financial Mail* supplement, 'Gauging JCI's Mettle', Johannesburg, 25 September 1970, p. 18.

4. *Sunday Times*, 21 November 1971.

5. 'Gauging JCI's Mettle', op. cit., p. 18.

6. H. Oppenheimer, interviewed in *Financial Mail* supplement, 'Inside the Anglo Power House', Johannesburg, 4 July 1969, p. 13.

7. Quoted in Timothy Green, *The World of Gold*, Michael Joseph, 1968, p. 51.

8. Robert Ramsey, *Men and Mines of Newmont – A Fifty Year History*, Octagon Books, New York, 1973, p. 11.

9. 'Gauging JCI's Mettle', op. cit., p. 18.

10. *Compass* (ALCAN house magazine), Vol. IX, No. 10, December 1967, quoted in C. Tugendhat, *The Multinationals*, Penguin Books, 1973, p. 130.

11. *African Development*, July 1972, p. 66.

12. *Financial Times*, 27 March 1969.

13. H. Oppenheimer, quoted in 'Inside the Anglo Power House', op. cit., p. 13.

14. ibid., p. 11.

15. 'Gauging JCI's Mettle', op. cit., p. 51.

16. 'General Mining: A Sense of Direction', *Financial Mail*, Johannesburg, 5 October 1973, pp. 53–4.

17. Ramsey, op. cit., pp. 8–11.

18. Amax *Annual Report 1975*. Note that since 1973 the aluminium

References

division has become a joint Amax–Mitsui wholly-owned subsidiary called Alumax Inc.

19. Tugendhat, op. cit., pp. 127–9.
20. Pechiney-Ugine-Kuhlmann *Annual Report 1971*.
21. *Financial Times*, 27 March 1969.
22. 'Top Companies', *Financial Mail* survey, Johannesburg, 16 April 1971, p. 75.

Chapter 14 Relations Between the Mining Groups

1. Alvin Wolfe, ' "The Team" rules Mining in Southern Africa', *Toward Freedom*, vol. xi no. 1, January 1962. Wolfe's work is interesting but it has serious conceptual limitations and factual inaccuracies. See M. L. O. Faber, 'Corporate Policy on the Copperbelt', in M. L. O. Faber and J. G. Potter, *Towards Economic Independence*, Cambridge University Press, 1971.

2. See Wolfe, ibid., and Faber, ibid., and Alvin Wolfe, 'The African Mineral Industry; Evolution of a Supranational Level of Integration', in *Social Problems*, fall 1963, pp. 153ff.; F. Taylor Ostrander (Amax), 'The Role of Foreign Private Capital in Africa', in J. A. Davis and J. K. Baker, eds., *Southern Africa in Transition*, Praeger, New York, 1966, p. 347. See also Chapter 13 above, and Kwame Nkrumah, *Neo-colonialism*, Nelson, 1965. For a discussion of these interlocks in a British context, see M. Barratt-Brown, 'The Controllers of British Industry', in K. Coates, ed., *Can the Workers Run Industry?*, Sphere, 1968, p. 36.

3. Nkrumah, op. cit., has a very good account of the extended nature of these links and how far they reach into the financial and banking circles of the metropolitan centres. Perhaps these links do not always have the significance placed on them, and there are several errors, but the connections he traces are very revealing.

4. S. A. Ochola, *Minerals in African Underdevelopment*, Bogle L'Ouverture, 1975, pp. 76, 78.

5. R. Ramsey, *Men and Mines of Newmont*, Octagon Books, New York, 1973, p. 316.

6. ibid., p. 234.

7. Jack Halpern, *South Africa's Hostages*, Penguin Books, 1965, p. 297.

8. Chairman's Statement, Botswana RST 4th *Annual Report*, Gaberones, 1 July 1971, p. 6.

9. James Ainsworth, 'The Copper–Nickel Project in Botswana' in *Optima*, June 1972, p. 63. (*Optima* is the house magazine of the Anglo

552

group, and Ainsworth the Executive Vice-President (Technical) of Bamangwato Concessions.)

10. See *African Development*, 1968, Vol. 2, No. 3, p. 20, and *Mining Journal*, 23 July 1971, p. 66.

11. *African Development*, June 1972, p. 82.

12. *Mining Journal*, 13 July 1973, p. 26.

13. *Financial Mail*, Johannesburg, 27 March 1975.

14. *Financial Mail*, Johannesburg, 17 May 1974, p. 675.

15. F. Taylor Ostrander, 'The Selebi-Pikwe Mining Project in Botswana', Keynote Address at American Academy of Arts and Science, 1 August 1972, mimeo, Brookline, 1972, p. 22.

16. *National Development Plan 1970–5*, Gaberones, Government Printer, September 1970, p. 77.

17. Article by Richard Rolfe, *African Development*, August 1971, p. 10.

18. F. T. Ostrander, op. cit., p. 23.

19. Botswana RST circular to shareholders, 19 July 1971, p. 9.

20. *Africa*, July 1972, p. 84.

21. *Financial Mail*, Johannesburg, 8 August 1975, p. 518.

22. In Charles Simpkins, 'Labour in Botswana: recent disputes', *South African Labour Bulletin*, Vol. 2, No. 5, quoted in *Africa Currents*, No. 4, Winter 1975–6, p. 2.

23. ibid.

Chapter 15 Mining in Africa Today

1. See R. J. Barnett and R. E. Muller, *Global Reach: the Power of the Multinational Corporations*, Simon & Shuster, New York, 1974, p. 13; N. Girvan, *Corporate Imperialism: Conflict and Expropriation*, Monthly Review Press, 1976, Chapter 1, Corporate Imperialism in Mineral Export Economies, pp. 11f., 45, 195; and Robin Murray, 'Underdevelopment, the International Firm and the International Division of Labour,' Institute of Development Studies, University of Sussex, mimeo, 1972.

2. Anglo American *Annual Report 1972*, p. 37.

3. De Beers *Annual Report 1971*, p. 20.

4. Amax *Annual Report 1972*, p. 23.

5. *Mining Annual Review 1973*, Mining Journal, 1973, p. 13.

6. See various speeches of Sir Ronald Prain (RST), quoted in the *Mining Journal*, 27 April 1973, p. 337; 11 May 1973, p. 382; and 29 March 1974, p. 231.

7. *African Development*, August 1970, p. 11.

References

8. United Nations, *Mineral Resource Development with Particular Reference to the Developing Countries*, New York, Reference ST/ECA/123, 1970, pp. 70-73.

9. United Nations Development Programme, *Pre-Investment News*, March 1971.

10. R. Ramsey, *Men and Mines of Newmont*, Octagon Books, New York, 1973, p. 316.

11. G. Arrighi, 'International Corporations, Labour Aristocracies, and Economic Development in Tropical Africa', in G. Arrighi and J. S. Saul, *Essays on the Political Economy of Africa*, Monthly Review Press, 1973, p. 132.

12. These and subsequent examples taken from 'The Prospects for New Mine Investment' by Andrew Gordon, in M. Bostock and C. Harvey, eds., *Economic Independence and Zambian Copper*, Praeger, New York, 1972, p. 192.

13. C. Levinson, *Capital, Inflation and the Multinationals*, Allen & Unwin, 1971, p. 152.

14. ibid., p. 153.

15. F. Taylor Ostrander, Assistant to Chairman of Amax, in an address to the 8th Industrial and Agro-Industrial Development Management Education Programme of Arthur D. Little Inc., American Academy of Arts and Science, 1 August 1972, p. 15.

16. *Financial Mail* supplement, 'Gauging J C I's Mettle', Johannesburg, 25 September 1970, pp. 51-3.

17. Source: conversation with company officer.

18. Advertisement for Selection Trust, p. 528, *Skinner's Mining Year Book 1972*.

19. M. Barratt-Brown, *Essays on Imperialism*, Spokesman Books, 1972, p. 76.

20. N.A.C.L.A. *The New Chile*, New York, North American Congress on Latin America, 1972, p. 113.

21. ibid., p. 96. Even though Chile taxed the copper companies at 80 per cent of their income, Anaconda's local subsidiary, Chilex, averaged 18 per cent net profit on its capital, while Kennecott's El Teniente operation averaged a 25 per cent return on its capital.

22. See *Revenue from Mining Industry*, Ontario New Democratic Party Research Office, mimeo, 17 July 1974, quoted in J. Deverell et al., *Falconbridge – Portrait of a Canadian Mining Multinational*, James Lorrimer & Co., Toronto, 1975, p. 111. The study showed that income taxes accounted for 53 per cent of taxable profits but only 13 per cent of the true net profit before tax exemptions for depreciation, exploration developments, depletion cost and loss-making operations.

23. S. A. Ochola, *Minerals in African Underdevelopment*, Bogle L'Ouverture, 1975, p. 89.

24. See R. W. Clower, G. Dalton, M. Horwitz and A. Walters, *Growth without Development*, Northwestern University Press, Evanston, 1966, Chapter 8.

25. Deverell, op. cit., p. 151.

26. See, for example, *Engineering and Mining Journal*, New Jersey, October 1974, p. 63.

27. *Mining Magazine*, September 1975, p. 185.

28. *Mining Annual Review 1974*, Mining Journal, p. 193.

29. *Mining Magazine*, January 1975, p. 3, and survey, pp. 41-9.

30. ibid.

31. For study of Bechtel, see *Fortune* magazine, Chicago, August 1974, p. 121.

32. See *Mining Journal*, 2 March 1973.

33. B. Davidson, *Black Star*, Allen Lane, 1973, p. 151.

34. Ian MacGregor in speech to Rocky Mountain Mineral Law Institute, quoted in *Engineering and Mining Journal*, September 1972, p. 94.

35. 'Mining in the Euro-markets', *Mining Annual Review 1974*, Mining Journal, pp. 25-7.

36. MacGregor, op. cit., p. 94.

37. Ostrander, op. cit., p. 15.

38. See, for example, *Mining Annual Review 1974*, Mining Journal, pp. 25-7, and the advertisement placed by the Rothschild's Bank in *Skinner's Mining Year Book*, 1973, p. 726.

39. *Mining Annual Review 1971*, Mining Journal, p. 9.

40. *Africa Report*, July/August 1974, p. 28.

41. See for example Wim de Villiers, Managing Director of General Mining, in *Financial Mail* survey, 'A Sense of Direction', 5 October 1973, p. 38; and *Engineering and Mining Journal*, November 1972, S.A. survey, pp. 101ff.

42. For a similar policy by North American copper companies in South America, see N.A.C.L.A., op. cit., p. 111.

43. *1971 Minerals Yearbook*, Vol. III, US Bureau of Mines, p. 1010. Pechiney's primary aluminium plant was one of only three in Africa in 1971.

44. *Mining Journal*, 1 March 1974, p. 150.

45. N. C. Pollock, *Studies in Emerging Africa*, Butterworth, 1971, p. 174.

46. W. A. Hance, *African Economic Development*, revised edition, Praeger, New York, 1967, p. 77.

47. *Mining Journal*, 13 December 1974, p. 501.

48. ibid., p. 502.

49. Sir Raymond Brookes, Chairman of GKN (a British steel company), in an address to the International Iron and Steel Institute, quoted in *X-ray*, March 1973, p. 4.

50. Eugene T. Rossides, *US Customs, Tariffs and Trade*, Graham and Trotman, 1977, pp. 709-11.

51. ibid., pp. 720-25.

52. 'EEC Mining', *Mining* Magazine, August 1972, p. 118.

53. S. H. Frankel, *Capital Investment in Africa*, Oxford University Press, 1938, p. 374; and K. Warren, *Mineral Resources*, Penguin Books, 1973, pp. 60-65.

54. Pollock, op. cit., p. 128.

55. ibid., p. 140.

56. A. Sutulov, *Minerals in World Affairs*, Utah University Press, Salt Lake City, 1973, pp. 72-3; see also *New Internationalist*, No. 28, June 1975, pp. 16-19.

Chapter 16 The Marketing of Africa's Minerals

1. United Nations, *The World Market for Iron Ore*, prepared by Economic Commission for Europe, New York, 1968, No. E.69 II. E.10, p. 88.

2. ibid., p. 88.

3. ibid., p. 69.

4. Douglas E. Bunce, 'The Structure of the British Non-Ferrous Metal Industry', *The Journal of the Institute of Metals*, London, September 1966, quoted in M. S. Brown and J. Butler, *The Production, Marketing and Consumption of Copper and Aluminium*, Praeger, 1968, p. 147.

5. ibid.

6. Brown and Butler, op. cit., p. 149.

7. *Financial Mail* supplement, 'Gauging JCI's Mettle', Johannesburg, 25 September 1970, p. 31.

8. *Financial Times* special survey, 'Platinum', 2 December 1971, p. 14.

9. Botswana RST Limited, rights issue, 28 April 1972, p. 12.

10. *Engineering and Mining Journal*, New York, February 1975, p. 40.

11. 'Gauging JCI's Mettle', op. cit., pp. 39-40.

12. *Financial Mail* supplement, 'General Mining: A Sense of Direction', Johannesburg, 5 October 1973, p. 77.

13. *Mining Journal*, Analysis of Rand and O.F.S. Quarterlies, 27 April 1973, p. 1.

14. *Financial Mail* supplement 'Gold', Johannesburg, 17 November 1972, p. 38.

15. *Mining Annual Review 1971*, Mining Journal, 1971, p. 29.

16. Robert H. Losemann, ed., 'Copper', an *Engineering and Mining Journal*, Metals and Minerals Market Guide, 25 October 1965, p. 11.

17. ibid., p. 13. See also *Copper – A Materials Survey*, Washington Bureau of Mines, 1965, Information Circular 8225, pp. 261–3; and Ronald Prain, *Copper – Anatomy of an Industry*, Mining Journal Books, 1975, for a general view of the industry.

18. United Nations, *Copper Production in Developing Countries*, report of UNIDO seminar held in Moscow, October 1970, published UN, New York, 1972, UN sales no. E72 II B.13, p. 23.

19. Brown and Butler, op. cit., pp. 127 and 129.

20. Quotation in *Metal Bulletin*, special issue 'Copper', London, May 1965; quoted in Brown and Butler, op. cit., p. 127.

21. United Nations, *Non-Ferrous Metals Industry*, UNIDO Monograph on Industrial Development, No. 1, New York, 1969, sales no. E.69 II. B. 39 Vol. 1, p. 42.

22. *Mining Annual Review 1972*, Mining Journal, 1972, p. 37, and *Mining Annual Review 1971*, Mining Journal, 1971, p. 29.

23. See for example Brown and Butler, op. cit., p. 164, and Zamanglo, Chairman's Statement 1967, by H. Oppenheimer.

24. *Mining Journal*, 13 July 1973, p. 22.

25. ibid.

26. *Financial Times*, 21 April 1975.

27. United Nations, *Non-Ferrous Metals Industry*, op. cit., p. 24.

28. Fourth International Tin Agreement, Article 1, Objectives, p. 9.

29. *Mining Annual Review 1971*, Mining Journal, p. 41; *Mining Annual Review 1975*, Mining Journal, p. 49.

30. *Mining Annual Review 1971*, Mining Journal, p. 41.

31. Kenneth Warren, *Mineral Resources*, Penguin Books, 1973, p. 152.

32. *Mining Journal*, 23 March 1973, p. 226.

33. ibid.

34. *Mining Journal*, 24 August 1973, p. 147.

Chapter 17 *Africa and the World Diamond Monopoly*

1. *UN Statistical Year Book 1974*, Table 78, p. 204.

2. Godehard Lenzen, *The History of Diamond Production and the Diamond Trade*, Barrie & Jenkins, 1970, p. 189.

3. Quoted in Theodore Gregory, *Ernest Oppenheimer and the Economic Development of Southern Africa*, Oxford University Press, 1962.

4. De Beers, *Annual Report 1977*, p. 8.

5. ibid., p. 32.

6. *Financial Mail*, Johannesburg, 14 January 1972.

7. De Beers, op. cit., p. 13.

8. 'De Beers Benevolent Glitter', *The Times*, 4 September 1968; *Financial Mail*, Johannesburg, 25 April 1975. Anti-Trust charges were first brought in 1942; see A. Hocking, *Oppenheimer and Son*, McGraw-Hill, Johannesburg, 1973, p. 216.

9. A. Hocking, op. cit., p. 221.

10. Theodore Gregory, op. cit., p. 149.

11. H. L. Van der Laan, *The Sierra Leone Diamonds*, Oxford University Press, 1965, p. 149. This book has a full history of the diamond rush and SLST's dispute with the CSO.

12. *African Development*, August 1970, p. 2.

13. ibid.

14. ibid.

15. *West Africa*, 5 March 1973, p. 304.

16. *African Development*, April 1971, p. 51.

17. *West Africa*, 5 March 1973, p. 303.

18. *African Development*, March 1972, p. 4.

19. ibid.

20. *African Development*, April 1972, Sierra Leone supplement, p. 23.

21. For an informed account of the alternatives to Sierra Leone's present marketing and pricing policies, see Martyn Marriott, 'Wanted, A Better Price For Diamonds', *African Development*, April 1972, Sierra Leone supplement, p. 23.

22. H. Oppenheimer in 1961, quoted in De Beers *Annual Report 1970*, p. 38.

23. *African Development*, August 1970, p. 12.

24. For example, David Nicholson, ex-High Commissioner to London, and S. Mathari (who was quoted in *African Development*, June 1975, 'There was a time when I was very critical of Dicorwaf'), are both employed by DICORWAF.

Chapter 18 Power Politics and the Diplomacy of Private Enterprise

1. Robin Murray, 'Second Thoughts on Ghana', in *New Left Review*, No. 42, March 1967, pp. 25 ff.

2. *African Development*, March–April 1967.

3. Figures from 1976 Annual Reports, GNP statistics from world Bank Atlas and IMF statistics.

4. S. Cronje, M. Ling and G. Cronje, *Lonrho: Portrait of a Multinational*, Penguin Books, 1976, p. 38 (Kenya), p. 51 (Ivory Coast). See also *Review of African Political Economy*, No. 2, January 1975, p. 7.

5. *African Development*, March 1974, p. 7.

6. 'The CIA as Equal Opportunity Employer in Africa', *Ramparts*, San Francisco, reprint, n.d.

7. W. Minter, *The Portuguese in Africa*, Penguin Books, 1972, p. 162.

8. See 'The Duncan Report: a Recipe for Disengagement', Richard Jolly in *African Development*, January 1970, pp. 22–3.

9. Louis Gerber, *Friends and Influence – the Diplomacy of Private Enterprise*, Purnell, Cape Town, 1973, p. 23. Gerber worked for the South Africa Foundation.

10. ibid., p. 88.

11. ibid., pp. 98–100.

12. ibid., p. 150.

13. ibid., p. 151.

14. ibid., p. 146.

15. ibid., pp. 89–91.

16. See *Sunday Times*, 7, 14 and 21 November 1971.

17. Elaine Potter, *The Press as Opposition – the Political Role of South African Newspapers*, Chatto & Windus, 1975, pp. 56–65.

18. ibid., p. 54.

19. Leonard Lazar, *Namibia*, Africa Bureau, 1972, p. 90.

20. *African Development*, July 1972, p. 67.

21. *Financial Mail*, 18 October 1974, p. 236.

22. See H. W. Singer, 'Distribution of Gains Between Investing and Borrowing Countries', quoted in Charles E. Rollins, 'Mineral Development and Economic Growth', in Robert I. Rhodes, ed., *Imperialism and Underdevelopment*, Monthly Review Press, 1970, p. 184; N. Kessel, 'Mining and the Factors Constraining Economic Development', in C. Elliott, ed., *Constraints on the Economic Development of Zambia*, Oxford University Press, Nairobi, 1971, p. 257.

References

23. See G. Bell, *Le Projet de pôle électro-métallurgique de FRIA: L'énergie hydro-électrique et le développement*, L'Institut de Science Economique Appliquée, Paris, 1963.

24. James Moxon, *Volta, Man's Greatest Lake*, André Deutsch, 1969, p. 50.

25. ibid., pp. 83–6.

26. ibid., p. 90.

27. ibid., p. 203.

28. M. S. Brown and J. Butler, *The Production, Marketing and Consumption of Copper and Aluminium*, Praeger, 1968, p. 12.

29. Moxon, op. cit., p. 232.

30. A. Krassowski, *Development and the Debt Trap*, Croom Helm, 1974, p. 51.

31. ibid., p. 53.

32. Moxon, op. cit., p. 207.

33. Pierre Bonté, 'Multinational Companies and National Development: MIFERMA and Mauritania', *Review of African Political Economy*, No. 2, January–April 1975, p. 93.

34. R. Green and A. Seidman, *Unity or Poverty ?*, Penguin Books, 1968, p. 117.

35. Bonté, op. cit., p. 99.

36. Green and Seidman, op. cit., p. 118.

37. S. Amin, *Neo-colonialism in West Africa*, Penguin Books, 1973, p. 79.

38. ibid., p. 80.

39. Bonté, op. cit., p. 100.

40. Amin, op. cit., p. 80.

41. ibid.

42. Green and Seidman, op. cit., p. 116.

43. Bonté, op. cit., p. 105.

44. Bonté, op. cit., p. 109.

45. S. A. Ochola, *Minerals in African Underdevelopment*, Bogle L'Ouverture, 1975, p. 76.

46. *African Development*, June 1972, Liberia supplement, p. 82.

47. Men like 'Chuck' Lipton (ex UN) and Martyn Marriott (ex De Beers), and a group of economists at the Commonwealth Institute which includes Mike Faber (ex Zambian government adviser) and Roland Brown (ex Tanzanian government adviser, responsible for the 1966 report on miners' pay in Zambia, see Chapter 11).

48. Sir Jock Campbell, *The New Africa*, p. 12; quoted in M.L.O. Faber and J. G. Potter, *Towards Economic Independence*, Cambridge University Press, 1971, p. 38.

49. See Chapter 12. If African countries were in any doubt about their position, they had only to look at the severe problems in getting spare parts which faced Cuba after that country had nationalized the nickel mines. See P. Sweezy and L. Huberman, *Socialism in Cuba*, Monthly Review Press, 1969, pp. 97–8, and E. Boorstein, *The Economic Transformation of Cuba*, Monthly Review Press, 1967, pp. 55–7.

50. *African Development*, December 1975, p. 19.

51. ibid., p. 20. See also *African Development*, April 1976, pp. 375, 383–5.

52. M. Bostock and C. Harvey, *Economic Independence and Zambian Copper*, Praeger, 1972, p. 19.

53. ibid., p. 239.

54. See for example *Investor's Chronicle*, 25 June 1971, 27 October 1972, and 20 April 1973, p. 263, urging investors to buy Zambian 'bonds'.

55. *Financial Times*, 'World Mining Survey', 16 August 1974, p. 17.

56. Ian MacGregor, Chairman of Amax, quoted in *Engineering and Mining Journal*, September 1972, p. 96.

57. *Mining Review 1974*, Mining Journal, p. 9.

58. *African Development*, April 1976, p. 387.

Chapter 19 The Oppenheimer Complex

1. *African Development*, June 1974, p. 32.

2. *Financial Mail*, 'Top Companies Special Survey', 16 April 1971.

3. These and all subsequent rankings taken from *Financial Mail*, 'Top Companies Survey 1978', 16 June 1978, pp. 50, 55.

4. *Sunday Times*, Johannesburg, 26 April 1970.

5. Brian Bunting, *The Rise of the South African Reich*, Penguin Books, 1969, p. 464.

6. *Financial Mail* supplement, 'Inside the Anglo Power House', 4 July 1969, p. 21.

7. ibid., pp. 17, 19.

8. *Die Afrikaner*, 20 February 1970, p. 1.

9. *Rand Daily Mail*, 28 April 1970.

10. *Sunday Times*, Johannesburg, 27 April 1970.

11. Anglo *Annual Report 1963*.

12. See S. Cronje, M. Ling, G. Cronje, *Lonrho: Portrait of a Multinational*, Penguin Books, 1976.

13. *Star*, Johannesburg, 26 May 1957.

14. *Rand Daily Mail*, 22 June 1957.

References

15. *Star*, 6 August 1957.
16. ibid.
17. *Star*, 16 May 1958.
18. *Star*, 5 November 1959.
19. *Star*, 6 August 1957.
20. *Rand Daily Mail* 29 September 1959.
21. Keith Gottschalk, *Black Sash* magazine, Johannesburg, 1971.
22. *Rand Daily Mail*, 5 March 1964.
23. *Sunday Times*, Johannesburg, July 1970.
24. *Rand Daily Mail*, 28 April 1970.
25. Timothy Smith, *The American Corporation in South Africa; An Analysis*, Council for Christian Social Action, New York, 1971, p. 33.
26. *Rand Daily Mail*, 30 June 1970.
27. Progressive Party Fact Sheet, February 1971.
28. *Star*, 16 May 1958.
29. *Rand Daily Mail*, 30 June 1970.
30. Chairman's Report, Anglo American *Annual Report*, 1975, p. 4. For some of many similar statements see *Financial Mail*, 'Top Companies Survey 1975', op. cit., p. 34.

Chapter 20 Namibia – The Last Colony

1. Leonard Lazar, *Namibia*, Africa Publications Trust, 1972, p. 75.
2. R. Murray, 'The Namibian Economy: an analysis of the role of foreign investment and the policies of the South African administration', in R. Murray, J. Morris, J. Dugard, N. Rubin, *The Role of Foreign Firms in Namibia*, Study Project on External Investment in South Africa and Namibia, Africa Publications Trust, 1974, p. 31.
3. Lazar, op. cit., pp. 3–5.
4. ibid., p. 12.
5. For a full account of the history of the mandate, see Lazar, op. cit. See also R. First, *South West Africa*, Penguin Books, 1963; and the papers prepared for the 1972 Namibia International Conference.
6. Lazar, op. cit.
7. Murray, op. cit., p. 31, for 1969 figures; 1977 estimate also by Roger Murray.
8. ibid., p. 43.
9. Roger Murray, *Foreign (British and Western) Investment in the Economy of Namibia (S.W. Africa)*, Africa Bureau, 1972, p. 6.
10. Murray, 'The Namibian Economy', op. cit., p. 9.
11. ibid., p. 42.

12. ibid.

13. R. Ramsey, *Men and Mines of Newmont*, Octagon Books, New York, 1973, p. 127.

14. *Windhoek Advertiser*, 17 April 1974, quoted in Murray, 'The Namibian Economy', op. cit., p. 46.

15. Roger Murray, *Namibia: Initial Survey*, Namibia International Conference, Brussels, 1972, p. 6.

16. Quoted in Lazar, op. cit., p. 25.

17. Murray, 'The Namibian Economy', op. cit., p. 79.

18. Quoted in Murray, *Namibia*, op cit., p. 3.

19. Quoted in Lazar, op. cit., p. 77.

20. ibid.

21. Murray, 'The Namibian Economy', op. cit., p. 80.

22. Murray, *Namibia*, op. cit., p. 5.

23. Murray, 'The Namibian Economy', op. cit., p. 80.

24. Quoted in Jennifer Davis *et al.*, *The Sacred Trust Exploited: American and Canadian Private Investment in Namibia*, American Committee on Africa, 1972, p. 27.

25. Lazar, op. cit., p. 82. See also Robert J. Gordon, *Mines, Masters and Migrants*, Ravan Press, Johannesburg, 1977.

26. J. Kane Berman, 'Wages and Payment in Kind in the Mining Industry of SA and SWA', mimeo, 1971.

27. L. Douwes Dekker, D. Hemson, J. S. Kane-Berman, J. Lever and L. Schlemmer, 'Case Studies in African Labour Action in South Africa and Namibia', in R. Sandbrook and R. Cohen, eds., *The Development of an African Working Class*, Longmans, 1975, pp. 227–30.

28. John Kane-Berman, *Contract Labour in South West Africa*, South African Institute of Race Relations, Johannesburg, 1972, p. 9.

29. Douwes Dekker, Hemson *et al.*, op. cit., p. 230.

30. ibid., p. 232.

31. Murray, 'The Namibian Economy', op. cit., pp. 107–9.

32. ibid., pp. 111–12.

33. Lazar, op. cit., p. 77.

Chapter 21 Mining Companies and the Underdevelopment of Africa

1. See for example Sir Ronald Prain (RST), 'Copper, the Anatomy of an Industry', *Mining Journal*, 1975; F. Taylor Ostrander (Amax), 'The Role of Foreign Private Capital in Africa', in J. A. Davis and J. K. Baker, eds., *Southern Africa in Transition*, Praeger, New York, 1966, p. 347; F. Taylor Ostrander, 'The Place of Minerals in Economic De-

velopment', *Mines*, 1963; Harry Oppenheimer (Anglo American), in his 1975 address to the Institute of Mining and Metallurgy, quoted in *Mining Journal*, 9 May 1975, p. 355; and the speech made by Sir Val Duncan (RTZ) to the Institute of Directors, 8 July 1968.

2. See also Charles E. Rollins, 'Mineral Development and Economic Growth', in Robert I. Rhodes, ed., *Imperialism and Underdevelopment*, Monthly Review Press, 1970 pp. 181ff; Norman Girvan, *Corporate Imperialism: Conflict and Expropriation*, Monthly Review Press, 1976, Chapter 1.

3. See, for example, *Mining Magazine*, December 1972, p. 519, and February 1973, p. 67, and *Mining Annual Review 1973*, Mining Journal, p. 185.

4. Robin Murray, 'Underdevelopment, the International Firm and the International Division of Labour', Institute of Development Studies, University of Sussex, mimeo, 1972.

5. Michael Barratt-Brown, *From Labourism to Socialism*, Spokesman Books, 1972, Chapter 1, 'The Demands of the New Technology'.

6. Michael Barratt-Brown, *Essays on Imperialism*, Spokesman Books, 1972, p. 160.

7. Giovanni Arrighi, 'International Corporations, Labour Aristocracies, and Economic Development in Tropical Africa', in G. Arrighi and J. S. Saul, *Essays on the Political Economy of Africa*, Monthly Review Press, New York, 1973, p. 125.

8. John S. Saul, 'The Post Colonial Societies', in *Socialist Register 1974*, Merlin, 1974.

9. Ruth First, *The Barrel of a Gun*, Penguin Books, 1972, p. 101.

Company and Mine Index

Mines are in italic type. A full list of the major mines in Africa is in Appendix 1.

General Index